CALCULATING
CATASTROPHE

CALCULATING
CATASTROPHE

$$f(\lambda 1/ \lambda 3) = f(\lambda 1/ \lambda 2) f(\lambda 2/ \lambda 3)$$

地
球

Gordon Woo

Imperial College Press

Published by

Imperial College Press
57 Shelton Street
Covent Garden
London WC2H 9HE

Distributed by

World Scientific Publishing Co. Pte. Ltd.
5 Toh Tuck Link, Singapore 596224
USA office: 27 Warren Street, Suite 401-402, Hackensack, NJ 07601
UK office: 57 Shelton Street, Covent Garden, London WC2H 9HE

British Library Cataloguing-in-Publication Data
A catalogue record for this book is available from the British Library.

First published 2011
Reprinted 2012

ISBN-13 978-1-84816-738-4
ISBN-10 1-84816-738-5
ISBN-13 978-1-84816-739-1 (pbk)
ISBN-10 1-84816-739-3 (pbk)

Printed in Singapore by World Scientific Printers.

Dedicated to the memory
of C.K.W.

Contents

Cover Photograph

Anak Krakatau

The photographer, Marco Fulle, is based in Trieste, Italy. Trained as a scientist in Genoa, he is passionate about capturing on film the majestic power of one of the great forces of Nature, taking personal risks for the advancement of volcano photography.

Marco's notes indicate that this picture happened by chance. He saw and quickly shot the image at 8 p.m. on 4 June 2009, as he was passing by the beach of Pulau Rakata, which is the southernmost of the three small Indonesian islands forming the rim of the caldera of Krakatau volcano. The young active volcano of Anak Krakatau lies at the centre of the caldera. The lights visible in the picture on the sea, in the front centre area of Anak Krakatau, are from the boats of the local fishermen.

The beach was formed by the deposits of the catastrophic 1883 eruption, and by the subsequent landslides, and was soon colonized by a tropical jungle. The sea is eroding the new land at a rate of several metres per year, causing old trees on the shoreline to fall. During the night, stars rotate around the volcano, so that above Anak Krakatau, the Big Dipper points approximately towards the erupting vent.

Special thanks to Alexandra Knaust for all her support and encouragement to write this book, for selecting the cover photograph, and her cover design and photograph of the Fiji fan palm from Tonga; to Lindsay Murray for technical assistance; and to RMS, for providing an ideal working environment for a catastrophist.

Prologue

Chaos, Crisis and Catastrophe

The German writer and polymath Johann Wolfgang von Goethe noted that 'Mathematicians are like Frenchmen: whatever you say to them they translate into their own language and forthwith it is something entirely different'. In Molière's play, *Le Bourgeois Gentilhomme*, Monsieur Jourdain learns he has been speaking prose for forty years without knowing it. Mathematics is a language which is generally associated with symbols as unfamiliar and incomprehensible as Chinese characters or Egyptian hieroglyphs. More fundamentally, mathematics is a language of ideas that people may express without knowing it.

Although there are some equations, this book is written to communicate maximally in prose the key ideas of catastrophe science. Progressing beyond an anthology of catastrophes, and the narrow silo exposition of individual modes of disaster, a deeper appreciation comes from a 360 degree perspective, linking together common concepts.

Catastrophe is a Greek word originally signifying a down-turning in a theatrical tragedy. Anyone who has watched a Greek tragedy unfold knows how rapid and calamitous this down-turning can be. In the third millennium, the modes of catastrophe are more numerous and more devastating than ever. In a letter to President Roosevelt shortly before the outbreak of World War II, Albert Einstein was prescient of the impact of an atomic bomb: 'A single bomb of this type, carried by boat and exploded in a port, might very well destroy the whole port together with some of the surrounding territory.'[1] This warning is still heeded for threats from rogue states and terrorists.

Ironically, Einstein was dismissive of the probabilistic quantum theory of atomic particles: 'God does not play dice.' He would have been further surprised by the inherent fundamental limits to the deterministic

1

predictability of classical Newtonian mechanics. *Chaos* is twinned with catastrophe. A third word of Greek origin linked with catastrophe is *crisis*, originally meaning a decision or judgement. Every significant down-turning of events is accompanied by vexed decision-making under uncertainty over what may happen. In Marisha Pessl's dark novel, *Special Topics in Calamity Physics*,[2] a university seminar on the Quintessence of Predicaments ends thus: 'One or two individuals in times of crisis turn into heroes, a handful into villains, the rest into fools.' The cleverest can be fooled, even Isaac Newton himself.

In 1720, the English government transferred its massive war debts to the South Sea Company, which was allowed to issue shares that could be exchanged for government bonds held by the public. The higher the market price of these shares, the better it was for the government. The share price soared to a peak of £1000, and then fell back to £135, its level eight months earlier. A prize victim of the South Sea Bubble, Newton bought shares at the top of the market, and even more as the price was sliding.[3] He lamented, 'I can calculate the motions of the heavenly bodies, but not the madness of people.' Ironically, the elegant mathematical framework that Newton devised for his astronomical calculations leads to a theory of dynamical chaos, which can explain complex system behaviour such as stock market bubbles.

Some of the most significant contributions to catastrophe science have been made by individuals whose thoughts were years ahead of their time. A key member of the Rogers commission investigating the 1986 space shuttle Challenger disaster was the Physics Nobel laureate, Richard Feynman. He recounted his commission experience in the book, *What Do You Care What Other People Think?*[4] Like Feynman, the English scientist, Lewis Fry Richardson, was eccentric in a highly creative way. A colleague wrote, 'Richardson was a very interesting and original character who seldom thought on the same lines as did his contemporaries, and often was not understood by them.' He found respite on the Great War battlefield figuring out how to compute the weather, and developing quantitative ideas on the causes of human conflict. He later switched career from meteorology to focus on peace research,[5] so pioneering an interdisciplinary approach to calculating catastrophe, that stands as an inspiration to all stepping into his shadow.

Chapter 1

Natural Hazards

I would find it easier to believe that
two Yankee professors would lie than
that stones should fall from the sky.
President Thomas Jefferson

'There is no crash at the moment, only a slight premonitory movement of the ground under our feet.' The context of this warning was a mid-19th century crisis in England; not a seismic one, although tremors are felt from time to time, but one involving the Bank of England, soon after it assumed the responsibilities and liabilities of a central bank. Metaphors from the landscape of natural hazards, such as seismic shock, storm, tsunami, and tidal wave, are commonly used to describe man-made catastrophes such as financial crashes and political violence. This is not mere linguistic hyperbole; there are common roots in their calculational framework which make a knowledge of natural hazards relevant for those aspiring to deepen their understanding of man-made hazards, and to lessen the degree of surprise they may cause.

One of the most insidious aspects of natural hazards is the protracted timescale of hundreds of thousands of years over which they occur. Collective memory of a natural disaster, such as an earthquake, tends to fade into amnesia after several generations of seismic quiescence. No wonder that a fatality from an earthquake on a fault that last ruptured during the Ice Age should seem as incredible as a victim of a woolly mammoth. There are many arcane geological hazard phenomena which would meet with similar incredulity and awe were they to recur in our own time, save for evidence of their occurrence preserved for posterity in the geological record.

3

The path to comprehending natural hazards has been arduous, not least because such events are not well suited to laboratory study. All natural hazards are macroscopic phenomena, governed fundamentally by the laws of classical physics which were known in the 19th century. Although the laws of physics are sufficiently concise and elegant as to fill a large tablature of mathematics, the emergence of complex spatial structures cannot be explained so succinctly, if indeed sufficient observations exist to permit quantitative explanation. Writing down large sets of nonlinear equations is one matter, solving them is another.

Yet hard problems do have solutions. Among these are physical situations where microscopic fluctuations do not average out over larger scales, but persist out to macroscopic wavelengths. A breakthrough in the understanding of such phenomena was made by the theoretical physicist Ken Wilson, whose Nobel prize-winning ideas of the renormalization group centred on modelling the dynamical effects of scale changes,[1] and whose early and opportunist use of computers allowed him to overcome major technical obstacles in replicating calculations at different scales. Experimental evidence suggests a strong analogy between the equilibrium phase transitions studied by Wilson and the statistical behaviour of types of turbulent flow.[2]

A fundamental understanding of fluid turbulence is not only needed for windstorm research, but corresponding ideas from statistical physics hold promise in furthering the understanding of earthquakes and volcanic eruptions. Strands of seismological evidence support the view that, prior to a major earthquake, a critical state may be approached where one part of the system can affect many others, with the consequence that minor perturbations may lead to cascade-type events of all sizes. Even though the fundamental tectonic mechanisms for earthquake generation are now quite well understood, the role of small external perturbations in triggering earthquakes is still scientifically contentious. Indeed, even though there was an accumulation of anecdotal evidence for one earthquake triggering another at a large distance, it took the Landers, California earthquake of 1992 to provide an unequivocal seismological demonstration. Whether it is one seismic event triggering another, or a volcanic eruption triggering an earthquake, the causal dynamical associations between hazard events need to be unravelled.

1.1 Causation and Association

On 10 April 1815, the 13,000 foot Indonesian volcano Tambora exploded in the most spectacular eruption recorded in history. One hundred and fifty km^3 of material was ejected, and the eruption column soared as high as 43 km, which left a vast cloud of very fine ash in the upper atmosphere. This cloud reduced significantly the amount of solar radiation reaching the Earth's surface, and caused a dramatic change in the climate of the northern hemisphere in the following year. To this day, the year 1816 is recollected as the year without a summer.

According to Mary Shelley, staying in Geneva, 'It proved a wet, ungenial summer, and incessant rain often confined us for days to the house.' Her poet husband Percy Bysshe Shelley rued the cold and rainy season. Upon the suggestion of their literary neighbour, Lord Byron, they all spent their confinement indoors writing ghost stories. Byron sketched a tale of vampires – she wrote *Frankenstein*.[3] A tenuous chain of causation thus links the world's greatest gothic novel with its greatest documented eruption. Tambora was neither a necessary nor sufficient condition for *Frankenstein* to be written. But the following *counterfactual* statement can be made: without the eruption of Tambora, *Frankenstein* most likely would never have been created. Akin to the writing of *Frankenstein*, the occurrence of a hazard event may be tenuously, yet causally connected with a prior event, which might have taken place at a significant separation of time and distance.

In deteriorating weather, on the evening of 27 March 1977, two Boeing 747 jets collided on the ground at Los Rodeos airport in Tenerife, killing 583 people.[4] Neither plane was even scheduled to be there. Both had been diverted from Las Palmas airport on the island of Gran Canaria, where separatist terrorists had earlier exploded a bomb in the passenger terminal. The following counterfactual statement might be made: if it had not been for this terrorist attack, the accident would not have happened. The long delayed KLM pilot would not have been in the predicament where he was very anxious to take off, even without proper clearance. But it cannot be said that the world's worst aviation disaster prior to 9/11 was also caused by a terrorist attack.

A formal discussion of the causation issue is worthwhile, because causal claims may have a subjunctive complexity. If a woman says her hair is brown because she dyes it, we infer that if she had not dyed her hair it would have been some other colour. This kind of counterfactual conditional is not necessarily correct: a brunette can dye her hair brown.[5]

After a succession of two hazard events, the public may enquire whether the first event caused the second. The reply is often unsatisfactory. The formal scientific response is to decline to admit a causal connection unless a direct physical link can be established and its effects demonstrated. Where a massive mountain rockslide dams a river and forms a lake, the cause of a subsequent outburst flood is clear: both the rockslide and the lake are visible, and the situation can be monitored remotely by satellite.

It is a frustration of Earth science that the interior of the Earth can be so opaque to human observation. Thus a geophysicist might freely speculate on, but not elaborate in precise numerical detail, the connection between the 1902 Caribbean volcanic eruption of Mt. Pelée and that of St. Vincent on the previous day, just 165 km to the south.

Whenever there is some constancy with which events of one kind are followed by events of another, scientists may wish to claim an association between the two kinds of event. But from the positivist philosophical viewpoint, this statement of empirical correspondence does not warrant drawing any inference on causation.[6] In his probabilistic theory of causation, the mathematical philosopher Suppes required that the cause should raise the probability of the effect.[7] Thus, even if occasionally an Indian rain dance is actually followed by a downpour, we do not say that the rain dance caused the rain. Similarly, even if occasionally a tornado near Topeka, Kansas is followed by an earthquake in California, we do not say that the tornado caused the earthquake.[8]

But how is the transition to be made from mere association to causation? This is particularly hard to establish when the effect of a preventive cause is an event, such as catastrophe, that does not materialize. Unfortunately, counterfactual statements of the kind, 'If this had not happened, then that would not either', have their weaknesses.[9]

The dictum of the statistician Ronald Fisher was to make the theories more elaborate. There are two ways in which this can be achieved. The first way, which is standard in pharmaceutical drugs testing, is by performing experiments, with a statistical design carefully chosen to discern causal factors. If variation of one feature X causes variation in another Y, then Y can be changed by an intervention that alters X. This procedure unfortunately is not feasible for observational sciences, because experimental conditions are those imposed by Nature.

The alternative mode of elaboration is to relate the phenomenon to scientific knowledge. Thus, epidemiological results are best interpreted in terms of an underlying biochemical process. Recalling the studies demanded by Ronald Fisher to establish, beyond the doubt of a sceptical geneticist, a causal link between smoking and lung cancer, the gaps in knowledge of the causal links between natural hazards seem more excusable, if no less regrettable.

Recognizing the dynamical complexity of the systems involved, there is advantage in representing event associations in a way which allows their relationships to be scientifically explored. Alas, the associations between some pairs of hazard events are far from transparent, and the infrequency of the phenomena and sparsity of data make hard work of attempts at statistical correlation. One of the measures for coping with small event datasets is to aggregate the data, some of which relate to binary variables, taking values of 0 or 1 according to whether something did or did not happen. But an analyst must beware of statistical illusions such as Simpson's paradox: there can be a positive association between two binary variables, even though, conditional on a third variable, the association may actually be negative.[10]

With a view to gauging the effect of even minor perturbations, the dynamical basis of each natural hazard is sketched here in an interdisciplinary way. This style of presentation is uncommon in the Earth and atmospheric sciences, despite the fact that some of the most senior seismological institutes have been accommodated with meteorological institutes; a vestige of an era when scientists thought there was such a phenomenon as 'earthquake weather'. A period German barometer even marked earthquake at the end of the dial after severe storm. Had the maker lived in Nordlingen, within the Ries Basin of southern Germany, the site of a major meteorite crater, perhaps the very end of the dial might have signified meteorite impact.

1.2 Extra-Terrestrial Hazards

Galileo was the first scientific observer of lunar craters, but it was three and a half centuries after the publication of *Sidereus Nuncius* (The Starry Messenger) in 1610 that the impact of large meteorites was appreciated as their cause, rather than giant volcanoes. Even after the physicist Chladni had published, at the beginning of the 19th century, memoirs on stony and metallic meteors falling from space, professional astronomers were very reluctant to accept impact theories for seemingly patent geometrical reasons: most lunar craters are circular rather than elliptical. The fact that high velocity impacts are similar to explosions, and hence form circular craters, was not appreciated until a century later.

Four hundred years after Galileo, another Italian made an important meteorite impact observation – using not a telescope focused on the moon, but satellite images on Google Earth. Vicenzo De Michele, former curator of the Natural History Museum in Milan, spotted the 45 m wide Kamil crater in the southern Egypt desert in 2008. It is reckoned this was caused by an iron meteorite hurtling to Earth at more than 12,000 km/hr. This is a notable discovery, because weathering makes such well-preserved impact craters very exceptional.

Supplemented by terrestrial research, such as the iridium analysis which gave Luis Alvarez an initial clue to a meteorite impact at the boundary between the Cretaceous and Tertiary periods,[11] planetary physicists have been able to quantify the mechanics of the cratering process, and to model the environmental consequences of large impacts.[12] Such studies show that, if sufficiently energetic, an impact by an asteroid or comet would be capable of causing a global catastrophe.

There are three main populations of potential extra-terrestrial impactors. First, there are asteroids which are in Earth-crossing orbits of moderate eccentricity. Such orbits overlap that of the Earth and undergo intersections due to orbital precession: a swivelling of orientation due to the gravitational attraction of the planets. These asteroids are composed largely of iron and rock, and are far less easy to spot than comets. Originating predominantly from the main asteroid belt, they may wander into orbits whose orbital period is harmonically related to that of Jupiter.

The gravitational effects of Jupiter can force these asteroids into orbits taking them repeatedly through the inner solar system.

The second population of potential impactors consists of comets in orbits similar to those of the above asteroids, which stay within the inner solar system. None of the discovered comets could collide with the Earth, at least for the next few centuries, and those in the Jupiter family may be more likely to hit Jupiter instead or be ejected from the solar system. By contrast, it is much harder to detect so-called extinct comets, which no longer display cometary activity and thereby appear point-like.

The third population of potential impactors includes occasional comets with periods longer than twenty years. The latter typically have greater impact velocities of 50 km/s, compared with about 20 km/s for the asteroids and short period comets. The known long period comets include members of the Halley family. But the chance that any of these known comets would collide with the Earth is minuscule. For Halley's Comet itself, it is as low as 0.5% in a million orbits. But the number of Earth-crossing active and extinct Halley-family comets is thought to be much larger than the number discovered, and these remain an unidentified and unquantified threat.

According to Steel *et al.*, the major concern for humanity is not so much the large global impact which might occur once in a hundred thousand years, or more rarely still, but regionally devastating impact events, which occur in clusters every thousand years or so, during epochs of high influx.[13] The Chinese historical record of meteorite observations, which dates back to the 5th century, attests to the danger posed by meteor clusters. In 1490, many were killed when stones, some the size of goose eggs, reportedly fell like rain.

Early in the 20th century, on 30 June 1908, it was Siberia that experienced a major impact event. Trees were flattened over an area of more than 2,000 km² in the region of the Tunguska River. A century later, in 2010, a Russian expedition deploying ground penetrating radar located a crater, carrying the icy signature of a comet, rather than a meteorite. Had it struck 4 hours and 47 minutes later, St. Petersburg would have been obliterated. Such a possible natural catastrophe is one of the most intriguing counterfactuals of 20th century politics, with untold consequences stemming from the end of the Romanov dynasty.

1.2.1 Solar storms

Galileo was the first to observe and appreciate the imperfections of the Sun, known as sunspots. Two and a half centuries later, on 1 September 1859, in the course of his daily sunspot observation, an English amateur astronomer, Richard Carrington, observed and reported for the first time a solar flare, which is a sudden, rapid, and intense variation in brightness of the Sun. This was so extremely bright that the associated 1859 space weather event remains one of the largest ever observed, as well as the first. A recurrence of this solar superstorm in the 21st century would severely affect satellite resources. The terrestrial impact of solar storms may also be widespread because they cause disturbances in the Earth's geomagnetic field, elevate radiation levels due to fluxes of high-energy particles and induce radio blackouts due to solar X-ray emissions.

A major advance in the understanding of space weather came with the discovery of coronal mass ejections (CME's) in the 1970s, and with the recognition that these ejections of matter into the outer corona are the cause of non-recurrent geomagnetic storms.[14] Eruptive flares and CME's result from the release of energy stored in the Sun's magnetic field, and occur most often around the period of greatest solar activity, which has an eleven year cycle. CME's and flares can occur independently of one another; however, both are generally observed at the start of a space weather event that leads to a large magnetic storm.[15]

Transient disturbance of the Earth's magnetic field can induce electrical currents in the long wires of an electrical power grid, and cause imbalances in electrical equipment. In March 1989, such a disturbance caused a blackout in Quebec, Canada. Oil well drilling from an offshore platform may also be impacted in situations where well bore navigation depends on its direction relative to the local Earth's magnetic field.

Other adverse effects of extreme space weather on modern technology include high-frequency communication blackouts and degradation of Global Positioning System navigation signals. GPS signals originate from satellites at about 12,000 miles' altitude, and these signals have to pass through the ionosphere in order to reach GPS receivers on the ground. An example of signal fade occurred during a significant solar flare event in December 2006.

1.3 Meteorological Hazards

Of the many forms of extreme terrestrial weather, specific types of weather system can generate violent conditions of wind and precipitation with massive destructive energy. These include tropical cyclones, extra-tropical windstorms, as well as tornadic and hail-bearing thunderstorms of such size and intensity as to be distinguished as supercells.

Atmospheric circulation patterns may be related over large areas, which need not be contiguous. Such teleconnections are often associated with atmospheric oscillations, the best known being the El Niño – Southern Oscillation phenomenon,[16] driven by interactions between the oceans and the atmosphere across the Indo-Pacific region, and having near-global effects due to the dynamics of the planetary atmosphere. Teleconnections affect meteorological hazards: e.g. those between North Atlantic sea-level pressures and precipitation variability over North America and Europe influence the Atlantic hurricane season.[17]

1.3.1 Tropical cyclones

A cyclone is a circulating weather system. In the northern hemisphere, the rotation of the Earth makes air move in an anti-clockwise direction around a low pressure system. In the southern hemisphere, the motion is clockwise. Cyclones which form over ocean waters within the equatorial region between the Tropics of Capricorn and Cancer are called tropical cyclones. Sub-tropical cyclones, which develop outside the tropics from mid-latitude low pressure systems, can also turn into tropical cyclones, as a result of thunderstorms in their centre. These weather systems are generically called tropical storms when the maximum sustained surface wind speeds lie within the range of 18 to 33 m/s, and are elevated to the status of hurricanes when the maximum sustained wind speeds are greater than 33 m/s.

A mature hurricane is an engine which converts heat energy from the evaporation of ocean water into mechanical wind energy. The amount of heat that can be injected into a hurricane is proportional to the amount of sea water that can be evaporated. This is limited by the relative humidity of air near the sea surface: when this reaches 100%, the air becomes saturated. Thankfully, not all of this heat energy can be converted to mechanical energy. According to the principles of thermodynamics, the maximum fraction is $[T(in) - T(out)] / T(in)$, where $T(in)$ is the temperature at which heat is added to the engine, and $T(out)$ is the temperature at which it is removed. For a hurricane, the input temperature is that of the sea surface, which is typically about 28°C. The output temperature is that of the air flowing out of the top of the storm, which is around –75°C. Expressed in terms of degrees Kelvin, the maximum fraction of heat energy convertible into mechanical energy is about one-third.

Whether a tropical disturbance develops and becomes a hurricane or not depends on a number of factors. One of the most significant is weak vertical wind shear, which is the rate at which the background horizontal wind changes with altitude. Strong vertical wind shear diminishes the concentration of thunderstorms associated with a tropical low pressure system. Conducive conditions, other than weak vertical wind shear, include pre-existing low surface pressure; a very humid atmosphere; an ocean temperature in excess of 26°C; a separation distance from the equator of about five degrees of latitude; and high pressure in the upper troposphere so that air is evacuated away from the region of the cyclone. The physics of tropical cyclones, such as it is understood, can be transcribed mathematically into equations of motion of the cyclone winds and associated thermodynamic relations.

1.3.2 *Tornadoes*

A tornado is not a storm system in itself, but rather an offspring of a thunderstorm. The potential energy stored within a parent thunderstorm is not a direct major hazard, but when converted into kinetic energy close to the surface, enormous damage can be inflicted on communities which happen to be nearby. A tornado vortex is the dynamical mechanism for this destructive energy conversion. A mathematician who had never witnessed or heard of a tornado, but could solve the Navier–Stokes equations for axisymmetric flow in a rotating cylinder, might surmise that Nature would make use of this frightening solution. For although a tornado occurs in a region of quite strong three-dimensional turbulence, the rotational forces impede the cascade of turbulent energy, thus allowing the core vortex to dominate.

Supercells, so-called because of their extended spatial and temporal dimensions, are responsible for producing the largest and most violent tornadoes, as well as hail and torrential rain. A supercell may have a diameter as great as 50 km, and last for several hours. The combination of strong winds aloft countered by weaker winds near the ground gives rise to a horizontal spinning vortex motion which can be transformed to vertical vortex motion by convective updrafts. Air which is both rising and rotating has a corkscrew motion which may be quantified in terms of *helicity*, which is defined as the alignment of wind velocity and vorticity vectors. Because of its helical nature, a supercell is less prone to viscous energy dissipation to smaller scales. Thus the gyratory wind field of a supercell is itself a key stabilizing factor in prolonging its life span.

Centrifugal force is considerable for winds rotating around a tornado, but the Coriolis force is negligible. The tangential wind velocity V_{tan} at a radial distance R from the centre can thus be approximately expressed in terms of the pressure gradient $\partial p / \partial R$, and the air density ρ as: $V_{tan} = \sqrt{(R / \rho)\, \partial p / \partial R}$. Inside the funnel of a tornado, the pressure can drop up to 100 millibars, and wind speeds can reach 100 m/s; and much higher tornado wind speeds are attainable. Low pressure in the tornado core creates a vacuum-cleaner effect in causing air and assorted debris to be sucked in near ground level, where friction lowers wind speeds and so prevents the centrifugal force from balancing the pressure gradient.

Tornadoes occur in mid-latitude regions of both hemispheres, but violent tornadoes mostly strike the continental United States, especially the area of the Central and East-Central United States, known as Tornado Alley. In April 1974, a super-outbreak of 148 tornadoes struck a 13-state area east of the Mississippi. At least six of these tornadoes carried wind speeds in excess of 100 m/s. More devastating was a tornado of March 1925, which remained on the ground for 220 miles. In Missouri, Illinois and Indiana, 700 people were killed, several thousand were injured and several towns were flattened.

Public warnings have since steadily reduced fatalities. Comparing a Mississippi tornado that struck without warning in 1936, with a bigger tornado that struck the state on 24 April 2010 and killed just ten, the official death toll in the earlier event was 216. But this tally excluded a similar number of black fatalities, which at that time were not counted in the South. The study of natural hazards cannot be decoupled from the political environment, and any natural catastrophe is liable to have a political dimension, which influences the segmentation of the population at risk, injured, killed, re-housed and compensated.

Tornadoes associated with tropical cyclones
The menace of tropical cyclones is heightened by their capability of spawning squalls of tornadoes, although these are not as ferocious as those on the Great Plains. At least as early as 1811, these have been recognized as occurring within some landfalling tropical cyclones. About a quarter of US hurricanes have been documented to spawn tornadoes. The level of tornado activity increases with both the intensity and size of the parent tropical cyclone. Hurricane Beulah in 1967 produced no less than 141 tornadoes. There is good spatial agreement between the patterns of hurricane tornadoes and enhanced ambient helicity. Sounding observations indicate that the maximum ambient helicity occurs in the right-front quadrant of the landfalling hurricane, which helps explain the prevalence there of tornado activity.[18]

1.3.3   *Extra-tropical windstorms*

In middle latitudes, the large-scale variability of the weather is dominated by extra-tropical cyclones. There are large-scale horizontal temperature gradients in the atmosphere in these latitudes, which arise from differential radiative heating between high and low latitudes. The poleward decrease in the temperature is usually concentrated narrowly in so-called *baroclinic* zones, where the air density depends significantly on temperature as well as pressure. Subject to wave perturbations, these zones become unstable, and the westerly airflow breaks up into large vortex structures known as cyclones. Some of the most active weather events are associated with instabilities which occur at fronts, which are discontinuities that form in strongly baroclinic zones of the atmosphere. One of the most important fronts is the polar front, which was discovered by the Norwegian meteorologists Bjerknes and Solberg around 1920. It is not coincidental that the radical concept of discontinuity should have gained acceptance in meteorology at the same time as the revolution of quantum mechanics; discontinuity in Nature had been anathema to earlier generations of scientists.

The polar front, which approximately girdles the Earth in the middle latitudes, separates polar air from tropical air. Along parts of the polar front, colder and denser polar air advances towards the equator to form a cold front; parts moving poleward form a warm front. The temperature contrast between the warmer and colder air masses is especially large in winter; a factor which explains the far greater severity of winter storms. Individual meteorological factors favouring strong extra-tropical cyclones over the eastern North Atlantic Ocean include an enhanced north–south temperature contrast in the troposphere, associated with a very strong jet stream in the upper troposphere directed towards Europe.

Winds can be very strong, but seldom attain speeds typical of severe tropical cyclones; they rarely exceed 55 m/s. Nevertheless they may be destructive, and there may also be flooding. The threat of extra-tropical windstorm losses in Northern Europe is exemplified by the storm of January 1990, called Daria. This was a very intense, damaging storm with a minimum pressure of 947 millibars. In January 2007, a winter storm occurred with a less deep minimum pressure of 962 millibars,[19] but a larger area of damaging winds. Kyrill left a trail of heavy damage across Europe, with particularly severe disruption to infrastructure: several million homes were without electricity in Central Europe, airports were closed, and ferry and railway services were suspended.

1.4 Geological Hazards

Subterranean faults and magma chambers present practical problems of observational access, which make geological hazards rather deceptive as a source of potential danger. For instance, communities may be oblivious of the local presence of an active earthquake fault or dormant volcano. Seeing is believing; but people may not see indirect evidence without believing in it first. Timely warning of geological hazards is difficult, not least because a critical change in the dynamical state of a fault or volcano may be triggered by a wide variety of perturbations.

1.4.1 Earthquakes

Science benefits from the cross-fertilization of ideas between contrasting disciplines. Fresh insights often come from across an academic corridor. California may be associated more with sunshine than with ice, but it took an expert on the movement of glaciers, Harry Fielding Reid, to pioneer geodetic studies of ground movement in the vicinity of the San Andreas Fault. Observing significant horizontal displacements both before and after the 1906 earthquake, Reid formulated the elastic rebound theory to explain the occurrence of earthquakes. Reid theorized that crustal stresses cause strain to accumulate around faults. Sudden frictional sliding on a fault occurs when the strain reaches a threshold beyond that sustainable by the weakest rocks.

The study of fracture processes in rock is a branch of rock mechanics, which is a basic discipline in the mining engineering profession. It is ultimately the breaking of atomic bonds which creates the instability of a fault rupture.[20] Traditionally, most seismologists have been concerned less with the mechanics of fault rupture than with the ground vibrations subsequently generated. More slowly than by satellite, news of an earthquake is spread rapidly around the world by seismic waves which are registered on seismological instruments. From distant recordings, seismologists are able to locate, via a triangulation process, when and where a seismic event occurred, as well as to estimate its size.

Vibrations distant from the epicentre consist of small elastic deformations, i.e. strains, which result from the action of rock stresses. Deformation depends on material properties such as rock density, rigidity and compressibility. Generalizing Hooke's law that elastic deformation is proportional to load, the classical mathematical theory of elasticity relates stresses to strains.

There are two fundamental types of seismic waves in solids, corresponding to wave solutions of the basic elastic media equations. First, there are compressional waves, known as (Primary) P-waves, corresponding to particles moving forward and backward in the direction of wave propagation. Secondly, there are shear (Secondary) S-waves, which cannot exist in air or in liquids, but can propagate in solids, because of a degree of rigidity allowing particles to move to and fro, transverse to the direction of propagation.

For granite, the P-wave velocity is about 5.5 km/s, which is approximately twice the S-wave velocity. The resulting difference in travel times of the primary P and secondary S-waves can be used to locate epicentres. This used to be a lengthy process, but with enough seismic instrumentation, modern digital data processing can perform this in a matter of seconds. The capability to identify rapidly the occurrence of a large distant earthquake can provide sufficient early warning for some countermeasures, such as slowing trains and shutting gas lines.

Earthquakes associated with other earthquakes

Following the large 1992 Landers earthquake in California, which occurred near the San Bernardino region of the San Andreas Fault, there were widespread observations of increases in seismicity in areas far from the epicentre. The publicity given to this phenomenon encouraged a retrospective search for similar occurrences elsewhere, and examples of long-range triggering of earthquakes have been found in zones as distant as the Valley of Mexico and Rabaul in Papua New Guinea. The physical causes of long-range interactions between earthquakes are not well understood, but various suggestions have been made, including transient deformation and increasing pore pressure. Lomnitz undertook a statistical analysis of a global 20th century catalogue of large shallow earthquakes, with results suggesting a degree of universality of the triggering process: a significant number of consecutive events had a separation distance ranging from 400 to 1,000 km.[21]

Closer to the epicentre of a large earthquake, seismicity may be triggered by a change in the static stress field. To assess whether the occurrence of one earthquake would make another earthquake more (or less) imminent, it would help to know how rocks fail under stress loading. For the failure stress, there exists a formula due to the French physicist Coulomb, which has become a mainstay of rock mechanical theory. The advance (or delay) in the time of occurrence can be estimated as the ratio of the increase (or decrease) in Coulomb failure stress to the long-term stressing rate.

The change, ΔCFS, in the Coulomb failure stress can be expressed as: $\Delta CFS = \Delta \tau_{slip} + \mu (\Delta \sigma_n + \Delta p)$. Consequent on the first earthquake, $\Delta \tau_{slip}$ is the change in the shear stress resolved in the direction of slip of the second earthquake; $\Delta \sigma_n$ is the change in the normal stress resolved orthogonally to the second fault plane (a positive value signifies increased tension); μ is the coefficient of friction; and Δp is the change in pore pressure. As an example of a static stress change analysis, the 1992 Landers earthquake sufficiently reduced the normal stress on part of the San Andreas Fault so as to advance, by one or two decades, the next large earthquake having a rupture initiating in that part of the fault.[22]

Earthquakes associated with volcanoes
As the strain field changes within a volcanic system, due to changes in the pressure in magma channels and chambers or the intrusion of magma into dikes and sills, so volcanic earthquakes commonly occur. Indeed, most volcanic eruptions are associated with a build-up of seismic activity. Multiple events may cluster over a short period of time: swarms of earthquakes have followed many major eruptions. Apart from local volcanic earthquakes, volcanic processes may trigger distant tectonic earthquakes. In the manner that earthquakes can change stress, so also can the transport of magma. Calculations of Coulomb stress changes have been undertaken to show how magma chamber inflation has triggered earthquakes on the Izu Peninsula, Japan.

Earthquakes associated with tropical cyclones
It is well known that the passage of tropical cyclones over the oceans can be detected by seismometers, through changes in the low level microseisms associated with ocean waves. The possibility cannot be excluded that the sudden drop in pressure as a tropical cyclone passes might be a sufficient perturbation to *trigger* an earthquake. However, because there are many other triggers for earthquake activity, it is no

easy task to extract from synoptic catalogues of earthquakes and tropical cyclones convincing statistical evidence.

Meanwhile, several intriguing coincidences remain on file. Most famously, the 1923 Kanto earthquake in Japan was preceded by a typhoon, which, if it did not actually trigger the earthquake, certainly fanned the flames of the fire that burned 35 km² of Tokyo. Less well known is the sequence of disasters which were to postpone the US purchase of the Virgin Islands. On 29 October 1867, a strong hurricane passed through the Virgin Islands; the lowest measured pressure being 965 millibars at St. Thomas. Only a few weeks later, on 18 November 1867, a destructive earthquake occurred, damaging almost all of the plantation houses in St. Croix. There and in St. Thomas, the height of the ensuing tsunami exceeded five metres.

1.4.2 Volcanic eruptions

The interior of a volcano is a natural physics and chemistry laboratory for extreme states of matter rarely found elsewhere. But Nature's underground experiments on brittle solids, ductile magma, and pressurized gases, and even the spatial layout of the laboratory, are largely obscured from direct human observation. The geometrical configuration of the plumbing system of dikes and conduits, and the associated multi-phase dynamics of solid, liquid and gaseous material, can only be inferred by making postulates based on joint studies of the products of explosive eruptions, instrumental monitoring and computer modelling exercises. The source of erupted material below a volcano is the magma chamber, which accumulates gravitational and elastic potential energy, like a mechanical capacitor.

Volcanic eruptions associated with earthquakes
Although volcanic earthquakes tend to be small compared with the possible size of tectonic earthquakes, they can trigger landslides, which can in turn trigger a volcanic eruption. This sequence of events took place on 18 May 1980 on Mt. St. Helens: the ground shaking from a

modest earthquake triggered a massive landslide on the north slope of the volcano, which released a blast of superheated steam and rock.

Earthquakes tend to trigger eruptions more directly. The time interval after a major regional earthquake can often be a period of heightened volcanic risk. A change of stress (+ or -) could trigger an eruption. Increased stress surrounding the magma chamber may squeeze magma upward; a decrease of stress may promote the formation of gases and the unblocking of conduits above the magma chamber. In 1975, a Hawaiian earthquake generated seismic waves which destabilized the dynamics of the magma below the Kilauea volcano, and, within an hour, caused lava to be issued from fissures. From historical experience, perhaps the most notable candidate for eruption triggering is Mt. Fuji in Japan. The most recent example, which dates back three hundred years, is also the most striking. Less than two months after the great Hoei earthquake had hit the coast of mid-Honshu on 28 October 1707, a violent eruption of Mt. Fuji began on 16 December 1707.

A particularly well recorded set of observations comes from the Long Valley caldera region of California, which experienced a significant deformation transient coincident with the 1992 Landers earthquake in Southern California, which triggered other earthquake activity. From the global historical record of earthquakes and eruptions, Linde *et al.* have found that, within a few days of large earthquakes, there are many more eruptions within 750 km than would be expected.[23] Furthermore, the triggering of volcanic eruptions by earthquakes may be a factor in the apparently excessive number of eruptions which occur in near unison.

Two volcanic eruptions in the Sumatra–Andaman arc that followed within a few months of the great Sumatra earthquake of 26 December 2004 seem to have been seismically triggered. Walter *et al.* present evidence indicating that earthquake-induced decompression of the volcano magma systems leads to such eruptions.[24] Numerical modelling reveals that the Sumatra and other megathrust earthquakes in Kamchatka (1952), Chile (1960) and Alaska (1964) induced volumetric expansion in the areas where volcanoes erupted. This yields a plausible dynamical eruption mechanism: abrupt decompression of a magma reservoir or possibly its feeding system may initiate processes that increase magma overpressure, and can ultimately lead to an eruption.

1.5 Geomorphic Hazards

The first named storm of the 2010 Pacific hurricane season dumped torrential rain on Guatemala, and left a remarkable imprint: a cavernous 18 m diameter round sinkhole, which swallowed up a three-storey building. Such sinkholes may form when the underlying rock is dissolved by circulating groundwater. This is a hazardous example of a catastrophic change in landform, which occurs suddenly.

Earthquakes are a prime cause of geomorphic hazards. A surface fault rupture can result in sudden permanent ground deformation, which can dislocate pipelines and roadways, as well as foundations. But the primary catastrophic geomorphic hazards are associated with mountainous regions. For communities living within or close to regions of high terrain, existence is made more precarious by the potential for slope instability, resulting in landslides, debris flows and avalanches.

The enormous destructive energy of these geotechnical hazards comes from the force of gravity. The proclivity for soil, rock, water, snow, and ice masses to move down a slope under gravity may be described by its *disposition;*[25] a term which carries echoes of old mountain legend. The basic disposition of a slope is governed by factors such as geology, topography and climate, which may change over long periods of time, but are comparatively stable in the short term. Each slope also has a temporally variable disposition, which alters according to the effect of weathering processes and seasonal changes, such as the extent of snow cover, density of vegetation and water saturation. At certain times, the slope disposition may attain a critical state of instability, whereupon a landslide or rockfall may spontaneously occur. Besides such sporadic release of potential energy, the same type of event may be precipitated by an external trigger, such as heavy sustained rainfall, earthquake shaking, volcanic eruption, or freeze–thaw effects.

Snow avalanches are especially treacherous, because they can be set off by small changes in pressure and temperature. When large ice masses break away from glaciers, their impact below can be catastrophic: some 4,000 were killed and 9 villages destroyed around Mt. Huascarán in the Peruvian Andes in 1962 from an avalanche of snow and ice that mixed with soil and rock. Once a snow avalanche or rock fall starts, it may move downslope across a wide mountain zone. Alternatively, snow may also avalanche in winter down channels for mountain torrents. This reflects a natural interconnection between the different manifestations of mountain hazard. Fluvial erosion processes and landslides provide another example: landslides and debris flows often follow the paths of steep runs and channels, before coming to rest in deposition zones.

1.5.1 Landslides

A landslide is a movement of soil or rock downslope under gravity, occurring as a result of a discrete shear failure. The resistance to shear of a material depends on both the coefficient of friction under stress load, as well as on its cohesion. The latter factor results from the mutual attraction between fine particles, which tends to bind them together. The average effective shear strength s of a saturated slope can be expressed as a sum of cohesion and friction terms by the Coulomb relation: $s = c + (\sigma - u)\tan\varphi$. The first term c is the material cohesion: this is very large for clay, but very small for sand. In the second friction term, σ is the total normal stress on a shear plane; u is the pressure of the water in the voids between solid particles of soil, i.e. the pore water pressure; and $\tan\phi$ is the coefficient of friction. φ itself is called the effective friction angle. Experimental and field studies of soil mechanics establish the above Coulomb criterion as appropriate for surfaces where frictional failure occurs.

Strength degradation can arise through reductions in any of the Coulomb relation factors. For major landslide disasters, a reduction in $\sigma - u$ is most typical. Landslides which occur for the first time are often associated with landscaped slopes in urban areas, where insufficient account of landslides has been taken in design. But even landslides which occur repeatedly may be blamed on human ignorance or negligence: intensive cultivation of land, and the heaping of fill, can reduce the material cohesion c; over-steepening of slopes by excavation can reduce the effective friction angle φ; and large-scale irrigation, leaky sewers and water pipes, can increase the pore water pressure u.

An empirical threshold for landsliding may be estimated from joint observations of rainfall intensity and duration. For a given rate of rainfall, landslides will tend to be triggered when the duration of continuous rainfall exceeds a critical number of hours. A combination of rainfall, seismic activity, tree-felling and other human interference render some regions exceptionally prone to landslide activity. Case studies almost too numerous and dreadful to list emerge from the Gansu province in north-west China, where sites of more than 40,000 large-scale landslides are known, covering a quarter of the total area of the province. In the 20th century alone, the number of lives lost through landslides in this hazardous, but densely populated mountainous area, runs into six figures. A high level of risk persists in the 21st century: on 8 August 2010, a rain-triggered landslide killed more than a thousand, as it engulfed the small valley town of Zhouqu.

1.5.2 Debris flows

When a mixture of solid and fluid constituents travels down a slope under the force of gravity, one of the most formidable of natural hazards is created: a *debris flow*. Areas particularly susceptible are characterized as geologically active, with steep unstable slopes. Whereas solid forces govern the physics of rockslides and landslides, and fluid forces govern the physics of mountain torrents, a combination of interacting solid and fluid forces generate a debris flow. For as many ways that solid and fluid forces may combine on slopes, so there are different phenomena which can be described in terms of debris flow. These include debris slides, debris torrents, mudflows and lahars. By weight, debris flows are mostly composed of solids such as gravel, cobbles and boulders (up to 10 m in diameter), with minor amounts of clay. A landslide that becomes disaggregated as it moves down a steep slope can turn into a debris flow if it contains enough water for saturation.

Debris flows can originate externally, such as a pyroclastic flow entraining snow and ice, or a flood incorporating large quantities of sediment. However, most debris flows are mobilized by slope failure, for which the landslide Coulomb criterion applies. Changes in pore pressure distributions arising from rainfall or meltwater have been known to trigger many a debris flow through causing slope failure. Debris flows can involve individual slope failures or many small coalescing failures. The interaction of solid and fluid forces can drive a debris flow to great destructive power. Like avalanches, such flows can travel at high speeds, and can occur with little warning, smashing most objects in their path. Like water floods, debris flows can travel long distances and inundate vast areas.

Once mobilized, debris flows tend to move like wet cement as unsteady and non-uniform surges.[26] This loping movement can develop without intermittent damming or slope failures: wave fronts can coalesce and produce large amplitude surges, which may become unstable. Fluid viscosity, sliding friction, and particle collision are important in the process of momentum exchange within debris flows; factors too complex to be adequately represented by standard fluid models. As a debris flow moves downslope, its energy degrades, converting from gravitational energy to translational kinetic energy, to grain vibrational kinetic energy plus fluid pressure energy, to heat. Flows will extend farther the more efficient this conversion process proves to be.

Alluvial fans are landforms created by the deposition of eroded sediment at the base of mountain ranges. Despite being zones of high geomorphic activity, they are often densely populated, because construction is much more difficult on adjoining steep mountain slopes. Alas, otherwise attractive human habitats may well be particularly hazard-prone. The stark risk–benefit trade-off can end in catastrophe. In December 1999, about 19,000 died along the Cordillera de la Costa in northern Venezuela, when massive rainfall of almost a metre triggered destructive debris flows.

Debris flows and landslides caused by tropical cyclones

Water is the principal agent of failure of natural earth slopes, as well as of the slopes of levees, dams, highways and railway cuttings. Rainfall is often exceedingly high as a tropical cyclone makes landfall, especially if the very moist air is forced up and over mountains. Given the sustained torrential rain brought by tropical cyclones, it is to be expected that massive debris flows and landslides should accompany their passage over high and steep terrain. But the lack of adequate preparation for them can be as astonishing as the scale of slope failures.

Within a single 24-hour period in September 1989, Hurricane Hugo dumped 20 to 30 cm of rain in the steeply sloping mountains of eastern Puerto Rico, and triggered four hundred landslides. The largest of these was a debris avalanche which moved about 30,000 m^3 of soil and rock 600 metres downslope. In 1994, more than 1,000 Haitians died as landslides were induced by thunderstorms at the fringe of Tropical Storm Gordon. Very much greater a storm was Hurricane Mitch, which had an extremely low central pressure of 905 millibars; at the time of occurrence in October 1998, this was the fourth lowest central pressure recorded for any western hemisphere hurricane. Prodigious rain brought massive landslides in Guatemala and Honduras, and exposed chronic weaknesses in disaster preparedness. In August 2009, typhoon Morakot dumped 200 cm of rain on southern Taiwan, causing devastating mudslides.

Torrential rain is not the only mechanism by which tropical cyclones can cause slope failure. Submarine landslides can also happen through the action of huge water waves on submarine slopes, resulting in wave-induced stresses, an eventual loss of shear strength, and ultimate slope failure. Evidence of such a submarine landslide comes from Hurricane Camille in 1969, which created enormous waves in excess of 20 metres on the Mississippi Delta.

Debris flows and landslides caused by earthquakes

Acting on slopes, seismic forces may directly cause sliding, or induce additional pore water pressure in the soil, which lowers the resistance to sliding. Furthermore, the amplification of ground motion by the overlying deposit may cause differential movements between loose soil and the solid bedrock. In some earthquakes, landslides have caused as much damage as other seismic hazards combined.[27] Notable among these events was the 1964 Good Friday earthquake in Alaska, during which numerous buildings near Anchorage were destroyed as near-surface material slid along underlying wet clay.

Just as a single large earthquake can damage buildings over a very wide area through ground shaking, so this can happen through landslides. On 12 May 2008, the Wenchuan, China, earthquake triggered more than

100,000 landslides. Earlier, in 1920, a large earthquake in Haiyuan, northern China, set off a dense series of landslides over a vast area of 4,000 km², which buried many villages and tens of thousands of inhabitants. Landsliding in the loess deposits was exacerbated through *liquefaction*: a process where large deformations in saturated cohesionless soil occur, following a build-up of pore water pressure induced by earthquake stresses.

Multiple landslides can be caused even by moderate earthquakes. This is a concern for landslide-prone cities, such as Tijuana, Mexico, where seismic activity is occasional. The past is often the key to gauging the future potential for surprise in natural catastrophes: several hundred landslides were generated in 1986 by a moderate earthquake in El Salvador. As in the Grand Banks earthquake off Newfoundland in 1929, landslides may occur on undersea slopes bearing unconsolidated material. Particles of mud, silt and sand become suspended in a turbidity current, which increases in intensity, in a self-stoking turbulent manner, as it flows down-slope.

Debris flows and landslides caused by volcanoes

The international vocabulary of volcanic action is drawn from the vernacular of hazardous regions. Thus, the Javanese word *lahar* is universally used for a debris flow along volcanic slopes, occurring either during or after an eruption. Lahars have insidious ways of displaying their menace, exploiting as many sources of water as may be found at a volcano, e.g. lakes, snow-caps, rivers, and rainfall. They may also emerge when a pyroclastic flow reaches a river.

Some of the most destructive lahars have been caused by eruptions through crater lakes. The 1919 eruption of Kelut volcano in Java violently mixed 38 million m^3 of water with volcanic debris. Lahars killed more than 5,000, and destroyed more than a hundred villages.

The melting of snow and ice has produced many notable lahars. With a maximum discharge of 48,000 m^3/s, a lahar originating from the snow-capped peak of Nevado del Ruiz in Colombia buried 22,000 in Armero in 1985. Lahars, caused by the rapid melting of the Eyjafjallajökull ice cap in Iceland in April 2010, posed a dangerous hazard to people near the volcano, quite apart from the continental aviation disruption.

1.6 Hydrological Hazards

The dependence of human life on water for subsistence, irrigation, transport and recreation exposes people and property to a diverse range of marine perils, the catastrophic effects of which may, in times of anguish, call into question the benefits of proximity to water. The rapid mobility of large volumes of water makes hydrological hazard a common secondary cause of loss following the incidence of other forms of natural hazard. The principal manifestations of hydrological hazard are the flooding of rivers, and storm surges and tsunamis in coastal regions.

1.6.1 River flooding

Heavy sustained rainfall, snow or icemelt, can lead to a high runoff from a catchment into a river, which may result in flow beyond its banks and consequent flooding. The dependence of flooding on rainfall varies according to the nature of the catchment. There are some types of catchment where the scale of flooding is directly related to rainfall, and conditions prior to the deluge are not important. These catchments include areas of clay or soil crusting. On the other hand, there are catchments with permeable soils which are able to store immense volumes of storm water. The wetter these catchments are prior to a deluge, the greater the likelihood of flooding. Soil absorption capacity is a key factor to be accounted for in hydrological rainfall-runoff models developed for flood forecasting.

Historically, the greatest flood disasters are those associated with the major rivers which drain south from the Himalayas; flow through eastern China; and down the Central US. From these mighty rivers down in scale to small tributaries and streams, river flooding is an almost universal peril. Bangladesh, which lies at the confluence of three major rivers (Ganges, Brahmaputra and Meghna) is a field study in river flooding: the annual runoff suffices to cover the entire country to a depth of eight metres. Besides regular rainfall floods, there are monsoon floods, where the rivers may stay at high flows for many weeks, as submerged a fifth of Pakistan in 2010. There are also flash floods where short duration heavy rain in the mountain catchments results in rapid runoff. In Bangladesh, more than a fifth of the country is flooded one year in two; but then annual fresh water inundation is essential to agriculture. Floodplain ecosystems are naturally adjusted to periodic inundation, even if artificial ecosystems established on floodplains are not.[28] The dynamic interaction between the human and river environments was well illustrated in 1993, when sustained heavy spring rain augmented by snowmelt brought about the worst flood in the 20th century in the Central US: almost a thousand miles of the Mississippi and Missouri rivers rose above normal flood levels.

Floods caused by tropical cyclones
Sustained torrential rain accompanying tropical cyclones inevitably brings the risk of flash flooding of rivers: over a single day in September 1963, as much as 126 cm fell over Pai Shih in Taiwan, as a typhoon passed. The flooding produced by the rainfall accompanying a tropical cyclone can be so intense as to break maximum discharge records on rivers. In September 1967, Hurricane Beulah caused floods of record-breaking magnitude over a vast 100,000 km² area of south Texas and northeastern Mexico; on the Rio Alamo watershed in Mexico, about 90 cm of rain was measured. As with flood hazard in general, the propensity for flooding induced by the passage of a tropical cyclone is often exacerbated by human encroachment into areas of high flood potential.

Floods caused by landslides
Landslides may generate a river flood hazard through the sudden formation of a debris dam, behind which ponding may occur. The size of the dam can be monumental: in 1893, a large section of rock dropped into a narrow Himalayan gorge, and formed a dam 300 m high and 1 km wide. The potential for severe damage was starkly demonstrated in the 1993 Paute Valley landslide, near Cuenca, Ecuador. A large rockslide of volume about 25 million m^3 dammed the Paute River at La Josefina. The inevitable ponding first caused upstream flooding, and then downstream flooding, once the debris dam was overtopped. The downstream flood wave had a peak discharge of almost 10,000 m^3/s, and caused serious damage to an area, which fortunately had been evacuated.

Floods caused by volcanic eruptions

The melting of glacier ice above an erupting volcano can lead to torrential flooding. Although these floods are known to occur in the Andes, they are most notorious in Iceland, whence their Icelandic name *jökulhlaup*, which sounds purely onomatopoeic, but has a stark meaning: 'glacier burst'. Beneath the broad Vatnajökull icecap, there are many volcanic centres. About 60 eruptions have occurred over the past 1,100 years, Grimsvötn being the most active. At the end of September 1996, a fissure eruption started close by, which caused meltwater to fill the subglacial lake at Grimsvötn. When the inevitable *jökulhlaup* finally occurred, the deluge was overwhelming – at its peak, the flow rate was 50,000 m^3/s. Some of the gigantic blocks of ice debris weighed more than 1,000 tons.[29]

1.6.2 Storm surges

Storms increase the tidal range beyond the mean predictions of tide tables, and so threaten coastal areas with inundation. The rise in water level begins with a local atmospheric low pressure system that lifts the sea surface through an inverted barometer response. A rise in sea level of approximately 1 cm accompanies a decrease in atmospheric pressure of 1 millibar. This relation was first observed in the winter of 1848–1849, when records of sea level and atmospheric pressure were kept on a ship trapped in the Canadian Archipelago, but the first quantitative dynamical discussion was given by the geophysicist Harold Jeffreys. Strong winds that rush into the low pressure area compound the rise in sea level. Depending on the direction of the wind, the surge may move towards the shore as a positive storm surge, or away from the shore as a negative storm surge. The most dangerous storm surges occur when the arrival of a storm happens to coincide with a spring tide, so that the overall water level is maximal.

Storm surges caused by tropical cyclones

A very strong tropical cyclone can generate a storm surge more than 6 m in height. About a metre of this might be attributable to the lower atmospheric pressure at the centre of the storm; the rest is due to the driving effect of strong winds and the configuration of the adjacent continental shelf. At landfall then, the storm surge is highest where the onshore winds are strongest, and where ocean bottom bathymetry focuses the wave energy. When a storm travels parallel to a coast without making landfall, a storm surge will also occur, but will either precede or follow behind the storm centre, according to when the winds blow onshore.

Preparedness for a storm surge was once a matter of notching water heights on offshore marker poles. The task is now facilitated by the computational modelling of the surge process. To model a storm surge, a set of differential equations describing water motion and surge height is discretized, and applied to a two-dimensional grid covering the area over which a forecast is to be made. This area may include bays, estuaries, channels and barriers.

The impact of a storm surge is generally greatest on beaches and islands; the surge height diminishes by a foot or so for every mile inland. However, very serious inundation inland can follow if the storm surge coincides with a high astronomical tide, as happened in 1989 when Hurricane Hugo struck the South Carolina coast. Inland loss from storm surge can be catastrophic: 1,836 people died in 1928 when Lake Okeechobee in Florida was blown into the surrounding lowlands.

Far more catastrophic loss of life has occurred around the North Indian Ocean, especially along coastal regions of India, Bangladesh and Myanmar. As Cyclone Nargis made landfall in Myanmar on 2 May 2008, storm surges as high as 4 m were observed, in line with computer model simulations.[30] A sorry, if all too predictable, confluence of cyclone and political risk delayed the arrival of international aid, and tens of thousands perished.

Storm surges caused by extra-tropical storms
Outside the tropics, severe storms can cause flooding around the low-lying margins of shallow seas. The coastline bordering the southern North Sea is very susceptible to storm surges; as far back as the 2nd century BC, a great flood of the Jutland and northwest German coasts led to the migration of the Celtic population. The east coast of England is

prone to flooding from northerly gales in the North Sea, due to the Coriolis force: currents flow to the right of the wind direction in the northern hemisphere. The greatest British storm surge disaster occurred in 1953. As with many large regional flood disasters, the storm surge coincided with a spring tide. Since then, numerical storm surge models have been developed, based on solving the hydrodynamic equations for sea motion under tidal and meteorological forcing.

1.6.3 Tsunamis

Etymology provides a curious anthropological guide to regional natural hazards. In the *Nambi-Quala* dialect of tribes in the Amazon Rainforest, there is no indigenous word for earthquake, so aseismic is the region. In Portuguese, which is the principal language spoken in Brazil, there is a word *terramoto* for earthquake, and also a word *maremoto* for an earthquake epicentred at sea, such as devastated Lisbon in 1755.

In the English language, there is no equivalent single word for a sea quake, nor is there an indigenous word for a sea wave generated by a non-meteorological source. *Tidal wave* is sometimes used, (in reference to UK storm surges), but this is a misnomer. Instead, ever since a disaster in 1896, the Japanese word for harbour wave has been used: *tsunami*.

The waves which threaten harbours may have been initiated by earthquakes, volcanic eruptions, landslides (or even asteroid impacts) thousands of kilometres away. Tsunamis are associated with coasts which are tectonically active, but because of their great travel distances, they can also have significant effects on coasts and hinterland areas far from zones of high seismicity.

Because of the focusing effect of variations in Pacific bathymetry, and the steering action of the Coriolis force, wave energy from distant tsunamis is often concentrated in the Japanese Archipelago. Deposits of past tsunamis are imprinted on the coastal geomorphology, notably on the Sendai plain, where a tsunami flooded several miles inland in 869. On 24 May 1960, the whole Pacific coast of Japan was struck by a tsunami. This was no local event; but rather a trans-oceanic tsunami generated off the Chilean coast the previous day by the greatest 20th century earthquake. Despite the geometrical spreading of waves from the Chilean source, on the opposite side of the Pacific, tsunami heights reaching 8 m were observed on the Japanese coasts.

Since 1960, tsunami observation has improved with the acquisition of better bathymetric data, and more recordings of wave heights obtained on coastal tide gauges. However, the Indian Ocean was still poorly monitored when a giant earthquake struck on 26 December 2004 off the northwest coast of Sumatra. This triggered a catastrophic tsunami, which killed a quarter of a million people around the Indian Ocean Basin.

For an earthquake tsunami, the geometry and kinematics of the fault source can be inferred indirectly by working backwards from seismograms regionally recorded. With sufficient seismological data, the fault source should be quite well constrained by this mathematical inversion procedure. Once the source has been characterized, the displacement of the seafloor can be computed using the equations of elastodynamics. The displacement forces the water column above to move, which then produces the tsunami. The labour of tsunami simulation is eased by the negligible coupling between the water and the Earth. Thus the deformation of the surface of the elastic Earth caused by an earthquake can be computed first, and then used as a boundary condition for hydrodynamic computation.

Tsunamis caused by volcanic eruptions
Tsunamis are generated by volcanoes in various ways: through pyroclastic flows, explosions and submarine eruptions, but half are associated with calderas, or cones within calderas. Some of the most cataclysmic volcanic eruptions involve a process of subsidence and caldera collapse which can result in massive tsunamis. An example from 3,500 years ago is the explosive volcanic eruption on the Aegean island of Santorini, which discharged tsunami waves around the eastern Mediterranean Sea.[31] In 1792, 10,000 people lost their lives in a tsunami resulting from a flank collapse on Unzen in Japan, and 36,000 were washed away by waves up to 40 metres high following the 1883 eruption of Krakatau. The modelling of tsunamis generated by a large submarine explosion differs from that of earthquake-generated tsunamis, because the excitation force lies within the ocean, rather than below the ocean

floor, and hence can directly act on the ocean water. The resulting equations yield a special combination of elastic, sound and gravity waves, which depict in mathematical symbols a scene of frightful terror.

Tsunamis caused by submarine slides
A tsunami generated by a submarine slide can be a dangerous hazard in fjords, bays, lakes and straits, where there are unstable sediment accumulations. Lituya Bay in Alaska has witnessed several tsunamis caused by landslides, including one in 1958, which generated a wave which removed trees to a height of 500 metres.[32] This size of wave emanated despite the low 2% efficiency of the conversion process from landslide potential energy to tsunami wave energy.

The historical record of catastrophic tsunamis can be extended back much further through *palaeotsunami* evidence, such as observation and dating of a distinct layer of sand in a peat outcrop. One prehistoric slide studied in some detail occurred in the Storegga area of the Norwegian Sea about 8,000 years ago. Reconstruction of this slide from tsunami deposits suggests that the resulting tsunami was one of the largest in the past 10,000 years. It affected coastal areas bordering the eastern North Atlantic Ocean, the Norwegian Sea and the northern North Sea. A simulation model of the tsunami developed by Harbitz indicates that a landslide moving at an average velocity of 35 m/s would have led to substantial runup heights of between 3 and 5 metres along neighbouring coasts of Greenland, Iceland and Western Norway.[33]

A remarkable feature of tsunamis generated by submarine slides is the colossal scale of the slides known to have occurred in the geological past; a scale that dwarfs any measure of historical slides. Such landslides are recognized as an integral part of the evolution of volcanic islands. For example, individual debris avalanches on the flanks of the Hawaiian Islands can involve 5,000 km^3 of material, giving rise to tsunami heights on the coast of Oahu as high as 50 to 60 metres. In the Canary Islands, a large debris avalanche has been found by sonar to be covered by angular blocks more than a kilometre across and 200 metres high.[34] This landslide is dated back about 15,000 years. Atlantic coast residents may take assurance from the geological evidence that the average time interval between major landslides is several times longer than this.

Chapter 2

Societal Hazards

To be alive at all involves some risk.
Harold Macmillan
UK Prime Minister

Natural hazards have sculpted the Earth's surface, and are endemic on the planet. Their severity may be influenced by actions of man, such as with future climate change, but great volcanic eruptions, earthquakes, hurricanes, tsunamis, and floods would occur if there never had been life on Earth. These are external hazards to which *Homo Sapiens* has always been exposed since emerging out of Africa; a development process that survived the supervolcanic eruption of Mt. Toba on Sumatra 74,000 years ago. Such is the power of Nature, that in seeking the cause for the decline of ancient civilizations, archaeologists often look for residual evidence of an external hazard, such as a great geological or hydrological catastrophe.

Apart from external natural hazards, there are also essentially internal hazards, the severity of which is driven by the development of human society. A common characteristic of societal hazards is the organized response of society to deal with threats, through codes of social and business conduct, corporate rules, and government regulations. The metaphor of a human immune system has been used to convey the coping mechanisms developed within society in the face of dangers, that may be likened to pathogens. Resilient organizations and communities adapt to changing patterns of anti-social or criminal behaviour, whether it is violence, fraud, or negligence, and exert some degree of system control over the consequent potential for catastrophe.

First among societal hazards is political violence, manifested through declared war, insurgency, and terrorism. The historian Edward Gibbon wrote of the Eastern Mediterranean earthquake of 365 AD, in which 5,000 were drowned by tsunami in Alexandria: 'Man has much more to fear from the passions of his fellow human beings than from the convulsions of the elements.'[1] The same is true of the spread of deadly infectious disease. Until their prohibition by the Geneva Convention, biological weapons were used as a lethal yet uncontrollable weapon of war. In 1346, Tartar forces catapulted plague-ridden corpses over the walls of a Black Sea besieged city, forcing the defending forces to retreat to Venice, from where the Black Death spread throughout Italy.

Whatever the terrorist intent to perpetuate biological warfare in the 21st century, even the most advanced biological laboratories cannot reproduce the most dangerous novel genetic reassortments of Nature. As a consequence, infectious disease pandemic remains Nature's biological weapon, with the global capability of killing millions of people.

Much smaller but still significant numbers of deaths may arise from the technological advance of society through industrial and transportation accidents. As demonstrated by the Chernobyl nuclear disaster in the Ukraine, the Exxon Valdez oil tanker disaster in Alaska, and the Deepwater Horizon oil spill disaster in the Gulf of Mexico, such accidents can be ecologically as well as economically destructive. As the geographical frontiers of exploration and industrialization have expanded, the potential has grown for catastrophic accidents.

Financial disasters may not be intrinsically lethal, but they can ruin lives and trigger political upheaval. The road to financial ruin may be partially closed by effective financial regulation, but individual and corporate fraudsters lack neither the ingenuity nor incentive to find routes to *catastrophize* the personal scale of 21st century fraud losses into the billion dollar range. Fear and profit motivate even honest financial traders, pushing markets out of equilibrium towards dynamic instability, and the perpetuation of systemic boom–bust cycles. Add honour to fear and profit, and the Greek historian Thucydides characterized the psychological motivation for the 5th century BC Peloponnesian War between Athens and Sparta. Shared human emotional drivers generate common dynamical patterns of societal risk.

2.1 Political Violence

It has been said of Thucydides that he wrote not only the *History of the Peloponnesian War*, but also the history of the Napoleonic Wars, World War I, World War II, and the Cold War. Alliances, balances of power, and choices in war between war and appeasement have remained similar over the millennia.[2] There is a timeless universal logic of hostility that is captured by Thucydides in his analysis of grand strategy. Indeed, whilst military technology is ever changing, it may be doubted whether modern strategists know anything about strategy that was unknown to him.[3] As in natural science, where there is universality there is underlying implicit mathematical structure to be explored and elucidated.

In the second half of the 20th century, the use of mathematical concepts in the formulation of military strategy was raised to a highly advanced technical level at the RAND Corporation in California, where creative minds such as John von Neumann, Oskar Morgenstern, and John Nash developed applications of the mathematical theory of conflict: game theory. Just as with strategy for the Cold War, RAND has also had a pivotal role in developing counterinsurgency strategy since the 1950s, through the establishment of an Insurgency Board.[4]

Intellectually, modern developments owe much to the strategic thinking of Antoine-Henri Jomini, who used a geometric vocabulary to convey his approach of putting superior force at the decisive point. Jomini served in the Napoleonic wars, and would have learned much from Napoleon's mathematical mastery of the military manoeuvre.

Thucydides is one of a number of grand military theorists over the ages: Kautilya in India, Julius Caesar in Rome, Machiavelli in Florence, and of course Clausewitz in Prussia. A close contemporary of Thucydides, but a civilization apart, was Sun Tzu. Two and a half thousand years ago, he wrote a treatise on the Art of War for the King of Wu in China. This masterpiece of military strategy, which was translated into French in the 18th century, retains its relevance for contemporary military conflicts, insurgencies, and terrorism. In his time, it was not unusual for leading thinkers to be employed as strategists by the sovereign. Many of the principles of the Art of War are strategy solutions that have no space–time boundary of geography or historical era, and might have originated from a mathematical mind.

It was Sun Tzu who first described guerrilla warfare, a type of informal conflict where surprise is a key weapon. In his revolutionary doctrine on guerrilla warfare, Che Guevara quoted Sun Tzu, and echoed the need for cleverness and surprise, using a Latin American idiom, 'The guerrilla fighter is the Jesuit of warfare'.[5] The term *guerrilla*, meaning 'little war', was originally coined in the Spanish War of Independence, following Napoleon's invasion of Spain in 1808. The British and Portuguese armies supported Spanish partisans, who would now be called guerrillas. Occurring in most societies around the world, the most common type of conflict is indeed guerilla war.

Following in the footsteps of Sun Tzu as a Chinese theorist of guerrilla war was Mao Zedong.[6] Mao's theory centred on a three-stage model. First is the organization of base areas, around which a network of sympathizers would be created. An aquatic Maoist metaphor is a guerrilla moving among the people and being sustained by them like fish in water. Second is the expansion of the base areas, with military action being taken to kill collaborators of the enemy. The third stage of Mao's guerrilla warfare is the destruction of the enemy. Following the precepts of Sun Tzu, Mao's Red Army attacked when strong and retreated when weak, and eventually overcame the nationalist forces in 1949.

Ideas on military strategy flow readily across borders. Mao's advice was influential in Vietnam in enabling Ho Chi Min to trap the French army at Dien Bien Phu in 1954. Across continents, the Peruvian terrorist organization, Sendero Luminoso (Shining Path), followed Mao's teaching. In Europe, several of the founders of the Italian Red Brigades and the French Action Directe belonged to Maoist groups. Their heyday of terror was in the 1970s and 1980s before the fall of the Berlin Wall stripped them of ideological backing and popular support.

The demise of terrorist groups has been analyzed by Cronin,[7] who has emphasized the dynamic tripartite nature of a terrorist campaign, involving not just the terrorist group and the target government, but also the audience influenced by the violence. The complex interactions between these three protagonists govern the life cycle of a terrorist campaign, with its wave-like phases of expansion and contraction.

2.1.1 The wave theory of terrorism

Ralph Elliott was an accountant who originated the wave principle of financial markets, which, he suggested, are moved by swings in investor crowd psychology. Less influential than Elliott waves in the financial markets has been his work on Nature's law of waves, 'A phenomenon that appears to mark the progress of all human activities.'[8] Just as there are cyclical geodynamic drivers of natural catastrophes, there are generational drivers for man-made cataclysms. The theory of plate tectonics epitomizes a paradigm shift in natural science, of the kind Thomas Kuhn analyzed in his philosophical study of the structure of scientific revolutions.[9] In political science, an analogy has been drawn with the structure of large-scale policy changes.[10] The overthrow of communism in Eastern Europe and dictators in the Middle East are salient examples of transformational political waves, impacting like tsunamis on unpopular regimes which have stood for too long.

In his *Four Waves of Modern Terrorism*, David Rapoport outlined a unified theory of terrorism, presenting a broad picture of terrorism as a recurrent manifestation of political violence, forcing and reacting to major policy shifts.[11] The first wave identified by Rapoport was the anarchist wave, which grew out of the failure of democratic reform, and was the first example of global terrorism. It began in the 1880s in Russia, where the terrorist was lauded as a martyr and hero. After seven failed attempts, *The People's Will* succeeded in deploying a bomb to assassinate Czar Alexander II in 1881. Within a decade, anarchist violence struck in Western Europe, the Balkans, and Asia. In the 1890s, the close of the century marked the end for a host of political leaders, assassinated by anarchists. But a generation later, the wave of anarchic terrorism was dissipated by the political upheaval of the Great War.

The second anti-colonial wave began in the 1920s, gained momentum from a *zeitgeist* of national self-determination, and lasted four decades. Foreign states predictably acted in their own self-interest, which a game theorist would interpret as rational behaviour, and lent support to nationalist movements. Thus Greece backed the Cypriots against the British, and Arab states supported the Algerian National Liberation Front against the French.

Emerging in the 1960s, and amplified by the Vietnam War, was the New Left wave aligned with communist objectives. With Soviet encouragement, many western groups, such as the American Weather Underground, the West German Red Army Faction (RAF), the Italian Red Brigades, and the French Action Directe battled on the streets with establishments styled as reactionary. With the end of the Vietnam War in 1975, the Palestine Liberation Organization (PLO) was championed.

During the third wave, numerous hijackings, kidnappings, and assassinations took place, and Americans were especially targeted. The Palestinian hijacker, Leila Khaled wrote confidently, 'We shall win because we represent the wave of the future'.[12] But with the dissolution of the Soviet Union, support for extreme left-wing violence faded, and towards the end of the 20th century only a few active groups remained. One of these, founded in 1964, was the Revolutionary Armed Forces of Colombia (FARC), which started out as a group of peasant families, and developed into a sizeable rural guerrilla army.

In 1979, as the extreme left-wing terrorism wave began to ebb, a religious wave emerged which strengthened into the 21st century with the Islamist attacks against America on 9/11. The overlap between ethnic and religious factors has been significant in many territories, including Armenia, Macedonia, Ireland, Cyprus, Chechnya, Israel, Palestine, and Sri Lanka. In the latter country, which is predominantly Buddhist, the largely Hindu Tamils aimed to create a separate state. The Liberation Tigers of Tamil Eelam (Tamil Tigers) fought a bitter and brutal secessionist campaign for three decades, until their military defeat in May 2009. The prospect of a military solution had seemed a remote achievement a few years earlier.

Even if the timing of the end of a terrorist campaign is hard to predict, the wave image of terrorism provides an approximate time period over which a decline in activity may be anticipated. Rapoport has remarked on the durability of religious communities, suggesting that the fourth wave may last longer than its predecessors.

One of the factors impelling the first wave in Russia was doctrine, such as the nihilist exposition of Sergei Nechaev. In common with Osama bin Laden's Al Qaeda training manual, Nechaev's *Revolutionary Catechism* stressed a central tenet of terrorism modus operandi: learning from experience to gain efficiency. Each wave has had its own literature on efficient practices. Georgios Grivas's *Guerilla War* was a manifesto for the liberation of Cyprus from British colonialism. Carlos Marighella's *Mini-Manual of the Urban Guerillas* envisaged cities, rather than the countryside, as the geographical centre of revolutions.

A manifesto could also be produced by a terrorist intellectual acting on his own. Such a manifesto was written by a Berkeley mathematics professor turned wilderness cabin recluse, Ted Kaczynski. One of the most wily and elusive of lone-wolves, Kaczinski embarked on a sporadic US bombing campaign from 1978 to 1995, killing several people and injuring a few dozen. Known as the Unabomber for targeting universities and airlines, Kaczynski had his long reign of micro-terror ended by his own brother, who recognized his social manifesto and tipped off the FBI.

2.1.2 Cyber attack

After the end of World War II, in 1947, a monument to commemorate the Soviet war sacrifice was erected in Tallinn, the capital of the Baltic state of Estonia. Sixty years later, the Estonian government decision to move the bronze statue to a suburban military cemetery sparked an outbreak of virtual international hostility, termed Web War I.[13] It started on 9 May, the anniversary of Soviet victory in World War II, when specific Estonian sites were overwhelmed by a massive cyber attack, coordinated across Russian-language chat rooms to retaliate for the removal of the statue on 27 April.

Trans-national cyber attacks are a constant and persistent threat: NATO's computer systems are attacked many times a day. But the coordination and sophistication of this attack cast doubt on whether nation states could secure and retain control of their infrastructure and systems against a relatively inexpensive form of highly leveraged attack, categorized as the poor man's weapon of mass destruction.

The 2007 assault on government and private sector networks in Estonia was a turning point in cyber risk awareness. Attack escalation seriously impacted government websites and systems and shut down newspaper and financial networks. The Estonian government closed large parts of the country's network to outside traffic to take charge of a crisis aggravated by the difficult cross-border pursuit of cyber criminals. Traffic involved in attacking Estonia was inter-continental, being traced to countries from the USA to China, Vietnam, Egypt, and Peru.

Estonia had to summon international help urgently in tracking and blocking suspicious internet addresses and traffic. Computer security experts from across the western alliance were brought in to assist Estonia, and learn its lessons. Other highly networked small states, such as Singapore, perceived their own national vulnerability on the risk horizon and took notice. In May 2008, the need for NATO to boost its cyber defence capability was recognized through the establishment in Tallinn of the Cooperative Cyber Defence Centre of Excellence.

Web War I involved cyber criminals, known as botmasters, each of whom had illicit control of a *botnet* of thousands of computers, on which rogue software was planted. These infected hijacked zombie computers repeatedly sent out communications as part of a denial of service operation. The network configuration of a botnet is a key factor in its resilience against being shut down. Like human terrorist networks, a decentralized computer network topology reduces communication efficiency, but adds robustness.

Russian involvement in virtual international hostilities moved from targeting Estonia to Georgia in 2008. Georgian government websites were shut down by a distributed denial of service attack, launched during the Russia–Georgia conflict over South Ossetia. This was a more orthodox example of auxiliary cyber warfare, conducted strategically to support a military campaign and suppress civic response.

Sun Tzu stressed the importance of winning the information war. A state-sponsored cyber attack capable of achieving political aims without the need for overt military action might also have been inspired by the strategic philosophy of Sun Tzu. Cryptography sections of intelligence agencies are taking responsibility to thwart such cyber provocation, which is far from science fiction. Discovered in 2010, the *stuxnet* worm had the technical sophistication and precision targeting of a digital cruise missile. It introduced cyber attack into the play-book of political espionage in an audacious way not even imagined in Hollywood.

2.2 Infectious Disease Pandemics

Among the Nobel laureates in physiology and medicine, one who stands out for applying mathematics to medical discovery is Ronald Ross, who made many contributions furthering the understanding of malaria, notably demonstrating the mosquito transmission of malaria, and developing mathematical models for the study of its epidemiology. As relevant to infectious as parasitic disease is his mathematician's modest apology: 'The mathematical method of treatment is really nothing but the application of careful reasoning to the problems at issue.'[14] The exercise of careful reasoning lies at the heart of all catastrophe calculations. In particular, the mathematical analysis of infectious disease pandemics involves not so much extensive knowledge of mathematics, although professional epidemiologists need some technical facility, as a reasoned practical appreciation of the problems at issue.

A century after Ross's careful reasoning, mathematical biologists have a key role supporting laboratory colleagues in mitigating the ravages of infectious disease. Contributions include constructing evolutionary models to predict viral mutations, estimating the likelihood of pandemics, and analyzing the population spread of an infectious disease. Advice on public policy issues covers a range of awkward decisions. Is it necessary to track the contacts of those infected, or is isolation sufficient? At a societal level, advice is needed on the efficacy of transportation restrictions, closing public meeting places, the use of anti-viral treatments, and scheduling a programme of public vaccination.

Ronald Ross grasped early the global importance of western scientists studying diseases in the tropics. A survey of global trends in emerging infectious diseases shows that more than half of emerging infectious diseases are caused by pathogens having an animal source, most of which have a wildlife origin.[15] A prime example is the 2003 outbreak of Severe Acute Respiratory Syndrome (SARS) in Guandong Province, China. From construction of an evolutionary tree of the SARS coronovirus, the source turned out to be in the bat population, which is a natural reservoir for many human viruses, including Ebola. In packed Asian animal markets, infected bats passed on the SARS infection to civets, from which cat-like species the virus jumped to humans.

Ominous as the potential threat is from emerging infectious diseases, influenza stands out as the persistent historical and future human threat. Influenza is not an eradicable disease. In wild ducks, influenza viruses cause no disease signs, ensuring their perpetuation in the aquatic bird reservoir, which contains all known subtypes of influenza A. This is the type presenting the greatest danger to humans, and is able to cause disease in birds, pigs, and other animals. Influenza viruses of avian origin are implicated in outbreaks in pigs as well as in domestic poultry. The main reservoirs are the vast flocks of birds in China, which are in close contact with large human populations.

Type A viruses are divided into types based on differences in two viral surface proteins called haemagglutinin (H) and neuraminidase (N). There are 16 known H subtypes and 9 known N subtypes. Only certain influenza A subtypes H1N1, H1N2, and H3N2, generally circulate in the human population. Others are found most commonly in animal species. The process by which an influenza virus mutates to evade immune systems is called antigenic variation. Seasonal influenza epidemics are caused by such mutations.

Occasionally, a more serious antigenic shift occurs involving an exchange of gene segments between human and animal influenza viruses. In a significant proportion of both adults and children, protective antibody levels are absent, and a global pandemic results. Mathematical biologists map the antigenic drift of the influenza virus to detect patterns,[16] but there is still a significant random element to the reassortment of genes leading to a pandemic.

As a consequence, epidemiologists look to history for guidance on the frequency of influenza pandemics, which is approximately every 30 years on average. During the 20th century, there were pandemics in 1918 (H1N1 Spanish flu), 1957 (H2N2 Asian flu), and 1968 (H3N2 Hong Kong flu). The 1918 pandemic killed about 40 million people worldwide and was more lethal than the Great War itself. The 1957 pandemic killed an estimated two million people, and the 1968 pandemic killed about one million people. Genetic analysis of the H2N2 and H3N2 viruses has shown they arose by genetic reassortment between avian and seasonal human viruses.

If not killed by the host's immune system, the influenza virus replicates in the respiratory tract and damages host cells. The main complication of the influenza virus is pneumonia which accounts for much of the mortality. A disproportionate number of young adults died in the 1918 pandemic, due to an excessively vigorous immune response known as a *cytokine storm*, in reference to signalling molecules called cytokines which signal immune cells to travel to the site of infection. Whereas seasonal influenza puts at risk mainly the young and elderly, an influenza pandemic can be a grave danger to a much wider age group of the population, thus posing a greater challenge to immunization public health policy.

2.2.1 Vaccination

Vaccination against an infectious disease is an important public health measure which still evokes political controversy in the 21st century, especially where there is an awkward balance between the cost and safety of vaccination and its effectiveness. The excess production of H1N1 vaccine for the swine influenza pandemic which spread from Mexico in spring 2009 brought criticism upon the World Health Organization, which declared a pandemic in June 2009. By December 2009, half a billion vaccine doses had been produced, but this was still insufficient to cover 10% of the world's population. As it turned out, the virus was much less lethal than feared, and this reduced the global demand for vaccination. However, to protect the developing as well as developed world against a future severe influenza pandemic, improved public policy on vaccination will be needed, including possibly some degree of pre-pandemic immunization.[17] Whatever the policy, it will have to be supported with robust mathematical calculations of anticipated efficacy and safety.

Mathematical epidemiologists have a key role in advising governments on vaccination strategies, which may be politically controversial, especially where there are potential adverse reactions to vaccination. The first mathematician to take on such controversy was Daniel Bernoulli, who published a paper in 1766, aimed at influencing attitudes towards *variation*, which was the technique introduced from Turkey to England, of injecting a mild strain of the smallpox virus to gain full immunity. Such advocacy was badly needed. Voltaire had derided the English as fools for giving their children smallpox to prevent their catching it. Bernoulli's insightful mathematics is an exemplary lesson in catastrophe risk analysis. It shows how objective scientific calculations, comparatively simple and straightforward as they may be, can yet cast quantitative light onto important issues of societal concern, and suggest beneficial solutions to problems that would not be resolvable by qualitative arguments or mere conjecture.

The following analysis of his, reproduced by Körner, assumes independence of age for the annual probability p of contracting smallpox, and for the probability q of an infected person dying from smallpox.[18] The annual probability of dying from another cause is denoted by $u(t)$. Let $r(t)$ denote the number who survive to age t, and let $s(t)$ denote the number who survive to this age without catching smallpox. Then $s'(t) = -s(t)(p + u(t))$ and $r'(t) = -r(t)u(t) - s(t)pq$.

The unknown $u(t)$ can then be conveniently eliminated, and the differential equation simply solved: $s(t) = r(t) / [q + (1-q)\exp(pt)]$. As a reference for $r(t)$, Bernoulli used survival rates from Edmund Halley's pioneering 1693 table of mortality, derived from church record data kept in the German city of Breslau of births and deaths. Age at death was recorded, but not cause of death. Bernoulli accordingly applied the simple solution to the differential equation to estimate the numbers dying of smallpox each year. Allowing for the risk of death associated with vaccination, which Bernoulli reckoned to be less than 0.5%, the life expectancy gain of vaccination at birth could be calculated. This was about three years on the average mid-twenties life expectancy at birth.

The French mathematician D'Alembert criticized Bernoulli, arguing that it is worse to do harm by action than inaction, and posed the following life-and-death conundrum. Suppose an elixir existed which guaranteed a full life, but carried a small risk of killing you. How small would this risk have to be before you were tempted to accept? For the relatives of King Louis XV of France, grieving his loss from smallpox, variation was willingly accepted as offering protection that privilege and royalty did not. In the 20th century, the modern smallpox vaccine risk became so tiny, less than one in a million, that its widespread adoption eradicated smallpox by 1979, except as a weapon of fear in the terrorist mind. Even where vaccination is only for seasonal protection against a mutating disease, such as influenza, the small residual risk is accepted by society. Vaccines for the 2009 swine flu influenza pandemic had safety profiles comparable to seasonal influenza vaccines.

But the trade-off between vaccination risk and the benefits of immunization to the individual and society will always remain. D'Alembert had endorsed the moral principle that a certain present good should not be sacrificed in the hope of a larger uncertain future good. Asked to choose between receiving $100 with certainty, and $200 or $0 on the toss of a coin, most would choose the former. Worried mothers may act on D'Alembert's principle. In 1998, an alarmist autism scare, that confused correlation with causation, resulted in UK vaccination rates for the combined Measles-Mumps-Rubella vaccine dropping from 92% to below 80%. The fall is important, because if vaccination rates are high enough, those not immunized may yet benefit from collective herd immunity. But with more children susceptible, UK measles cases increased, with some associated deaths.

2.2.2 SIR analysis

Classic modelling of infectious disease assumes a homogeneous population and that transmission contacts are uncorrelated. An approximate calculation of the population spread of an epidemic can be performed using *SIR analysis*. The acronym stands for Susceptible-Infectious-Removed. The disease progression can be represented as: $S \rightarrow I \rightarrow R$. A susceptible individual may become infected by the disease, whereupon he or she may recover and be immune, or may die, or otherwise be removed from the population through isolation. At time t, the population is written as $N(t)$, which is split among the susceptible, infectious, and removed classes as $N(t) = S(t) + I(t) + R(t)$. The movement between the classes is modelled by three differential equations: $S' = -\beta IS$, $I' = \beta IS - \gamma I$, $R' = \gamma I$. The βIS term in the first two equations embodies the law of mass action that the force of infection is proportional to the number infected $I(t)$ and the number susceptible $S(t)$, with β being the pairwise infectious contact rate. In reality, an epidemic is the result of the interaction of many heterogeneous agents, some of whom may have particularly high contact rates. In the absence of specific population data on social networks, the law of mass action is a reasonable initial simplifying assumption.

In the solution of these equations, a key parameter is the basic reproductive number $R_0 = \beta N / \gamma$. The numerator βN is the rate at which a single infected person makes infectious contacts within a population of size N. The denominator γ is the reciprocal of the expected duration of being infectious. Thus R_0 is the expected number of contacts made by an infected person. If this is less than 1, the disease-free state is stable, but not if $R_0 > 1$, when an epidemic may occur. The size of the epidemic is given by the number eventually in the removed class. This is Nw where w is the positive root of the equation: $1 - w = \exp(-R_0 w)$.

As an illustrative example, consider smallpox. One of a number of indigenous populations in the Americas decimated by this infectious disease was the Aztec empire. In 1520, Aztecs contracted smallpox from a Spanish soldier who died of the disease. Assuming an infective period of 2 weeks, $\gamma = (52/2) = 26$. Taking a local population of 1,000, and an infectious contact rate $\beta = 0.1$, R_0 is about 4. The equation for w then forebodes disaster, with only a few dozen remaining uninfected. But, hypothetically, had there been 70% immunity, then the size of the epidemic would have only been about 80.

The basic reproduction number R_0 is quite high for smallpox, and is one of the key factors identified by Fraser *et al.* that govern the controllability of an infectious disease.[19] A second is the disease generation time, which is the mean time interval between infection of one person and infection of those he or she infects. A third is the proportion of transmission θ occurring prior to symptoms. This determines the potential effectiveness of symptom-based public health control measures in reducing the number infected. Control through isolation alone would only work if this transmission proportion is adequately low: $\theta < 1/R_0$. For higher values of θ, isolating infected people is not enough; their contacts also need to be traced.

Comparing R_0 and θ for smallpox, Severe Acute Respiratory Syndrome (SARS), and influenza, SARS is the easiest to control because of its low values for these key factors. Indeed, effective isolation of symptomatic patients can control an outbreak. Smallpox is the next easiest to control. Even though isolation is insufficient on its own, taken together with effective contact tracing, an outbreak can be controlled. However, even with 90% quarantining and contact tracing, influenza is very difficult to control because of the high level of pre-symptomatic transmission. In contrast with SARS and smallpox, influenza is far less lethal, having a case fatality rate in the general range of 0.1% to 2%. However, the number of cases tends to be very large, due to the difficulty of controlling an outbreak, and high transmissibility. Seen from an evolutionary perspective, it is not in the survival interests of a virus to over-exploit its hosts, suggesting there might be a negative correlation between lethality and transmissibility.

2.3 Industrial and Transportation Accidents

The memory of catastrophe should never be allowed to fade, lest vital safety lessons are forgotten and disaster history repeats itself. For almost two months in 1908, a catastrophic oil well fire at Dos Bocas, Mexico, burned out of control, consuming 90,000 barrels a day, which flooded swamps, streams, lagoons, and rivers.[20] A century later, local soil remains contaminated with large tar balls. The overall volume of oil spillage was similar to that from the Deepwater Horizon offshore oil platform accident in the Gulf of Mexico in 2010.

As a class of observable phenomena, accidents are amenable to structured analysis, which helps understand how, where and why they happen, and how they might be avoided through enhanced resilience. There are a variety of accident models.[21] Conceptually the most straightforward are sequential models, comprising sets of barriers, which may fall like dominos. Such accident models involve a linear series of causes and effects, or multiple sequences of events. Propagating outwards from a root cause, the evolution of the consequences is represented by a fault tree diagram.

Disasters seek out the weakest links in safety and quality management. A contrasting perspective on accidents is provided by system models which crucially recognize systemic latent factors which establish conditions conducive to an accident. Such factors include the corporate culture, organizational processes, and risk management procedures. All accident investigations identify systemic problems. Had the latent factors not existed, then the accident under investigation may well not have occurred. But this does not imply that the latent factors actually caused the accident. This is termed by John Reason, 'the counterfactual fallacy'.[22] The latent factors are conditions but not causes.

Thankfully, major industrial catastrophes are rare: the right combination of circumstances is required for a catastrophe to evade the layered defence-in-depth in the presence of the prevailing latent factors, and actually occur and cause loss. Nevertheless, the progressive improvement in industrial safety standards in the late 20th century still provides opportunity for catastrophes, even in the most highly industrialized nations. A prime example is a disastrous US accident which occurred on 23 March 2005 at the Texas City refinery, 40 miles from Houston. Due to an overfilling drum problem, there was a geyser-like release of highly flammable liquid and vapour onto the grounds of the refinery, causing a series of explosions and fires: 15 people died, and 180 were injured. Alarms and gauges that should have warned of the overfilling equipment failed to operate properly on the fateful day.[23]

Perhaps the single most effective tool for mitigating industrial risk is a proficient risk management system. A risk manager will have to engage all employees actively in a safety programme, because human error is one of the most significant contributors to industrial risk. Safety management cannot be entirely prescriptive. There has to be a degree of self-organization, so that members of the workforce can respond with some initiative to threats as they arise. Individual groups of the workforce would then be empowered to help maintain the integrity of local defensive barriers against system loss. In order to mitigate human errors in barrier protection, there is a need to understand the relationships and roles of individuals within systems.[24]

On a plant-wide scale, to combat the battery of hazards, a risk manager will organize a series of defensive barriers, the purpose of which is to prevent these hazards from ever materializing into a loss. Some barriers will offer defence against multiple hazards; others may be designed to meet one specific threat. It is important to appreciate the dynamic nature of these barriers. The most mundane maintenance or testing operations can alter the pattern of protection offered by a series of barriers. For the Texas City refinery, as with other industrial installations, there were three generic sets of barriers, varying from hard to medium to soft:

[1] Plant: *engineering hardware, control systems, and layouts*
[2] Processes: *management systems to identify, control and mitigate risks*
[3] People: *leadership skills, relevant knowledge, and experience*

A risk manager will strive to ensure there are no latent hazards lacking any barrier protection, and would acknowledge that hard barriers are more reliable than soft barriers. But, crucially, they all rely on people; hence the need for experts in human factors.

James Reason conveyed the imperfect functioning of a set of barriers using the visual metaphor of *Swiss Cheese*.[25] The Swiss Cheese model has become the *de facto* model of accident causation, and has been adopted for investigation in many industries. This has had a beneficial constructive effect, shifting the focus of accident investigations from just addressing human error to more basic organizational explanations.

Holes are distinctive appealing features in Emmental cheese, but not in defensive barriers. There may be gaps in any barrier, which could vary in extent and position from time to time, according to human as well as external factors. An accident will happen if, at some time, a particular hazard succeeds in finding gaps in all the barriers set against it. This situation is shown in Fig. 2.1. Barrier failure is the cardinal principle that can explain the occurrence of all the major historical industrial disasters, most notably at Chernobyl, where successive layers of defence were intentionally removed. Conversely, residual barrier integrity is the guiding principle explaining why the loss after an initiating event was not considerably worse, such as at Three Mile Island in 1979 where the nuclear plant containment was not breached by a strong pressure surge.

Risk can be mitigated through *safety performance indicators*: leading indicators which plug holes before an accident happens, and lagging indicators which reveal holes through the occurrence of incidents.

[a] Initial configuration of defence barriers, with some gaps.

[b] Later configuration, showing changes in gaps, and barrier removal.

Figure 2.1. Diagram showing how various combinations of defence barriers act to prevent a latent hazard from materializing into a system loss.

To illustrate the defence-in-depth concept, consider the earthquake threat to a gas storage tank in a petrochemical refinery. Compounded by fire, such a threat is serious at many refineries in seismic regions of the world. Where past earthquake-induced losses at refineries have been severe, defence has lacked depth. An early exposure of a defence with holes came in 1952 with the Kern County, California earthquake, the epicentre of which was a mere 25 km from the Paloma plant, which stored five 2,500 barrel butane tanks. The inadequately braced supports of two of the spherical tanks collapsed when the ground shook, and gas was released which was spontaneously ignited by electrical flashes from a transformer bank. The barriers preventing a rupture should include seismic design measures to ensure tank stability and integrity under strong ground shaking. To mitigate the consequences of any rupture, the tank might be covered by an earth mound to minimize gas leakage, *and* be close to fire-fighting equipment, *and* be distant from ignition sources.

As a psychologist, James Reason was keen to identify cultural drivers of accidents, and he quoted Sigmund Freud's concern to understand the motive forces that drive people into erroneous behaviour. James Reason argued that, in hazardous commercial work, an organization's safety culture is a key motive force. In such work, he suggested that time pressure, cost-cutting, indifference to hazards, and the blinkered pursuit of commercial advantage, all act to propel organizations down pathways to error. In mentioning oil exploration and production as an industry where a commercial trade-off exists between the risk of accidents and financial return, he noted that, to stay competitive, many companies must operate in the moderate risk regime, with occasional excursions beyond.

In the assessment of any future commercial opportunity, the prospective cash flows have to be weighed against the financial risk, which includes losses arising from potentially catastrophic accidents. Quantitative techniques for evaluating this trade-off decision include *real options* analysis, which considers the branching possibilities of future market circumstances, and the financial sensitivity to the oil price.

Each offshore oil well-drilling operation is subject to twin pressures of safety and cost-effectiveness. Procedures need to be established which enable engineers to demonstrate that the operational plan minimizes the chance of undetected errors, and subsequent damaging consequences to the offshore platform and the environment. Best practice in conceptual thinking in anticipating remote hazard contingencies is exemplified by an innovative quantitative risk assessment of subsurface well collisions undertaken by BP Exploration for North Sea offshore operations.[26] The possibility that two directional wells drilled from the same platform might collide at depth was not merely hypothetical – it had happened elsewhere in the North Sea. Through calculating practical error tolerances for drilling operations, the well collision risk could be adequately minimized, if not eradicated.

After the Gulf of Mexico oil spill catastrophe of 2010, where the environmental and business disruption losses amassed over months of spillage to tens of billions of dollars, an accident investigation report issued by BP identified the following eight defensive physical or operational barriers in place to eliminate or mitigate hazards: the cement barrier; mechanical barriers; pressure integrity testing; well monitoring; well control response; hydrocarbon surface containment; fire and gas system; and the blowout-preventer emergency operation.[27] In the Swiss Cheese model, eight key report findings represent eight holes that lined up enabling the Deepwater Horizon accident to occur. Had any of these critical factors been eliminated, the catastrophe might have been averted. A systems analyst might figure the chance that these eight holes should have lined up. If they were independent, the accident likelihood would have been minuscule. However, the presence of latent factors might have eroded their independence, inducing a degree of correlation.

Every manager has to balance safety and performance. The Columbia shuttle disaster of 1 February 2003 was ostensibly due to tile damage incurred during launch. However, investigators concluded that the organizational causes of the accident were rooted in history and culture.[28]

2.3.1 The learning curve

It might have been an engineer, but it was a philosopher, George Santayana, who wrote: 'Those who fail to learn from the mistakes of their predecessors are destined to repeat them.' Some mistakes are survivable, engineering mistakes are often not. As a matter of Darwinian natural selection, users of technology who do not learn from the mistakes of their predecessors tend not to be the future role models. When the US Air Mail service was founded after World War I, as many as 31 of the first 40 pilots were killed in action.[29] But as technologies develop and mature, and human knowledge and experience accumulate, so the rate of errors declines.

The classic human learning curve is derived from the assumption that the rate of learning or error reduction is proportional to the number of errors made.   Duffey and Saull have considered the industrial applicability of this simple assumption, which has both a theoretical basis in reliability analysis and empirical support from data comparison.[30]   At any stage, the rate of reduction of errors A is proportional to the number of errors: $A' \propto -A$. The errors then decline to a minimum rate via a universal exponential learning curve.

For the world's commercial shipping fleet, a century of learning experience has progressively brought down the annual percentage of ships lost, more or less in line with the learning curve.   With GPS navigation systems to keep ships firmly on course, a prospect of more rapid safety advancement is dimmed by the universality of human error, which can never be eradicated.   The scale of human error can defy credulity. In April 2010, a bulk coal carrier took an illicit route from Australia to China.   Fifteen nautical miles off course, the ship ran aground on the ecologically precious Great Barrier Reef.

Another key transport component of the world economy is aviation. According to official statistics from the International Air Transport Association, IATA, the 2010 global accident rate, as measured in hull losses per million flights of Western-built jet aircraft, was 0.61. Compared to the rate in 2001, the accident rate had been cut by 42%. Short of hull loss, the learning curve for aircraft can be costly: a couple years after the maiden Qantas flight of an A380 superjumbo jet, engine failure and wing damage led to an insurance loss of $70 million.

Much is learned after each accident, but for every accident, as with every catastrophe, there are numerous near-misses, which also offer valuable lessons in air safety in that they are amenable to statistical analysis of process control.   Sidney Dekker has stressed the importance of a *just culture* for responding to such incidents and accidents, a safety culture that encourages the open reporting of failures and problems.   As an air safety expert, Captain Sullenberger had a copy of Dekker's book on board US Airways flight 1549, which he landed in the Hudson River on 15 January 2009, after an encounter with a flock of birds had disabled both engines.   This miracle of airmanship has encouraged research into the survivability of planes in water, from which yet more will be learned.

2.4 Fraud Catastrophe

One of the books of timeless relevance published in the first half of the 19th century was an account of extraordinary popular delusions, written by Charles Mackay.[31] Reprinted with the subtitle of *The Madness of Crowds*, Mackay explained that his object had been to collect the most remarkable instances of moral epidemics, and to show how easily the masses have been led astray. One of these moral epidemics is avarice. This can entice some individuals of lesser moral fibre into fraudulent actions, which might be explained, if not excused, by self-delusion, bordering on a psychological disorder a layman would recognize as madness. Petty fraud is commonplace; fraud on a million dollar scale is not unusual; but fraud catastrophes on a billion dollar scale are rare.

Catastrophe fraudsters suffer the intoxicating delusion, shared with inveterate gamblers, that, however large the losses, they may eventually somehow be put right. All are blissfully ignorant of a basic theorem about gambling: if a gambler risks a finite capital over a large number of plays in a game with a constant single-trial probability of winning, losing, and tying, then any and all betting systems lead ultimately to the same value of mathematical expectation of gain per amount wagered.[32]

From 1984 to 1995, Toshihide Iguchi lost a billion US dollars for Daiwa Bank in unauthorized bond trading. He told *Time* magazine, 'I think all traders have a tendency to fall into the same trap. You always have a way of recovering the loss.' Sketching the operational loss exceedance curve associated with this trap, Iguchi has observed that 'Many traders have engaged in unauthorized trading to recoup unreported losses. Some were discovered at an early stage, but some lost $10 million, $100 million, or even a billion.'[33]

Topping the 20th century list of bank trading frauds was the Barings Bank loss of £827 million in 1995, attributed to the self-styled English rogue trader, Nick Leeson.[34] It all started with just a simple error made by a Singaporean trader colleague, who bought rather than sold 100 contracts, worth around £8 million – under 1% of the final loss. But in attempting to recoup this amount through trading, a modest loss turned into a catastrophe. A back-office tremor evolved into a corporate earthquake. Perhaps fittingly, whilst gambling on the Japanese Nikkei

Index rising, Leeson's last chance at trading out of his forlorn position was stymied by a destructive earthquake which struck the Japanese port city of Kobe on 17 January 1995. Over this notable causal link between the financial markets and natural catastrophe, Leeson lamented, 'They were selling shares to pay for the damage. The market was butchered.'

Leeson's loss of £850 million might have been logged as an approximate upper bound for operational losses, spanning the observed historical range. As such, it could have been used to anchor statistical analyses of operational losses. But because of the open-ended prospect for trader fraud at major financial institutions, such analyses would give a misleading impression of the heavy tail of the operational loss curve.

2.4.1 Ponzi schemes

It could be said of the Italian dictator, Benito Mussolini, that he offered his people much more than he could deliver. In a financial rather than political sense, nobody offered more than he could deliver than Charles Ponzi, who briefly worked for Mussolini back in his native Italy having spent ten years in American prison for fraud. The original Ponzi scheme, which helped give the English word *scheme* the pejorative American connotation of *scam*, closed in July 1920, having opened just after the previous Christmas. He had offered to double the money of investors in 90 days. Yet he had no way of realizing any significant amount from investing this money. His ability to pay investors came from the inflow from new gullible investors, who lined the streets to his office.

No double-your-money scheme lasts very long, even with political support. Such schemes proliferated in Eastern Europe after the fall of communism. In Romania, more than a million joined a pyramid scheme called *Caritas*, which is Latin for charity.[35] Living up to its name for a short while, it paid 800% a month for deposits of three months – until the scheme folded. Investors were also lured by Russian treasury bills paying 50% returns in dollars. The day of reckoning came on 17 August 1998, when Russia ran out of foreign exchange reserves in defending its pegged exchange rate. The returns seemed just too good to be true. As with all Ponzi schemes, they were.

But a Ponzi scheme offering a more modest 10% per year might keep going for years, taking advantage of rising stock markets until some major financial downturn drastically curtails high-yield re-investment opportunities, and cuts asset values. It was amidst such a downturn, with investors asking for more and more of their money back, that Bernard Madoff was arrested in December 2008, having amassed liabilities in the financial catastrophe range of tens of billions of dollars.[36]

Those thinking of offering Ponzi schemes would be advised to read Artzrouni's article on the mathematics of Ponzi schemes – before, rather than in prison.[37] Denote by $S(t)$ the amount in the scheme at time t. The inflow and withdrawal of money are denoted as $I(t)$ and $W(t)$. The latter depends on the promised Ponzi rate of return, which typically far exceeds the rate of return r earnable by the fund manager. Then the differential equation governing scheme solvency and collapse is: $S'(t) = rS(t) + I(t) - W(t)$. As the initial condition, $S(0)$ is the opening deposit contributed by investors, possibly supplemented by access to other start-up funds.

Artzrouni solves this equation to determine the parameter ranges for scheme solvency and collapse. The dynamical instability of a Ponzi scheme is striking: if the inflow of new investor money is too large, or the withdrawal rate is too low, the fund can grow quickly, but be at risk later as withdrawals increase. However, if the inflow of new money is too small, or the withdrawal rate is too large, then funds may be unavailable to meet the withdrawal demand.

Steered precariously between these perils, some schemes can survive for a remarkably long time, especially if they have start-up funds and can avoid regulatory suspicion. Bernard Madoff's experience of serving on the board of governors of the National Association of Security Dealers helped him to evade detection from the recession of the early 1990s to the time of his arrest in 2008, during another recession.

But sooner or later, he would have his day in court. When this came, he testified: 'When I began the Ponzi scheme I believed it would end shortly and I would be able to extricate myself and my clients from the scheme. However, this proved difficult, and ultimately impossible, and as the years went by I realized that my arrest and this day would eventually come.'[38]

2.4.2 Operational risk

Most of Madoff's institutional investors were mutually reinforcing in their credulity.   Not so the French bank Société Générale, which dispatched an investment bank team to New York in 2003 to discover a strategy which could not work.   But the bank's diligence over Ponzi schemes was not matched in its own control of operational risk.   This is the risk of unexpected losses associated with human error, systems failures, inadequate controls and procedures, and unauthorized activities.

Risk management teams are expected to determine the scope of operational risk.   Losses on a catastrophic scale due to internal fraud have been a primary cause of bank failure.   Among the most notorious cases have been the collapse in 1982 of the Vatican Bank Ambrosiano, and in 1991 of BCCI, which perpetrated illegal acts and was mired in drugs trafficking and money laundering allegations.[39]

Within financial institutions, small and moderate operational losses are not uncommon.   However, large operational losses are contained by strict trading controls which are checked daily.   But where an employee of a financial institution is smart and devious enough to circumvent company controls, losses can occur on a massive scale.   The circumvention of internal procedures is possible because of an ineffective organizational environment.   But, as with all catastrophe risks, operational risk is pushed to record levels by the law of unintended consequences.   In the case of the young trader, Jérôme Kerviel, the extra factor was another manifestation of criminal activity on a catastrophe level: terrorism.

On 4 July 2005, a Parisian trader, Jérôme Kerviel, working in Société Générale, speculated €15 million on a fall in the share price of the Allianz insurance group.[40]   He had hoped to unwind his position during the day, so it would not seem that he had passed his trading limit.   But the market did not go the way he hoped.   A few days later it did.   On 7 July, four Jihadi suicide bombers struck the London transport network. Kerviel made a trading gain of €500,000.   This was not blind luck.   He had been told that, prior to 9/11, there had been strong derivatives market movements relating to US airlines, presumed to be Al Qaeda financial opportunism.   Kerviel had observed similarities between the share movements of Allianz and the US airlines. His hunch paid off unduly well, considering the UK threat level had been lowered shortly before the bombings, and even MI5 had been taken by surprise.

If Kerviel had only recognized the significant random element in his trading gain, he might have quit ahead. Instead, he was fooled by randomness.[41] The Allianz windfall gain opened Kerviel's eyes to a style of speculation beyond his authorized trading limit which brought further short-term trading success, but inevitably brought about his downfall. Kerviel's risky trading ultimately cost Société Générale about €5 billion, a record for operational risk. Indirectly, a terrorist attack on London public transportation had leveraged a financial blow to a French bank.

Insight into Kerviel's avaricious mentality and that of other traders is gained from his quotation from Greek mythology of the legend of Icarus, who flew on wings of feathers and wax. Ever higher he flew, ever closer to the Sun, but the wax melted and he fell: *'Toujours plus haut, donc toujours plus proche à la fois du soleil et de la chute.'* Serious fraud evolves into catastrophe through the Icarus effect. Just as Icarus ignored his father's wise words of caution, so a trader may ignore authorized trading limits. The path to disaster is a sequence of such illicit trades: just one more trade beyond the limit, then another, and another.

Writing of his exclusive billion dollar education, paid for unintentionally by the Daiwa Bank, Toshihide Iguchi presented his own version of Kerviel's apology: 'Trading is a tough business. To trade well, one must often go against human nature. In doing so, one must ignore inner warnings and take a course that seems self-destructive. It's much like turning the wheels of a car toward the direction of skidding. It takes enormous discipline to do this day-in and day-out.'

A financial victim of the South Sea Bubble, Isaac Newton had the trader's self-destructive impulse to keep buying a failing stock. Thus he might have empathized with Iguchi, whilst explaining the steering analogy from his laws of mechanics. While the front wheels skid, the driver has no directional control of the vehicle. In turning the wheels in the direction of the skid, the wheels start rolling in the direction of motion again. Only once the wheels are rolling can a driver turn them and affect the vehicle direction. Iguchi's problem was that the office environment at Daiwa Bank gave him license not just to drive a car, but a large trailer-truck, capable of causing catastrophic skid accidents.

Chapter 3

A Sense of Scale

*Sea coasts provide an apt illustration
of how insignificant causes
can produce very noticeable effects.*
Lewis Fry Richardson,
Statistics of Deadly Quarrels

As an amateur ornithologist, Murray Gell-Mann was gifted with a multi-lingual knowledge of the names of birds, which astonished the author once in Aspen, Colorado. His Caltech colleague, Richard Feynman, also a Physics Nobel laureate, noted, 'You can know the name of a bird in all the languages of the world, but when you're finished, you'll know absolutely nothing whatever about the bird. I learned very early the difference between knowing the name of something and knowing something.'[1] This quote has resonated with many thinkers about risk, not least Nicholas Taleb, who has cited Richard Feynman as one of his intellectual heroes.

Taleb's celebrated Black Swan is a special bird for risk analysts to know about in any language.[2] It is a creature of the wild world of *Extremistan*, where a single observation can disproportionately affect the aggregate of many observations. A primary law of catastrophe, not to be forgotten, especially by financial traders, is that our world is Extremistan. By contrast, in a mild more predictable world, named by Taleb as *Mediocristan*, it is hardly possible for any single observation to achieve such a Black Swan surprise. It is a world essentially devoid of earthquakes, spectacular terrorist attacks, pandemics, or financial crashes. Living in Mediocristan, a resident of an arid desert kingdom would never be so unfortunate as to drown in a flood. Yet, on 25

November 2009, more than a hundred perished in a flash flood in Jeddah, Saudi Arabia, as a consequence of more rain falling in 6 hours than within 150 average November days.

According to the Greek historian Herodotus, geometry originated from the resurveying undertaken in the aftermath of the annual flooding of the Nile valley. If measurement is the quintessence of mathematics, so *scale* is the quintessence of natural hazards. The vast range of scales of natural hazards contrasts with the narrow range of scales that bound human existence and all but the most fabulous legend. Not only are many natural hazard phenomena beyond the realm of common experience, some stretch the limits of human credulity and imagination, in a manner approached in the 21st century by trillion dollar financial hazards.

Atmospheric processes have scales ranging downwards from the macroscale (thousands of kilometres), associated with global climate; to the mesoscale (tens or hundreds of kilometres), characterized by regional atmospheric circulations; to the turbulent microscale, measured in metres. Turbulent fluxes of momentum, heat, and moisture play an essential role in windstorm development. There is a dynamic interaction between processes at different scales, so that those acting at a smaller scale can affect the evolution of the state of the atmosphere: without this interaction, the proverbial butterfly of chaos theory would have no chance of affecting a distant storm system.

Likewise, geological processes have scales ranging downwards from continental (thousands of kilometres), associated with convection in the Earth's mantle; to regional faulting (tens or hundreds of kilometres), on which major earthquakes occur; to rock asperities, measured in metres, which influence the extent of fault rupture.

Physicists have learned that transformations of spatial scale play a crucial role in natural processes. Objects which are so small as to appear point-like at one scale are revealed, on closer observation, to have spatial structure at a smaller scale. Like a series of nested Chinese boxes or Russian dolls, this sequence cascades down from rocks to crystals to molecules, to atoms, to the smallest constituents of matter. The scientific curiosity to model changes in scale is often rewarded with the gift of deeper understanding of the underlying empirical observations, and with the discovery of new phenomena.

3.1 Size Scales of Natural Hazards

From the disorder wrought by natural catastrophes, a mathematician would seek order: information that would allow hazard events to be classified by size. Such an intellectual salvage operation may be as challenging as physical reconstruction. There is no unique choice of a consistent classification scheme, because of the multiple spatial–temporal attributes of each event. How does a slow-moving but massive event rank in size against one which is fast-moving but compact?

Associated with each type of natural hazard is a common geometrical structure, reflecting fundamental distinctive spatial attributes. Thus the spiral swirl of a tropical cyclone is instantly recognizable from a satellite image. Associated also with each type of hazard is a dynamical structure which introduces a temporal aspect to the size classification. This is typically expressed in terms of a time-dependent variable such as velocity, rate or flux, or simply duration.

For a classification scheme to be practical as well as rational, an estimate of event size should be parsimonious in its demands on instrumental data, since measurements may be as geographically sparse as they are economically costly. Furthermore, use of qualitative information should be legitimate in circumstances where instrumental data are poor or non-existent. This applies in particular to historical events predating the era of instrumental recording; the time window of instrumental data is only a brief exposure period for displaying extremes of hazard phenomena. In any observational study, whether of comets or earthquakes, historical archives provide a unique resource for calibrating and validating models.

Once a particular definition of size has been chosen, the number of grades and their partitioning remain to be decided. In principle, one would think it beneficial to have an ample number of grades. However, because of observational uncertainty, there is an inherent restriction: the resolution of the partitioning cannot be so fine as to confuse the assignment of individual grades. An excess of grades and ambiguity would be a recipe for error, and would discourage use of the size scale.

A mark of a good scale is order in its grade increments. If grades are assigned mainly for administrative bookkeeping purposes, with minimal concern for subsequent numerical analysis, any irregularity or non-uniformity in grade definition might be immaterial. However, a well graduated scale has the merit of expanding the horizon of detailed statistical investigation, which holds the promise of a more quantitative understanding of the hazard phenomena. This objective is easier to accomplish if size is distinguished numerically, rather than qualified by adjectives which would be considered vague even in common discourse.

With individual scales developed specifically for each type of natural hazard, the sizes of events from different hazards are not intelligibly exchanged among scientists, let alone shared easily with the media and the general public. Conscious of this public relations neglect, Arch Johnston devised a comparison based on a common size measure.[3] Recognizing that all natural catastrophes are associated with the uncontrolled release of energy, the obvious, if not unique, choice is the energy released in the event. (For windstorms, this is the kinetic rather than thermal energy.) Relative to the atomic bomb dropped on Hiroshima in 1945, a moderate tropical cyclone has 100 times the energy; the 1980 eruption of Mt. St. Helens, Washington, had 1,000 times the energy; and the 1811 New Madrid, Missouri, earthquake, which was perceived over an area of five million square kilometres, had 10,000 times the energy.

3.1.1 Tropical cyclones

An ominous stage in the development of a tropical cyclone is a rapid decrease in central pressure. This is a crucial variable for gauging the size of a tropical cyclone, because it is the horizontal difference in pressure across the cyclone which drives the cyclonic winds. Given the central pressure p_c, and the ambient pressure away from the cyclone p_n, then the surface pressure p at a radial distance r from the centre of the eye of a tropical cyclone may be calculated from a semi-empirical formula, such as one developed by Holland:[4]

$$p = p_c + (p_n - p_c)\exp(-R/r)^b$$

R is the radius of maximum wind, because at this distance from the centre of the eye, the maximum wind speed (as estimated by balancing the pressure gradient and centrifugal force) is attained:

$$V_{max} = \sqrt{b\,(p_n - p_c)\,/\,(\rho\,e)}$$

where ρ is the air density, and e is the base of natural logarithms. The parameter b lies between 1 and 2.5. Applying various wind correction factors, and allowing for forward motion of the tropical cyclone, the severity of wind speed at the surface can be estimated. Because central pressure is related to surface wind speed, the latter observable can be used directly in a strength scale for tropical cyclones.

Such a practical scale was devised in the 1970s by Robert Simpson, director of the US National Hurricane Center, and Herbert Saffir, a Florida consulting engineer. Rather like its better known cousin, the Richter Scale for earthquakes, the Saffir–Simpson Scale was originally devised to provide public information: a requirement which would have had a significant influence on the scale design. Earlier versions of the Saffir–Simpson Hurricane Scale incorporated central pressure and storm surge as components of the categories. The central pressure was used during the 1970s and 1980s as a wind speed proxy, because accurate wind speed intensity measurements were not then routinely available.

Storm surge used to be quantified by category in the earliest published versions of the scale. However this may be misleading because local bathymetry, topography, the hurricane's forward speed, and angle to the coast also affect the surge. In September 2008, Hurricane Ike, with hurricane force winds extending as far as 125 miles from the centre, made landfall in Texas just as a Category 2 hurricane but had peak storm surge values as high as 20 ft. To avoid such conflicts, *The Saffir–Simpson Hurricane Wind Scale* does not address the potential for storm surges, rainfall-induced floods, and tornadoes. Instead, it focuses on general descriptions of wind damage to commercial and industrial buildings, residences, mobile homes, canopies, trees, fences, commercial signage, as well as water and power outages. The degree of damage is dependent on local building codes and their enforcement.

3.1.2 Tornadoes

Tornadoes are highly variable in intensity as are all extreme weather phenomena, but it was only in the late 1960s that a scale for tornado intensity was developed. Based on wind speed, and descriptions of damage obtained from post-tornado survey information, the six-grade Fujita scale was designed to connect with the upper end of the maritime Beaufort wind scale, and the lower end of the aeronautical Mach number scale, which is anchored to the speed of sound. An able meteorological detective, Ted Fujita (Mr. Tornado) had the facility of reconstructing storm history from limited instrumental data.

As happens with all hazards, a crucial research milestone was initiated by a severe event. In May 1970, a powerful tornado struck Lubbock, near the campus of Texas Tech University, thus catalyzing a sustained research focus into wind engineering.[5] As noted by TTU wind scientists, the primary limitations with the Fujita scale were a dearth of damage indicators, no account of construction quality and variability, and the absence of any definitive correlation between damage and wind speed. As a result, tornadoes were inconsistently rated, and wind speeds were sometimes overestimated, notably where there were weak links in construction, or the storm was slow-moving.

Over more than three decades of use, the limitations of the Fujita scale had become increasingly apparent. Accordingly, in February 2007, an enhanced six-grade Fujita scale became operational, reflecting tornado damage surveys more accurately, and aligning wind speeds more closely with damage. The *Enhanced Fujita Scale* is referred to as the EF Scale to distinguish it from the original Fujita Scale.[6]

This scale makes distressing reading for the millions of US residents of mobile homes, who might even be safer in their vehicles than in their homes during an EF1 tornado. Their plight is increasingly shared by house-dwellers, whose homes also become mobile the further up the intensity scale a tornado reaches. The maximum EF scale grade is 5. Unlike the top category of the former scale, the EF5 scale recognizes the possibility of extreme super-tornadoes by not defining an explicit upper bound wind speed above 200 mph, the grade threshold.

3.1.3 Volcanic eruptions

For Fujita, the inventor of the tornado severity scale, the volcanoes of Kyushu were a childhood memory, but it was not until 1982 that eruptions of Aso, Sakurajima, and other volcanoes of the world could be assigned a *Volcanic Explosivity Index* (VEI). Newhall and Self defined the nine indices of increasing explosivity in terms of a mixture of quantitative and qualitative measures. The three quantitative parameters are: (a) the volume of tephra (m^3); (b) the height of the eruption column (km); (c) the duration of the volcanic blast (hr).[7] The qualitative parameters include the amount of injection into the troposphere and the stratosphere, as well as a verbal description of event severity.

Pyle spotted the need for independent size scales for volcano magnitude and intensity.[8] For the same overall size of eruption, a very vigorous eruption merits a higher intensity than a gentle slow eruption. From an estimate of the mass (kg) of magma erupted E_M, volcano magnitude can be defined as: $M = Log(E_M) - 7.0$. For most eruptions, this yields a similar size assignment to VEI. From the estimated eruption rate E_R expressed in kg/s, volcano intensity can be defined as: $I = Log(E_R) + 3.0$.

Inspection of the global catalogue of volcanic eruptions shows that there are numerous small events, a fair number of medium-sized events, and comparatively few really large events. Using the VEI scale, it is possible to improve upon a qualitative account of volcanism, and make some quantitative remarks about worldwide volcanic activity.[9] Thus, somewhere on the Earth, a VEI 2 event occurs every few weeks; a VEI 3 event (e.g. Nevado del Ruiz, 1985) occurs several times a year; a VEI 4 event (e.g. Galunggung, 1982) occurs every few years; a VEI 5 event (e.g. Mt. St. Helens, 1980) occurs about once a decade; a VEI 6 event (e.g. Krakatau, 1883) occurs rather more often than once a century; and a VEI 7 event (e.g. Tambora, 1815) occurs once or twice a millennium.

Geological investigations have been conducted to find latent evidence of VEI 8 events, such as are associated with Yellowstone in the USA, Toba in Indonesia and Taupo in New Zealand. Such supervolcanic eruptions, with ejecta greater than 1,000 cubic kilometres, are thankfully rare in the world, occurring less often than once in ten thousand years.

3.1.4   Earthquakes

Up until the end of the 19th century, earthquake information came not from instrumentally recorded seismograms, but from documented accounts of the varying severity of damage and felt effects in the region surrounding the epicentre.   Such local accounts serve to distinguish different grades of earthquake *Intensity*.   The first version of an Intensity scale was produced by Rossi and Forel in the 1880s, but it was a geophysicist, Mercalli, whose name is most widely associated with Intensity scale development.   His Intensity scale has XII grades, identified by Roman numerals, which not only honour his Italian heritage, but distinguish this qualitative macroseismic scale from any instrumental scale based on recorded traces of seismic waves.

From the time that seismograms were first recorded, several decades elapsed before Richter arrived at a practical definition of earthquake *Magnitude*, based on the peak amplitudes measured.   The Richter Magnitude Scale has since ceded ground to the Moment Magnitude Scale, which relates Moment Magnitude M_W to the seismic moment of an earthquake M_0, which is a fundamental measure of the strength of an earthquake, proportional to the fault slip and the fault area.   Even though these are geometrical fault properties, seismic moment can be estimated from seismograms.

Richter demonstrated with his colleague Gutenberg a simple universal relationship for the annual number N of earthquakes of Magnitude greater than or equal to M : $Log(N) = a - bM$. In this formula, a is a measure of activity rate of seismicity, and b is a measure of the relative number of small to large earthquakes. A typical value for b is unity; a lower value indicates a greater preponderance of large events, whereas a higher b value indicates the converse.

The Gutenberg–Richter relation is taught in every elementary course in seismology, but as phenomenology without the following underlying dynamical systems explanation. Driven by slow tectonic deformation, a finite part of the Earth's crust is susceptible to large response when subject to small external perturbations.   Over geological time, certain spatial domains of the crust enter into a *self-organized state* of instability, where small perturbations can lead to localized fault rupture.

3.1.5 Tsunamis

On 11 March 2011, one of the largest recorded earthquakes (M9.0) struck Northeast Japan. Tsunami heights of 10+ m were in accord with a tsunami magnitude scale devised by Abe after a major Japanese tsunami in 1993. This yields values close to earthquake Magnitude.[10] Given the distance R in km from the epicentre, and the maximum amplitude of tsunami waves H in metres, a tsunami magnitude may be defined as:

$$M_T = Log(H) + Log(R) + 5.8$$

Just as earthquake Magnitude is logarithmically related to seismic energy release, so it is also possible to define a tsunami magnitude in terms of the logarithm of the tsunami source energy, which includes both the potential energy due to the seafloor uplift, and kinetic energy due to the horizontal displacements of the continental slope. The seafloor displacements may be calculable using data from coastal GPS stations.[11]

3.1.6 River floods

Where flood hydrographs exist which chart the time dependence of water surface elevation and discharge, the size ranking of floods might be thought to be straightforward; but it is not. As a single index, the absolute volume of flood water is unsatisfactory, because the flood water may be widely but thinly dispersed; but neither satisfactory is the discharge per unit area, which may be concentrated and have limited overall volume. A multiplicative compound index, suggested as being particularly appropriate for China, involves the product of the peak discharge, the flood volume, and also flood duration.[12]

As a function of basin size, the absolute flood volume generally increases, while the discharge per unit area generally decreases. One size index, which has been developed to improve flood management of large dams, is the Myers' rating $Q / \sqrt{A}$. In this rating formula, Q is the maximum discharge in m^3/s, and A is the basin area in sq. km. This varies with climate, topographical, and geological characteristics.

3.1.7 Space weather

Like earthquakes, the energies of solar flares range over many orders of magnitude,[13] and a formal power–law size classification exists based on peak flux. Classes are labelled in increasing intensity: B, C, M, and X. Space weather scales were introduced by NOAA around the start of the 21st century as a way to communicate to the general public space weather conditions and their possible severity effects on people and systems. Separate scales are defined for three categories of solar hazard phenomena. For each of these, there are five grades: minor, moderate, strong, severe, and extreme.[14] Analogous to hurricanes, tornadoes, and earthquakes, the severity scales list a range of possible effects.

- *Geomagnetic storms*: disturbances in the geomagnetic field caused by gusts in the solar wind that blows by the Earth;
- *Solar radiation storms*: elevated levels of radiation that occur when the numbers of energetic particles increase;
- *Radio blackouts*: disturbances of the ionosphere caused by X-ray emissions from the Sun.

3.1.8 Extra-terrestrial impacts

A meteoroid is a body in space with size varying from interplanetary dust up to about five to ten metres. Most originate from comets passing through the inner solar system. A solid fragment of a meteoroid which survives entry into the Earth's atmosphere is termed a meteorite. Larger than meteoroids are asteroids, which range in diameter up to a maximum of about 1,000 km, this being the dimension of asteroid 1 Ceres.

The scale of an extra-terrestrial impact depends both on the mass and velocity of an impactor. From observations of small Earth-crossing asteroids, frequencies of Earth impacts have been estimated, which agree with lunar cratering data. Expressed in terms of the kinetic energy of the impactor at the top of the Earth's atmosphere, a power–law scaling formula provides a good fit for the cumulative Earth impact frequency, and should be valid up to asteroid impacts of 100,000 Megatons TNT.

3.2 Hazard Spatial Scales

Features in the natural environment often have the same average appearance after a change in scale, and so display statistical *self-similarity*. The self-similarity of rocks was observed by the Victorian art historian, John Ruskin, who argued that art should devote itself to the accurate documentation of Nature. He noted, 'Things have a scale. The small may be a model of the large, and the large of the small. A stone, when it is examined, will be found to be a mountain in miniature.'[15]

The notion of an absolute length of a jagged coastline is illusory: the length is proportional to l^{1-D}, where l is the measuring scale used, and the exponent D is the fractal dimension of the coastline. For the rugged west coast of Britain, D is about 1.25; a value inflated above 1.0 by the countless coastal bays and inlets.

Benoît Mandelbrot opened the eyes of the world to the amazing vistas of fractals,[16] having serendipitously unearthed a posthumous paper by Lewis Fry Richardson,[17] who had observed anomalous discrepancies between the lengths of the common frontiers of neighbouring states, such as Spain and Portugal, and Belgium and the Netherlands.[18]

Invariance principles often provide useful constraints on mathematical representation, and scale invariance is no exception.[19] Consider a natural hazard parameter κ, the value of which is related to the value of another parameter λ in a scale invariant way. If the measuring scale changes, both the ratio of the values of κ, and the ratio of the values of λ, only depend on the degree of the scale change, hence $\kappa_1 / \kappa_2 = f(\lambda_1 / \lambda_2)$. Suppose there are two consecutive measuring scale changes, so that: $\kappa_1 \rightarrow \kappa_2 \rightarrow \kappa_3$, and $\lambda_1 \rightarrow \lambda_2 \rightarrow \lambda_3$, then:

$$f(\lambda_1 / \lambda_3) = \kappa_1 / \kappa_3 = \{\kappa_1 / \kappa_2\}\{\kappa_2 / \kappa_3\} = f(\lambda_1 / \lambda_2) f(\lambda_2 / \lambda_3)$$

Cauchy originally proved that the only non-trivial continuous solution of this functional equation is $f(\lambda) = \lambda^q$, for some real number q. A classic hydrological example of power-law scaling is Hack's Law, which relates the length L of the longest stream in a drainage region to its area A. The scaling relation here is: $L \propto A^{0.6}$.

Each natural hazard event is associated with a dual spatial structure: one element relates to the geometry of the event itself, which often has self-similar characteristics; the other element relates to the area over which the environment is disturbed. Risk assessment requires both to be quantified. To take a seismological example, an earthquake is associated both with the rupture geometry of the causative fault, as well as the area over which the ground is noticeably shaken.

Lessons in both types of hazard geography have traditionally been learned by local populations from past loss experience. But this approach can never make citizens more than apprentices in disaster management. During the historical period of human settlement, the spatial structure of possible events may only be partially revealed: rare types of hazard event may have had no witnesses. Another caveat is the encroachment of urban development into areas hitherto thinly populated.

3.2.1 *Tropical cyclones*

In his book, *Visual Explanations*, which is a geometer's delight, Edward Tufte has emphasized the importance of attaching spatial scales to supercomputer animations of severe storms.[20] How else would one know that a supertyphoon had a continental, rather than a county-wide scale? The most obvious geometrical characteristic of a tropical cyclone is the radius of winds in excess of the tropical storm speed threshold. The largest on record is 1,100 km. This prodigious figure is associated not with any Atlantic hurricane, but with Typhoon Tip, which struck the Western Pacific in 1979. But absolute spatial size is, in itself, not a sufficient guide to damage potential: relative size of cyclone and target city matters, as residents of Darwin, Australia, discovered when their homes were devastated by Tracy in 1974, one of the most compact tropical cyclones, having a tiny 50 km radius.

A more restrictive spatial measure of a tropical cyclone is the radius of maximum wind, which is the radial distance to the band of strongest winds within the wall cloud, just outside the eye. This radius varies within a range of a few tens of kilometres, according to a number of parameters, including central pressure and latitude.

3.2.2 Earthquakes

The greatest of Swiss mathematicians, Leonhard Euler, was a native of Basel, and would have known of the destructive earthquake there in 1356, the largest historical event in Northwest Europe. If not a seismologist, he was a prolific geometer, and proved one theorem which is literally pivotal to the understanding of earthquake occurrence. Euler's theorem states that the rigid motion of any surface area of a sphere, across the sphere's surface, can be expressed as an angular rotation about some pole. It implies that the drift of a continent across the Earth's surface should be describable simply by an angle of rotation and a choice of pole. Although ideas of continental drift circulated even in Euler's own time, it was not until 1965 that Euler's theorem was used to find a close mathematical fit between continental shelf edges on either side of the Atlantic. Thereafter, the theorem has been invoked to construct the relative motions of the Earth's tectonic plates, the boundaries of which delineate the major zones of earthquake activity.

Through the kinematics of the tectonic plates, the spatial distribution of seismicity is thus largely explained, except for residual intraplate earthquakes, which reflect rather broadly the nature and direction of stress within plates. The spatial scales of seismicity are intrinsically linked with the hierarchy of spatial scales of faults. There are geometrical scaling relationships describing fault populations which provide insight into the development of faulting. These scaling relationships cover the size distributions of fault lengths and displacements, and the spatial pattern of faulting. Field studies indicate that fault patterns display scale invariance over several orders of magnitude.[21] It is scale invariance which makes it so difficult to gauge the true scale of a graphical image of faulting, without a reference object of standard size, such as a geologist's hammer.

Over a length range,[22] the number of faults $N(L)$ above a given length L may be observed to fall off as a power C of fault length: $N(L) \propto L^{-C}$. If each fault is associated with its own characteristic earthquake, so there is a one-to-one correspondence between faults and earthquakes, the Gutenberg–Richter Magnitude–frequency relation would then follow from the logarithmic correlation between earthquake Magnitude and fault length, which is empirically substantiated.

To understand the spatial characteristics of faulting, it is helpful to appreciate how major faults evolve. In the case of the Earth's brittle crust, short-range interactions govern the elastic stresses, and long-range elastic interactions contribute to organizing the pattern of faulting, as well as triggering distant earthquakes. Models of fault growth indicate that, with the gradual passage of geological time, crustal deformation can become increasingly concentrated on large dominant faults.

Zones of earthquake effects

Engineering seismologists bridge the domains of seismology and civil engineering, and concern themselves not only with the mechanics of large earthquakes, but also the distances over which they cause damage. Some of these distances are vast. To cite a European example, on 12 October 1856, a great Eastern Mediterranean earthquake epicentred off Crete caused the collapse of a church bell tower 1,000 km to the west in the old capital city of Malta. The spatial scales of earthquake effects may be viewed from maps of Intensity isoseismals, contoured from assignments of Intensity at many individual locations. Such maps chart the attenuation of ground shaking with distance from the fault rupture.

Isoseismals are approximately elliptical in shape, reflecting the length and orientation of fault rupture, and some directivity in the attenuation of ground motion from the fault: the aforementioned 1856 event illustrates the latter wave propagation effect. Although Intensity is a qualitative parameter, attributes of size can be calculated from an isoseismal map. One such attribute, which is now facilitated and expedited by online reports, is the felt area A of an earthquake. This is the area within an outer isoseismal.

Studies for many parts of the world have shown the felt area of an earthquake to be correlated with instrumentally measured Magnitude M, according to regression relations of the following form, which may involve the peak Intensity I_0 as well as A: $M = a + b\,I_0 + c\,Log(A)$. Thus, apart from depicting the geographical pattern of earthquake effects, a map of Intensity isoseismals constitutes a valuable surrogate resource for quantifying the size of a historical earthquake.

3.2.3 Volcanic eruptions

The most powerful physical theories explain not one but a multiplicity of seemingly different phenomena. Plate tectonics is in this category, for, apart from residual intraplate activity, it explains not just the origin of most of the world's seismicity, but also the geography of most of the world's volcanism. The converging plate margins surrounding the Pacific Basin are populated by active volcanoes, which form a ring of fire. Subduction volcanoes are found between 100 and 200 km from the deep ocean trenches marking the edges of the converging plates. Apart from the mid-ocean ridges where the oceanic plates are created, and the subduction zones where the oceanic plates are consumed, some volcanism is associated with continental rifts.

The volumes of lava which can flow from basaltic fissure eruptions are best described in terms of flooding. Indeed, widespread discharges of basalts from swarms of fissures and shield volcanoes are termed flood basalts. Great sheets of basalts cover vast continental areas: the Jurassic Paraná flows of Paraguay and Brazil cover more than 750,000 sq. km., and the mid-Miocene Columbia River basalts of the Northwest USA cover more than 200,000 sq. km.. Lava eruptions are intermittent, often with thousands of years of quiescence between flows. Once they occur, individual flows can be gargantuan: depending on their storage reservoirs, they can extend for hundreds of kilometres.

A volcano eruption column with its billowing ash clouds, is one of the most spectacular sights in the natural world. Distinctly unspectacular are chimney smoke-stacks, but the universality of physics allows the height of eruption columns to be gauged from the mundane observation of plumes rising from industrial chimneys. The plume height above a smoke-stack vent is proportional to the thermal flux to the power of one quarter. Denoting the eruption column height as H , and the discharge rate of magma as Q , a regression analysis using data from several dozen historic volcanic eruptions yields a power-law for H , with a scaling coefficient slightly greater than one quarter.[23]

A volcano eruption column is generated by the explosive upward motion of hot gas and pyroclasts. In the lower part of the column, the initial motion of the gas and pyroclasts is dissipated by turbulent eddies which mix in air from the surrounding atmosphere. Larger eddies produce smaller and smaller eddies through inertial interaction, thereby transferring energy to the smaller eddies. The air which is turbulently entrained becomes heated, and so expands and rises. At some height, the initial upward momentum of the volcanic discharge may be reduced to a level where subsequent ascent is driven by the thermal buoyancy of the mixture of entrained air, gas, and fine pyroclasts. If this happens, then an eruption column develops, and the material is transported high into the atmosphere. The material then permeates the upper atmosphere, forming an umbrella cloud over the column, which can result in widespread debris fallout over hundreds or thousands of square kilometres.

Yet more devastating is an alternative eruption scenario. This is a fountain collapse, which occurs when the upward motion of the air, gas, and pyroclast material stalls before the material achieves buoyancy. The consequence is the lateral spreading of a dense mixture of ash and gas from the top of the fountain, and the flow of dense hot ash around the volcano. This cusp in dynamical behaviour was observed in the eruption of the New Zealand volcano Ngauruhoe in 1975, and in several of the 1980 explosions of Mt. St. Helens.

Spatial reach of eruption effects
For explosive volcanoes, the effects of an eruption extend well beyond the mountains themselves. Apart from local pyroclastic flows, the principal hazard arises from the fall of airborne fragmental debris, ranging from blocks to ash particles, collectively known as tephra. In the vicinity of the eruption column, the fallout will mainly be of ballistic origin, being hurled away from the margins of the column. Beyond this zone, the fallout originates from the umbrella cloud or plume, and the thickness of tephra decreases exponentially with distance.[24]

The transport of volcanic ash over distance is significantly influenced by the process of aggregation. Fine ash particles form aggregates both in the eruption column and in the ash cloud, and are responsible for mass deposition maxima. Aggregates have a fractal geometry, with the number of primary particles in an aggregate increasing with its solidity.[25]

Atmospheric effects

The consequences of a major explosive eruption may be especially far-reaching because of atmospheric effects. Volcanic gases may undergo chemical reactions, and form volcanic aerosols. Together with volcanic dust, these aerosols shroud and thereby reduce the amount of solar energy on Earth. In the 1970s, the climatologist, Hubert Lamb, devised a Dust Veil Index (DVI) as a measure of the impact of an eruption on climate. This index involves parameters which reflect three salient factors: the duration of the volcanic veil; the latitude of injection (which affects the geographical cover of the veil); and the potential of the eruption to influence the climate, such as indicated by the volume of material ejected. As an illustration, an eruption within tropical latitudes, e.g. that of Tambora in 1815, has twice the weighting of a more northerly eruption such as of Vesuvius.

There is also a seasonal effect for great eruptions. A supereruption in summer at Yellowstone might spread aerosols almost globally, whereas the aerosol cloud would be more restricted to the northern hemisphere with an eruption scenario in winter.[26] As with the supereruption of Toba, 74,000 years ago, global temperatures might take a decade to recover after plummeting by 10°C.

3.2.4 Environmental pollution

Since Roman times of lead pollution from smelters, industrialization has come at a cost of environmental pollution. The spillage of oil, heavy metals, acid, poison, or other deadly chemicals into waterways not only degrades the environment, but can be injurious or lethal to people. Whereas drinking polluted water or eating contaminated food may often be avoided, breathing air of dangerously poor quality may be unavoidable for inhabitants of a region unevacuated from the shadow of a toxic plume. Two of the most catastrophic atmospheric releases of toxic plumes are indelibly imprinted in the annals of industrial accidents simply as Seveso 1976 and Chernobyl 1986.

About 15 km north of Milan, a small company was producing a compound used for the synthesis of herbicides. On 10 July 1976, a pressure anomaly caused a breakage in the chemical reactor, which led to the production of dioxin that was released over several hours into the atmosphere. With the wind blowing at about 5 m/s, the powdery dioxin was deposited along a 4 km by 7 km corridor in the town of Seveso.

A large Soviet nuclear power plant stood in the Ukrainian town of Chernobyl. On 26 April 1986, two explosions occurred, leading to the emission into the atmosphere of several tons of uranium dioxide and myriad radionuclides, which were dispersed by high altitude winds over many thousand square kilometres of Europe.

A feature of the spatial distribution of the fallout of dioxin and Caesium-137 is its spotty 'leopard skin' characteristic, involving hotspots, which complicate risk assessment and dose monitoring.[27] Within the region polluted by dioxin, the density varied over about five orders of magnitude from 0.1 to 27,000 micro-gram per m^2; for soil deposition samples measured in Europe, the Caesium-137 concentration also ranged more than five orders of magnitude from 1 to 261,000 Becquerels per m^2. Areas of ever higher concentrations correspond to regions of lower and lower fractal dimensions. Hotspots accordingly can be associated geometrically with *multi-fractal* structures. For the Seveso fallout of the heavy molecule dioxin, the multi-fractal parameters turn out to be compatible with rainfall, whilst for the lighter Chernobyl fallout, the parameters are very compatible with cloud formation.[28]

3.2.5 Debris flows

Debris flows are the scourge of many mountainous regions of the world, most notoriously in Asia and the Americas. The dangerous mixture of steep, unstable slopes with torrential rain or meltwater is to be found in many geologically active yet densely populated regions. Many different soil types provide conditions suitable for debris flow; a low clay content expedites mobilization. Removal of vegetative cover increases soil erosion and the likelihood of a debris flow occurring.

The volume of a debris flow depends on a diverse range of factors, including vegetation, soil type, antecedent moisture, as well as drainage area and channel geometry. As an initial approximation, the extent of a debris flow might be estimated simply as a function of drainage area, or as the product $L.B.e$, where L is the channel length with uniform erodibility; B is the channel width; and e is the mean erosion depth. But the validity of this expression is limited: for a given watershed, the volume of a debris flow may vary by orders of magnitude from one event to another.[29] This is most obvious for snow-capped volcanoes, where the volume of lahars depends not just on the magma ejected in an eruption, but also on the volume of meltwater. If a large amount of snow and ice is melted, even a modest eruption may generate a massive lahar. In the 1985 eruption of Nevado del Ruiz, Colombia, the lahar generated had a tremendous volume of almost 100 million m^3 – about 20 times the volume of magma output.

3.2.6 Landslides

Although universal as a high terrain phenomenon, there is no formal scale index for the size of a landslide, save the area covered by a landslide, or the volume of landslide material, but there is still a geometrical structure to landslides. The blocks forming a large landslide may have a self-similar geometry, and studies have estimated the fractal dimensions of landslides.[30] Such blocks may cascade downwards in size in a power-law fashion. Let l be a measure of spatial extent, and let $N(l)$ be the number of slide blocks with width (or length) greater than l. Then, from some Japanese landslide studies, a fractal scaling law has been obtained: $N(l) \propto l^{-D}$. With respect to landslide width, the fractal dimension D lies between 1.2 and 1.4. With respect to landslide length, the range of D is somewhat higher, between 1.4 and 1.5.

The characteristic of fractal scaling is significant, as it is linked with slope stability and mass movement. In Taiwan, fractal scaling has been exhibited by thousands of landslides generated by typhoon rainfall and also by earthquake action.[31] Fractal scaling has been replicated over three orders of magnitude in a computer landslide model developed by Hergarten *et al.*.[32] According to Per Bak, fascinated by the self-organization of sandpiles, fractal scaling over still more orders of magnitude has been exhibited by mountain landslides in Nepal.[33]

3.2.7 Tsunamis

Tsunamis are very effective at transmitting energy away from their source, be it an offshore earthquake, eruption on a volcanic island, submarine landslide, or meteorite impact. This explains their threat to so many coastlines around the world, most notably around the Pacific Rim. The evidence for great earthquakes in the Cascadia zone offshore from Oregon, Washington, and British Columbia, partly rests on written records of a tsunami in 1700, affecting 1,000 km of Japanese coast. By contrast, the far-field tsunami threat from earthquakes in the Indian Ocean was barely reflected in the historical record. Indeed, before the calamitous tsunami of 26 December 2004, verifiable damage was reported only on the Australian coastline in 1977 from a tsunami emanating from Sumbawa, Indonesia, and in the Seychelles in 1833 following a tsunami generated in South Sumatra.[34] Typical of extreme natural hazard events, worse than 2004 may yet be to come: many areas in the Indian Ocean Basin could experience higher tsunami amplitudes.

From an earthquake source, tsunami energy is mainly transmitted orthogonal to the causative fault, both in the direction of the near shore, and along a great circle path on the opposite side of the ocean.[35] According to Costas Synolakis, an eminent *tsunamista*, inhomogeneities along the travel path may cause tsunamis to spread out directionally in fingers of energy, known figuratively as 'fingers of God'.

Approaching land, the waves slow down and bunch up, resulting in an increase in height. A tsunami will intensify if it encounters a coastal scarp or underwater ridge, or if it enters a bay with a broad but narrowing entrance. The height of tsunami runup in a coastal area depends crucially on local bathymetric factors. As evidenced by tragic images of destruction of coastal areas of Northeast Japan on 11 March 2011, tsunami speed on land is a powerful damage multiplier.

3.2.8 River floods

As with most natural hazards, the spatial variability of flooding for a river network in a drainage basin, and for different rivers of a geographical area, lends itself to a fractal description. The applicability of these concepts follows from empirical study of the self-similarity characteristics of drainage networks, the accuracy of which owes much to the availability of digital elevation models of river basins. Because of the scale invariance of the hydrological processes governing rivers throughout the world, the mathematical description of river basins is rich in power-law relations, most of which reflect, through their probabilistic formulation, the statistical aspects of self-similarity.

Consider first the total *contributing area* at a catchment site. This area is defined in terms of the size of the upstream network which is connected to the site, and is a measure of the flow rate under constant spatially uniform rainfall over the river basin. Over three orders of magnitude, a study by Rodríguez-Iturbe *et al.* of five basins in North America has shown that the probability of a total contributing area exceeding a value A scales in power-law fashion as $A^{-0.43}$. It is through energy dissipation that river networks are carved, and with a related scaling exponent, a power-law for the spatial distribution of energy dissipation also holds, similar in some respects to the Gutenberg–Richter relation for earthquakes. Both river discharge and seismic activity are manifest across a spectrum of length scales, and may be interpreted as reflecting a state of self-organization of a spatially extended system.[36]

The discharge Q is related by a runoff coefficient β to the area A contributing to a catchment site. As suggested by the principles of scale invariance, this relation is well represented as a power-law: $Q = \beta A^m$. Where the rainfall rate is constant for long periods, m is 1, and the runoff coefficient then is just the runoff rate. The widespread validity of such scaling relations suggests that, underlying the formation of drainage networks, are common optimality principles such as the minimization of energy expenditure in the river system, both as a whole and over its parts. Similar minimization principles have previously been applied in geomorphic research. These economical but powerful optimality principles can explain the tree-like spatial structure of drainage networks, their internal connectivity structure, and their main flow characteristics. They also provide important insight into particularly dangerous forms of flooding, during which spatially distributed potential energy from rainfall on hillslopes is rapidly converted into kinetic energy.

3.2.9 Extra-terrestrial impacts

Meteorite and asteroid impacts are an episodic component of the Earth's history, and remnant craters may be found scattered across its surface. There is a large random element in their landfall, but because of the pull of the Earth's gravitational field, there is a gravitational effect focusing more impacts near the equatorial region than near the poles.

The dimensions of a crater may be approximately estimated from scaling laws relating the crater diameter D to the kinetic energy W of the impactor.[37] The argument is simple, and requires no solving of differential equations. Ignoring gravity terms, the equations of hydrodynamics are invariant under the transformation which increases the time and length scale by the same factor α, but keeps the density the same. Under this scaling transformation, the kinetic energy increases by α^3. Hence the diameter of a crater scales as the cube root of the impactor energy: $D \propto W^{1/3}$. For very large impacts, gravity has a significant effect on limiting crater size, because of the need to raise the excavated mass by a vertical distance which is proportional to D. The diameter corresponding to a given impact energy is thus smaller; being proportional to the one-quarter power rather than the one-third power.

3.3 The Human Disaster Toll

Somerset Maugham told the legend of a merchant in Baghdad who sent his servant to buy provisions.[38] The servant returned, saying, 'Master, just now when I was in the marketplace I was jostled by a woman in the crowd and when I turned I saw it was Death that jostled me. She looked at me and made a threatening gesture. Now, lend me your horse, and I will ride away from this city and avoid my fate. I will go to Samarra and there Death will not find me'. The merchant lent him his horse. Then the merchant went down to the marketplace and saw Death standing in the crowd and said, 'Why did you make a threatening gesture to my servant when you saw him this morning?' 'That was not a threatening gesture', Death said. 'It was only a start of surprise. I was astonished to see him in Baghdad, for I had an appointment with him tonight in Samarra.'

On 22 February 2006, the Al Askari mosque in Samarra, one of the holiest sites in Shi'a Islam, was bombed by Al Qaeda in Iraq. In the ensuing sectarian violence, refugees from the bloodshed in Baghdad may have found Death awaiting them in Samarra. It would be demoralizing if there were some absolute irrevocable law of mortality from catastrophes; a mathematical fate which populations could not elude, try as they might. There happens to be just such a law, originally formulated by Lewis Fry Richardson for the number of fatalities of a war. The relative frequency of a number X of fatalities is proportional to $X^{-\alpha}$.

For the Iraq War, the power α is close to the number 2.5, which can be arrived at from studying patterns of violence, and formulating a model of evolving self-organized groups of attackers.[39] This is similar to the power obtained from terrorism in general.[40] A smaller value may pertain for inter-state wars, where mass casualties are more likely, but mitigated by defensive safety measures. This is illustrated by the *Luftwaffe* bombing campaign during World War II. Statisticians could estimate the number of casualties for sheltered and unsheltered English populations.[41]

In war-time as with terrorist bombing, fate plays a part in choosing which individuals become death statistics. On 17 December 1983, the author missed the IRA bombing of the Harrods department store in London by a few hours. A lawyer, John Woods, narrowly escaped death from terrorism no less than three times. On 21 December 1988, he was scheduled to fly on Pan Am flight 103, which exploded over Lockerbie, but he cancelled late. On 26 February 1993, he was unharmed on the 39th floor of the World Trade Center when it was bombed by Ramzi Yousef. On 9/11, a calendar day remembered for the Al Qaeda attack masterminded by Yousef's uncle, Khalid Sheikh Mohammed, the lucky lawyer left his office just before it was struck.[42]

Persi Diaconis, magician and mathematician, has made a study of coincidences, and has pointed out that vast numbers of apparent coincidences arise from hidden causes that are never discovered. In the case of John Woods, the causes are clear. If terrorism targeting were largely random, he would have been extremely unlucky to have been in the wrong place at three wrong times years apart. But terrorist targeting is anything but random: the aviation route from London to New York is especially targeted by terrorists, as is Manhattan.

Anyone searching for a law of mortality might well be guided by the works of George Zipf, a self-styled statistical human ecologist, whose eponymous law of word frequencies is but one example of his fervent belief in the near-universal applicability of scaling distributions to social science statistics. Indeed, Zipf's Law has been found to represent more data than any other. Zipf's Law holds for the population distribution of cities, so it might be expected to hold also for disaster casualties.

Suppose we are interested in a human population variable Z; in the present circumstances, this might be a catastrophe death toll. Rank the N largest values over a period of time according to size, the first being the largest: $Z_1 \geq Z_2 \geq Z_3 .... \geq Z_N$. Considering the largest values in the tail of the dataset, the sizes may be found to satisfy Zipf's Law, a scaling distribution:

$$Log(Z_N) = -\left(\frac{1}{\delta}\right) Log(N) + C$$

From an analysis of the population of global earthquake death tolls, with the 1976 Tangshan, China earthquake as the highest ranked human disaster, Knopoff and Sornette found a value of about 1.0 for the scaling parameter δ.[43] The stability of sums of power-law distributed variables implies that the same scaling holds for deaths in individual countries, albeit with a population-dependent upper limit. Tectonics played a role in shaping the pattern of early human settlement. Tectonic movements created the mountain ranges that provided natural defences against the ravages of barbarians. Earthquake loss associated with an active tectonic habitat, and flood loss associated with a river fortification, have been accepted as prices for military security.

Using a similar approach, Pyle has analyzed global volcanic eruption death tolls, with the 1883 Krakatau eruption as the highest ranked human disaster, and found a lesser value of about 2/3 for δ.[44] Since the highest ranked death toll, Z_1, scales with the dataset size as $N^{1/\delta}$, one might expect, over time, a greater human tragedy to unfold from a cataclysmic volcanic eruption than even a great earthquake. The geological evidence of pre-historic eruptions would add fear to such an expectation. Unbounded losses are of course not credible, but the highest ranking loss may always be exceeded: worse may yet be to come, especially with rising populations.

To illustrate the consequent risks associated with increasing population densities, consider the earthquake threat. A large earthquake may inflict serious building damage over an epicentral area of a few hundred square kilometres and moderate damage may extend over an additional peripheral area of a few thousand square kilometres. Already, population densities exceeding 10,000 per square kilometres are attained in urban areas of the developing world, and even as much as 1,000 per square kilometres in some rural areas of the Middle and Far East. Thus for earthquake scenarios where the epicentre is in an urban area, the population at risk may well be of the order of millions, and the spectre looms of very high earthquake casualties in areas with poor housing and with seismically vulnerable health facilities, such as Tehran.[45] Poor governance adds to the woes inflicted by Nature, and compounded the scale of Haiti's earthquake tragedy of 12 January 2010.

In his 1798 essay on the principle of population, Thomas Malthus declared, 'The most tremulous convulsions of nature, such as volcanic eruptions and earthquakes, have but a trifling effect on the population of any state'.[46] This was written when the world population was about a billion, and when death rates in his native England were several times higher than now. With a world population seven times larger, the statement would still be true. Appalling though the loss of 300,000 lives was, the Bangladesh cyclone of 1970 killed a fraction of 1% of the citizens of one of the most densely populated countries.

Wars have the capability of killing far higher percentages of populations. In the time of Malthus, about 2% of the world population was lost through war. Napoleon could permit a monthly loss of 20,000 to 30,000 men. The French *polemologist*, Gaston Bouthoul, was familiar with the prey–predator differential equations of Lotka and Volterra, which quantify the oscillatory dynamics of biological populations. He noted dispassionately that, regardless of the cause of war, the ruthless effect is to trim down a growing population.[47] As observed by Malthus, who was mathematically trained at Cambridge, an unchecked population increases in a geometric ratio. Mathematically, the population at time n exceeds that of an initial reference population by a growth factor λ^n.

Apart from war and pestilence, famine has been a considerable check on Malthusian population growth. Although drought is a primary driver of food shortage, famine is largely a man-made disaster. Harvest failure is not a necessary cause of famine. The Great Bengal Famine of 1943 followed a harvest only 5% below the five year regional average. A review of famine in history suggests that Nature is more the proximate cause or trigger of famine than the final determinant.[48] Political doctrine has starved tens of millions to death.

3.4   Models of a Fractal World

The ubiquity of approximate power-law relations in catastrophe science is the simplest reason why our world has the characteristics of Nicholas Taleb's *Extremistan*: catastrophes are extreme events that occur far more often than would happen in *Mediocristan*, where short-tailed Gaussian distributions hold sway, and witnessing a natural catastrophe might be as rare an experience as seeing a human eight foot tall. From the *Guinness Book of Records*, the ratio of the heights of the tallest to the shortest adult men is about five, whereas the ratio of the sizes of the largest to the smallest natural catastrophes is measured in orders of magnitude.[49]

Whenever a major catastrophe occurs, media coverage is dominated by reports of bad news. But the salient bad news is already here, and always has been here, even though it is left unreported: our world is governed by power-laws. But there is also good news, as will be evident to readers of Mandelbrot's book, *The Fractal Geometry of Nature*.

Mandelbrot, who was brought up in a house full of maps, left a legacy of visually captivating illustrations of imagined fractal landscapes that never were, (sometimes called fractal forgeries), generated using computer colour graphics. For a global readership unfamiliar with self-similarity, and unused to seeing such simulated images, they came as a powerful revelation of the creative potential of computer-generated imagery. These jagged landscapes were broadly reminiscent of hills and islands we see on Earth, although nowhere in particular. Favoured for special effects scenes on television commercials, they were yet different enough for two mathematics graduate students to exploit fractal methods in simulating the landscape of a mythical world for a sequel to George Lucas's *Star Wars* movie.

Especially interested in fractals have been geomorphologists, whose expansive field of study is the surface of the Earth. Beyond cataloguing and describing landscape changes qualitatively, they seek to explain the changing features of a landscape through mechanistic models. Geohazard analysts are also interested in the study of *morpho-dynamics*, since this is intertwined with the study of river floods, landslides, debris flows, soil failures, storm surges, and earthquake fault movements.

In reviewing geomorphic transport laws for predicting landscape form and dynamics, Dietrich *et al.* have considered a range of alternative landscape evolution models.[50] A basic question addressed is what degree of physical approximation should be acceptable in the scientific pursuit of explanation. Consider, as an example, the basic geomorphic process of river channel transport and incision into alluvial beds. The sediment transport q can be related to the drainage area A and the local slope S via the power-law formula: $q = k \cdot A^m \cdot S^n$. Compact idealized models such as this serve a useful purpose, in that they are based on process mechanics and can be parameterized. However, they have obvious simplifying limitations, which explorers of alternative modelling approaches would seek to overcome.

3.4.1 Model representations

The philosopher of science, Nancy Cartwright, is well known for her abrasive polemical statement: 'A model is a work of fiction.'[51] There are different types of scientific model: theoretical, computational, heuristic, phenomenological, small scale, etc.. The more realistic the assumptions underlying the model are, the less 'fictitious' it will be. Newtonian mechanics sets an exemplary standard for scientific model validation. Galileo's classic experiment of rolling a ball down an inclined plane can be explained very well with a simple mathematical model of the force of gravity, ignoring the effect of air resistance. Rolling a boulder down a rough mountain slope is one of Nature's avalanche experiments; one that poses a more severe landscape modelling challenge.

Over large spatial and time scales, interior geodynamic processes influence the topography observed on the surface of the Earth. Some direct subterranean observations are possible through deep drilling, but the development of scientific understanding, on human rather than geological time scales, depends on the construction of models. Powerful computer technology has made mathematical modelling increasingly popular, but laboratory models are useful as well.

The wonder of Galileo's elegant inclined plane experiment is that the findings on gravity scale up to the size of the Earth. Scaled laboratory models of geodynamic processes can be constructed, provided model materials and experimental conditions satisfy some physical similarity criteria. The derivation of such similarity criteria can be based on dimensional analysis, and the so-called Pi-theorem for determining scale transformations for solutions to the equation systems.

Through the use of mathematical and laboratory models inspired by plate tectonics, geodynamical theories have progressed greatly. But however much global data are consistent with these theories, scientists should have the humility to heed the injunctions of philosophers of science that they cannot be fully validated as fact: geophysicists can be mistaken, as they have been on the occurrence of rare great earthquakes. Further refinement of scientific theory is always possible, and comes with patient observation over a sufficient period of time to collect anomalous and discordant evidence.

As with underlying geodynamics, so there are practical limitations in modelling changes to the Earth's surface. The pace of landscape change is generally very slow on a human timescale. This encourages the search for a high-speed laboratory of geomorphology. One such laboratory is the picturesque and explosive Indonesian volcanic island of Anak Krakatau. After the cataclysmic eruption which pulverized Krakatau in August 1883, it only took four decades before three new ash-cone islands appeared in the late 1920s. These were destroyed by marine erosion and submarine sliding on the slope of the submerged caldera. But Anak ('child') Krakatau succeeded in establishing itself in 1930, and gained geological maturity and security thirty years later through the extrusion of lava which solidified into a rock bulwark against wave erosion.

Numerical models of coastal geomorphology have been developed for simulating the complexities of the sand transport and ocean wave erosion process.[52] But anyone attempting to predict landscape form and evolution should be realistic about what level of reliability might be practically achievable. Landscape modellers cannot reproduce in a forecast the megapixel accuracy of a photograph.

3.4.2 Landscape models

If, at a formal philosophical level, a model narrative might be classified within a genre of fiction rather than as documentary reality, then a model visual image might be classified within a genre of art rather than as photographic reality. Within this philosophical paradigm, a fine art metaphor has been chosen by Dietrich *et al.* to characterize the different types of realism to which landscape modellers may aspire.

At the same time, these geoscientists convey an important general message about the basic nature of numerical model development, in situations where prediction is not practically testable because of the protracted timescales involved. Real landscapes generally change far too slowly for the forecasting of future states to be checked, and the same slow pace applies to the occurrence of rare catastrophes, including those that may affect topography. Lacking benchmarks against evolving reality, workable quantitative metrics for rejecting incorrect models and constraining dynamical laws are hard to construct, especially since similar results may arise from different dynamical processes.

To illustrate the concept of fractals, which weave art with science, Mandelbrot referred in *The Fractal Geometry of Nature* to some great art works of the world depicting meteorological and oceanographic themes: *The Deluge* by the Italian renaissance genius Leonardo Da Vinci, and *The Great Wave* by the Japanese artist Hokusai, whose prints influenced artists in mid-19th century Paris. To illustrate the type of output generated by different categories of landscape model, Dietrich *et al.* offer comparisons with several styles of French 19th century landscape painting. As a guide to this interdisciplinary cultural exercise, an authoritative reference is Kenneth Clark's treatise *Landscape into Art*. [53]

Suppose a specific terrain is chosen, and imagine that three artists are invited to paint their view of the landscape before them. One artist paints like Gustave Courbet, who led the realist movement in 19th century French painting. A second paints in the style of the primitive artist, Douanier Rousseau, who incorporated into his landscapes incongruous dream-like images, such as a jungle animal, earning him the sobriquet *'Monsieur Rêve'*. The third artist paints in the structural post-impressionist style of Paul Cézanne, who abstracted geometry out of observations of Nature through simplified forms and faceted planes.

The rich detail offered in the first landscape style looks very realistic. But such *detailed realism* is far beyond the capability of any predictive geomorphic numerical model. Even equipped with supercomputers, no modeller can anticipate the future sequence of climatic and tectonic events that might affect the landscape. Indeed, for beach erosion, which is very sensitive to the random occurrence of storms, efforts at prediction may be useless and futile.[54]

The second landscape style of the *apparent realism* school is also rich in detail, and may pass a credibility check on individual constituents: the trees have leaves, the plants have stems, the grass is green etc.. But the ensemble may be impossible. Rousseau was fond of representing jungle scenes in his landscapes – but he never left France. In landscape numerical prediction, what may purport to be reality may be nothing more than the superficial fortuitous outcome of some large-scale numerical model, where the failure to acknowledge the scale limitations of some geomorphic transport laws may yield quite misleading results.

The third landscape style of Cézanne captures the essential topographic features, but stops short of providing fine detail. The associated style of geomorphological modelling recognizes at the outset that landscape cannot be precisely predicted. This is because of the spatial variability in material properties, the temporal variability in the forces driving topographic change, and the fundamental nonlinearity of erosion processes. Accordingly, the *essential realist* does not attempt to portray the exact topography, which is dynamically indeterminate, but rather is satisfied to capture the key elements through dynamical models that can be parameterized from field measurements. Numerical modelling in practical applications is about essential realism.

3.4.3 Uncertainty in model depictions

Writing on exactitude in science, Jorge Luis Borges imagined an empire where cartography had been perfected to a level where the printed map of a single province occupied an entire city.[55] In the 21st century, digital mapping and computer graphics can aspire to such fine resolution, where the underlying data have been adequately mined. But there is no cartographic tradition for the uncertainty associated with maps to be displayed any more than for French landscape paintings.

In early maps of the world, a distinction was not drawn between parts of the world familiar to the cartographer, and those completely unknown. So a 14th century map of Western Europe produced in Catalonia for King Charles V of France was admirably reliable for Spain and France, but woefully unreliable for Scotland and Ireland. Poor maps cost lives. In 1588, reliance on poor navigational charts and an encounter with a savage Northwest European windstorm caused numerous ships in the Spanish Armada to be shipwrecked off the fractal coasts of Scotland and Ireland. Some 4,000 of the Armada's men were drowned; the greatest loss of life in this attempted Spanish invasion of Elizabethan England.[56]

In the 20th century, maps of active earthquake faulting did not make clear those areas where resolution was poor due to fundamental deficiencies in geological investigation capability. Californian geologists were surprised by large earthquakes occurring on hidden blind thrusts, such as at Coalinga in May 1983 and Northridge in January 1994.

Whether drawn by hand or computer-generated, any map is ultimately only a visual guide to reality. Some images may only present general statistical information, and not purport to provide anything resembling a full picture. Other maps may offer a high resolution image with a considerable amount of detail, albeit of partial accuracy. Thus maps of tsunami risk along a coastline may fail to recognize shortfalls in data on local bathymetry, a key amplification factor of tsunami runup heights. Seismic microzonation maps for a city may ignore shortcomings in the geotechnical database on soil profiles under buildings.

Of major practical concern are detailed model depictions which are superficially real, but might bear little relation to reality. A caveat is required for the contemporary usage of some natural hazard maps. For example, some dated flood maps may ignore the impact on rainfall runoff of modern urban development and hillside deforestation. Some maps of earthquake building damage potential ignore the prevalence of code non-compliance. As a consequence, they may be as idealized as some pre-scientific drawings of earthquake destruction.

Most open and useful are model depictions which give an immediate indication of imperfect resolution, rather as in a Cézanne landscape painting. A mountaineer planning to climb Mont Sainte-Victoire in France, might gain some idea of the scale of the task from Cézanne's classic Provençale landscapes, but could not fail to appreciate the need for further topographic information.

In the 21st century, a civil engineer contemplating building in a seismically active zone might be left unaware, from inspecting a regional fault map, of the inhomogeneous spatial coverage in geological investigation. Some empty spaces on a map may correspond to areas partially explored, rather than areas known to be free of active faults.

Overlaying uncertainty on maps, which is facilitated by modern computer graphics, provides a practical way of conveying uncertainty to a viewer,[57] rather as in some post-classical styles of landscape painting. An open and explicit visual display of uncertainty serves to avoid a false impression of undue data quality or a misleading sense of model accuracy. Model transparency is gained by rendering output images opaque with the associated degree of uncertainty.

Dietrich *et al.* suggest that even the geomorphological models of the second *apparent realism* school have some value in affording insight into linkages between uplift, erosion, and topography at a very coarse scale. But such insight is worthless without frankness over the limitations of the models and their domain of applicability.

Cartographers are accustomed by venerable tradition to mapping available knowledge, such as it is. But lack of knowledge is in itself also noteworthy information to share. Indeed, while ignorance is to be deprecated, whistle-blowing on ignorance is to be encouraged. The charting of uncertainty and ignorance would provide a helpful and informative supplementary guide to end-users of maps, whether they are residents, tourists, engineers, insurers, or decision-makers of public policy. This would be a milestone in catastrophe visualization.

Chapter 4

A Measure of Uncertainty

The only certainty
is that nothing is certain.
Pliny the Elder,
Naturalis Historia

In his novel, *Dr Fischer of Geneva or The Bomb Party*, Graham Greene tells a story of an apocalyptic Christmas party held at Dr Fischer's mansion to which six guests are invited.[1] In a corner is a barrel containing six crackers, five of which contain a cheque for two million Swiss francs; the sixth cracker may or may not contain a lethal quantity of explosive, placed by the generous yet treacherous host. One of the guests rushes forward, 'Perhaps she had calculated that the odds would never be as favourable again.' If she did, she miscalculated. In fact, the chances of detonating the bomb were the same for all, as is clear if one imagines a cracker being given to each guest, and all the crackers then being pulled simultaneously. It is a popular misconception, long studied by psychologists, that there is a difference between rolling a set of dice one at a time, and rolling them all at once. With the dice rolled separately, some think wishfully they can exert an influence over the outcome.

This fictional episode would have appealed to the French mathematician Pierre Simon Laplace, who deemed probability to be 'good sense reduced to calculus', and whose logical theory of chance consisted of reducing all events of the same kind to a number of equally probable cases.[2] Acting as much out of good sense as courtesy, he would have been happy to let ladies first to the cracker barrel.

Laplace's theory works well in situations such as at the bomb party, but there are many cases where the criterion of equal probability involves a significant measure of subjective judgement, and mere rationality is insufficient for evaluating a risk. Such situations arise, for example, where probabilities of individual events are required: a common predicament in hazard forecasting and risk assessment. Notions of probability and uncertainty are central to decision-making over the threat of catastrophes. However, scientists and civil engineers are mainly schooled in the mathematics of determinism, and tend to be more fluent in Newtonian calculus than the calculus of probabilities; an educational bias which the present exposition seeks to redress.

4.1 The Concept of Probability

As befits the study of randomness, the subject of probability has evolved in a rather haphazard fashion, with an essentially informal mathematical approach guiding the interpretation and application of probability over the centuries. The foundations of the theory of probability theory were laid only as recently as 1933 by Andrei Kolmogorov,[3] one of the great mathematicians of the 20th century, whose parallel contributions to classical dynamics and turbulence alone would have earned him acclaim as a major architect of the modern understanding of hazard dynamics. Inspired by the axiomatic basis of geometry constructed by the Göttingen mathematician David Hilbert, Kolmogorov devised a simple but powerful axiomatic approach to probability. Although an acquaintance with initial axioms is not often necessary for practical applications, in the case of catastrophes it is desirable as well as instructive. Given the sparsity and inhomogeneity of data, the range of extremes, and common divergence in the opinions of scientists, methods for measuring uncertainty may be devised which, perhaps unknowingly, conflict with these axioms. An application of practical significance where such conflict has actually arisen is the ranking of geological faults according to their threat to a nuclear power plant. However vague the data and urgent the application, a tower of probabilistic risk calculations needs solid mathematical foundations.

Kolmogorov admitted that his task would have been hopeless but for earlier original French work on integration calculus which suggested the analogy between the probability of an event and the measure of a set. The axioms are thus defined abstractly in terms of a family of subsets of a set Ω, each of which is assigned a non-negative real number, which is called its probability. This number is unity for Ω itself. As a simple illustration, for a single toss of a coin, the set Ω consists of two points, corresponding to Heads and Tails. According to the axioms, if two subsets are disjoint, so that they have no element in common, then the probability of the combined subset is just the sum of the probabilities of the two individual subsets. Thus the probability of Heads plus the probability of Tails equals the probability of Heads or Tails, which is unity. Note that the axioms do not dictate the probability assigned to Heads or Tails: this depends on perception as to the fairness of the coin.

There are some immediate corollaries of the axioms, two of the most important being the total probability theorem and Bayes' theorem. Given sets A and B, we denote the probabilities assigned to A and B as $P(A)$ and $P(B)$ respectively. Denoting the intersection of sets A and B, i.e. the elements common to both, as $A \cap B$, then provided $P(A)$ is greater than zero, the conditional probability of B given A is defined as:

$$P(B \mid A) = P(A \cap B) / P(A)$$

Suppose that the whole set $\Omega = A_1 \cup A_2 \cup ... \cup A_n$, where the subsets A_i are mutually exclusive, i.e. non-intersecting, and let X be an arbitrary set. Then the probability of X is given by the following total probability theorem:

$$P(X) = P(X \cap A_1) + P(X \cap A_2) + ... + P(X \cap A_n)$$
$$= P(A_1)P(X \mid A_1) + P(A_2)P(X \mid A_2) + ... + P(A_n)P(X \mid A_n)$$

Given that $P(A_i \mid X)P(X) = P(A_i \cap X) = P(X \mid A_i)P(A_i)$, the above formula provides the denominator for Bayes' theorem:

$$P(A_i \mid X) = \frac{P(A_i)P(X \mid A_i)}{P(A_1)P(X \mid A_1) + P(A_2)P(X \mid A_2) + ... + P(A_n)P(X \mid A_n)}$$

A feature of the axiomatic system is its abstractness. This may not advance universal understanding, but it has the signal merit of generality; such generality, in fact, as to allow for various alternative practical interpretations. Of course, the theorems derived from the fundamental axioms, such as the total probability theorem and Bayes' theorem, hold true regardless of interpretation. According to the axioms, to each of the sets A, a probability $P(A)$ is assigned: but in what various ways can this be done? There are subjective, frequentist, and logical schools of probability, which differ in their interpretations of the concept of probability.

Within the subjectivist school, it is accepted that rational people may legitimately hold contrasting views about the probability of an event. A phrase introduced to represent the variation in views, and which is fitting for the present hazard context, is a barometer of probability. To use the vivid language of the historian Edward Gibbon, this barometer can swing from the lowest degree of credulity (a simpleton who blindly believes in the event) to the highest pitch of scepticism (someone who resolutely refuses to believe in the possibility of the event). When new evidence becomes available, beliefs may of course change. But the manner by which beliefs change is not usually logically structured. How would Gibbon's beliefs on the decline of the Roman Empire have changed with new information of a volcanic eruption of global climatic impact?

According to Bayesian practice, changes in belief upon receipt of new information are reflected in the transition from a prior to a posterior probability.[4] Bayes' theorem is used as part of the process of learning from new data. Thus if A_i is a particular event, and X is some data, Bayes' theorem can be used to update the prior probability $P(A_i)$ to obtain the posterior probability $P(A_i \mid X)$. Bayes himself stated his result only for a uniform prior, but more informative priors may be judged to be appropriate. Resort to a uniform prior reflects a lack of preference between alternative events.

In contrast with the subjectivist, the frequentist assigns a measure of uncertainty to an individual event by considering it to belong to a class of similar events having similar randomness properties, and associates probability with some notion of limiting frequency. Thus the outcome of a single toss of a *fair* coin is embedded within a hypothetical set of trials where the coin is tossed many times. Let the proportion of Heads after n trials be P. Then the law of large numbers states that as n gets larger, P tends towards the value of a half, which is taken to be the probability of Heads.

In circumstances where large numbers of independent observations are made, the frequentist and subjectivist views become reconciled. For, regardless of the differences of prior subjective judgements, through the Bayesian updating procedure, the posterior probabilities will converge arbitrarily closely, provided there are sufficient observations. To illustrate this mathematical theorem, suppose that an individual believed initially that a coin was heavily biased in favour of Heads. Then his posterior belief will tend towards fairness as more and more tosses are made, if the ratio of the number of Heads to the number of Tails approaches ever closer to one.

Finally, some comment should be made about the connection between the subjectivist and logical theories of probability. The classical proponents of the logical theory would argue that the symmetry in a situation can determine assignments of probability. In the absence of any meteorological information, this would be the basis for assigning equal probabilities for hailstorm damage to neighbouring fields of agricultural crops. A Bayesian might be happy to use spatial symmetry to inform his or her prior distribution. However, asymmetric loss experience of hailstorms over time would afford empirical grounds for updating this distribution.

4.2 The Meaning of Uncertainty

In former times, when hazards such as earthquakes, hurricanes, and volcanic eruptions were perceived by some cultures as wilful acts of supernatural powers, mitigation of risk might sensibly have focused on appeasing the external agents of disaster. Such events would not have been regarded as a matter of chance, (in the Aristotelian sense of absence of purpose, order, or cause), so to try to predict a hazard event would have been dismissed as an absurd or reckless pursuit.

A contrasting world view is the fundamentalist dogma that the future is pre-ordained: for good or ill, we happen to be ignorant of what the future has in store. This belief inevitably engenders a sense of fatalism, which may have its social virtues, but to one who holds such a belief, determinism must undermine the value and thus question the purpose of risk mitigation. Ironically, given that *hazard* is a word of Arabic origin, fundamentalist beliefs are held in areas of the world exposed to some of the highest levels of natural and man-made hazard.

From a fundamentalist viewpoint, chance, as in the casting of dice, would be firmly associated with the hand of fate. The French mathematician De Moivre viewed statistical regularity as evidence of a grand design. However, within the overall grand design, chance might be allowed a minor role in effecting less desirable outcomes, which might not be an expression of providential intent. Exploiting this loophole, the Victorian naturalist William Paley, whose watch-maker metaphor embroidered his argument for design in Nature, was prepared to countenance a chance explanation for disfiguring warts.

The premise that, given the past state of the world, any event happening now was necessarily bound to happen, is not one to which only fundamentalists would have subscribed. This is the mantra of metaphysical determinism, repeated by some of the leading figures in the European enlightenment, such as Jakob Bernoulli and Pierre Laplace. Perceiving chance as a reflection of imperfect human knowledge, Augustus de Morgan believed that, in the presence of such ignorance, past experience would furnish no basis for assessing future probabilities.

Celebrating the success of Newtonian mechanics in predicting eclipses, there was a confident belief in mathematical circles that all events were predictable in principle. Bernoulli insisted that the outcome of the throw of a die was no less necessary than an eclipse. Only the ignorant would gamble on the dates of eclipses: a layman's contingency is an astronomer's necessity. Yet it is in the dynamics of apparently clockwork celestial mechanical systems, that the origins can be traced for the breakdown of classical 18th century determinism.

The starting point is the formulation of Newtonian mechanics constructed by the Irish polymath William Hamilton. The merits of Hamiltonian mechanics lie not so much in its facility to help solve practical problems, but rather in the deep insight afforded into the underlying structure of the theory of dynamics. For a system with N degrees of freedom, a state is specified by N position coordinates and momentum variables. The equal status accorded to coordinates and momenta encouraged new, more abstract ways of presenting and interpreting mechanics, including a mathematical equivalence with geometrical optics, which paved the way to the atomic world of wave-particle duality.

Under Hamilton's formulation, the dynamics of a system is completely defined by a single function, called the Hamiltonian, which is equivalent to the energy of the system, if the forces acting within the system (such as gravitational) are not time-dependent. We know from our own very existence on Earth, that, despite the gravitational pull of Jupiter and other planets, the Earth's orbit around the Sun has remained comparatively stable. But just how stable are Hamiltonian systems to perturbation? Many would have paid for an answer, had King Oskar II of Sweden not saved their expense. More than a decade before Nobel prizes were awarded, the Swedish monarch offered a prize of 2,500 gold crowns for proof of the stability of the solar system. The prize went to Henri Poincaré, who greatly advanced the study of dynamics, and invented much new mathematics – without actually cracking the problem. This had to wait another half century for the attention of Kolmogorov.

An outline of the solution was presented in 1954 by the same Andrei Kolmogorov, who several decades earlier had laid the rigorous foundations of probability theory. In 1962 and 1963, following Kolmogorov's lead, Arnold and Moser published proofs of the theorem, known by the acronym KAM. Fortunately for the Earth and its inhabitants, it turns out that most orbits can survive small perturbation. But more than answer the question, the KAM theory has helped illuminate the inner mysteries of dynamical uncertainty, and show how apparent randomness can emerge from the midst of determinism.

The source of indeterminism is manifest in attempting to find stable solutions for a perturbed Hamiltonian system. One can look for a trial solution of the form: $S_0 + \varepsilon S_1 + \varepsilon^2 S_2 + ...$, where ε is the scale of the small perturbation. But if one writes a Fourier wave expansion for S_1, one finds a series expression of the form:[5]

$$S_1 = \sum_m \frac{H(\boldsymbol{m})}{\boldsymbol{m} \cdot \omega} \exp(i \, \boldsymbol{m} \cdot \omega)$$

This formula includes the denominator: $\boldsymbol{m} \cdot \omega = m_1 \omega_1 + m_2 \omega_2 + ... + m_N \omega_N$ where $\boldsymbol{m} = (m_1, m_2, ..., m_N)$ is a vector with integer components, and $\omega = (\omega_1, \omega_2, ..., \omega_N)$ is a N component frequency vector. For most frequencies, the denominators are non-zero, and a solution to the equations of motion exists which tends to that of the unperturbed system, as the perturbation diminishes. However for specific resonant frequencies, a denominator may vanish, and a pathological situation develops.

The problem with small denominators is that, because the frequencies depend on the dynamical variables of position coordinates and momenta, trajectories associated with resonances wander erratically in a seemingly random manner, in contrast with well-behaved non-resonant trajectories. This apparent randomness can evolve into chaos, with neighbouring trajectories diverging exponentially. It is important to appreciate that these resonances do not occur at a particular point location or moment in time. They are nonlocal, and lead to a diffusive type of motion: from an initial starting point, it is not possible to predict with certainty where a trajectory will be after an elapse of time. A probabilistic characterization of dynamics is required, which leads on to the formalism of statistical mechanics, and thermodynamics.[6]

The notion that observed thermodynamical behaviour depends on suitable instabilities or disturbances had occurred to James Clerk Maxwell, who recognized the deficiencies of pre-KAM deterministic mechanics. Maxwell was a leader in applying probabilistic thinking in the natural world, having seen its applications in other realms of human activity. In developing the kinetic theory of gases, he saw an analogy with social statistics, and argued that, since we cannot know the causes of gas molecule motion in detail, we can only aspire to a statistical description of the physical world. The twin 20th century revolutions of quantum and chaos theory do not deny the truth of this perceptive argument.

True to his determinist convictions, Laplace had conceived of a secular super-calculator which could ordain the future of the universe, 'All events are as necessary as the revolution of the Sun.' We now know better. From Heisenberg's uncertainty principle of quantum mechanics, we know there is a finite limit (i.e. Planck's constant) to the accuracy with which the location and momentum of a particle can be simultaneously determined. So the state of a physical system cannot be specified exactly. Furthermore, even if this were possible, a simple dynamical system, once perturbed, can defeat the goal of a general deterministic prediction of time evolution. Laplace was amongst the first to warn of the catastrophic effects of the impact of a comet on Earth; a warning which would not be muted by two centuries of additional knowledge about comets and their dynamics.

4.3 Aleatory and Epistemic Uncertainty

From the viewpoint of 18th century classical determinism, probability connoted only lack of knowledge, that is to say only *epistemic uncertainty*. Lack of knowledge was a deficiency which might be remedied in principle by further learning and experiment. From quantum mechanics and dynamical chaos, we now know that there is much more uncertainty in characterizing the physical world than mere epistemic uncertainty, arising from lack of knowledge. There is an intrinsic uncertainty associated with the need for a statistical perspective in order to comprehend the physical world. Whether it is the motions of gas molecules in the atmosphere, or water molecules in the ocean, or silica molecules in sand, the need for a statistical physics formulation introduces an irreducible element of uncertainty.

This type of uncertainty associated with randomness is called *aleatory*, after the Latin word for dice. Aleatory uncertainty can be estimated better, but it cannot be reduced through advances in theoretical or observational science. This contrasts with *epistemic* uncertainty, which arises from imperfect information and knowledge, which is potentially reducible through data acquisition, even though, for some hazard observations, this may take generations.

The two forms of uncertainty reflect the underlying duality of probability. On the one hand, probability has a statistical aspect, concerned with stochastic laws of random processes; on the other hand, probability has an epistemic aspect, concerned with assessing degrees of belief in propositions with no statistical basis. In the absence of statistics, these beliefs may be based on logical implication or personal judgement.

This duality might best have been marked etymologically with distinct English words for *aleatory* and *epistemic* notions of probability. As the French mathematicians, Poisson and Cournot, pointed out, such words exist in their arguably more precise language: *chance et probabilité*. Commenting on the confusion over terminology, Hacking has drawn a comparison with Newton's distinction between weight and inertial mass.[7] Imagine the bother if only the word 'weight' existed for the two concepts, and engineers had always to qualify the word as active or passive to avoid being misunderstood.

Writing of the different types of probability in 1939, decades before this distinction was appreciated in probabilistic seismic hazard assessment, the mathematical geophysicist Harold Jeffreys returned to the simple illustration of the toss of a coin.[8] According to Jeffreys, we may suppose that there is a definite value p_H for the probability of a Head, which depends on the properties of the coin and the tossing conditions. In ignorance of p_H, (and without automatically assuming it to be one-half), we may treat it as an unknown with a prior distribution over a range of values. We can then estimate p_H from the results of tosses. Such estimates involve epistemic probabilities. Thus we can speak of an epistemic probability of 0.7 that the aleatory probability, p_H, lies between 0.4 and 0.6. With the labour of many repeated tosses, under the same standard conditions, the epistemic uncertainty would be progressively reduced.

Even if dice are not intentionally loaded, fairness may not be exact. In the late 19th century, when home entertainment distractions were few, a young English biometrician, W.F.R. Weldon, conducted a laborious manual experiment involving no less than 26,306 rolls of 12 dice. These were painstakingly performed down a slope of corrugated cardboard to avoid throwing bias. He found 106,602 instances of 5 or 6, which is 1,378 more than the expected number of 105,224, and corresponds to an excess of 0.0044 in the probability above 1/3. This small discrepancy was explained as a displacement of the centre of gravity towards the faces with fewer pits for marking numbers.

A measure of Weldon's endurance is that this basic experiment in probability was only automated in 2009.[9] This found an anomalous frequency of instances of 1, (attributable to a minute imperfection in the dice dimensions), showing the practical sense in enquiring into the probability that the probability of throwing 1 is 1/6.

This may remind some readers of the Russell paradox of 'the class of all classes'. However, Jeffreys argues that it is logically legitimate to speak of a probability that a probability has a particular value, as long as the subtle distinction between the two types of probability is respected. That the different forms of probability should elude the grasp of non-mathematicians is easier to understand than the differences themselves. Most people who use probability are oblivious and heedless of these differences; subtleties perceived as beyond their need for comprehension.

Mathematicians might be looked upon to set a clear example in distinguishing these probabilities. Actuaries do take care to make this distinction. But decisions about dealing with the two forms of uncertainty are clouded by an element of discord within the ranks of professional mathematicians. Strict Bayesians regard any probability assignment as having an unavoidable subjective element, whereas strict frequentists deny the objective reality of probability concepts which are not firmly rooted in observed frequencies. In practice, most applied statisticians are pragmatic, and will choose whichever method of statistical inference is deemed most appropriate for a specific problem.

As an actual example of how epistemic uncertainty may be reduced, consider the forecasting of the number of Atlantic hurricanes in a forthcoming season. In the absence of any current climatic information, a historical average figure might be calculated, and the probability of any particular number might be based simply on a histogram of historical relative frequencies. On the other hand, suppose it known that it is an El Niño year, which means that the wind shear conditions are not favourable for hurricane generation. With this information alone, the probabilities would be weighted down somewhat towards fewer hurricanes, as was the case for the quiet 1983, 1997, and 2009 seasons. However, El Niño is only one of a number of factors relevant to the severity of an Atlantic hurricane season, other causal factors have been identified and analysed by Gray *et al.*.[10]

As more knowledge is accumulated on hurricane generation, and numerical medium-term weather forecasting models become more sophisticated, the predictions of the hurricane count should become more accurate, and there should be a corresponding decline in epistemic uncertainty, which in any case is not absolute, but model dependent. Indeed, were it not for dynamical chaos, forecasting might be refined enormously. Lorenz, whose name is synonymous with meteorological chaos, speculated that, but for its chaotic regime, the atmosphere might undergo rather simple periodic oscillations.[11] Hurricanes might then have similar tracks and maximum wind speeds each year. Uncertainty in wind loading on structures would be drastically reduced. This would give planners extra authority in prohibiting construction in well-designated areas of high threat; confidence in prescribing wind design criteria in areas of moderate exposure; and peace of mind in allowing construction elsewhere with only modest wind resistance. In this chaos-free idyll, windstorm catastrophe should be largely avoidable.

Surveying the bewildering damage from some historical hurricanes, an outside observer might wonder whether builders were suffering under the delusion of a chaos-free environment: one governed by underestimated deterministic forces. Of course, in reality, dynamical chaos is intrinsic to the atmosphere, and contributes significantly to the aleatory uncertainty in wind loading. It may take more than the flap of a butterfly's wings to change a hurricane forecast, but chaos imposes a fundamental practical limit to windstorm prediction capability.

If the meaning of uncertainty has long occupied the minds of natural philosophers, it is because, as Joseph Butler put it, 'Probability is the very guide to life.' The practical consequences for decision-making in the presence of uncertainty are everywhere to be seen: from engineering design and construction to financial risk management. In the design of a critical industrial installation, for example, an engineer may cater for an earthquake load which has a very low annual probability of being exceeded: perhaps one in a thousand or even one in ten thousand. By contrast, for an ordinary residence, the building code may stipulate a less onerous load with an annual exceedance probability of one in a hundred.

Best estimates of these annual exceedance probabilities can be obtained recognizing the aleatory uncertainty involved in the loss process. However, should better knowledge be gained of factors contributing to epistemic uncertainty, these probabilities are liable to a degree of amendment. Although not always quoted, confidence bounds can be estimated which reflect the epistemic uncertainty. As exemplified by flood risk in the German city of Cologne on the Rhine River, these bounds may be quite large.[12] In so far as it may have a tangible impact on the height of river defences, the logical concept of a probability of a probability is not a mere philosophical abstraction.

4.3.1 Wavelets and aleatory uncertainty in seismic ground motion

The distinction between epistemic and aleatory uncertainty is especially significant in estimating the severity of ground shaking G arising at some distance R from an earthquake of a given Magnitude M.[13] This estimate is an essential component of the procedure for establishing design criteria for seismic loads, and typically is based on a parametric attenuation relation: $G = f(M, R)$, which is derived from regression analysis of data recordings of strong ground motion at various monitoring stations. Implicit in its suitability for a single site is the assumption that spatial scatter, as embodied in such a statistical attenuation relation, is a good guide to the temporal variability in ground motion at a particular site. Borrowing the terminology of statistical mechanics, Anderson *et al.* named this the ergodic hypothesis.[14]

In this earthquake engineering context, aleatory uncertainty arises partly from the erratic nature of the fault rupture process. For an earthquake of a given Magnitude, the rupture geometry and dynamics are not fully determined. Differences in ground shaking which are due to wave propagation path or site effects also contribute to aleatory uncertainty, given the presence of random heterogeneities in a geological medium. But only an idle seismologist would blame all of the uncertainty in ground motion on aleatory factors. A significant component of this uncertainty is epistemic, which should be ever more reducible, in principle, as increasing amounts of data are acquired on repeat earthquakes recorded at the site.

In scientific terms, epistemic uncertainty is the modelling uncertainty due to incomplete knowledge about the physics governing the earthquake rupture and wave propagation process, and insufficient information about local geological and geotechnical conditions. These deficiencies should be rectified through further seismological monitoring, and geological and geotechnical field investigation.

The dynamics of a fault rupture may be indirectly inferred from seismograms recorded sufficiently close to the fault that propagation path and recording site effects are minimized. From analysis of these seismograms, seismologists can attempt to reconstruct the details of the earthquake rupture process. A potentially important part of the rupture process is the breakage of strong patches on the fault at different times, giving rise to sub-events. The timing of these breakages, and the frequency content of the seismic energy released, are significant factors in determining the characteristics of surface ground shaking. The best way of obtaining information on the timing and frequency content of a rupture uses the method of *wavelets*, which are a modern extension of Fourier analysis.

Whereas a standard Fourier transform decomposes a time series according to frequency alone, making the recovery of time information from phase data extremely inefficient, a wavelet transform expresses a time series in terms of a set of wavelets, each of which has a specific time window and a frequency bandwidth. Rather akin to a mathematical microscope, the width of a wavelet window can be squeezed or stretched, while the number of oscillations remains constant, thus increasing or decreasing the frequency. Large wavelets filter out all but low frequencies, and small wavelets filter out all but high frequencies.

The consequence is that, at low frequencies, the wavelets are broad and poorly localized in time, whereas at high frequencies, the wavelets are well localized in time, but the frequency bandwidth is large. This inherent characteristic of wavelet resolution is reminiscent of Heisenberg's uncertainty principle. In mathematical terms, for a time series $v(t)$, the wavelet transform is defined as follows:[15]

$$W(a,b) = \frac{1}{\sqrt{a}} \int_{-\infty}^{\infty} dt \, v(t) \, \psi\left(\frac{t-b}{a}\right)$$

Where $\psi(t)$ is a window function known as the analyzing wavelet, a is a scale factor which compresses or dilates the wavelet, and b is a translation factor which localizes the wavelet in time. Given the frequency-dependent scattering of seismic waves by discontinuities in subsurface media, seismograms may be naturally viewed as composed of wavelet structures. There are a variety of alternative wavelet function sets which have been devised by mathematicians, but they all trade off resolution of time with frequency: the uncertainty principle is inviolable.

Wavelet analysis has been undertaken on seismograms recorded from a number of major earthquakes. Where aleatory uncertainty takes the form of near-fault directed ground motion, such directivity effects may generate notable wavelet pulses. An early application of wavelet analysis was on seismograms recorded during the devastating M8.1 Michoacan, Mexico, earthquake of 19 September 1985. The records were taken from a station, La Union, close to the fault. A late phase on one seismogram has been characterized as producing a prominent peak on one wavelet with an arrival time of about 38 seconds.[16] This particular wavelet has a narrow time window resolution of about one second, and an associated frequency band of 0.25 Hz to 1.0 Hz, which is noteworthy because it encompasses the frequency range of substantial amplification at lake sediment sites in Mexico City, where the worst damage was inflicted. The origin of this wavelet is uncertain, but it might be attributed to the late breaking of a strong patch of the fault, called an asperity. This is illustrated schematically in Fig. 4.1.

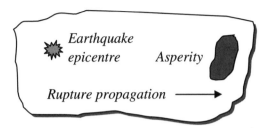

Figure 4.1. Cross-sectional diagram of a fault surface, showing an asperity at the extremity of rupture propagation, which can have a significant influence on the characteristics of ground shaking.

4.4   Probability Ambiguity

If six fair dice are thrown, the chance that each of the six faces appears exactly once is $(1/6)^6 \times 6! = 0.015432$. This would be a rare event, potentially yielding a handsome payoff for a gambler. In ancient classical times, when a pantheon of gods ruled the affairs of men, a *venus* was a gambling metaphor for an unlikely event. This was a particular outcome of the throw of four sheep or goat bones, called *astragali*, where each of the four possible labelled faces occurred exactly once.[17] But, unlike dice, astragali were highly irregular, and no two astragali were identical. So the chance of a venus was specific to the four astragali thrown. Apart from being small, its actual value was imprecise.

An experiment to assess this chance was undertaken by the founder of the Hungarian probability theory school, Alfréd Rényi. This involved throwing a single astragalus a thousand times to gauge the four relative face frequencies: 0.408, 0.396, 0.091, and 0.105. If this astragalus were thrown independently four times, the venus probability would be the combinatorial factor 24 times the product, which yields 0.0371. An experiment with four different astragali would have been closer to authenticity, but closer also to the limits of human patience, even that of Rényi for whom mathematics was a perpetual source of happiness.

The throw of four astragali, with the inherent ambiguity over the outcome chance, provides a paradigm of an unlikely catastrophe. Suppose that a hurricane is tracking across the Atlantic. An anxious resident of Bermuda, mindful of the destruction wrought on the island by Hurricane Fabian in September 2003, may ponder the following four questions. What is the chance that the hurricane will track close to Bermuda? If it does, what is the chance that it will be a major hurricane? Given that the hurricane does pass close to Bermuda as a major hurricane, what is the chance of high wind speeds where he lives? What is then the chance of his roof blowing off?

Catastrophes are rare and occur typically as a sequence of misfortune. It takes the right combination of circumstances to produce a catastrophe. Perrow has termed this 'the Union Carbide factor',[18] in reference to the deadly release of toxic gas in Union Carbide's plant in Bhopal, India, in December 1984, which killed and injured many thousands of people.

Thus a catastrophe might arise if E_1, E_2, E_3, E_4,... were to occur. The catastrophe probability is then given by the product:

$$P(E_1) \ . \ P(E_2 \,|\, E_1) \ . \ P(E_3 \,|\, E_1, E_2) \ . \ P(E_4 \,|\, E_1, E_2, E_3).$$

Four generic factors typically form the core of a catastrophe sequence: initiation of a hazard; the evolution of the hazard size; the spatial severity of the hazard; and the societal impact. At each stage of an associated probability tree, drawn schematically in Fig. 4.2, the number of branches proliferates according to the range of alternative consequences.

As with throws of different astragali, at each stage in this sequence there is ambiguity as to the probability of a particular outcome, which accumulates over the whole sequence of misfortune.

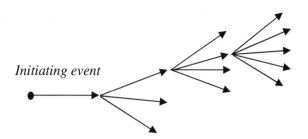

Initiating event

Figure 4.2. Probability tree showing the branching associated with contingent events. Each arrowed branch is assigned a probability weight.

4.4.1 Knightian uncertainty

As with the throw of an astragalus, the laws of physics ultimately govern the flip of a coin, the roll of dice, and the spin of a roulette wheel, which are the most familiar realizations of the laws of chance. The rotation of a coin in mid-air is amenable to elaborate mechanical analysis, even down to the detail of its wobble. Indeed, the physics of the wobbling of a coin is similar to that of a dinner plate, which inspired the young Richard Feynman on his road to scientific discovery and the Physics Nobel Prize.

One of Feynman's students was Albert R. Hibbs. In 1947, Hibbs and a fellow Caltech student, Roy Walford, painstakingly recorded numbers from roulette wheels in Nevada, and were able to establish confidence limits for identifying biased roulette wheels. At that time, one wheel in four was sufficiently unbalanced for them to achieve a measure of financial success. Bias can be caused by the weakening or bending of the frets between the numbered compartments, by irregular bearings, and other mechanical imperfections. Lack of knowledge of such imperfections contributes to ambiguity in the probability that a ball will land on a specific number – if a particular fret is very flexible, the probability for the corresponding number would increase significantly.

As with a spin of the casino roulette wheel, a spin of the revolver barrel in Russian roulette randomizes the chance that the next shot fired will be lethal. But how well do we know this chance? After the Congo gained its independence from Belgium in 1960, it became a Cold War African battleground. The local CIA station chief, Larry Devlin, found himself in a room of local militia, who amused themselves at his expense by playing a game of Russian roulette. The first shot was fired without incident, and then the second. As if he needed reminding, Devlin was told that one-third of the Russian roulette options had passed. A third shot was fired, then a fourth, and then a fifth. When the sixth shot was fired, laughter broke out among the onlookers. There was no bullet in the revolver after all.

The laws of physics govern the spin of a revolver barrel, but not the chance of an empty barrel. Often, the hapless victim may witness a single bullet being inserted, but otherwise there is some slight prospect that the barrel is empty, the chance of which is entirely at the whim of the gunman. Clearly, there is no objective way of assessing this chance. A serial gunman might develop a history for leaving the barrel empty sometimes, but otherwise each game of Russian roulette is different, like each astragalus. For this type of uncertain situation, Frank Knight, one of the most eclectic economists of the 20th century, is often quoted: 'There is no possibility of forming in any way groups or instances of sufficient homogeneity to make possible a quantitative determination of true probability. Business decisions deal with situations which are far too unique, generally speaking, for any sort of statistical tabulation to have any value for guidance. The conception of an objectively measurable probability of chance is simply inapplicable.'[19]

This is a passage out of Knight's influential 1921 dissertation, *Risk, Uncertainty and Profit*, from which originated the term *Knightian uncertainty*, covering situations where probabilities are not objectively knowable. During the financial crisis of 2008–2009, when many business risk decisions proved so unsound, Knightian uncertainty was cited as an explanation if not excuse for financial failure. The rise of behavioural economics and finance as disciplines relevant to global markets driven by emotions of fear and greed reflects the need for notions of probability to be adapted for different contexts. In his review of philosophical theories of probability, Gillies distinguishes the epistemological interpretation of probability advocated by Keynes for the application to economics from the objective interpretation of probability associated with application in the natural sciences.[20]

Although the study of natural catastrophes is founded firmly upon the laws of Nature, the rarity of major disasters renders impractical a purist objective interpretation of probability, which would require an abundance of data beyond doomsday imagination. There are natural hazard analogues to a Russian roulette revolver which is presumed to be loaded, but which turns out not to be. A magma chamber beneath a volcano may appear primed for eruptive activity, but there remains some residual probability to the contrary, which is not objectively measurable. Just as the unwitting victim of a Russian roulette game cannot see directly into a revolver chamber, so a volcanologist cannot see directly into a magma chamber. Indirect and imprecise geophysical observations of a magma chamber form the empirical basis for probability inference.

The academic pursuit of volcanology as a natural science may not require such a probability to be estimated. However, when volcanism is recognized as a natural hazard with significant implications for public safety, then volcanology becomes in practical application also a social science, and such probability estimation may be desirable if not obligatory as part of a risk assessment informing decision-makers.

4.4.2 Subjective probability

The rarity of catastrophes will always exasperate attempts at achieving full scientific consensus on critical hazard issues. Two seismologists, sharing the same information about regional seismotectonics, and presented with the same seismological and geological data, may quite rationally arrive at contrasting degrees of belief about the imminence of an earthquake. As a critical example for post-disaster reconstruction, the lack of a surface rupture associated with the 12 January 2010 Haiti earthquake, created significant scientific uncertainty over subsequent local fault hazard potential.[21]

The brilliant young Cambridge mathematician, Frank Ramsey, contemplated the notion of a *psychogalvanometer* to measure an individual's degree of belief.[22] But this is not directly measurable as an electric current would be by a galvanometer. Independently, he and Bruno de Finetti discovered the subjective theory of probability, where a degree of belief is measured by the action to which it leads.[23] A suitable action for such measurement is betting. Whether to accept a bet or not is a matter of judgement, and a subjective probability might be termed a judgemental probability.[24] In their training, scientists are not usually exposed to this notion of probability, unless specially instructed. De Finetti had his students bet on the outcome of Italian football matches.

Probabilities have always had a pivotal role in the transaction of insurance. Indeed, the commercial expansion of insurance was an early driver of probability theory, and insurance market development continues to depend on probabilistic analysis. Unsurprisingly, when the French mathematician, Henri Poincaré, was searching for a concrete argument for objective probability, he thought of the insurance industry:

'There are many insurance companies that apply the rules of the probability calculus, and distribute to their shareholders dividends, whose objective reality is incontestable.' Insurance risk modellers would be flattered at this compliment from an eminent mathematician. However, the loss of shareholder value and occasional ruin from catastrophe insurance losses are also incontestable. These financial outcomes may be attributable to a wide range of insurance risk management factors, such as inadequate information about individual risks and poor control of risk accumulations. Insurers, like most people, prefer certainty over ambiguity. Consider two properties: one in a region with an estimated 50% level of seismic code compliance; the other in a region of similar seismic hazard, but with no information on code compliance. In keeping with the *Ellsberg paradox*, most insurers would prefer to underwrite the first property.

To the extent that probability is a measure of an individual's degree of belief, it is also a reflection of subjective judgement. Unlike physics, where universal symmetry transformations exist to relate measurements of separate observers, there are no general transformations linking the probabilities assigned by two people. So if one scientist assigns probability P_A to an event, there is no universal way of relating it to the probability P_B assigned by another scientist. There is no mathematical formula which can enumerate and explain the discrepancy. However, these probabilities are far from being arbitrary; there are logical principles by which they can be compared.

Although subjective degrees of belief are not physically observable, they must conform to the axioms of probability theory if they are to be coherent. If an individual's degrees of belief fail to be coherent, then he would be prepared to accept a Dutch Book type of wager: a series of bets that he would be certain to lose. Realizing such incoherence, an individual would usually wish to revise his degrees of belief. It is by no means uncommon for compulsive gamblers to take sure-loss bets unwittingly; but to do so knowingly would reflect pecuniary indifference or irrationality. There is a close parallel between the principle of consistency in subjective probability and the financial principle that there should be no risk-free profit in trading, i.e. no arbitrage.

Subjective probabilities are constrained by Bayes' theorem. First, there are some constraints on prior probabilities. The classical Laplacian definition of probability revolved around symmetry. Knowledge of symmetries is naturally incorporated into subjective probability via prior distributions according equal chance to each alternative under the symmetry. As an example, in the absence of any opportunity to examine a coin, it would be rational, on symmetry grounds, to assume a prior probability of one half to either Heads or Tails. However, after inspection, an individual may come to believe that a coin is biased.

Another constraint on subjective probability is provided through the acquisition of further evidence, such as frequency statistics. Relative frequency data are naturally incorporated into subjective probability assessment through the computation of posterior probabilities. The prior probabilities assigned by individuals are updated to posterior probabilities through Bayes' theorem. Regardless of the initial divergence of opinion, as more and more data are accumulated which enable relative frequencies to be calculated with increasing accuracy, the opinions should converge ever closer.

Experts whose probabilities satisfy all the logical constraints imposed by the axioms of probability may nevertheless find that their degrees of belief are not the same. There are two main explanations for such discrepancies.[25] One scientist may have more substantive knowledge and expertise than another about the specific variable in question. But also, one individual may have more normative expertise, i.e. have more skill at expressing beliefs in probabilistic form. The former source of discrepancy can be addressed to some extent by pooling data, documentation, and experience among all scientists. The latter source of discrepancy in probabilistic judgements can be addressed by training scientists in essential normative skills.

It should not be forgotten that, except for some bookmakers, gamblers and mathematicians, human beings do not routinely carry probability values and distributions around in their heads. In order to avoid bias and error, these values and distributions need to be considered thoughtfully. They may need to be constructed systematically, possibly through a staged process of decomposing the factors underlying an event probability into constituent elements and sub-elements.

4.5   The Weighing of Evidence

Substantial theories of evidence have been laid out by outstanding Anglo-Saxon jurists such as Bentham and Wigmore: matters in dispute are to be proved to specified standards of probability on the basis of the careful and rational weighing of evidence, which is both relevant and reliable. Statistical science is recognized as an academic discipline and studied much more than *evidence science*, which lays the intellectual foundation for the weighing of evidence of all kinds, and is especially crucial for catastrophe risk applications.

Through its sparsity and susceptibility to alternative interpretations, geological evidence is particularly prone to debate over the weighing of evidence. Such debate is far from academic when the evidence concerns active faulting close to a critical industrial installation or centre of population. Geological investigation defines a spatial sampling process, to which every trench and geophysical survey makes some contribution. This sampling process is partially systematic, with specific faults targeted on the basis of their perceived chance of revealing neotectonic evidence. However, there is also a serendipitous aspect, with fault offsets observed in exposed quarries and road cuts, or inferred from scanning hydrocarbon exploration data. This kind of erratic sampling procedure, which falls far short of any laboratory experimental design, is prone to many forms of statistical bias.

In actual neotectonics practice, inferences are traditionally drawn on the seemingly rational basis of what is locally observed. But the 17 January 1995 Kobe earthquake taught geologists the lesson that the activity of a local fault cannot be assessed in isolation, without reference to the active status of regional faulting. This Japanese earthquake was much more powerful than expected, because of an extended rupture of several neighbouring fault systems, previously regarded as uncoupled.

An uncertainty audit of neotectonic investigation would catalogue the host of deficiencies in empirical data, and accuse deterministic seismic hazard analysts of wishing data to be absolute. The very existence and extent of apparent fault offsets can be misleadingly asserted if geophysical data are of poor quality and quantity, which often they are. Observed displacements in fault trenches need not necessarily be neotectonic, but may be superficial. And even if displacements are properly identified as neotectonic, interpretation of offset information in terms of specific event occurrences and Magnitudes is beset with ambiguities over the proportion of deformation unrelated to earthquakes; the number of individual events; and the stability of the statistical correlation between earthquake Magnitude and the observed offset.

Entering the controversy in seismic hazard assessment between probabilism and determinism, the geologist Clarence Allen expressed preference for a probabilistic approach as providing the only hope of quantifying earthquake hazards in a meaningful way for formulating equitable public policy. But the probabilistic approach is not yet fully refined in its practical applications. One essential element prone to misinterpretation is the weighing of neotectonic evidence.[26]

A common error made in weighing evidence of all kinds is known as the *fallacy of the transposed conditional*.[27] If the evidence is denoted as E, and the proposition to be established is G, then $P(E|G)$, the conditional probability of the evidence given G, is often erroneously and unknowingly substituted for $P(G|E)$, which is the conditional probability of G given the evidence E. Consider the context of a site designated for major construction. If E is neotectonic evidence, and G is the proposition that a local fault is active within the current tectonic regime, then there may be practical regional interest in estimating $P(\neg G|E)$ (i.e. the probability of the fault being inactive, given the neotectonic evidence). However, this may be falsely equated with $P(E|\neg G)$, which is the likelihood of the evidence given that the fault is inactive in the current tectonic regime.

A geologist, who has laboured long in the field searching for strands of neotectonic evidence, may be motivated to take a positive view of his findings, and tend to be reluctant to accept an alternative negative explanation for his evidence; e.g. fault creep or landslides. The geologist may thus personally, and quite understandably, feel assured that $P(E|\neg G)$ is very low. So it may well be, but this does not then necessarily imply that $P(\neg G|E)$ must also be very low. Confusion over this transposition can lead to the scientific elevation and proliferation of dubious claims for neotectonics, and artificially inflate regional levels of seismic hazard.[28]

4.5.1 Bayesian epistemology and Black Swans

Epistemology inquires into the nature of knowledge and what justifies a belief. Donald Rumsfeld's enigmatic and celebrated US Department of Defense news briefing on 12 February 2002, baffled a global media audience with the concept of the 'unknown unknowns'.[29] This was a commendable if somewhat bemusing attempt to address fundamental epistemological issues, which indeed are as relevant to knowledge of natural catastrophes as those that are man-made. During the First Gulf War against Iraq in 1990, US general Colin Powell challenged his intelligence officers with these orders, 'Tell me what you know, tell me what you don't know, tell me what you think – and tell me the difference.' In any list of what the intelligence officers did not know, there would have been omissions: the unknown unknowns. This is a consequence of the fact that the world of possibility in which intelligence is gathered is undeniably large.

In a comment of conceptual if not practical interest, the philosopher of economics, Ken Binmore, has pointed out that, in a small world, not knowing what one doesn't know is equivalent to knowing.[30] He cites the example of a girl, Pandora, playing a card game, who doesn't know that she doesn't know that she has been dealt the Queen of Hearts. But she would know that she hadn't been dealt the Queen of Hearts if she had been dealt some other card. So she knows she was in fact dealt the Queen of Hearts. During the Second Gulf War against Iraq in 2003, the faces of the most wanted Iraqi leaders were placed on playing cards so they could be widely recognized. As an architect of this war, Donald Rumsfeld should have been pleased if somebody didn't know if he didn't know that he had seen the Ace of Spades.

Taking a more orthodox philosophical reference than Rumsfeld, Nassim Taleb has used the paradigm of the *Black Swan* to question induction from past observational experience: no amount of observations can deny the possibility of a surprise. Following a bird allegory, he has pointed to the predicament of the US farm turkey which is well treated daily by humans until the approach to Thanksgiving Day, which comes as a terminal surprise.

An event may come as a complete surprise, but then there may be some surprising information of varying reliability, upon which a risk-mitigating decision can be made. As an experienced Wall Street analyst, Posner has argued that probability trees help bracket the odds of Black Swan-like outcomes.[31] But traders have to be mindful of change blindness, which is a failure to recognize slow change. This is 'the boiling frog syndrome'. During the early years of the 21st century, the sub-prime mortgage lending problems at Fannie Mae and Freddie Mac were coming to the boil. But most financial analysts were insensitive to the rising temperature, and suffered for it, like the mythical frog.

Change blindness is one example of a broader psychological malaise: cognitive dissonance. This is a psychologist's expression for the discomfort felt at a discrepancy between what you already know or believe, and new information or interpretation. According to Leon Festinger, who was the first authority on this subject, 'When dissonance is present, in addition to trying to reduce it, a person will actively avoid situations and information which would likely increase the dissonance.' Catastrophes, real or imagined, tend to evoke such dissonance. One of Festinger's case studies involved a doomsday group whose disappointment and frustration that the flood to end the world did not arrive induced a dissonant reaction of increased group bonding.[32]

In 1697, a Dutch explorer, Willem de Vlamingh, was investigating a shipwreck in Western Australia, when he was spooked by the sight of something which is now associated etymologically with disaster: a black swan. On its own, a single strange report such as this might be dismissed as fanciful. But the collective value of surprising information increases with the number of independent reports. A weird story, repeated by independent witnesses, may be just too odd not to be true. Aggregating information available is a task for evidence science, and involves the use of the technique of Bayesian updating. Epistemology informed by evidence science constitutes the joint discipline of Bayesian epistemology, which has the intellectual firepower to hunt Black Swans, provided there is some observable shred of evidence of their existence.[33]

Denote by X a binary variable corresponding to the presence or absence of a witness report constituting evidence for a hypothesis H. Let R denote the reliability or unreliability of the witness. The chance that an unreliable witness makes the report is characterized by the randomization parameter: $S = P(X \mid H, \neg R)$. Generally, the more surprising the report is, the lower this randomization parameter is. Denote by ρ the prior probability that a witness is reliable: $\rho = P(R)$. Then the ratio of the likelihood of the report, if the hypothesis were false, to the likelihood of the report, if the hypothesis were true, is given by the expression $S(1-\rho) / (\rho + S(1-\rho))$. This ratio decreases with the report's surprising content. With multiple independent surprising reports, the posterior probability of the truth of the hypothesis can therefore increase substantially.

This analysis of the value of surprising information has clear military application. Despite some surprising intelligence evidence, the US Navy was blindsided by the Japanese air attack on Pearl Harbor in 1941. The prior probability had been low, because of the long flying distance from Japan to Hawaii. The Yom Kippur war of 1973 was similarly a cognitive failure of Israeli military intelligence.

This analysis is also relevant for regions of the world endangered by rare natural hazards, which may never have been witnessed in centuries. Especially in these circumstances, self-organization of population response through person-to-person risk communication remains important for the dissemination of warnings.

A prime example of such a rare natural hazard, with no precedent in living memory, was a tsunami on the coast of Thailand, generated by a giant earthquake off Sumatra. Tragically, a tsunami so caused drowned many holidaymakers in Phuket on 26 December 2004. The strange sight of the water receding a long way, (for which Hawaiians have a special word), was disregarded as a threat by many, but not ten-year-old English schoolgirl, Tilly Smith, whose shouted warning saved the lives of a hundred on the beach. Her world view had been shaped by a recent geography lesson at school, thus illustrating the practical use of risk education in defeating cognitive dissonance, such as displayed by her mother, who thought it was just a bad day at the beach. Regrettably, this was an isolated tale of dissonance avoidance. In the Andaman Islands, northwest of Phuket, Indian navy officers also witnessed the tsunami, but did not communicate this surprising observation to Delhi, so missing an opportunity to provide a tsunami warning for their mainland compatriots.

Chapter 5

A Matter of Time

> *Time precedes existence.*
> Ilya Prigogine,
> *The End of Certainty*

For disaster historians, numbers have resonances with seminal events, e.g. 911. For the Indian mathematical genius, Srinivasa Ramanujan, every positive integer was a personal friend. As a number theorist, he had dazzling powers of numerical pattern recognition. Consider the following sequence of five integers: 13, 20, 9, 24, and 8. The mean of this sequence is 14.8, and the standard deviation is 7. This sequence is actually part of a deterministic Taylor series from Ramanujan's *Lost Notebook*, which was published posthumously. Few other than Ramanujan would have figured out the next number in the series,[1] which happens to be 32; almost two and a half standard deviations from the mean. Brief deterministic sequences can easily hold surprises.

The same integer, 32, happens also to be the fifth in the following sequence of five integers: 24, 20, 21, 12, and 32; numbers which have been written down in too many notebooks for them to be forgotten in the annals of seismology. These numbers are time intervals in years between occurrences of a characteristic earthquake of about Magnitude 6 on the Parkfield segment of the San Andreas Fault in California. The actual earthquake years were 1857, 1881, 1901, 1922, 1934, and 1966. To Bakun and Lindh in 1985, the 'remarkably uniform' times between events since 1857 suggested a recurrence model from which they estimated a narrow 95% confidence interval for the date of the next characteristic Parkfield earthquake to be 1988.0 ± 5.2 years.[2] A decade passed from 1985, with no sign of the Parkfield earthquake.

Despite its endorsement by the National Earthquake Prediction Evaluation Council, the Parkfield prediction failed.[3] The high confidence placed in this prediction was mathematically spurious: the earthquake kept seismologists and the phlegmatic Parkfield villagers waiting almost another decade, until 28 September 2004.

But imagine, as a seismologist, scanning a regional earthquake catalogue. Poring over a sequence of time intervals, by what criteria might the events be described as random? Intuition is not always a good guide to randomness. Psychologists have discovered that when asked to generate strings of random numbers, people tend to avoid repeating the same digit. Another example is provided by the fount of many probabilistic paradigms: the repeated tossing of a fair coin. Suppose after each toss, a tally is kept of the overall difference between the number of Heads and the number of Tails. To the uninitiated, the possible size of this difference, realized in actual trials, can seem anomalous. A large number of excesses somehow appears too ordered to arise randomly. *Homo Sapiens* has evolved to discern patterns against background noise – a life-saving skill in avoiding predators. In this context, the concept of randomness is somewhat alien: people often think they see patterns where none exist. The corollary is that people are not adept at recognizing randomness, which pervades our entire lives, and is commonly underestimated. The impression that a random streak may be due to extraordinary performance is known as the hot-hand fallacy.[4]

Murray Gell-Mann has recalled his surprise at finding an apparent errata sheet within a table of random numbers, produced by the RAND corporation.[5] How can random numbers not be random enough? The existence of random numbers is provable from Kolmogorov's probability axioms; the problem is finding a good method for generating them. Electronic noise has been used as a physical source, which may work well, but the numbers output need to be checked for bias. In the case of the RAND machine, faults impaired the randomness.

From the mathematical perspective of *algorithmic information theory*, the randomness of a sequence of digits may be defined in terms of how concisely they may be compressed into a computer program for calculating them. On this basis, even though the digits in the decimal expansion of π are thought to be spread evenly from 0 to 9, π is far from random. Neither random is the Ramanujan sequence, even though, for the layman, this sequence has almost null predictability. In contrast, due to algorithmic incompressibility, there are numbers whose digits cannot be predicted: tossing a fair coin is as good a way as any other to find them. Randomness in this respect is fundamental in mathematics.

Acknowledging the pervasive presence of randomness, the statistical prediction of occurrence times based on small event datasets needs to be treated with due circumspection. In order to extrapolate a sequence of observed hazard event times with some degree of assurance, we need some dynamical knowledge of the causal processes governing event generation, and we need some insight into the effect of environmental perturbations on these processes. At Parkfield, the characteristic earthquake model was an insufficient dynamical basis for the generation process, and the perturbing influence of extraneous regional seismicity was not fully appreciated. The search for dynamical understanding of seismicity catalogues has since advanced the study of the interactions between faults, and the mechanisms by which the stress released in one fault rupture can trigger another.

Even if the Parkfield earthquake disappointed some seismologists by failing to appear during the 1990s, a pair of interesting large earthquakes did show up in California, in the comparatively quiescent area of the Mojave Desert. The first was the M7.3 Landers earthquake of 28 June 1992 and the second was the M7.1 Hector Mine earthquake of 16 October 1999. These earthquakes occurred on fault systems about 24 km apart, with similar slow slip rates of about 1mm/year. From palaeoseismic evidence of dating past ruptures, this fault pair had a similar fault history, each rupturing about 5,000 to 6,000, and 10,000 years ago. Compared with a recurrence interval of about 5,000 years for events of this size, a short time difference of only seven years between recurrences on the two faults during the 1990s might be dismissed as a mere coincidence; a simple temporal pattern dictated by chance, of no more scientific significance than the apparently 'remarkably uniform' time intervals of the Parkfield sequence recorded up to 1966.

But could it be indicative of a deeper seismological truth, some dynamic phase locking of the seismic cycle of these faults, so that future earthquakes would be similarly clustered in time, as they appear to have in the past? Using examples from various countries, Scholz has suggested that certain fault systems can be self-organized in such a way as to synchronize fault ruptures.[6] Two such neighbouring faults might behave as oscillators, which progressively act in consonance, rather as adjacent pendulum clocks had been observed in 1665 by the Dutch scientist Huygens to keep exact time. In a letter to his father, Huygens wrote, 'Mixing up the swings of the pendulums, I have found that within half an hour, they always return to consonance and remain so constantly afterwards for as long as I let them go.'

With pendulum clocks, Huygens was able to undertake a number of experiments to explore the synchronization phenomenon, and understand it as due to vibratory interaction of their common support.[7] Mathematically, the synchronization of two coupled self-sustained oscillators with frequencies ω_1 and ω_2 can be described by a pair of equations, assuming a weak interaction between the phases φ_1 and φ_2:

$$\frac{d\phi_1}{dt} = \omega_1 + \varepsilon\, Q_1(\phi_1, \phi_2) \qquad \frac{d\phi_2}{dt} = \omega_2 + \varepsilon\, Q_2(\phi_2, \phi_1)$$

Through analysis of these equations, and their generalization to many oscillators, a quantitative level of understanding can be achieved for a rich variety of synchronization phenomena, involving not just inanimate, but also biological and human oscillators. Such phenomena may take engineering risk analysts by surprise. The Millennium Bridge across the Thames in London was not originally designed to allow for the self-organized synchronization of the walking steps of people as they tried to maintain balance on a wobbling bridge. This happened on opening day, on 10 June 2000, and forced its closure for engineering modifications.

Fault rupture synchronization might also impact engineering safety. It is possible that one large earthquake might trigger another, not just within years, but even within days. This happened in Bulgaria in 1928. Event clustering over a short time matters, because buildings weakened by the primary event may be especially susceptible to damage from subsequent large triggered events. With the Millennium Bridge, the synchronization problem was diagnosed quite quickly by a number of engineers, and notably by the Physics Nobel laureate Brian Josephson, whose eponymous junctions involve atomic synchronous behaviour.

In contrast with experimental science, the curse of an observational science like seismology is the length of time it takes to acquire adequate data to assess theories. This is of course true of all extremely rare events. Philosophers of science note that for natural historical sciences like zoology and geology, claims to knowledge have depended upon extensive observation rather than experimentation, and on classifying volumes of data rather than on deriving general laws.[8]

Leaps in theoretical understanding can be made, but validation of new concepts can never be rapid. Laboratory experiments can be done, but their relevance to the real earthquake environment is always questionable. The global database of synchronized earthquakes remains comparatively small, and the palaeoseismic data for any region of faulting provide only a short record of synchrony. So there is a shortage of empirical data for estimating the likelihood of one large earthquake triggering another. Nevertheless, it is an interesting scientific discovery that a potential mode of synchronized earthquake behaviour should be identified. The possibility of a rare Magnitude 7 earthquake triggering another Magnitude 7 earthquake on a neighbouring fault, with similar slip rate, is at least a known possibility.

The exploration of temporal catastrophe processes endeavours to distinguish causation from coincidence, signal from noise. Mathematical insights can probe beyond the narrow bounds of scientific observation. Idealized mathematical models and their qualitative analysis are favourite tools of Steven Strogatz, an applied mathematician who has used them to assess a wide range of complex system behaviour.[9]

Even in the absence of seismological data on synchronized fault rupture, idealized mathematical models might suggest novel intriguing modes of earthquake clustering. There is much to be explored. A trio of enormous tsunamigenic earthquakes occurred within a decade of each other around the Pacific Ring of Fire in 2004, 2010 and 2011. Each fault rupture was large enough to have some perturbative effect on other regional faults. What remains unclear is if there might be some large scale dynamic triggering mechanism capable of inducing some degree of global synchronization for the greatest earthquakes in the world.

5.1 Temporal Models of Hazards

Consider the date sequence: 1815, 1863, 1911, 1959, and 2007. The
time interval between these dates is 48 years. A disaster occurs with
metronomic regularity, which leads to massive crop destruction and
economic hardship in a remote northeastern corner of India. What could
this be? A plague of rats of biblical proportions is responsible for the
destruction of agriculture. It is not that the rat population keeps an
elaborate trans-generational biological clock; rather, they eat their way
through crops after gorging on the abundant seeds of a blossoming
bamboo, (*Melocanna Baccifera*), that just happens to flower
synchronously and gregariously about every 48 years. This botanical
alarm clock is rhythmically more precise than any geological hazard.
The predictability of this biological hazard affords some practical
opportunities for risk mitigation, but the lives of regional farmers are
regularly blighted by this curious peril of the living world, the scientific
origins of which remain to be explained at a plant genetics level.

Periodicity of a natural phenomenon, in the precise sense of a cyclic
repetition with some regular recurrence frequency, is one of the purest
forms of temporal order that can be conceived. Where environmental
factors which might influence hazard events are periodic in time, it is
natural to search for evidence of a similar periodicity in the data on event
occurrence. However, the sparsity of most natural hazard data makes
significant statistical evidence for periodicity difficult to glean, and a
convincing case for causality is thus hard to establish categorically.

For cyclic order, it is natural to search beyond the arithmetic
coarseness of seismic cycles, (such as purported at Parkfield), for cycles
of astronomical origin that would keep accurate heavenly time. The most
familiar are the Milankovitch cycles associated with variations of the
Earth's orbital eccentricity, obliquity, and precession, with periods
ranging from 19,000 years to 413,000 years. These variations cause
minor reductions in the intensity of radiation at high latitudes during the
summer, which is a critical factor in ice sheet development. Milutin
Milankovitch was a Serbian mathematician, who was dedicated to
calculating these reductions, and developed his astronomical theory of
ice ages partly in conjunction with Alfred Wegener, the pioneer of the

theory of continental drift, whom he met in Austria in 1924. It is a measure of the intricacies of climate science that, many decades later, precise theoretical explanation of the 100,000 year glacial cycle is still rather elusive.[10] Indeed, the plate tectonics heirs of Alfred Wegener might contend their understanding of the plate motion drivers of seismic cycles is not inferior to the climatologists' understanding of the drivers of the glacial cycles.

An astronomical phenomenon of approximate 11 year periodicity, which could potentially have significant damaging impacts on power and communications, is the solar cycle. This was discovered in 1843 by a German astronomer, Samuel Schwabe, who observed a periodic variation in the average number of sunspots seen from year to year. The solar magnetic cycle is governed by numerous separate physical processes, but within the classical Sun dynamo model, the cycle can be interpreted as an oscillation between magnetic fields. The cycle duration has an inverse-power dependence on the meridional circulation speed: faster circulation gives rise to shorter cycles.[11] Although there is a fair degree of variability in the periodicity, from 9 to 14 years, prediction of the behaviour of a sunspot cycle is reasonably reliable a few years after the minimum in sunspot number.

At the short end of the astronomical timescale are the daily variations of the tides. Speculation that earthquakes and volcanic eruptions might be associated with the action of the tides has been put to many an empirical test. Neuberg has shown there is strong evidence against tidal triggering on volcanoes, but for Stromboli in the Tyrrhenian Sea, there is a correlation between barometric pressure and volcanic activity.[12]

Data on tidal triggering of earthquakes are rather equivocal, and are continually assessed. The basic rationale for the suggestion that tides might trigger earthquakes is simple. Suppose that the tectonic stress on a fault builds up steadily over the recurrence interval for fault rupture. Given that recurrence intervals might be a hundred years or more, the rate of stress accumulation might average out at about 0.001 bars/six hours, which is a hundred times lower than tidal stress rates.[13] Of course, tectonic stress rates may increase rapidly prior to rupture, but the possibility remains that the stress increase attributable to tidal loading may be the proverbial straw that breaks the camel's back. If this is the case, then the time at which an earthquake occurs should depend to some extent on tidal stresses.

This time dependence can be tested statistically, using a method due to Schuster. First, the tidal stress components, including both solid Earth and ocean tide loading, are calculated at the location of an earthquake hypocentre. Secondly, at the time of an earthquake, a phase angle is assigned with reference to the time history of stress change: 0^0 for a stress peak and $\pm 180^0$ for the following and preceding stress troughs.

Suppose there are N earthquakes in a specific dataset. Let the phase angle assigned to the i th earthquake be ψ_i, and define:

$$A = \sum_1^N \cos{(\psi_i)} \quad \text{and} \quad B = \sum_1^N \sin{(\psi_i)}$$

Then the test parameter is $R = \sqrt{A^2 + B^2}$. If earthquakes occur randomly with respect to tidal phase, then A and B are distributed around zero mean with a variance of $N/2$, and R^2 satisfies the χ^2 distribution, with two degrees of freedom, as in a two dimensional random walk. This is simply the exponential distribution, so the probability that R or a larger value occurs by mere chance is given by the expression $P_R = \exp(-R^2/N)$. The parameter P_R is the significance level for rejection of the null hypothesis that earthquakes occur randomly with respect to the tidal phase angle.

Taking a global dataset of several decades of earthquakes of M5.5 and above, Cochran *et al.* have calculated a tidal stress time-series that includes the solid Earth tide and an ocean loading component, which can be large near coasts.[14] They found a correlation between the strongest Earth tides and shallow earthquakes of the thrust-faulting type, (where the rocks on the upper side of an inclined fault plane have been displaced upwards). For these events, Schuster's test is passed at a significance level of 1%. This is corroborated by a simple binomial test of the proportion of events occurring during the half of the tidal phase periods encouraging stress. The tidal stress amplitudes required to trigger earthquakes appear similar to thresholds suggested for the triggering of aftershocks.

5.1.1 Poisson processes

Keeping a tally of event occurrences over time is a simple but instructive way to learn about any natural hazard. In order to make some mathematical sense of such a tally, let us then define a counting process $N(t)$ to be the total number of events that have occurred up to time t. A counting process is said to possess *independent* increments if the numbers of events occurring in separate time intervals are independent. This means, in particular, that the number of events occurring between times t and $t+s$ is independent of the number that have occurred by time t. Furthermore, a counting process is said to possess *stationary* increments if the distribution of the number of events occurring in any interval depends only on the length of the interval. A Poisson process with intensity $\lambda \, (> 0)$ is a special kind of counting process, having stationary and independent increments, where simultaneous events are ruled out, and where the probability of an event in an infinitesimal time interval h is equal to $\lambda \, h$.

From this definition, the probability of n events being counted by time t is $\exp(-\lambda t)(\lambda t)^n / n!$, which of course is the familiar Poisson distribution. As a particular case, the probability of no events by time t is the exponential function $\exp(-\lambda t)$. Let X_k be the inter-arrival time between the $(k-1)$ th event and the k th event. Then the Poisson process can be characterized by the property that the time intervals $\{X_k, k = 1, 2, ...\}$ are independently exponentially distributed with parameter λ. Because a Poisson process restarts itself probabilistically at any point in time, it carries no memory of the past, unlike human societies which do have a collective historical memory – a contrast which clouds hazard perception, and can fool people.

An important result for the applicability of the theory of Poisson processes is a theorem due to Khintchine, which relates to the superposition of a large number of independent processes.[15] Provided that the points of each of the individual processes are sufficiently sparse, and that no processes dominate the others, then the superposition of a large number of independent processes is approximately a Poisson process. This theorem has widespread application in the evaluation of risk stemming from natural hazards, because hazard processes can often be treated as a superposition of many individual sub-processes. Consider the prime example of seismic hazard assessment. At a general site, the occurrence of earthquake ground shaking should be approximately that of a Poisson process. However there are exceptions: those sites exposed predominantly to high local fault activity, which may have a sufficient memory of the past as to be ill-described as Poissonian.

A variation on the time-independent Poisson model is to assume that the recurrence rate for hazard events is not constant, but has an increasing or decreasing trend. Thus the mean number of events in time t might be written as: $\mu(t) = (\lambda t)^\beta$ where β is unity for a Poisson process, but may be greater or less than unity, according to the perceived time trend in event data. A feature of this model is that the time to the first event arrival has a Weibull distribution.

5.1.2 Markov processes

Pushkin's masterpiece, *Yevgeny Onegin*, is written in that most structured fictional style: a novel in verse. The alternation of consonants and vowels was investigated by his Russian compatriot Andrei Markov. Suppose, at some point in the text, you want to guess whether the next letter is a vowel or a consonant. With information as to whether the preceding letter is a vowel or consonant, you can make a much better guess. But knowing the preceding two letters is no further advantage. This type of analysis is important for cryptography, but the underlying idea is applicable to a wide range of practical problems.

The basic concepts of a *Markov process* are simply those of a state of a system, and a state transition. For a system which may be regarded as having a finite number of states X_n, transitions between states define a so-called Markov chain, if the transition probabilities only depend on the current state, and not on past history. More formally, a stochastic process $\{X_n, n = 0,1,...\}$ is called a discrete-time Markov chain if, for each value of n:

$$P(X_{n+1} \mid X_0, X_1, X_2, ... X_n) = P(X_{n+1} \mid X_n)$$

One of the most basic applications is to the study of daily rainfall patterns. A stochastic model of rainfall is valuable for studies of flood potential[16] as well as drought forecasting, e.g. in Ethiopia. The simplest model of rainfall involves a two-state Markov process. State 0 may be taken to be a dry day, and state 1 may be a wet day. A classic study by Gabriel *et al.* of winter rainfall at Tel Aviv used 2,437 days of data, gathered over 27 years, to show that dry days were followed by dry days on 1049 out of 1399 occasions; and wet days were followed by wet days on 687 out of 1038 occasions.[17] The state transition probability matrix $P(X_i \mid X_j) = p_{ij}$ is then defined:

$$\begin{cases} p_{00} = 1049/1399 & p_{01} = 350/1399 \\ p_{10} = 351/1038 & p_{11} = 687/1038 \end{cases}$$

There is an elegant mathematical theory of Markov processes, central to which is the state transition probability matrix. From this matrix, many useful probabilities can be calculated, e.g. the probability of extended spells of dry or wet weather, and the probability of being in a specific state at some prescribed future time. In the atmospheric sciences, the availability of daily, weekly, or seasonal records can provide reasonably ample and consistent datasets for parameterizing a multi-state Markov model, even for tornadic activity.[18]

However, in the geological sciences, the rarity of extreme events, such as volcanic eruptions, may confound such modelling aspirations. Furthermore, due to the subterranean nature of geological hazard sources, states may not be physically observable. Accordingly, volcanological application of the theory of Markov processes has focused on so-called *hidden Markov models*.[19,20] Lawrence Rabiner has given the simplest illustration of such a model.[21] Imagine that somebody is conducting a coin-tossing experiment in a cellar below where you are sitting. You do not know how many coins are being used, or how biased they may be. But after every toss, the outcome is relayed to you from the cellar. How can the series of outcomes be explained? Each alternative coin corresponds to a state, characterized by a probability distribution of Heads and Tails. Transitions between the states, i.e. coin changes, are characterized by a state transition matrix. Given the observed sequence of outcomes, the model has to calculate the likelihood of the sequence, and find the best number of hidden states.

The principal application in Rabiner's mind was to speech recognition, which uncannily echoes the original labour of Markov in analyzing the letter sequence of words. A separate N-state hidden Markov model is required to recognize each spoken word. Within a volcanological context, a separate hidden Markov model is required to comprehend the recorded 'utterance' of each volcano. Such models have been developed for a few volcanoes, including Montserrat and Etna. However, errors, omissions, and other deficiencies in the historical volcano catalogues obstruct attempts to parameterize these models. But, hidden Markov models may be valuable to volcanologists deliberating over alternative dynamical eruptive mechanisms, which might confute the simple Poisson model for the temporal occurrence of eruptions.

5.1.3 *Waiting for the next event*

One of the most celebrated plays in the Theatre of the Absurd is Samuel Beckett's tragicomedy *Waiting for Godot*. Every hazard analyst has had the experience of waiting, and waiting...and waiting, and being unsure whether, as for Godot, the wait is in vain. Waiting in anticipation of a catastrophe which fails to materialize is absurd enough when, as with the millennium bug Y2K, the date is fixed. When the date is unknown, those waiting can seem extremely foolish, and the wait itself may seem as pointless as portrayed by Beckett. As time goes by, does one become more or less confident of the wait terminating soon?

Falk *et al.*[22] pose the problem of a tourist in a foreign city waiting for a bus, which normally runs at half hour intervals, but, like Godot, may or may not be appearing that particular evening. As time passes, the tourist can update her estimate of the probability of the bus arriving, using Bayes' theorem. Intuition can mislead, which makes it worthwhile pondering some mathematical aspects of waiting.

Consider a catastrophe version of the bus waiting situation, namely a bomb threat to a tourist site. A message (which may be a hoax) is received that a bomb will explode within three hours. Assuming that a real bomb has an equally likely chance of detonating in any of the six half-hour time intervals, the following generic risk analysis can be done.

Denote by $L[0]$ the prior probability that the bomb threat is genuine and the bomb will detonate. Denote by $L[i]$ the probability that the bomb will detonate, conditional on it not having done so in the first i of n time intervals. Further, denote by $S[i]$ the probability that the bomb will detonate in the next time interval, conditional on it having not done so in the first i time intervals.

Then $S[0] = L[0]/n$, and $S[i] = L[i]/(n-i)$. Bayes' theorem yields:

$$L[i] = \frac{[(n-i)/n]\,L[0]}{[(n-i)/n]\,L[0] + (1 - L[0])} = \frac{(n-i)\,L[0]}{n - iL[0]} \quad \text{and} \quad S[i] = \frac{L[0]}{n - i\,L[0]}$$

Setting L[0] = 60%, and $n = 6$, then $L[i] = (6-i)/(10-i)$ and $S[i] = 1/(10-i)$. As time ticks by, metaphorically or literally, the long-term function $L[i]$ decreases, reflecting the prospect of the bomb threat just being a hoax, but the short-term function $S[i]$ increases.

A variation on this bomb waiting scene was enacted at the French shrine of Lourdes, on one of the busiest days of the year, the annual Feast of the Assumption of the Virgin Mary. Shortly before noon on 15 August 2010, an anonymous caller threatened that four bombs were due to explode at the Sanctuary at around 3pm. Recognizing the possibility of explosions any time in the subsequent three hours, the police rapidly evacuated 30,000 pilgrims. Bomb threats and premature explosions have to be taken seriously: two days before Pope John Paul II's first visit to Lourdes in 1983, a bomb did go off and caused some damage. But hoaxes have also happened: in October 2002, an explosives alert prompted a partial evacuation. The 2010 scare was also a hoax.

Leaving aside the problem of the one-off catastrophe event, consider a sequence of hazard events. Suppose that a time t_0 has elapsed since the last hazard event. Let the probability density for the time interval between events be denoted by $p(t)$. The probability density for the next event occurring at time t_1 into the future is:

$$P(t_1) = p(t_0 + t_1) / \int\limits_{t_0}^{\infty} p(t) \, dt$$

Writing $p(t) = f''(t)$, Sornette and Knopoff have shown that the expected further waiting time can be expressed as:[23]

$$E(t_1) = -\frac{f(t_0)}{f'(t_0)}$$

Hence the expected waiting time increases as the hours go by, provided the following inequality holds: $f(t_0) f''(t_0) > [f'(t_0)]^2$.

If $p(t)$ is the exponential waiting time distribution, which corresponds to a Poisson distribution for event recurrence, $P(t_1) = p(t_1)$: the time to the next event does not depend on the time since the last event, and so the average waiting time does not change. However, this invariance does not hold for other distributions. Obviously, for a periodic event distribution, the average waiting time decreases steadily. But for many other distributions, it is not nearly so clear whether the average waiting time should increase or decrease. This is because there may be a cross-over point in time where the behaviour switches.

The tendency for the waiting time to lengthen or shorten with passing hours can be examined using criteria such as given above. Results obtained by Sornette and Knopoff show that for the lognormal and power-law distributions, there is a switch: for short elapse times, the expected waiting time decreases with the passing hours; but for long elapse times the expected waiting time lengthens. The latter is generally true of any distribution that falls off at large elapse times more slowly than the exponential. This mathematical analysis of waiting times highlights the sensitivity to the tail of the $p(t)$ distribution.

It is only through clarifying this distribution, that one's waiting expectations can be refined. For the earthquake recurrence process, a Brownian Passage Time distribution can be defined as a dynamically motivated and mathematically tractable alternative to simple parametric distributions, like gamma, lognormal, or Weibull. Let T be the first passage time to a level X by Brownian motion with drift rate λ and diffusion rate σ^2. Then the probability distribution of T is given by:[24]

$$\frac{X}{\sqrt{2\pi\sigma^2 T^3}} \exp\{-\frac{(X - \lambda T)^2}{2\sigma^2 T}\}$$

The distribution of the time a Brownian motion takes to reach a fixed level is called *inverse Gaussian*. It may be interpreted as representing the effective crustal stress reaching the Coulomb threshold at earthquake event times, and then dropping to a characteristic ground level as rupture relaxes the source region. As a reminder of the importance of physics in seismology, the first derivation of this law was given by Erwin Schrödinger in 1915.

5.2 Long-Term Data Records

When Jeanne Calment was 90 years old, she entered into a reverse mortgage agreement with a middle-aged French lawyer, whereby, in exchange for her apartment on her death, she was to receive 10% of its value each remaining year of her life. It was only a matter of time. But she ended up living to 122, breaking the record for human longevity. Indeed, she was already 120 years old in the year the lawyer died of cancer, aged 77, and commented with the wisdom conferred with old age, 'In life one sometimes makes bad deals.'

In the context of catastrophes, records typically have a negative association. But although, by definition, records are singular events, they have a mathematical structure which is both interesting, and even surprising. The mathematics of records is sufficiently rich as to provide an auxiliary tool for exploring event data on catastrophes, and so elucidate their temporal pattern of occurrence.

Some simple results follow from the dual assumptions that the events from which records arise are independent, and that each event is drawn from the same probability distribution, i.e. that the underlying causes of the hazard phenomena are not changing over the time period of observation. Although these assumptions are rather idealized, they provide a useful reference for exploring underlying data trends, and searching for possible scientific explanations. When a record event occurs, it is a common public attitude and media reaction to suspect some baseline trend, but the possibility that it might merely be a fortuitous event should not be discounted lightly.

For a sequence of n independent events, drawn from the same probability distribution, the expected number of records m, and the standard deviation σ of the number of records, are given by two summations:[25]

$$m = \sum_{1}^{n} 1/r \qquad \sigma^2 = \sum_{1}^{n} (1/r - 1/r^2)$$

The first sum approximates to $Ln(n) + \gamma$ for large values of n. (γ is Euler's constant 0.5772.) The logarithmic growth in the expected number of records is so sluggish as to defeat all but the most educated guesses. This result for the expected number of records is all the more fascinating, because it is so easily established by induction. It is obviously true for $n = 1$, since the first event is also the first record. Suppose that it is true for $n-1$ events. The expected number of additional records after the next nth event is $1/n$, since the nth event has the same chance of being a record as any predecessor. Hence the above expression for m also holds true for n events.

Part of the excitement of the Olympic Games lies in the anticipation of world records being broken. Usain Bolt's 9.69 seconds for the 100 metres in Beijing in 2008 was a memorable example. In the 40 years from the introduction of electronic timing in 1968 to the Beijing Olympics of 2008, there were some several thousand world class competitive men's 100 metre races, resulting in the world record being improved a dozen times. This information alone is indicative of notable developments in men's sprinting during this period. For without such developments, a new world record would have been expected mathematically only about eight times.

The oldest planned city in the world is Mohenjodaro, the centre of Indus Valley civilization. Since it was built, around 4,500 years ago, it has been destroyed at least seven times, and rebuilt directly on the top of ruins. Over such a very long time period, such a calamitous history may not seem so surprising, given that even with no adverse environmental change, nine record floods would be expected.

There is an immediate application of the theory of records to those hazard parameters which furnish a basis for a safety criterion, by way of their maximum historical value. As a yardstick for seismic design, the maximum Magnitude of any known regional historical earthquake is sometimes used, or, more conservatively, the maximum Magnitude plus half a Magnitude unit. Within the context of the design of coastal sea defences, similar use is sometimes made of the maximum sea water height registered on a local tide gauge, or this height incremented by half to one metre. These two ad hoc rules motivate an analysis of record earthquake and flood events. To apply the theory, extensive historical datasets of earthquake and flood observations are necessary. A country for which such data exist, and where ad hoc rules for maximum events have been used for engineering design purposes, is Britain.

The first example concerns historical earthquakes. Tectonically, the British Isles lie within the interior of the Eurasian Plate, and are subject to sporadic seismicity. Invaluable for analyzing records is the history of major events, extending back to the 12th century monastic chronicles. Earthquake history is also preserved in ancient buildings: Saltwood Castle, on the Kent coast, was damaged by Channel earthquakes in 1382 and 1580. The 1931 North Sea earthquake was one of the first to be instrumentally recorded;[26] a delight to the geophysicist Harold Jeffreys, who hailed it as 'almost a perfect earthquake'.

From extensive research of archive documents, Intensity assignments have been made, and Intensity plots have been produced for all historical British earthquakes. The contouring of these plots results in isoseismal maps, from which estimates have been made of the areas over which the events were felt. The logarithmic correlation between the felt area of an earthquake and instrumental (surface wave) Magnitude, Ms, established from 20th century data, allows the record events from the British earthquake catalogue to be tabulated below.

Table 5.1. Record historical British earthquakes.

Day/Month	Year	Location	Ms
15 April	1185	Lincoln	5.0
20 February	1247	Pembroke	5.2
21 May	1382	North Foreland	5.3
6 April	1580	Dover Strait	5.4
7 June	1931	Dogger Bank	5.5

Because of aftershock clustering in time, there is some dependence between the largest earthquakes occurring over a few years. However, over a time interval of about a decade, such dependence should be quite weak. For the dataset comprising the largest earthquake per decade, there are 82 observations within the time span from 1185 to the first decade of the 21st century. If it is assumed that these maximum decadal Magnitudes are independent, and drawn from identical distributions, (which is tectonically plausible), then the expected number of records is five, which is the same as the actual observed number of records.

In intraplate areas of low or moderate activity, the occurrence of an event larger than any in a brief historical catalogue should not be regarded as unduly surprising. The past is such a valuable data source for catastrophe science that every effort is made to extend historical catalogues back in time, and even to archive oral disaster traditions. This is especially true of regions of the New World lacking a long literary tradition. The 1985 sequence of earthquakes in the Canadian Northwest Territories not only exceeded in Magnitude the largest previously documented, but also the maximum size of earthquake hitherto anticipated. As with Canada, Australia is part of the New World with a comparatively brief but important documented history of disasters. In December 2010, Queensland was struck by record flooding, induced by a severe La Niña event. The state capital, Brisbane, recorded its wettest December since 1859.

As a flood illustration of use of records for exploring environmental data sequences, consider the annual maximum high water levels observed at London Bridge, situated on the River Thames. Until the construction of the Thames Barrier in 1982, London was exposed to a high risk of major flooding due to a storm surge travelling up the Thames Estuary, augmented possibly by heavy rainfall.

Over a period of about 200 years,[27] high water records were established in eight years: 1791, 1834, 1852, 1874, 1875, 1881, 1928, and 1953. According to the above formulae for records, the expected number of records is approximately six, and the standard deviation of the number of records is about two. Although not entirely inconsistent with the hypothesis of independent identically distributed data, the excess number of records does suggest there might be external factors elevating gradually the distribution of annual maximum high water levels. Indeed, this hypothesis would accord with known changes in the tidal regime of the Thames: there is ample geological evidence that the southeast of England has been slowly subsiding, and there is historical information about artificial changes in river geometry, occasioned by dredging.

5.2.1 River discharges

The preceding diagnostic analysis of annual high water maxima leads on naturally to an enquiry about the interdependence of geophysical data over the long-term. For annual river discharges, the work of Mandelbrot and Wallis suggests that there is generally a degree of long-term statistical interdependence.[28] The phenomenon of persistence in yearly discharge and flood levels was coined by Mandelbrot: *the Joseph effect*, after the Nile prophecy in the Old Testament book of Genesis.

The practical motivation for the statistical analysis of river discharges stems from a hydrological issue of dam reservoir capacity. For a reservoir to function well over a period of years, it should produce a uniform outflow. Its capacity depends on the difference between the maximum and minimum values of the cumulative discharge, over and above the average discharge. Given the biblical story of the Nile flood, and the subsequent historical evidence of famines, anyone embarking on preliminary 1950s studies for the Aswan High Dam would have been well advised to undertake a detailed statistical analysis of discharges. This task fell to Harold Hurst, affectionately known locally as Abu Nile, who stumbled across a universal scaling law worthy of the contribution made to mathematics by the Ancient Egyptians, and ever more insightful for flood management than the astrological prophecies of Nile flooding still being peddled in the Third Millennium. The mathematical background to this scaling law is summarized. Let $X(u)$ be the discharge rate at time u, and let the cumulative discharge at time t be written as:

$$X*(t) = \int_0^t X(u)\ du$$

For a lag time δ, the adjusted range of $X*(t)$, in the time interval up to δ, is defined as:

$$R(\delta) = Max_{[0,\delta]} \{X*(u) - (u/\delta)X*(\delta)\}$$
$$- Min_{[0,\delta]} \{X*(u) - (u/\delta)X*(\delta)\}$$

Denote the sample standard deviation by $S(\delta)$, and use these formulae to obtain the ratio $R(\delta)/S(\delta)$. If the annual discharges could be simply represented as white (Gaussian) noise, corresponding to the statistical independence of observations sufficiently distant in time, this ratio would tend to $\sqrt{\delta}$. Instead, for a number of rivers, this ratio is δ^H, where the exponent H, called the Hurst (or Hölder) index, is typically greater than 0.5, in some cases as high as 0.9. This size of index is indicative of long-term interdependence in the annual discharges. The Nile itself happens to be one of the rivers with an index value at the upper end of the range.

The non-stationarity of the annual flow process in the Nile may be partly attributable to oscillatory modes of ocean–atmosphere variability,[29] including the El Niño-Southern Oscillation (ENSO), which influences rainfall at the source of the Nile. Prophetically, there may also be evidence of a seven year periodicity associated with influence of the North Atlantic Oscillation (NAO). Not for the first time, scientific sense may be made of biblical references to disaster.

5.3 Statistics of Extremes

Hydrodynamic computational models of storm surges in the Netherlands have advanced considerably since, but flood protection along the Dutch coast once was based on taking a small ad hoc margin above the highest recorded water level. That was before 1 February 1953, when a great North Sea storm surge on a high spring tide caused serious dike failure, resulting in massive flooding, the evacuation of 100,000 people, and 1,835 fatalities. In almost all cases, inadequate height of the dikes was the root cause of dike failure, because overtopping waves were able to erode the inner slopes of the dikes. This disaster prompted the Dutch government to appoint the Delta Commission, which undertook an econometric analysis to arrive at an optimal level of safety against flooding. For practical design purposes in heavily built-up and populated areas,[30] the design water levels for dikes were set to have an annual exceedance probability of 1/10,000.

There have been few advances in mathematics as closely associated with a specific hazard application as the statistical theory of extremes is with floods. Laurens de Haan, who contributed significantly to the development of the theory, as well as to its application to flood control in the Netherlands, summoned mathematicians to action with his 1990 paper with the confrontational title: *Fighting the Arch-Enemy with Mathematics.*[31] The basic statistical data required for this type of armoury are observations of extreme values over a period of time. The seasonal nature of flooding makes water levels a suitable source of data where continuous measurements of high water exist for a number of decades. For the North Sea port at the Hook of Holland, high tide water levels have been recorded since 1887.

Consider a sequence $X_1, X_2, ..., X_n$ of independent and identically distributed random variables, with an unknown cumulative distribution function F, such that $F(x) = P(X \leq x)$. As a simple example, these random variables might be the annual maximum water levels at a coastal site. For the design of coastal defences, we may be seeking to determine a water level x_p such that $F(x_p) = 1 - p$, where p is some small probability tolerance such as 1/10,000. Because p is usually smaller than $1/n$, an assumption about the unknown distribution F needs to be made. Since our interest is restricted to the upper tail of the distribution, this assumption need only concern the asymptotic behaviour of the distribution.   Before the assumption is stated, note that, because the sequence of n random variables is taken to be independent:

$$P(\max\{X_1, X_2, .., X_n\} \le x) = \Pi_i \, P(X_i \le x) = F^n(x)$$

For an extreme value distribution to be stable as n increases, F^n should asymptote to some fixed distribution G, in which case F is said to lie within the *domain of attraction* of G. Given that a change of physical units of x should not make a difference to the form of the asymptotic distribution, one might suspect that a process of scaling and normalizing would be fruitful. Indeed, the key postulate is that there exist a sequence of numbers $a_n > 0$, and b_n, such that as n increases, $F^n(a_n x + b_n)$ converges to $G(x)$.

To form an idea of what kind of limiting distribution $G(x)$ would result, one can start by addressing the stability equation: $G^n(x) = G(x + b_n)$. Gumbel showed a straightforward way of finding the resulting distribution,[32] which is consequently named after him: $G(x) = \exp\{-\exp(-(x-\mu)/\sigma)\}$. More generally, it can be established that $G(x)$ must have the following characteristic functional form, which is called the *generalized extreme-value distribution*:

$$G(x) = \exp\{-[1 - k(x-\mu)/\sigma]^{1/k}\}$$

In this formula, the location and shape parameters μ and k may be any real numbers, the scale parameter σ must however be positive, as must $1 - k(x-\mu)/\sigma$. In the limit that k is zero, the Gumbel distribution is recovered; for values of k greater than zero, the extreme-value distribution is named after Weibull, and for values of k less than zero, the mathematician honoured is Fréchet.

Common probability distributions which are within the domain of attraction of the Gumbel distribution are medium-tailed distributions such as the Normal, exponential, gamma, and lognormal. Probability distributions which are within the domain of attraction of the Weibull distribution include the short-tailed distributions such as the uniform and beta distributions. Finally, probability distributions which lie within the domain of attraction of the Fréchet distribution are long-tailed distributions such as the Pareto, Burr, log-gamma, and Cauchy distributions.

Taking an exceedance probability of p as a flood hazard criterion, the corresponding water level height $z(p)$ is given by the expression:

$$z(p) = \mu + (\sigma/k)[\,1 - \{-\ln(1-p)\}^{\,k}\,]$$

The generalized extreme-value (GEV) model can be extended in a straightforward way to situations where the probability distribution of annual maxima is not stationary, but varies over time. For example, a simple constant trend in water-level height could be represented by making μ linearly dependent on time.

In its crudest form, the use of annual maxima to estimate statistical extremes makes rather modest demands on the completeness of historical observation and requires no physical knowledge of the underlying hydrological processes. It is a tribute to the power of extreme value methods over the purely empirical procedures once implemented with the sound judgement of water engineers, that these methods can play a prominent part in establishing guidelines for flood protection.

Forsaking simplicity in the pursuit of greater accuracy, a number of statisticians have attempted to refine the classical extreme value models. One approach is to model separately the component parts of the hydrological process: for coastal flood analysis this would be tide and storm surge.[33] Such a split is warranted because the tidal component is deterministic, although there is a dynamical interaction between tide and storm surge to be represented. A consequent development is the modelling of the spatial coherence between the water levels at different locations, due to the dynamics of tide and storm surge propagation. Because of the spatial interdependence, simultaneous use of all regional extreme event data is needed to derive GEV parameters for a stretch of coast prone to flooding.

Another route for improving upon the classical extreme value model involves the incorporation of information on all large events (exceeding some threshold) during a year rather than just the annual maxima. This leads to the *peaks over threshold* (POT) approach to the frequency analysis of river as well as coastal floods.[34] Compared with annual maximum flood modelling, POT models incorporate a more numerous set of events than just one event per year, but they fall short of a detailed time-series analysis of daily river discharge, which would explore the statistical structure of all the daily values, not merely the high values over the designated threshold.

The POT set is also more selective than the annual maximum set in as much as, in some dry years, the annual maximum event may not be severe enough to warrant description as a genuine flood event. Furthermore, it has been argued that POT models are better able to represent rainfall and snowmelt floods, which often occur at different times of the year, and may have different characteristics. There is a price to pay for statistical flexibility beyond that of the annual maximum approach, which is the obligation to accumulate and process more data. There is also some additional mathematics to be mastered, but the heavier burden of mathematical invention has been shouldered by new recruits to the mathematical fight against flooding.

Let the threshold be u, and let N be the number of exceedances of u during a given period. We suppose that the excesses above the threshold are independent with common distribution function H. One of the earliest models suggested for excesses above the threshold was the simple exponential, with mean value α:

$$H(y;\alpha) = 1 - \exp(-y/\alpha)$$

This happens to be the limit, as the parameter k goes to zero, of the generalized Pareto distribution:

$$H(y;\alpha,k) = 1 - \left(1 - k\frac{y}{\alpha}\right)^{1/k}$$

where α is positive. If $k \leq 0$, then y can be any positive number, but otherwise $0 < y < \alpha/k$. The mathematical rationale for considering this particular family of distributions was developed by Pickands.[35] He proved a necessary and sufficient condition for the generalized Pareto distribution to be a limiting distribution for excesses over a threshold. This condition is that the parent distribution lies within the domain of attraction of one of the extreme-value distributions. Another special property of the generalized Pareto distribution is threshold stability: the conditional distribution of $Y - u$ given that $Y > u$ is also a generalized Pareto distribution.

Furthermore, if N has a Poisson distribution, and $Y_1, Y_2, ..., Y_N$ are independent identically distributed generalized Pareto random variables, then their maximum has the generalized extreme value distribution. Thus, a Poisson model of exceedance times with generalized Pareto excesses implies the standard extreme value distributions.

Provided the threshold is taken sufficiently high, the generalized Pareto distribution can be of practical use in statistical estimation,[36] and there are various data analysis techniques for parameterizing the distribution.[37] Non-Poissonian models for the arrivals of peaks have been considered, and may be especially warranted where human intervention is a major cause of jumps in a flood series. Changes in land use and climate are some of the factors extending extreme value analysis to cover parameters changing over time.[38]

A high threshold may be viable for hydrological hazards, and also for windstorms,[39] but poses difficulties for geological hazards, such as earthquakes and volcanic eruptions, because of the limited amount of data on extreme events. Deligne *et al.*[40] showed that, with corrections for under-reporting bias of volcanic eruptions, extreme value analysis can yield robust frequency estimates for large Plinian eruptions, but not for caldera-forming eruptions, including those known as super-eruptions, much larger than the Vesuvius cataclysm witnessed by Pliny in AD 79.

Beyond flood and windstorm modelling, a further meteorological application of extreme value theory, developed at the European Centre for Medium-Range Weather Forecasts, involves leveraging numerical forecasting simulations to estimate recurrence intervals, referred to as return periods, for extremes of low and high temperature. These are catastrophe calculations: extreme cold snaps and heat waves may cause the premature deaths of the vulnerable. In August 2003, nearly 15,000 died in France, mostly the elderly, as dangerously high temperatures were sustained for more than a week.

Chapter 6

Catastrophe Complexity

A general collapse of credit, however short the time,
is more fearful than the most terrible earthquake.
Michel Chevalier,
Lettres sur l'Amérique du Nord

The reductionist approach to physics, aimed at understanding matter at ever finer resolution, has triumphed with the discovery of atoms and their constituents. Successful scientific prediction hardly gets better than Dirac's prediction of the existence of the positron, the anti-particle to the electron. Dirac's mystical relativistic wave equation, $(i\gamma.\partial - m)\,\psi = 0$, the source of this prediction, allows properties of the electron to be calculated with a decimal degree of accuracy that would confound a meteorologist and amaze an economist. Dirac asserted in 1929 that, 'The underlying physical laws necessary for the mathematical theory of a large part of physics and the whole of chemistry are thus completely known, and the difficulty is only that the exact application of these laws leads to equations much too complicated to be soluble.'[1]

The caveat is significant not just for philosophers of science, but for practitioners as well. Powerful as it is in predicting atomic and molecular characteristics, the reductionist approach has limited practical ability to explain the behaviour of larger physical systems. Even understanding the dendritic growth of a snowflake is a challenge.

The hierarchical structure of reality, requiring additional concepts at each system size level, was emphasized by Philip Anderson, who earned his Physics Nobel Prize four decades after Dirac in condensed matter physics. This branch of physics broadens knowledge gained of individual particles to consider their cooperative group behaviour in gases, liquids, and solids. The Physics Nobel Prize has been awarded numerous times to discoverers of fascinating emergent behaviour of groups of the basic constituents of matter, e.g. superconductivity, which would have been hard to anticipate outside the physics laboratory.

The observation of a bewilderingly rich variety of emergent group phenomena by physicists suggests that economists might also make important discoveries in the study of emergence. There is a respected tradition for economists to look towards physical science for key ideas. For example, classical thermodynamics had been a scientific inspiration for Paul Samuelson in his path-breaking mathematical development of economic theory. At the interdisciplinary Santa Fe Institute in New Mexico, co-founded by the erudite Murray Gell-Mann, the fertile collaboration of physicists and economists has pioneered joint developments in the field of complexity science.

Insight from physics suggests that a host of interesting socio-economic group phenomena should emerge from the various social interactions between people. Whereas extremes of group behaviour are limited if group members act individually, these extremes can be wild if group members act collectively as a herd. Representing people as agents, the interactions between them can be analyzed and studied in agent-based models of human behaviour. These models have grown in sophistication and capacity as computer resources have expanded in the 21st century.

From the interactions between crowds of people competing for resources, major departures from equilibrium behaviour can arise. A simple paradigm is the urban traffic jam. This would be hard to plan and coordinate centrally vehicle by vehicle, if it did not occur spontaneously. Road works and accidents can cause traffic jams, but gridlock can occur endogenously with an excess number of vehicles converging on busy intersections during rush hour.

Emergent risky phenomena can be collectively deleterious for society, if not catastrophic: financial markets can crash; infectious disease epidemics can spread; cities can be blacked out; wars can break out; and terrorist plots can be hatched. That so many societal catastrophes are inherently emergent risks is an important realization coming from complexity science. The practical consequences have yet to be analyzed fully and absorbed within public policy.

Ilya Prigogine, who received the 1977 Chemistry Nobel Prize for his contributions in nonequilibrium thermodynamics, extended his thinking to human systems. Characteristic of societies are the adaptability and plasticity of human behaviour, which are two basic features of nonlinear dynamical systems capable of performing transitions far from equilibrium.[2] Accordingly, societal application of complexity science should help to deepen understanding of emergent catastrophic phenomena, and create fresh initiatives for risk mitigation and warning.

In this respect, the role of social psychology as a discipline in catastrophe risk assessment is crucial. Individual behaviour changes dynamically with the changes seen in their neighbours, friends, relatives, and other social contacts. Rather than legislating change in public behaviour, it may be more effective to achieve desired social objectives through encouraging self-organization.

When Hurricane Katrina struck in 2005, the Walmart Chief Executive trusted his staff to self-organize, saying, 'A lot of you are going to have to make decisions above your level. Make the best decision that you can with the information available to you at the time.'[3] Over a hundred Walmart stores were closed due to power outages and damage. But while FEMA officials were figuring out how to requisition supplies, Walmart employees were taking individual initiative and action to find a way into their stores and distribute supplies.

A similar degree of self-organization is invaluable in complex military operations, since battle plans should not be expected to survive contact with the enemy, where tactical execution of strategy begins. The Allied Normandy landings on D-Day 1944 exemplify the tactical expedience of quick local decisions over excessive centralized decision-making.

In his manual on counterinsurgency, David Kilkullen has argued that complexity theory offers fresh possibilities for understanding the systems behaviour of insurgencies, beyond the reductionist classical counter insurgency approach which failed the Pentagon so abysmally during the Vietnam War.[4] As with all organic systems, insurgencies are complex and adaptive and are self-organizing. Crucially, they are nonequilibrium dissipative structures, requiring for stability the throughput of energy, such as violence, grievances, insurgent action, and counterinsurgency reaction. Once energy is drained, disruption then becomes possible.

6.1 Emergent Catastrophes

One of the most catastrophic of emergent phenomena, which led to the slaughter of millions, was World War I. The European political system was in a critical state on 28 June 1914 when a Serbian nationalist assassinated Archduke Franz Ferdinand on a visit to Sarajevo. The circumstances were accidental: the Archduke's driver had taken the wrong road, and the assassin happened to be in the right place at the wrong time. But this was an accident waiting to happen. Many catastrophes, natural and societal, are triggered by minor events which perturb systems on the edge of instability. So it was that a minor Balkan crisis that might have been containable, span out of control and inexorably set in train events leading to the outbreak of war.

The philosopher of war, Christopher Coker,[5] who has made a special study of complexity and war, has pointed out that there was good understanding in 1914 of the individual component parts of the European political system, such as the naval arms race, alliances etc.. But such understanding was lacking for the complex system as a whole. Out of this complexity emerged general instability, which led to an inevitable war which international diplomacy could not stop. Rather, as an avalanche can grow in scale from small to large to massive according to a power-law, so the hostilities in 1914 deepened and spread relentlessly to become the Great War. Ultimately, pulling the trigger seemed the least worst political option. As the French statesman Georges Clemenceau admitted, 'It is easier to make war than peace.'

It is also much easier to start an avalanche than to stop one. During the Great War, as many as 40,000 Austrian and Italian troops were killed by avalanches in the Italian Alps, set off by artillery shells; a triggering technique since copied by civilians to make ski resorts safer. Over the ages, forlorn attempts have been made to stave off hurricanes and earthquakes, but these remain so beyond the control of Man as to justify the historical insurance terminology 'Acts of God'. Despite human mastery of Nature's resources in the daily struggle for survival, it is humbling also to reflect that Man may have limited power to stop the descent of political strife into war. The mantra for increasing military expenditure, 'If you want peace, prepare for war', would have echoed in political forums long before its quotation by Flavius Regetius Renatus in Roman times. But arms escalation for peace creates its own inherent instability. An imbalance of military power may be an opportunity, excuse, invitation, and even imperative to strike first. The street fighter's logic of getting one's retaliation in first may be much more compelling to a politician than a pacifist call for unilateral disarmament.

The build-up of arms creates an inexorable process of increasing political strain, leading to a state of criticality, which a seismologist would recognize as dangerous. A progressive arms race may be no more possible to halt than the relentless incremental movement of the Earth's tectonic plates, which perpetuates a cycle of earthquake fault rupture. After crustal strain is released violently in an earthquake, the menacing process of strain accumulation starts anew. So it is with war, where the military push for re-armament may be fuelled by innovation and enhancement in the lethal effectiveness of weapons technology.

The Great Powers of the early 20th century armed themselves to deter others from warring against them. Steps to reduce the strain, such as slowing mobilization prior to 1914, were hard to implement unilaterally because of the competition of national interests. It is this competition which so characterizes the dynamics of complexity, and drives systems towards catastrophe: there is no earthquake to end all earthquakes, and no war to end all wars. Anticipating the sudden outbreak of hostilities may be no easier than a sudden earthquake fault rupture. In the late 1970s, a UK intelligence review was conducted of the track record in warning of foreign acts of aggression. Just a month after the final report was approved came the surprise Argentine invasion of the Falklands.

6.1.1 Conspiracies

The Serbian nationalist, Gavrilo Princep, who assassinated Archduke Franz Ferdinand, was one of seven conspirators who lined his Sarajevo route in readiness for an opportunity to perpetrate the act of terrorism for which they had been trained by the Serbian secret society 'The Black Hand'. Although it is possible for a lone terrorist to perpetrate deadly and damaging attacks on society, it takes a terrorist network to organize and execute spectacular plots with a high chance of success.

The formation and growth of a terrorist organization are characteristic of an emergent phenomenon. Thus, whilst Osama bin Laden provided guidance, funding, and inspiration for the development of Al Qaeda, it metamorphosed into a global self-organizing Jihad movement, with complex international dynamics of its own, which would have surprised its founder as much as dismayed its manifold victims of terror around the world. The social interaction, training, and indoctrination of members of a terrorist network, communicating and meeting in person, by phone, or online, can convert 'a bunch of guys' from an ordinary community into a fearsome and troublesome militant adversary of the state.

As far as the counter-terrorism security services are concerned, the group of active supporters of violence constitutes a very large social network, interlocking sub-networks of which may be involved in terrorist plots at any given time. Key to the disruption of plots is the discernment of links between nodes of a terrorist sub-network. The higher the likelihood of identifying a link between two terrorist nodes, the clearer a pattern of connections will become, and the easier it is to 'join the dots' to disrupt an emergent terrorist plot, and gain the necessary corroborative evidence for successful criminal prosecutions.

Suppose that, within the large disparate population of terrorist supporters, there is a group actively involved in operational planning at a particular time. It is in the general terrorist interest to tend to randomize network connections, to keep security services guessing about plot involvement, and defeat efforts at profiling. However, the disconcerting news for terrorists is that, even with randomization, there is a tipping point in the size of the group, beyond which the presence of a conspiracy should become increasingly manifest to the security services.

Population clusters forming within random networks may be analyzed graphically in terms of a basic small clique of three people, who all are interlinked. The better the link detection is, the more cliques that can be spotted. Mathematical graph theory analysis of the way such cliques can percolate through a network reveals a tipping point transition. This occurs when the link detection probability attains the value: $p = 1/\sqrt{2N}$ where N is the size of the group.[6] Inverting this formula, the tipping point arises where the size of the group exceeds one half of the inverse-square of the link detection probability.

The nonlinearity embedded in the expression for the link detection probability embodies in a concise and convenient manner the rapidly escalating dependence of counter-terrorism performance on surveillance capability. The greater the link detection probability is, the smaller the size of conspiracies that can be disrupted. Conversely, the smaller the link detection probability, the more tenuous is the prospect of identifying plots. To illustrate this rule, if the link detection probability is as high as 1/2, then the tipping point is at 2; if it is 1/10, then the tipping point is at 50; and if the link detection probability is as small as 1/50, then the tipping point is 1,250. In circumstances where the link detection probability is tiny, e.g. 1/100, then the tipping point is too far removed at 5,000 to be of practical interest.

Commenting on the intelligence failure to interdict the London transport bombings of 7 July 2005, the director-general of MI5, Eliza Manningham-Buller, remarked that, 'MI5 would have to be the size of the Stasi to have the chance of stopping every possible attack, and even then, it would be unlikely that it would succeed.' This is a stark and disturbing reflection on the superior capabilities and powers that police states have in combating dissidents.

A deeper understanding of this statement can be gained by examining it in simple arithmetic terms. The German Democratic Republic under Erich Honecker, was the epitome of a harsh and repressive security regime. Honecker's secret police, the feared Stasi, kept records on about 5 million of 17 million East German citizens. Even though so many were under Stasi scrutiny, the proportion that might have been actively supportive of a regime change, and prepared to risk arrest, was smaller. Recognizing that the dissident movement consisted largely of the educated middle class, up to around 10% of the population might have been potential activists, in which case the surveillance ratio of potentially radical citizens to 85,000 Stasi agents was about 20:1.

It is known that the Stasi recruited several hundred thousand informants. Assuming that an agent, in conjunction with a team of informants and police officers, could keep a reasonable watch-list of approximately five citizens, there would be a sizeable 1/4 chance that a member of a GDR conspiracy would be under surveillance. Since each link has two nodes, the chance of a link being detected between two conspirators would then be about twice this, or 1/2. According to the tipping point rule, for such a high link detection probability, the corresponding tipping point is 2: implying that any conspiracy against the East German state involving more than two people would have had very little chance of escaping detection. The state surveillance apparatus would implicitly have been sized to achieve this extraordinarily high level of state protection against conspiracy.

6.1.2 *Infrastructure cascade failure*

In October 2002, the mayor of Paris launched the first white night (*Nuit Blanche*) celebration dedicated to the arts. The name of the event is a reference to *White Nights*, a short story about a dreamer by Fyodor Dostoevsky, which was turned into a movie by Luchino Visconti. Given this Italian connection and the success of the French nocturnal event, the mayor of Rome organized a similar event (*Notte Bianca*), scheduled for the night of 27 September 2003. What would be the blackest nightmare for the organizer of a white night celebration with a million revellers in the city centre? A terrorist attack would be potentially more injurious, an earthquake more destructive, but most galling and ill-fated would surely have to be a power blackout. Only a *catastrofista*[7] would think of it. The odds of a catastrophic blackout on any specific night in Rome are tiny, of the order of thousands to one – but happen it did at about 3am.

Despite the lateness of the hour, many people were out on the streets and public transportation was still operating at the time of the blackout. Several hundred people were trapped in underground trains. Traffic jams developed as traffic lights failed, and one death resulted at an unregulated intersection. Coupled with heavy rain at the time, many people spent the night sleeping in train stations and on the streets in Rome. Hundreds of people had panic attacks. Fortunately, thanks to disaster preparedness, hospital electricity generators continued to function. As the crowds returned home in darkness, they must have pondered what could have caused the worst blackout in Italian history.

Overhead high voltage electricity lines are normally bare, and if an object gets too close it is possible that a 'flashover' can occur, where electricity will jump over a small distance to reach earth. A flashover to a tree was the proximate cause of the blackout, but a trigger is only an incidental cause of an emergent catastrophe of a complex system lacking resilience. There is an inherent fragility associated with infrastructure networks exhibiting dynamic self-organization.

The general industry practice for system security assessment traditionally had been deterministic, with the power system conventionally designed and operated to withstand the loss of any single element. This is usually referred to as the $N-1$ criterion because it examines the behaviour of an N component grid following the loss of any one of its major components, but not following multiple outages. But a blackout is rarely the result of a single catastrophic disturbance. Rather it is an event cascade, resulting in multiple outages, that stresses the complex network beyond its capability. So it was that a cascade blacked out the first *Notte Bianca*.

A tree flashover caused the tripping of a major line between Italy and Switzerland. The connection was not re-established because the automatic breaker controls were unable to re-close the line. This resulted in an overload on a parallel path. Since power was not redistributed quickly and adequately, a second 380-kV line also tripped on the same border due to tree contact. This cascading trend continued. In a couple of seconds, Italy started to lose power synchronism with the rest of Europe and the lines between France and Italy tripped. The same happened for the 220-kV interconnection between Italy and Austria. Subsequently, the final 380-kV corridor between Italy and Slovenia became overloaded and tripped. These outages left the Italian system with a power shortage of 6400 MW. As a consequence, the frequency in the Italian system was reduced. But the frequency decay was not controlled adequately to stop generation from tripping due to under-frequency. Over several minutes the entire Italian power system collapsed causing a country wide blackout.

A particular feature of the 2003 Italian blackout cascade, which exacerbated network failure was the way that the shutdown of power stations led to failures of nodes in the internet communication network, which in turn caused further breakdown of power stations. This loss amplification pathway is of broad international significance because there are numerous types of interdependent infrastructure networks, involving flows of communication, energy, material, people, and commerce. The interdependence of infrastructure networks provides a mechanism for failures in one infrastructure to propagate to other infrastructures, and cause catastrophic levels of disruption to lives, livelihoods, and businesses.

Buldyrev *et al.* have generalized the Italian interdependency to a network model where the failure in one network can lead to failure of nodes in a second network, that in turn can escalate failures in the first network.[8] This model explores network connectivity when nodes are removed. In a standard network, as more and more nodes are removed, a critical threshold is reached above which the network becomes totally fragmented. An interdependent network is more vulnerable: the critical threshold is lower, and the system breakdown occurs abruptly, making it more difficult to handle.

Vespignani has drawn attention to the organic growth of large-scale critical infrastructures, e.g. the internet, which transcend engineering and design issues.[9] Analyzing single system components is important, but it leaves open the challenge of understanding the global behaviour of a complex system stressed by the failure of a set of network nodes, and impacted furthermore by a natural hazard event. It is worthwhile commenting that a windstorm caused the initial flashover triggering the 2003 Italy blackout, and that heavy rain in Rome deteriorated conditions for both pedestrians and drivers, as well as the emergency services.

More weather critical for power networks than a rain storm is an ice storm. Meteorologically, an ice storm can be explained as follows. When the air at ground level is colder than freezing, liquid drops will freeze on contact, resulting in glaze: this is called freezing rain. A storm consisting of freezing rain is called an ice storm. When the ice builds up enough, it can snap power lines. When thousands of individual power lines snap, the task of restoring power is enormous, and may take days. Crews often have trouble just to reach the broken lines in icy conditions. Hence, of all the possible natural hazard triggers of a blackout, a sustained ice storm carries special economic danger. Most ice storms are fairly short-lived, lasting a day or so, as did an ice storm in April 2003, which badly disrupted power supplies in upstate New York. But, occasionally, ice storms last considerably longer. Four days in 1921 covered the worst ice storm in the New England record.

North America's worst ice storms are commonly associated with slow-moving low-pressure systems having very large temperature differences between colliding warm, moist Gulf air and very cold Arctic air in their northeastern sector. When these storm systems stall for an extended period over one region, heavy accumulations of ice may blanket a region, causing much destruction.

The great ice storm of January 1998 is an extreme example of a stalled storm. It brought to Eastern Canada 80 hours of freezing rain, spread over six days, and caused a loss of power to more than a million homes in Quebec and Ontario provinces. Outside Canada, northern parts of New England and New York State were also blacked out. A thick sheet of ice covered an area of 100,000 sq. km., which turned into a vast outdoor laboratory of emergent phenomena. Conversion of freezing water into ice is a classic emergence paradigm of physics. But within this frozen area, businesses and transport infrastructure were closed; agriculture was ruined; ironically, even water treatments plants were affected, so that residents had to boil water for drinking.

6.2 Financial Crashes

Inspired by the Newtonian concept of equilibrium in physics, the French economist Léon Walras developed a general equilibrium model for an economy, with prices and quantities determined by balancing supply and demand. As a 19th century innovator in theoretical economics, he was unduly opinionated about mathematical modelling in the social sciences: 'As for those economists who do not know any mathematics, who do not even know what is meant by mathematics and yet have taken the stand that mathematics cannot possibly serve to elucidate economic principles, let them go their way repeating that human liberty will never allow itself to be cast into equations.'[10]

The Walrasian model was used by Kenneth Arrow and Gerard Debreu to show that competitive price equilibrium is efficient (Pareto optimal) in that nobody could be made better off without making someone else worse off. In his 1972 Harvard Nobel lecture, Arrow extolled the remarkable coherence of individual economic decisions.[11] As incomes rise and demands shift, so do the labour force and productive facilities. He also asserted that, 'The economic system adjusts with a considerable degree of smoothness and indeed of rationality to changes in the fundamental facts within which it operates.' This is of course Adam Smith's invisible hand in operation in the market place.

This simplified rather impersonal view of Man as *Homo Economicus*, a calculating, rational, individual, has been criticized by behavioural economists who have sought to test the validity of the underlying assumptions on real human economic agents, especially in extenuating economic circumstances. Rather as Newtonian physics has evolved to consider systems far from equilibrium, so theoretical economics has progressed from the neoclassical idealized model of *Homo Economicus*, to consider other physics paradigms of economic behaviour, *econophysics*, which can capture better the dynamics of group behaviour.

When a stock market crash occurs, it is human nature for an enquiry to be set up to identify the underlying cause, and apportion responsibility, if not outright blame. The 1987 stock market crash was blamed on computer trading; the Asian currency crisis was blamed on hedge funds and the International Monetary Fund; the internet bubble was blamed on Wall Street analysts. The mathematical reality is that thin-tailed Brownian motion models of stock movements do not encompass the fat-tailed distributions that govern financial crashes. In the absence of a financial Richter scale, natural hazard metaphors have described the potential for financial disaster better linguistically than the Gaussian distribution has mathematically.

Enough crashes have occurred to demonstrate that a financial market operates as a self-organizing process, and that a crash is an emergent characteristic of a complex system driven to instability by some deep-rooted aspects of human nature: fear, greed, hubris, and panic. Increasing financial complexity may result in markets becoming destabilized, and driven to singular states.[12]

6.2.1 Complexity of a financial market

A survivor of the D-Day landing on Omaha Beach, Hank Greenberg guided AIG to becoming the world's largest insurer, with a triple-A credit rating. With this rating, AIG's lower cost of capital enabled it to take on from banks more and more credit default swap risk, until the trillion dollar risk balloon exploded catastrophically in 2008. In a call to investors in August 2007, the London head of the AIG financial products division had confidently proclaimed, 'It is hard for us, without being flippant, to even see a scenario within any kind of realm of reason, that would see us losing one dollar in any of those transactions.'[13] Risk which is not perceived is not explicitly collateralized.

Like terrorism, complexity is a term which is rather elusive to define, but you recognize it when you see it. The occurrence of extreme scenarios that may not be readily anticipated or foreseen is a common outcome of complexity, which can have potentially catastrophic consequences. The demise of AIG, which had the size and strength to underpin the market for credit default swaps, was one of the financial catastrophes which precipitated the financial system collapse in 2008.

Awareness of the attributes of a system displaying complexity is clearly needed by risk managers.[14] Mining his deep knowledge of physics, Neil Johnson has drawn up a list of complexity features. These apply to financial markets, and make them paradigms of complexity:[15]

[1]   The system displays feedback so that it remembers its past to some degree and is responsive to it.

[2]   The system is non-stationary, so that its dynamical and statistical properties may change over time.

[3]   The system contains many agents, interacting in time-dependent ways, and each endeavouring to improve performance through behaviour adaptation.

[4]   The system typically remains far from equilibrium and can thus exhibit extreme behaviour.

[5]   The system is coupled to the environment, making it hard to tell which effects are exogenous, and which are endogenous and self-generated.

In a financial market system, the traders are the agents, and the market prices track the system's dynamics. A market is deemed to be efficient if all the available information is instantly processed when it reaches the market, and reflected in asset pricing. In 1965, Paul Samuelson formulated the efficient market hypothesis, that no profitable information about future price movements can be obtained by analyzing past prices. Assuming rational behaviour and market efficiency, he was able to derive the following result which indicates that, in gambling terms, market investment is a fair game, i.e. the gambler's expected future wealth equals his present assets:

If Y_{t+1} is the expected value of the price of an asset at time $t+1$, then it is related to the previous values of prices $Y_0, Y_1, ..., Y_t$ by:

$$E\{Y_{t+1} \mid Y_0, Y_1, ..., Y_t\} = Y_t$$

From the perspective of algorithmic complexity theory, it is not possible to discriminate between trading on noise and trading on information.[16] The difficulty of beating the market, despite the large finance industry in business to gain a market edge for investors, gave credence to the theory. However, if enough traders believe they can discern a profitable pattern in the price series of some stocks, e.g. by scanning charts, their concerted actions could have the effect of developing such prices through the momentum of their trading actions. Irrational exuberance can build momentum for stocks and inflate bubbles and booms, whilst irrational pessimism can steepen downturns.

There are some intriguing parallels between financial and physical risk modelling. The dynamic movements of financial markets are turbulently nonlinear, like those of the natural environment. There are economic cycles as aperiodic as seismic cycles, and Elliott waves which ripple through global markets, having an impact like El Niño on the global climate. One essential difference is the Oedipus effect, a term coined by the philosopher of science Karl Popper for a prediction which can influence the very event which is predicted. Like a Greek oracle, it is possible for a powerful global financier or government minister to make a prediction of some market change, and by doing so precipitate, (perhaps unwittingly), the fulfilment of the prediction. When the financier happens to be as shrewd as George Soros, himself a student of the writings of Karl Popper, the effects are almost uncanny.

In the early 1970s, he forecast a boom and bust for real estate investment trusts which turned out exactly as predicted. In August 1998, he wrote a well-meaning and well-publicized newspaper letter suggesting that the best solution to the Russian financial crisis would be a modest devaluation of the rouble. Almost immediately, the deputy governor of the Russian central bank imposed some restrictions on the convertibility of the rouble, and the Russian stock market fell 15%. Within a week, the rouble was effectively devalued by up to 35%.

With decades of rewarding experience as a hedge fund manager in detecting and playing markets far from equilibrium, Soros has pointed out how unstable markets become because of reflexive decisions. On a fundamental level, the pricing of stocks is meant to reflect just their future earnings, dividends and asset values. However, the stock price itself affects the performance of a corporation in numerous ways, e.g. through executive stock options, which in turn can influence the stock price. This type of nonlinear interaction may send a stock price soaring above any notion of equilibrium. The dynamic instability of financial markets is reflected in the frequency of stock market plunges of 5% or more, which are indicative of self-reinforcing price movements. Soros has identified eight stages of a stock boom–bust sequence:[17]

[1]   The initial stage when the trend is not recognized.
[2]   A period of acceleration, when the trend is recognized.
[3]   A period of testing when prices suffer a setback.
[4]   Far-from equilibrium conditions become firmly established.
[5]   Reality can no longer sustain the exaggerated expectations.
[6]   People continue to play the game although not believing it.
[7]   Tipping point when the trend turns downwards.
[8]   Catastrophic downward acceleration: the crash.

These progressive stages of a boom and bust are imprinted on the schematic plot in Fig. 6.1 of the asymmetric rise, twilight, and fall of a stock price.

Price

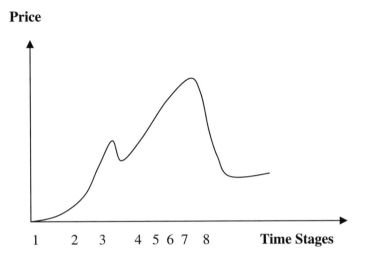

1   2   3   4 5 6 7 8   **Time Stages**

Figure 6.1. Soros schematic boom–bust model of a stock price, showing periods of upwards and then downwards acceleration.

This same sequence can be discerned in international banking crises. Joseph Stiglitz has observed that bubbles need to be recognized as a social as well as economic phenomenon. The herding instinct of traders is strong, and the cycle of affirmation is positive. Accordingly, the history of investment provides a tutorial in social psychology, with bitter lessons drawn internationally from 17th century Dutch tulip mania to 21st century American subprime mortgage mania.

The US provision of 'ninja' (no income, no job or assets) loans would have caused astonishment in Denmark, which has an enviably stable mortgage system, in which loans are prudently covered by the issuance of bonds, which are retained on the issuing bank's balance during the whole lifetime of the loan. Catastrophe risk analysts would note that the robust Danish mortgage system emerged like the phoenix from the ashes of the mediaeval part of Copenhagen, which burned down in a great fire in 1795. Arguably, this phoenix has saved Denmark from later financial catastrophes. The fire in 1795 was a lesser fire than that of 1728 which was the largest fire disaster in Copenhagen's history, and shared similarities with the more widely known 1666 Great Fire of London, in spreading rapidly through narrow mediaeval streets.

6.2.2 Financial market bubbles

Christopher Wren's architectural Monument to the Great Fire of London carries a Latin inscription commemorating the catastrophe. An engraving from 1722 by the satirical artist, William Hogarth, depicts an allegorical crowd scene around the Monument in 1720. The inscription on the base is altered to read, 'This monument was erected in memory of the destruction of the city by the South Sea in 1720.' This was the year of the first great stock market crash in England, which ended a frantic period of speculation, known as the South Sea Bubble. This might have been a footnote in English school history textbooks except for the lessons it continues to teach on international stock market dynamics.

In 1711, the South Sea company had a monopoly on all South Sea trade, including anticipated trade with the prosperous South American Spanish colonies. The short-term prospects were poor when Britain and Spain went to war in 1718, but the medium-term prospects were hyped as being extremely bright, and this fuelled unbridled speculation by a credulous investment community in England and elsewhere. When the bubble burst as the summer of 1720 faded, the avaricious who had borrowed money to speculate, or only part-paid their shares, found themselves closer to bankruptcy than to riches.

The particular circumstances of the South Sea Bubble may have been particular to 18th century colonial Europe, but dreams of riches on the horizon entice investors in every age. During the dot.com boom of the late 1990s, the revolutionary transformational nature of internet technology lulled investors into a belief, self-reinforced by an internet stock buying frenzy all over the world, that this would be no bubble. Yet the underlying principles of bubble dynamics are universal.

Consider a new wonder stock which promises to have fantastic growth potential, but the company issuing the stock is not yet profitable, and pays no dividends. Denote the discount rate by r. Suppose that the anticipated dividend growth rate of the stock, adjusted downwards for the perceived risk, is d. Let the difference $r - d$ be denoted by b for bubble. When b is negative, holding money might seem to be a sad waste of financial opportunity. Indeed, b is like a negative interest rate, advantage of which might be taken by borrowing all or part of the money to buy the stock, and selling later at a generous and effortless, although not riskless, profit. The negative b regime is associated with herd market sentiment that the upwards rise in stock price has far to go, and that the rapid expansion of the company equates with rosy prospects of future dividend growth.

Speculative phases may last a while, but may be halted by rises in the discount rate. This happened in the Wall Street Crash of 1929, when it was raised from 3.25% to 6%. Such rises may bring b closer to the critical crash point of zero. The tendency for traders to act cooperatively, copying, buying, and selling as others in the market, is timeless human nature, documented by J.K. Galbraith for the Great Crash,[18] and in the 1980s by Wall Street dealers.[19] To a socio-physicist, it suggests a system analogy with critical phenomena in physics. An advantage of looking to the physical world for analogies is that an abstract idea, such as an investment bubble, can have some tangible physical realization.

One of the most intriguing and beautiful fundamental concepts in physics, originated by Jeffrey Goldstone, is that of a system mode, or oscillation, which tends to restore a spontaneously broken symmetry. This is the kind of general knowledge, for its own sake, that economists might be glad to have, even if it lacked the relevance to market trading that Sornette has suggested.[20] He has likened a stock market bubble to a Goldstone mode. He argues that fluctuations of the bubble price restore the independence of the stock price with respect to dividend. Whatever the depth of explanation, the practical lesson for investors is to beware of a company whose share price spontaneously gains value without earnings support. An irony of this analogy is that Goldstone himself would sooner have given money to an impecunious graduate teaching assistant, as the author once was, than speculate with it.

6.3 Ancillary Hazards

The devastation wrought by Hurricane Katrina in 2005 brought to public attention and urged upon civic authorities the necessity for diligence in analyzing, and vigilance in watching, ancillary hazards associated with direct perils. When an earthquake, hurricane, or other hazard event strikes, the main focus is on the direct impact of ground shaking, wind speed etc.. But in addition to direct action, there is also the possibility of loss arising indirectly due to an ancillary hazard event, triggered by the primary hazard event. Such secondary loss can severely exacerbate the primary event loss in both human and financial cost.

An ancillary hazard event may be another natural hazard contingency emanating directly from the primary event, such as a landslide or tsunami. An ancillary hazard event may also be the outcome of a man-made failure, such as inundation, pollution, explosion, or power blackout following primary hazard damage to an industrial facility. Where the facility is a nuclear plant, fears of a catastrophic core meltdown arise when there is a loss of reactor coolant. With modern reliability engineering, this is a rare occurrence, but it happened on 11 March 2011 at the Fukushima plant in Japan, after an unprecedented M9.0 earthquake and massive tsunami had disabled the cooling water supply system.

Situated below sea level, and surrounded by water, New Orleans has long been recognized to be vulnerable to flooding. Hurricane Betsy caused flooding in New Orleans in 1965, and as recently as 1998, when Hurricane Georges skirted the city, gales pushed the water of Lake Pontchartrain over the man-made sea wall and onto roads and yards that face the lake. Prior to the landfall of Hurricane Katrina, meteorologists at the National Hurricane Center did brief FEMA on the potential incipient threat of levee over-topping. But meteorologists are not experts in civil engineering and the reliability of flood defence systems. The levee breaches and the subsequent overwhelming scale of the resultant flooding induced by Hurricane Katrina surprised the civic authorities.

Civil protection decisions may be fraught, even with the best engineering advice. A massive vapour cloud explosion at an oil depot at Buncefield, southern England, on 11 December 2005, astonished even experienced safety engineers. The hazard mechanism was unfamiliar: oil overtopping a fuel storage tank gathered at the base, and led to the formation of a large explosive vapour cloud.[21] As unfamiliar and surprising would have been overtopping caused by earthquake ground shaking. This particular unusual industrial disaster scenario lends purpose to identifying, categorizing, and analyzing potential ancillary hazards associated with natural perils.

The impact of a natural hazard on any human construction is liable to have some external consequences. In a strong windstorm, debris from even a modest residential home may become flying missiles endangering the safety of local people and property. As shown by Hurricane Katrina, the external consequences of a levee failure can be catastrophic. New Orleans is far from unique in its vulnerability to levee failure, induced by a natural peril. In California, building development in the Sacramento–San Joaquin delta, where flood control efforts first started in the mid-1800s, is exposed to an environmental threat recognizable to that faced by New Orleans. The Sacramento–San Joaquin delta receives runoff from more than 40% of California. Much of the land is below sea level and relies on more than a thousand miles of levees for protection against flooding. It is the main source of water for more millions of Californians. A major earthquake could breach the delta's levee system, and so cause significant regional inundation.

Earthquakes pose a threat to dams as well. There have been a number of instances of the failure of small dams in earthquakes, and there have been some very narrow escapes from flood disaster. In the M6.7 San Fernando, California, earthquake of 1971, the Lower San Fernando dam, built more than half a century earlier to inferior seismic safety standards, suffered severe damage and forced the evacuation of homes in an area six miles long. The dam was very close to failure. Had the reservoir been at its maximum height, water would have overtopped and eroded the dam, and flooded the valley.

6.3.1 Tipping points

A key attribute of ancillary hazards is nonlinearity in the loss potential developing with the size of the initiating event. The fragility of buildings is typically a convex function of hazard intensity: beyond the specification of building codes, considerable damage may be anticipated. This implies that if there are two similar properties where hazard intensities of X and Y are experienced, doubling the damage at the mean hazard intensity of $(X+Y)/2$ could well seriously underestimate the combined loss from both properties.

When considering a large number of properties, the dynamic analysis of complex systems is needed. The overall system loss may increase gradually with the size of the primary event until some tipping point is reached, whereafter the system loss escalates rapidly. For the spread of fire, which is a contagion process, once a critical number of fire outbreaks are attained, the resources of the fire services become insufficient for gaining control, and the fire will spread rapidly.

The tipping point for system loss may have both a physical and a behavioural origin. In the case of ancillary flood risk, the physical tipping point will occur when the initiating hazard event is sufficiently severe as to rupture a levee or dam. The corresponding behavioural tipping point would arise from the evacuation of the affected area, with the environmental consequences of unattended homes that may be dowsed with floodwater, deteriorated by mould and pollution, or ransacked by vandals.

In the case of the ancillary risk of toxic release from a chemical plant, the physical tipping point will occur when the initiating hazard event is sufficiently severe as to rupture a process unit, and generate a toxic cloud. The corresponding behavioural tipping point would arise from the safety evacuation of the affected downwind area. In July 1987, a powerful Canadian tornado narrowly missed the largest chemical plant in Edmonton, Alberta, as well as a power station. Even with this good fortune, 27 died and 300 were injured. A direct strike on the chemical plant could have significantly amplified the loss. Over the past few decades, improvements in engineering design against external hazards have been made, but whatever the design level of an installation, the possibility exists of a hazard event yet more severe. Design for the worst possible hazard circumstances is not feasible, because of the fractal power-law characteristics inherent in natural hazard severity scales.

Apart from freak waves and earthquakes, explosion and fire on an offshore oil installation can trigger a major disaster. On 6 July 1988, the Piper Alpha platform in the North Sea was destroyed in an explosion and fire which killed 167 men. On 20 March 2001, offshore Brazil, several explosions struck Petrobras 36, the largest floating semi-submersible oil platform in the world, causing the loss of 11 lives. A similar number of fatalities occurred on 20 April 2010, when an explosion occurred on the

Gulf of Mexico semi-submersible rig, Deepwater Horizon. Fed by months of continuous oil leakage, expanding oil slicks polluted the Gulf coast, causing the worst US environmental catastrophe.

6.3.2 Randomness and order

The concept of order as a dynamical parameter was introduced by the Russian Nobel laureate Lev Landau to describe the physics of phase transitions. The properties of a system may alter considerably with a change in its state or phase. A domestic example is the solidification of water into ice: a phase transition from a fluid with disordered water molecules to an ordered crystalline phase, where the molecules are packed within a lattice. Another familiar example involves magnetism. Below a critical temperature, local magnetic polarizations of atoms are aligned in an ordered way, giving rise to collective magnetization. By comparison, the higher temperature phase is a disordered phase.[22] This phenomenon can characterize a diverse range of abrupt socio-economic system changes, such as the transient 9% 'flash crash' in the Dow Jones Index, which was triggered by a sudden rush of market sell orders on 6 May 2010, sparked by a single massive sale of stock index futures.[23]

Physicists gain valuable insight into the cooperative behaviour of atoms through simple didactic models amenable to mathematical solution. A classic prototype is the so-called *Ising* model, which is the simplest model of interacting degrees of freedom.[24] The state of an element in an Ising model has one of just two alternative polarization values: either up or down. Due to neighbour interactions, clusters of similarly aligned polarizations can form. The success of the Ising model in statistical mechanics has encouraged its broad application to the general study of systems in which individual elements, which might be atoms, biological membranes, humans etc., modify their behaviour so as to conform to the behaviour of others in their vicinity.

A generalization of the binary state Ising model allows for a larger vector of alternative states, beyond the smallest number of two. This *Potts* model is sometimes also called the clock model, because the alternative vector states may be arrayed as directions around a clock face.

In its physical representation of self-organized critical phenomena, the Potts model has been applied to a wide range of practical socio-physics problems, such as the formation of coalitions, the development of ghettos, and the structure of complex social networks.[25]   It can also be applied to losses from a natural peril event at a grid of geographic locations. At each site location, the loss can take one of a discrete range of possible values, which may be represented as a vector orientation, as illustrated in Fig. 6.2.

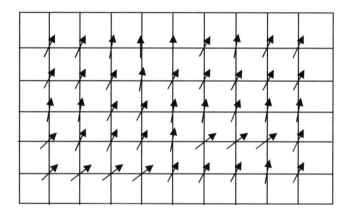

Figure 6.2. Potts model 2-D grid showing loss vector states at each site oriented as on a clock face. North corresponds to zero loss; South to total loss.

System energy is raised by contrasting loss between neighbours. Potts dynamics encourage the alignment of loss at neighbouring sites. As a result, clusters of different scales may develop within which losses are well aligned. Consider a group of N properties exposed to a hazard scenario. At the k th property location, let the standard deviation of the loss be denoted by σ_k. The loss correlation matrix is written as ρ_{ij}.

The aggregate loss standard deviation can be expressed as a weighted mixture of two terms, corresponding to loss being completely correlated and completely uncorrelated:

$$\sigma^2_{Total} = \sum_{i,j} \sigma_i \sigma_j \rho_{ij} \quad \text{where} \quad \sum_i \sigma_i^2 \le \sum_{i,j} \sigma_i \sigma_j \rho_{ij} \le \left(\sum_i \sigma_i\right)^2$$

Denoting the aggregate loss standard deviation correlation weight factor by w, which is typically set around the modest figure of 0.2 for ordinary hazard events:

$$\sigma_{Total} = w \sum_i \sigma_i + (1-w) \sqrt{\sum_i \sigma_i^2}$$

In a major hazard event, consideration of physical and behavioural neighbour loss interaction suggests that the group of properties will fragment spatially into a disjoint set of spatial domains, within each of which loss is highly correlated. A basic measure of the property loss caused by a hazard event is the number of properties falling within its spatial footprint. These properties will tend to group in clusters, which are the spatial domains corresponding to the fragmentation above. A statistical method for analyzing the loss potential considers the expected number $N(K)$ of clusters of size K.[26]

A power-law rule for the cluster size distribution is generated by the Potts model, and is suggested by various considerations drawn from the physical, environmental, and behavioural sciences, socio-physics, complex dynamic systems analysis, the intensity footprints of environmental hazards, as well as geographical studies of urban building density. The expected number of clusters of size K is assumed to be proportional to some power V of K, i.e. $N(K) \propto K^{-V}$. The cluster index V will generally be governed by a key local ancillary event.

For N similar properties having σ as the individual loss standard deviation, a clustering factor $C(N)$ is defined as:

$$C(N) = (\sigma_{Total} / \sigma) / N$$

For a cluster index V of 2, which corresponds to weak clustering, $C(N) \rightarrow 1/\sqrt{Ln(N)}$ for large N. This diminishes slowly but remains above the baseline of 0.2 for ordinary hazard events, even when N is huge, and is 0.3 for 100,000 properties. However, for a cluster index V of 1, which corresponds to strong clustering, $C(N)$ tends at large N to $\sqrt{(1/2)} = 0.707$, which amounts to significantly high correlation.

Chapter 7

Terrorism

If you are turning to Milestones
for light reading or amusement, stop here.
Sayyid Qutb,
Milestones

For natural perils, hazard calculation may be technically and computationally demanding, but modellers can take comfort from Einstein's dictum, 'Nature may be subtle, but is not malicious.' Terrorists, on the other hand, are notoriously both subtle and malicious. Apart from managing insurance, the need to quantify terrorism risk arises because finite resources are allocated to deal with hazards of all kinds, man-made as well as natural. To what extent is it worth protecting urban infrastructure against terrorism as well as earthquakes and floods?

Obviously, a different approach to terrorism risk modelling is required to the traditional reductionist approach used for modelling the world of engineering physics: the human dimension has to be incorporated. Calculating terrorism risk encompasses analysis of the terrorist threat, tradecraft, choice of weapon mode, targeting, and loss estimation. Any quantitative model has to be based on conceptual understanding of the underlying behavioural processes, without the bias of value judgements about political militants. This sentiment is well expressed in a quote from the Dutch philosopher, Baruch Spinoza, cited by Gilles Kepel in his exposition of the roots of radical Islam: 'In order to preserve in political science the freedom of spirit to which we have become accustomed in mathematics, I have been careful not to ridicule human behaviour, neither to deplore nor to condemn, but to understand.'[1]

With natural perils, an understanding of the underlying principles governing these phenomena is essential if modelling is to progress beyond statistical data analysis. Historical disaster catalogues are a valuable resource for flood hazard assessment, but this should be guided by basic hydrological principles, which find elegant mathematical expression in optimality criteria originated in 1744 by the French savant, Pierre de Maupertuis: 'The great principle is that, in producing its effects, Nature always acts according to the simplest paths.'

It is not just Nature that follows the path of least resistance. Avoiding strength, and attacking weakness is a fundamental precept for asymmetric warfare, expounded by the master strategist Sun Tzu in the *Art of War*, 'Now an army may be likened to water, for just as flowing water avoids the heights and hastens to the lowlands, so an army avoids strength and strikes weakness.'[2]

The notion that the principle of least resistance may guide the probability distribution of certain human actions originated in sociology, and may be considered in the context of attack mode preferences. One of the main signposts on the path of least resistance is adaptive learning. As with warfare in general, terrorists are eager to learn from past experience the successes and failures of attacks perpetrated by their own network, and by other terrorists around the world. During the decade of Jihad against the Soviet invaders, the Afghan mujahideen perpetrated not a single suicide attack. But learning the use of human vehicle bombs and suicide jackets from the Iraq War, there were as many as 136 in 2006, causing more than a thousand casualties.[3] Terrorists tend to copycat methods, such as martyrdom missions, that either have proven to be successful, or are perceived to have promise.

The basic arsenal for terrorists contains a range of conventional weapons: improvised explosive and incendiary devices, and standard military weapons such as automatic rifles, rocket-propelled grenades, mortars, and surface-to-air missiles. Sticking with off-the-shelf or tried-and-tested weapons might seem to be the easiest strategy, but further variety in attack modes is needed to evade counter-terrorism action. From this necessity emerges the invention of unconventional attack modes: sabotage, aviation hijacking and bombing, and use of chemical, biological, radiological, and nuclear (CBRN) weapons. Although terrorists aspire to use weapons of maximum force, the principle of least resistance is inculcated in the preaching of Abu Hamza,[4] inspirational imam of the notorious Finsbury Park mosque in North London, 'You can't do it by a nuclear weapon, you have to do it by the kitchen knife.' A British MP bears the stab wounds from a kitchen knife assault by a young intelligent Muslim woman, avenging his vote for the Iraq War.

For practical terrorist innovation, there is concern over computer crime. In cyberspace, a Trojan horse is an apparently innocent piece of code containing hidden instructions for the unauthorized collection, exploitation, falsification, or destruction of data. Given the linkage between cyber and physical security, security forces need to be watchful for a coordinated virtual and physical Trojan horse attack. This might bring down a computer control and security system at a target site, followed by an actual destructive physical attack.

A hallmark of Al Qaeda operations is having multiple synchronous points of attack. High multiplicity moves Al Qaeda towards its objective of inflicting maximal loss, and success is still claimable even if some of the synchronous attacks fail, as happened on 9/11. Furthermore, multiple benefits can be gained from a specific surprise attack mode; defence against such a mode would be hardened afterwards, as with aircraft impact. As the multiplicity increases, so more targets need to be surveilled, more funding and attack weaponry procured, and more terrorists engaged in planning and preparation. Progressively, the chance increases of the whole plot being compromised by a security lapse. At some point, it would be foolhardy to expand the attack size; instead it would be best to rein back ambition, and stick with the existing multiplicity. The dilemma faced by a terrorist organization in increasing attack multiplicity is analogous with other types of criminal activity, such as poaching and burglary. Operational research analysis defines when it is optimal to stop, rather than continue and risk existing gains.[5]

Nobody can predict the precise timing of the next major terrorist attack. Randomness plays a significant part in any human conflict. Going to war is a choice for unpredictability; as Otto von Bismarck remarked, 'When you draw the sword, you roll the dice'. Furthermore, as astutely noted by Thucydides in the 5th century BC, the longer a war lasts, the more things tend to depend on accidents.

But, as with natural hazards, there are causal non-random factors in man-made hazards as well. These shape the conflict landscape, and influence the temporal pattern of successful attacks. In constructing a stochastic model of the recurrence of terrorist attacks over time, these non-random factors need to be taken into account through an appropriate conceptual paradigm: cybernetics. Magnus Ranstorp has referred to Al Qaeda operatives as parasites on globalization. In common with other prey–predator situations, the conflict between the forces of terrorism and counter-terrorism may be represented using the principles of cybernetics.

In a democracy, there are rigorous checks and balances imposed on the law enforcement and security services. As director-general of MI5 faced with the IRA terrorist threat, Stella Rimington observed that it is a feature of a democracy that a security service will follow a new security threat, rather than foreseeing it. The British neuroscientist and mathematician, Ross Ashby, was one of the earliest thinkers about self-organizing systems,[6] such as terrorist organizations typically are. Highly relevant to counter-terrorism is Ashby's Law of Requisite Variety: 'If a defender's move is unvarying, then the variety in outcomes will be as large as the variety in the attacker's moves; only variety in the defender's moves can force down variety in the outcomes.'

With variety in counter-terrorism moves, terrorism can be controlled. However, in democracies, counter-terrorism action must remain commensurate with the threat, whether high or low. Each successful attack is met with a counter-terrorism response suppressing the threat of future attacks, albeit infringing some civil liberties. But the subsequent restoration of these liberties and a relaxation of security during a tranquil period may create opportunity for a resurgence in terrorist activity.

Michael Chertoff, a leading US judge as well as resilient Secretary of Homeland Security, has drawn special attention to the inextricable nexus between terrorism and organized crime. Terrorists are, at the same time, both warriors and criminals; a complex legal duality which Chertoff has likened to the wave-particle duality of the laws of quantum mechanics.

A democracy with a legal system adaptive and flexible enough to allow terrorist attacks to be anticipated well is the French Republic. The counter-terrorism environment in France, effectively developed by magistrate Jean-Louis Bruguière, has been particularly hostile for the formation of conspiracies. Comparing the Jihadi threat against France as against the UK or the USA, he would have approved constructive French diplomacy in the Middle East, but not appreciated Hollywood recreation of the French contribution to the crusades. Described by a Cambridge historian as Osama bin Laden's view of history, Ridley Scott's epic 2005 film, *The Kingdom of Heaven*, featured a French crusader leader as hero. Crusaders voyaging to the Holy Land are assured, 'To kill an infidel is not murder, it is the path to heaven.' Despite such incitement, it is not the crusaders who prevail; rather victory goes to Saladin. For Osama bin Laden and his deputy, Ayman al Zawahiri, the mediaeval crusades were never over. Indeed, Zawahiri chose the evocative title *Knights under the Prophet's Banner* for his post-9/11 book exhorting terrorism.[7]

Al Qaeda is a steadfast, determined, and patient adversary, prepared, indeed planning, to play the long game. The Palestinian journalist, Abdel Bari Atwan has warned, 'The West should never underestimate the intellectual prowess or scope of the Al Qaeda leadership, which is extremely learned, well-read and informed.'[8] When asked why he lost his World Chess champion's crown in 1961, the Russian Grandmaster, Mikhail Tal, remarked ruefully that he had underestimated his opponent's will to win. The Soviets underestimated the Afghan Mujahideen, who instructed their children in the obligation of the Jihad. What little mathematics young children learned included calculating the travel time for a bullet to strike a Russian forehead.[9]

7.1 A Thinking Man's Game

It is said of counter-terrorism campaigns that the most successful have been those where the terrorists have been *out-thought* rather than out-fought. Despite being heavily out-manned and out-gunned, terrorists are still capable of deftly out-manoeuvring the military and police resources of nation states. They are able to achieve success through meticulous operational planning, and adopting a thoughtful rational strategy, involving a measure of surprise to compensate for the lack of power. Surprise is a double-edged weapon. Of course, it improves the chance of success of an attack. But, as Clausewitz remarked, it also confuses the enemy and lowers his morale, and furthermore, it invigorates the forces effecting the surprise. After 9/11, Abu Al-Qurashi, one of Osama bin Laden's lieutenants, delighted in boasting that Al Qaeda had entered the annals of successful surprise attacks. In some military situations, tactical surprise can achieve an impact greater than a 2000:1 force ratio.[10]

Terrorists can maximize the surprise they can cause by randomizing alternative attack strategies, rather than having one specific strategy. From a terrorist's perspective, randomization has the benefits of countering efforts at interdiction by intelligence agents, and of throwing security services off balance. Counter-terrorist forces should not, therefore, be surprised by late changes in attack plan. The process of randomization need not be deliberate, such as rolling dice or seeking an augury of divine guidance; it may happen fortuitously through striking a target of opportunity that presents itself at the right place at the right time, or serendipitously through searching online, or watching a video that may suggest an alternative attack mode.

Terrorists have to be intelligent in order to make an impact in asymmetric warfare. Dr George Habash, co-founder of the Popular Front for the Liberation of Palestine, was known as *Al Hakim*, in recognition of his status as a medical doctor and conscience of Palestine. Of terrorism, he contemplated, 'This is a thinking man's game. Especially when one is as poor as the Popular Front is. It would be silly for us to even think of waging a regular war. We will continue our present strategy. It's a smart one, you see.'[11] It may be argued that the most powerful biological weapon in the terrorist's arsenal is not any lethal virus or poison, but the human brain itself.

In applying game theory, the mathematical theory of conflict, to terrorism, it is important to recall the formal mathematical definition of rational behaviour: actions are taken in accordance with a specific preference relation. There is no requirement that a terrorist's preference relation should involve economic advantage or financial gain. Much of the purpose of terrorism is psychological: inspiring the global Jihad; whipping up populist *schadenfreude* at seeing a great political power suffering loss; and terrorizing the general public. Nor is it necessary that a terrorist's preference relation conform to those of society at large. Game theory is not restricted to any one cultural or religious perspective.

But is it rational for a terrorist to undertake a suicide mission? Yes, according to the 17th century French philosopher, Blaise Pascal. Given the promise of eternal paradise after a martyr's death, and a non-zero likelihood of this promise being actually realized, it is perfectly rational for a terrorist to take Pascal's wager, and bet on this outcome of a martyrdom mission. It is known that some terrorists have followed this line of philosophical thought. In the words of one Palestinian, 'If you want to compare it to the life of paradise, you will find that all of this life is like a small moment. You know, in mathematics, any number compared with infinity is zero.'[12]

Baitullah Mehsud, who formed the Pakistan Taliban, believed that suicide bombers were a force that could not be defeated: 'They are my atom bombs.' Oblivious of Pascal, his teenage boys clamoured to be first to accept Pascal's wager. Their submersion in and submission to the Koran at the expense of other learning earned them certainty of the bountiful rewards of pressing the martyr's button on their suicide jackets. Nobody on Earth might persuade them that their probability of being greeted by beautiful girls in paradise was not very close to unity. Yet no Bayesian could assign zero to this probability, since no amount of supportive evidence could then yield a non-zero posterior probability. Never to believe in anything absolutely is a principle known by decision analysts as Cromwell's rule, in reference also to an ecclesiastical debate.[13] As an exercise in probability theory, this shows that the distinction between subjective and objective probability is not purely academic – it can be a matter of life and death.

The test of any mathematical risk model is its explanatory and predictive capability. Game theory predicts that, as prime targets are hardened, rational terrorists may substitute lesser softer targets. This prediction is essentially equivalent to the statement made by the CIA director, George Tenet, in his prophetic unclassified testimony of February 7, 2001, seven months prior to 9/11, 'As security is increased around government and military facilities, terrorists are seeking out softer targets that provide opportunities for mass casualties.' Explicit admission of this target strategy came later from Khalid Sheikh Mohammed, the Al Qaeda chief of military operations, in his interrogation following arrest in Pakistan.

Rationality pervades the operational modus operandi of terrorists. A classic terrorist attack mode is the vehicle bomb, referred to as the poor man's airforce.[14] The terror of the Japanese kamikaze pilot is replicated by the martyr with an explosive payload several orders of magnitude greater than a suicide vest.

The car bomb was introduced as a weapon of urban warfare in 1947, when the Stern Gang drove an explosive-laden truck into a British police station in Haifa, Palestine. The ammonium nitrate-fuel oil (ANFO) car bomb was later favoured by the IRA for its cheapness of construction and devastating power. A bomb explosion is fundamentally a chemical reaction generating transient air pressure waves. The maximum degree of decompression of the air at a blast wave front is measured by the peak overpressure. For an explosive charge mass W, at a distance R from the explosion, the peak overpressure is conveniently expressed in terms of the scaling distance parameter $R / W^{1/3}$. Modellers of blast loads in dense urban areas use computational fluid dynamics computer programs. These solve the Navier–Stokes equations of fluid flow, subject to boundary conditions at the ground and the surfaces of solid objects.

Narrow city streets funnel blast waves, which are reflected and refracted by buildings. Depending on the geometry of the urban landscape, blast pressures may damage buildings beyond the usual safe distances. At even further distances, falling building debris may injure people in the streets. Hazardous as remote bomb damage may be, building collapse is the civil protection nightmare scenario.

In the 10 April 1992 IRA vehicle bomb attack on the Chamber of Shipping in St Mary Axe, London, built in 1967, a number of columns were severed.[15] The load borne by these columns was not redistributed to adjacent columns, and the storeys above became deformed, and extensive collapse resulted. Gravity is a powerful force multiplier for a terrorist thinking to maximize loss. The collapse under gravity of the twin towers on 9/11 scaled up horrifically the initial impact in all measures of loss. As with aircraft hijacking, so also with other spectacular attack modes, the cunning use of force multipliers is capable of leveraging enormous economic losses for an initial modest outlay in terrorist resources. In asymmetric warfare, the intelligent exploitation of technological leverage is a potent equalizer of capability.

7.1.1 Targeting

The fundamental concept underlying terrorist targeting is that of substitution, and is an essential feature of any terrorism risk model. If two targets are equally attractive, terrorists will tend to target the less secure. Target substitution is a phenomenon very familiar to criminologists, and operates on all spatial scales: from individual to street, to city, to national level. At an individual level, the assassination of Theo van Gogh in November 2004 was a classic example: a knife in the film-maker's chest affixed a letter addressed to the source of the terrorist's fury, Ayaan Hirsi Ali, the self-styled infidel subject of his film. At the street level, the Bali cafés bombed on October 2005 had been chosen for their inferior security. At the national level, the IRA switched a truck bomb attack from London to Manchester, when the border security around the City of London was tightened. In the skies, Israeli security around their national airline El Al is so tight, that hijackers have turned their attention to American and European carriers.

The urban concentration of financial, economic, and political power in a major city makes for an attractive target. Key to the understanding of the Jihadi movement is the *Umma*, which is the global brotherhood of Muslims. Dr Ayman Al Zawahiri noted that the Umma is won over when Al Qaeda chooses a target that it favours. Cities with international name recognition thus come to the fore, as affirmed by postcard cities attacked within a few years of 9/11: Bali, Mombasa, Casablanca, Riyadh, Istanbul, Amman, Madrid, and London.

Unlike natural perils, the free mobility of terrorists means that there is no fixed geography for terrorism hazard. There is an earthquake engineering adage that an earthquake will expose the weakest link in a building. But if a number of structures are randomly distributed in a region, the pattern of seismicity does not alter so that the weakest structure is most likely to be shaken. Yet, with a terrorist threat to a number of prize targets, the most vulnerable may have the highest probability of being attacked.

In November 2003, Islamist terrorists struck a major city with high name recognition: Istanbul. The local US embassy was too hard a target to hit; it had been relocated out of the city for security reasons. Instead, terrorists struck the much softer target of the British consulate, where a desire to foster closer community links precluded such tightening of security. The lesson of Istanbul was learned fast. Concrete blocks were rapidly installed outside the British embassy in Sofia, Bulgaria. With a terrorist threat to a number of prize targets, the most vulnerable generally have the highest probability of being attacked. As with the installation of burglar alarms, self-protection carries the externality of shifting criminal attention to neighbours.

The dependence of target location on vulnerability introduces a nonlinear feedback in risk computation, which would tend to escalate the loss potential. This feedback may be recognized using game theory. Another knowledge domain important for terrorist targeting is urban geography. The social scientist, Manuel Castells, developed the idea of a new spatial logic for understanding inter-city relations.[16] In this logic, which terrorists exploit, cities are a process for network connection.

Consider the potential targets in a country, and suppose that they have been ranked in discrete city tiers (capitals, provincial towns etc.) and type classes (government offices, infrastructure etc.) according to the terrorist spatial logic. Symbolic and publicity value, name recognition in the Middle East, and economic and human loss consequence would be factors in gauging target utility. In order to express target prioritization in a quantitative way, the discrete ranking by city and target type has to be converted into continuous form. This interpolation is achieved by invoking Fechner's Law, which states that an arithmetic progression in perceptions requires a geometrical progression in their stimuli. This yields a parsimonious, simple, and economically sensible logarithmic formula for the utility of the city tier C, and for type class T.[17]

In order to arrive at a target likelihood distribution, a mathematical expression needs to be obtained for the functional dependence of target likelihood on utility. For this, game theory is required. It is known that Al Qaeda is committed to achieving success, is watchful that missions are cost-effective, and is sensitive to target hardening. In order to ensure, as far as possible, that a strike will be successful, irrespective of defensive action by security forces, Al Qaeda will effectively seek to minimize the impact of target hardening. From knowledge of its modus operandi, this goal is attained by Al Qaeda by adopting a mixed strategy of randomizing its target selection, meticulously undertaking surveillance on targets and avoiding targets where the level of security is very uncertain, whilst switching targets if the original target has hardened. This might happen if police departments operate extra random security patrols, as conducted by NYPD in New York.

For a mixed attack strategy, designed so as not to be impaired by changes in defence strategy, game theory optimization analysis yields a power-law for the dependence of attack relative likelihood on the city tier C, and on type class T. Thus a capital city might be a hundred times as likely a target as a small provincial town, and a foreign consulate might be ten times as likely a target as a small convention centre. The power-law formula encapsulates the key aspects of target likelihood: the terrorist threat is concentrated in major cities and focused on strategic economic and political targets. The threat gradient varies from country to country according to its degree of decentralization. But it is never so flat as to suggest that martyrdom missions against low value targets would be worthwhile, simply to terrorize people who might not consider themselves targets. As the Taliban military code of conduct dictates, 'Suicide attacks should be at high value and important targets because a brave son of Islam should not be used for low value and useless targets.' Targeting the latter would relieve pressure on the former, and violate the strategic principle of force concentration.

7.2 Defeating Terrorist Networks

Following the 10 metre tsunami that laid waste to Japanese towns on 11 March 2011, a tweet recorded the frustration of a small boy, 'Why can't the earthquake be arrested?' It is a key distinction from natural hazards that perpetrators of man-made hazards can be brought to justice.

The Renaissance political theorist, Nicolò Machiavelli, noted that conspiracies have to be kept small if they are to elude the attention of the authorities. The larger a conspiracy is, the greater the chance that it will fail haphazardly due to a tip-off from an inside informant or an observant member of the public, through indiscretion or betrayal by one of the conspirators, or the investigative diligence and detective skill of law enforcement authorities. After a hotel bomb explosion in October 1984 narrowly failed to kill the British Prime Minister, Margaret Thatcher, the IRA taunted the British authorities, 'We only have to be lucky once, you will have to be lucky always.' The individual responsible for the bombing, Pat Magee, was arrested shortly afterwards, but the comparatively small size of the IRA attack cell precluded the prior leakage of information to the British intelligence services. The larger the size of a conspiracy is, the likelier that the authorities will be 'lucky' in foiling it. Indeed, 80% of IRA plots were foiled, blunting the destructive force and political influence of the Irish republican terrorist campaign.

As the most notorious example of a plot that escaped prior detection, the 9/11 Al Qaeda operation was almost uncovered when Zacharias Moussaoui was taken into FBI custody on 16 August 2001. According to George Tenet, CIA learned a week later via the French security service, DST, that Moussaoui had Chechen terrorist links.[18]

All conspiracies organize to maintain operational secrecy as far as possible. The internal organizational structure can vary from top-down to bottom-up, with some plots being directed from a centralized leadership, and others being inspired by the central leadership, but emanating from more decentralized planning. Regardless of the internal structure of a terrorist cell, the key to its dismantling is the same as for storming a fortress, namely managing to find an entry point into the cell network. Once one member has been identified, then close surveillance of his movements and communications can unravel the network and ultimately expose most if not all of the other cell members. Thus, even though a Jihadi terrorist cell may be internally organized to minimize the potential for the leakage of plot information, a plot nevertheless can be compromised if a single entry point can be found into the cell network. Any cell member may inadvertently provide an entry point into the plot network through a link outside the network.

A small radicalized minority of Muslims are supportive of the Jihad. Within the ranks of radicalized Muslims are the extremists who would be prepared to have some secondary or peripheral involvement with a plot, to assist the hard-core men of violence. Abdullah Azzam, the mentor of Osama bin Laden, defined a pyramidal segmentation of the radicalized Muslim community as follows, 'A small group: they are the ones who carry convictions for this religion. An even smaller group are the ones who flee from this worldly life in order to act upon these convictions. And an even smaller group from this elite group are the ones who sacrifice their souls and their blood.'[19]

Recruitment of a Jihadi terrorist cell would draw upon the latter two categories. Apart from contacts within the cell, each terrorist cell operative will have some links with the broader radicalized community, presuming they would not assist substantively with any terrorism probe. Such links may be with an extended family, Jihadi forums and websites relating to their designated function within the cell, Islamist societies, Muslim organizations, and mosques.

However, an external link can be dangerous in various ways. A cell member may come into contact with someone who happens to be an informant or intelligence agent, or is under surveillance by the intelligence services. This contact can arise via a personal meeting or phone or electronic communication. Alternatively, the dangerous contact can arise through a virtual online meeting in a Jihadi forum. Intelligence agent postings may be outspoken in their advocacy of violence, and have been effective as honey pots in luring potential terrorists, and preventing nascent plots from developing into actual attacks.

7.2.1 Plot interdiction

Of all the ways in which resources might be allocated for combating terrorism, efforts to thwart nascent plots merit special priority. The arrest of terrorist suspects can prevent loss irrespective of the designated targeting. By contrast, resources focused on protecting a class of important buildings or infrastructure may just shift an attack elsewhere.

Paul Wilkinson, doyen of the academic study of terrorism, has likened fighting terrorism to being a goalkeeper: 'You can make a hundred brilliant saves but the only shot that people remember is the one that gets past you.'[20] The efforts of the intelligence and law enforcement services to interdict plots are crucial for mitigating terrorism risk. Indeed, such risk mitigation is akin to the protection afforded by flood defences: MI5 protects London from terrorism as the Thames Barrier does against flooding from storm surges. But where security is compromised by collusion or corruption, terrorists can prepare an attack with little fear of plot disruption. As pointed out by Magnus Ranstorp, an erstwhile colleague of Wilkinson, 'Once a terrorist moves towards his target, half the battle is already lost.'[21]

A high interdiction rate depends not so much on lucky tip-offs but on effective meticulous surveillance by the intelligence and security agencies. Each suspect is at the centre of a spiderweb of contacts, who have their contacts to be tracked electronically etc.. By building up concentric circles of information, connecting each suspect to others, intelligence agencies can piece together a conspiracy, without needing the intrusive authority to mine information on entire civilian populations, which would jeopardize fundamental civil liberties.

Social networks are very different from physical networks. Take three points on the Earth: A, B, and C. Then the distance between A and C is less than or equal to the sum of the distances between A and B, and between B and C. This need not be so for people in social networks. A may be close to B, and B to C, but A may not at all be close to person C.

In the analysis of social networks, an important concept is the small world phenomenon.[22] This is the experience of meeting a stranger and discovering a mutual acquaintance. In fact, any two people are connected by a surprisingly small chain of connections. It was the social psychologist, Stanley Milgram, who first demonstrated that this inter-connectivity was a general quantifiable feature.[23] Milgram's legacy for the understanding of terrorism includes also his obedience experiments which have had a revelatory effect on our perception of human evil.

The small worlds notion was popularized in John Guare's play *Six Degrees of Separation*, from which the following lines are taken: 'Six degrees of separation between us and everybody else on this planet. I find that (a) tremendously comforting that we're so close, and (b) like Chinese water torture that we're so close, because you have to find the right six people to make the connection.'[24]

For conspirators, (b) is the more relevant sentiment. Valdis Krebs, an expert in business networks, has been prominent in developing social network analysis as a mathematical method for connecting the intelligence dots. His analysis of the 9/11 terrorist network is particularly illuminating.   Two suspected terrorists linked to Al Qaeda, Nawaf Al-Hazmi and Khalid Al-Midhar, were covertly photographed attending a meeting in Malaysia in January 2000.   Krebs showed that all 19 of the 9/11 hijackers were within two degrees of separation of these two suspects known to the CIA in early 2000.   Indeed, had the Electronic System for Travel Authorization (ESTA) existed then, this data source would have identified links between 15 of the 19 hijackers.

Such is the extent of the social network of radicalized supporters of the Jihad within two degrees of separation of terrorist suspects, that any new conspiracy against the homelands of the western alliance has a significant chance of being uncovered through a dangerous link. Terrorist plots may be hatched through unregulated anger, hatred, and malevolence, but ultimately, more than human malevolent behaviour, terrorism is regulated by the laws of social networks, which are universal in applying as much to terrorists as anyone else: even terrorists have an extended family, friends, acquaintances, and virtual online connections. Indeed, Muslim community support, in person and online, is an essential step on the path towards radicalization.   Intelligence gathering of the contact details of links between members of supportive social networks is central to the identification of potential conspirators.

The larger and more ambitious the conspiracy, the greater is the chance that at least one conspirator will be uncloaked, and the plot disrupted.   The interdiction probability for a cell plot may be calculated by a computer simulation process which considers a large number of possible alternative external link configurations for the individual cell operatives.   For each configuration, the total number of distinct external cell links to known extremists, radicalized supporters of the Jihad, and informants is enumerated, and the interdiction probability is calculated as the complement of the likelihood that no cell link is dangerous.[25] Fig. 7.1 illustrates a schematic configuration of noteworthy community links outwards from a five-person terrorist cell.

Whilst small two-man plots have only an even chance of interdiction, spectacular attacks involving more than half a dozen operatives, have a high interdiction rate in excess of 80%. A key parameter modulating this chance is the ratio of the size of the counter-terrorism surveillance force to the size of the population under surveillance.

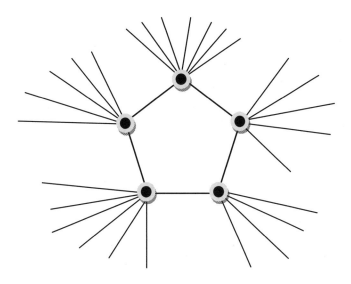

Figure 7.1. External community links emanating from a five-person terrorist cell.

Contract killings by individual professional hit men are crimes that are seldom solved.[26] Similarly, a plot by a lone terrorist would only have a comparatively modest chance of being interdicted. The human loss that an individual assassin can cause is nevertheless of tragic dimensions, as exemplified by Major Nidal Hasan's shooting rampage at Fort Hood, Texas, on 5 November 2009.

7.3 Counter-Radicalization

For the terrorist threat to be lowered in democracies unwilling to descend towards a police state, heightened surveillance is not the answer. There has to be a reduction in the sub-population who consider terrorism to be justified. A year after the 2005 London transport bombings, at Islam Expo, a major Muslim congress in London, the assertion by British MP, George Galloway, that, 'Israel, UK, and USA are the axis of evil' was greeted with rapturous applause by a British Muslim audience largely sympathetic with the Jihad, and disaffected with British foreign policy.

Psychology has been an art of war for millennia. In July 2005, Al Qaeda's chief strategist, Ayman Al Zawahiri, wrote as follows to Musab Al Zarqawi, 'I say to you: that we are in a battle, and that more than half of this battle is taking place in the battlefield of the media. And that we are in a media battle in a race for the hearts and minds of our Umma.'[27] Al Qaeda has been very adroit at using strategic persuasion to sell its extremist narrative to the Umma, and has committed substantial resources to its propaganda machine.

'Using strategic persuasion to sell your ideas' is the subtitle of a book, *The Art of Woo (Winning Others Over)*, written by two Wharton Business School professors, Richard Shell and Mario Moussa.[28] They mainly use business and political case studies as illustrations of principle. But as a critical paradigm, they highlight a classic military case study involving Napoleon as a young artillery officer at the siege of the southern French port of Toulon. On establishing an artillery battery in an extremely dangerous exposed position, he encouraged soldiers to man it voluntarily, not through coercion, but by proudly posting a large placard next to the cannons: 'The Battery of the Men Without Fear'.

Napoleon knew how to persuade his men to volunteer for suicidal missions. And so does Al Qaeda. From the forced viewing of shocking horror videos recording atrocities committed against their Muslim brethren to the preparation of heroic martyrdom videos, the process of radicalization and indoctrination of Jihadis is a diligent exercise in the social psychology of winning others over, involving these four key steps:

[1]   *Survey Your Situation*, including understanding social networks.
[2]   *Confront the Barriers*: poor credibility, communication mismatches, contrary belief systems, and conflicting interests.
[3]   *Make Your Pitch*, by presenting solid evidence and arguments.
[4]   *Secure Your Commitments*, at both the individual and organizational level.

The paramount importance of social psychology in understanding population behaviour has motivated the development of the quantitative discipline called socio-physics, rooted in the statistical mechanics of systems with many degrees of freedom, like crowds and swarms. The intelligent behaviour of a foraging swarm of bees or ants is a fascinating emergent consequence of self-organization.[29]   Even without central direction, simple rules of individual action and neighbour interaction enable an insect swarm to conduct an optimal search for food. Similarly, 'a group of guys' can self-organize and plan a terrorist conspiracy.

Socio-physicists have studied voting patterns, the rise and fall of societies, the madness of crowds, and the spread of rumours and fads. Thomas Schelling, the Economics Nobel laureate, was a pioneer of socio-physics in devising an elegantly simple model of the formation of ghettos, which develop spontaneously from basic individual preferences.

No socio-physicist would be brazen enough to believe in the prediction of any type of social behaviour; the value of quantitative analysis lies in understanding better the basic elements of mass behaviour, such as radicalization, and its sensitivity to strategic persuasion. The need for a statistical approach is evident from the element of individual randomness as to who becomes radicalized, and who does not: terrorists cannot be stereotyped. Alas for the authorities, it is not possible to tell amongst siblings who might become radicalized. Of three Muslim brothers born in Algeria and settled in London, it was the most secular and worldly brother who eventually became radicalized and involved in a major UK terrorist plot.[30]

A social characteristic of mass movements of political violence is a shared sense of common political purpose and direction, and a group feeling of 'coolness' which is attractive to new recruits who become drawn to the fad. Uli Edel's 2008 film, *The Baader Meinhof Complex*, about the Red Army Faction's reign of terror in Germany, vividly captured the anti-establishment mood of German youth in the 1970s. Social contagion in youthful behaviour can even extend to suicide. This is the *Werther effect*, after Goethe's novel, *The Sorrows of Young Werther*, which led to readers emulating the hero in taking their own lives, and the book being banned.[31]

Analytical work on social fads builds upon the work of the sociologist, Mark Granovetter.[32] A simple model can describe the incipient development of mass violence, such as a riot or terrorist campaign, where each individual's decision on joining depends on what all others are doing. For each individual, there is assumed to be a critical number of others involved in the violence before he or she is prepared to join. A probability distribution would describe the variation of this critical threshold number within the susceptible population. But even some specific elementary cases are instructive and insightful.

First, suppose that there is a uniform distribution of thresholds from 0 to 99 among 100 people. So one person has a threshold of zero, another has a threshold of one, and so on. Then the early adopters of the political violence fad are followed by the later adopters and then by the really late adopters until all sign up. This domino theory outcome turns out to be unstable, and very sensitive to perturbations of the threshold distribution. Just a slight increase in the critical number for the person with a low threshold of one would halt the fad right at the very start – just a lone maverick would cause trouble.

This illustration demonstrates how volatile the social dynamics of a group can be, and how effective strategic persuasion might be in curtailing recruitment through winning the hearts and minds of those who otherwise might be persuaded to follow a path of political violence. Collateral deaths of civilians in attacking terrorists are ultimately counter-productive. This is classical 1950s counterinsurgency wisdom, espoused by David Kilcullen, Australian military expert on guerilla war, and advisor to General Petraeus on counterinsurgency.

To understand Jihadi thought profoundly, one has to follow a line of enquiry of the philosopher Bertrand Russell: 'I wonder what it feels like to think that.' Kilcullen has admitted that if he were a Muslim, he would probably be a Jihadi for the sense of adventure, and being part of a big movement of history.[33] In order to avoid strategic surprise, one has to think how a terrorist might think he could cause surprise. This requires an appreciation of the terrorist's religious, cultural, historical, and political background. The psychologist, Simon Baron-Cohen, has coined the word *mindblindness* as a state of being blind to the thoughts, beliefs, knowledge, desires, and intentions of others.[34] Surprise may always happen; but those who misunderstand, or are insensitive to the terrorist mindset make themselves much more vulnerable to surprise. The less well that we understand Islamist militants, the easier it is for them to surprise, confuse, divide, and terrorize us. For as long as they understand us better than we understand them, the war on terror can have no end.

Chapter 8

Forecasting

*We have been absolutely unable
to hear a word from Galveston
since 4pm yesterday.*
G.L. Vaughan,
Manager, Weston Union, Houston
Telegram to: US Weather Bureau

Anyone who has witnessed an illusionist astound an audience with amazing feats of extrasensory perception (ESP) will have a sense of how difficult it can be to design suitable statistical tests for forecasting. As both a mathematician and magician, Persi Diaconis berated poorly designed and inappropriately analyzed ESP experiments as a greater obstacle than cheating. As a mathematician, he would know about the former; and as a magician, he ought to know about the latter. The conditions under which ESP tests are carried out often seem designed to obfuscate statistical analysis, and ploys by wizards may pass unnoticed by those untrained in the magician's craft, except for reading *Harry Potter*. With such obstacles to validating predictive or precognitive powers, one should be profoundly sceptical. But, as Diaconis has remarked, sceptics can be mistaken, citing President Thomas Jefferson and his refusal to countenance the fall of meteorites from the sky.[1]

As with the galactic sources of meteorites, the terrestrial sources of earthquakes are not easily accessible; but this has not prevented doomsday predictions being foisted on the public. There was Henry Minturn, whose forecast of a large Los Angeles earthquake in December 1976 was as bogus as his Ph.D.; Iben Browning, a biologist, whose maladroit prediction of an earthquake in New Madrid in December 1990 may have precipitated his own demise from heart attack; and Brian Brady, a physicist in the US Bureau of Mines, who falsely predicted a giant Magnitude 9 earthquake off Peru in 1981, comparable to the 1960 Chile earthquake. The prospect of future large Los Angeles, New Madrid, and Peruvian earthquakes is beyond argument – it is the timing that is so poorly constrained.

An earthquake prediction specifies the location, size, and time of an event within a compact parameter window. Less than a year before the great M8.8 Chile earthquake of 27 February 2010,[2] a seismological paper was published identifying its correct location in the Constitución seismic gap, (which was accumulating significant stress), and estimating a large Magnitude of 8.0 to 8.5. But the timing could only be very vague: not within a year, or five years, or even a decade, but in 'the coming decades'.[3] The last great earthquake in this gap had occurred in 1835, and was famously witnessed by Charles Darwin.

The inherent difficulties in making legitimate earthquake predictions can be appreciated from addressing dynamical instability. One approach, advocated by Liu *et al.*,[4] centred on an application of René Thom's mathematical theory of discontinuous phenomena, known universally as catastrophe theory.[5] This provides a geometric framework for dealing with singularities, where gradually changing forces produce sudden effects. To illustrate how catastrophe theory might be used in the present context, consider the elementary case of the collapse of a shallow arch under vertical loading applied at the centre. As the loading is increased, can one predict when the arch will collapse?

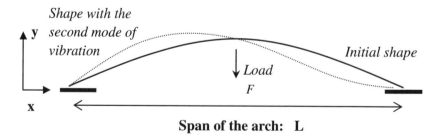

Figure 8.1. Diagram showing the initial shape and the altered shape including the second mode of vibration of the shallow arch. An increasing vertical load F is applied.

The profile of the arch $y(x)$ can be defined adequately by the leading two terms in a Fourier expansion: $y(x) = u \sin(\pi x / L) + v \sin(2\pi x / L)$, where L is the span of the arch. In the absence of loading, only the first term is present. Mathematically, the stability of the arch can be analyzed in terms of potential energy.[6] A constraint on the overall length of the arch allows u to be expressed in terms of the other Fourier coefficient v, and for the potential energy function to be written as follows:

$$V(v) = C_0 + C_2 v^2 + C_4 v^4$$

In this expression, the coefficient C_2 depends on the applied load F. The stable equilibrium position of the arch involves no second mode shape, i.e. $v = 0$. But there are two unstable equilibria with $v \neq 0$. As F is increased, these unstable situations occur with smaller and smaller absolute values of v, until a critical load is reached, when a collapse of the arch will be triggered by the tiniest perturbation. Within Thom's classification, this is described as a dual cusp catastrophe.

To embed the problem of earthquake prediction within catastrophe theory, Liu *et al.* consider the cumulative area of fault rupture in a seismic region as being a variable liable to sudden large change. As a function of time t, this variable is written as $S(t)$. Scaling arguments suggest the seismic energy release $E(t)$ is approximately proportional to $S(t)^{3/2}$.

This enables the cumulative area of fault rupture to be estimated from a compilation of seismological data on event size. Liu *et al.* posit further that, around the time origin, $S(t)$ can be represented by a finite Taylor series. They take as an example a quartic expansion:

$$S(t) \propto \sum E(t)^{2/3} = a_0 + a_1 t + a_2 t^2 + a_3 t^3 + a_4 t^4$$

The third-order term in this expansion can be easily removed by a simple change of variables, resulting in an equation of the form:

$$\sum E(t)^{2/3} = b_0 + b_1 t + b_2 t^2 + b_4 t^4$$

This algebraic expression exhibits a cusp catastrophe. Depending on the values of the coefficients of the quartic polynomial, an instability may exist which might be interpreted as indicating a heightened earthquake hazard. To this qualitative extent, catastrophe theory can provide a guide to the instability of dynamical systems governing earthquake generation, and cast a topological light on the inherent difficulty of earthquake prediction.

Unfortunately, the issues which have made practical applications of catastrophe theory contentious, arise here as well, and explain why, despite its alluring name, catastrophe theory has failed to figure prominently in the quantitative understanding of natural hazards. It provides a useful geometrical perspective on problems, such as the collapse of a shallow arch or the buckling of beams, where the dynamical energy equations are known. However, in order to apply the theory in a quantitative way to problems of poorer definition, assumptions need to be made about the functional form and parameterization of the relevant potential function, which may be beyond the resolution of empirical data or physical theory.

8.1 Earthquake Forecasting

Earthquake rupture is far more complex and subtle a dynamical process than the collapse of an arch, and its intrinsic predictability is one of the frontiers researched by the international *Collaboratory for the Study of Earthquake Predictability*. Tom Jordan has outlined a progressive 'brick-by-brick' approach, involving interdisciplinary investigations of active fault systems, and building upon system-specific models of stress transfer and earthquake triggering.[7]

The brasher 'silver-bullet' approach explores precursory signals that might be diagnostic of an impending fault rupture. These signals might include seismological, electromagnetic, hydrological, geochemical, and animal behaviour traits. From a Bayesian viewpoint, given the low prior probability of precursor existence, a substantial volume of evidence would be demanded to support claims. In this aspect, an analogy has been made between earthquake prediction research and the fruitless search for a fifth fundamental force of Nature beyond the gravitational, electromagnetic, weak, and strong nuclear forces.

Much of the acrimony over earthquake prediction has fallen back on the mathematical definition of prediction verification. Where the scientific argument for predictive power may appear tenuous or suspect, the focus of debate naturally turns to prediction verification through the sheer weight of empirical observation. This is not far removed from the 'lucky charm' principle: even if a method is not physically understood, as long as it works in practice, then some grain of truth could lie behind it, which sooner or later may become formally established.

Accordingly, for a forecasting methodology, scientists are interested in evaluating the relative hit rate to false alarm rate. A plot of this is called the *receiver operating diagram*, and is used in medical testing.[8] Indeed, there is a parallel with the testing of new drugs in the pharmaceutical industry. Experimental drugs may be found to be efficacious in practice, even though their biochemistry is poorly understood. Because of the difficulty in predicting the therapeutic power and side effects of new drugs, extremely rigorous multiple statistical trials are undertaken. For example, Phase II trials to test the efficacy of a treatment for a specific disease involve several hundred patients. A comparable level of rigour in earthquake forecasting would involve several hundred earthquakes. Unfortunately, being an observational rather than laboratory science, the accumulation of regional data on earthquakes takes generations.

Reviewing the history of earthquake prediction in China, Chen and Wang noted the conceptual analogy with traditional Chinese medicine: a degree of empirical success may make up for scientific ignorance of the underlying causal mechanisms.[9] But apart from the 1975 Haicheng earthquake, the empirical record of Chinese earthquake prediction is very much inferior to that of herbal remedies. Apart from other possible precursors, the Chinese have led the way in cataloguing accounts of anomalous behaviour of animals, ranging from reptiles and mammals to birds and insects. Such accounts were included in a study of nine major earthquakes in China, including the 1976 Tangshan calamity.[10] For the M7.9 Wenchuan earthquake on 12 May 2008, there was no forecast to save more than 80,000 lives, just some anecdotal reports of anomalies, such as changes in water wells and strange animal behaviour.

One of the first scientific studies to document animal behaviour before, during, and after an earthquake was reported by Grant *et al.*.[11] A population of reproductively active common toads was monitored over a period of 29 days, before, during, and after the M6.3 earthquake at L'Aquila, Italy, which occurred on 6 April 2009. Toads at the study site, 74 km distant from L'Aquila, showed a dramatic change in behaviour five days before the earthquake, abandoning spawning and not resuming normal behaviour until some days after the event. The zoologists cautioned, 'Whether toads would exhibit similar behaviour at other locations and preceding other large seismic events remains to be seen. Testing this hypothesis would, however, be very difficult, given the rarity and unpredictability of earthquakes.'

To establish whether anomalous toad behaviour is causally linked with an impending earthquake, scientific data would have to be gathered meticulously for numerous toad populations from many earthquakes. As it stands, a single observation looks no more than a mere coincidence. Diaconis and Mosteller have explored methods for studying coincidences, and have declared the Law of Truly Large Numbers.[12] This law states that, with a large enough sample, any outrageous thing is likely to happen. Prior to the earthquake, there must have been hundreds of thousands of creatures within 74 km from L'Aquila. According to the Law of Truly Large Numbers, surely some would have exhibited an amazing change of behaviour five days before the earthquake.

Belief in non-coincidence is shaken by unbridled zoological speculation as to what the explanation might be. Was the behaviour due to humidity; or a foreshock on 30 March? Was the behaviour due to ionospheric perturbations? Electromagnetic signals released by the crushing of rock crystalline structures might lead to changes in the ionosphere. Was the behaviour due to anomalies in levels of radon gas in groundwater? Radon may be released from cavities and cracks as the Earth's crust is strained prior to an earthquake. However, as with animals, the false positive rate is very high: many phenomena other than large earthquakes also result in radon emission, including rainfall and atmospheric pressure change. Radon anomalies were indeed observed by Giampaolo Giuliani, a local nuclear technician, who had been monitoring radon emissions. Like others who have assumed powers of earthquake prediction, he had scant seismological background.

For the first three months of 2009, small tremors were felt sporadically around L'Aquila. In itself, this is not at all an unusual occurrence in Italy. On 27 March, Giuliani sent a message to the mayor of L'Aquila, warning that there could be an earthquake within 24 hours. This was a false alarm: there were only small tremors. Giuliani then apparently detected a greater threat to the southeast, towards the city of Sulmona, 50 km from L'Aquila. This was again a false alarm, and led to an injunction being served on Giuliani on 30 March against sounding further alarms.

As it happened, this turned out to be just a week before a large earthquake did strike L'Aquila. From a scientific perspective, Giuliani's evidence was far too flimsy for practical earthquake forecasting. Radon at the surface is only an indirect measure of radon at seismogenic depths. Furthermore, to test scientifically the hypothesis of a link with radon emission, hundreds of detector devices would need to be deployed along a fault zone.

8.1.1 Stochastic triggering model of earthquake occurrence

Forecasting a major earthquake remains a rather distant and elusive seismological aspiration. A less ambitious but more realistic practical objective is to analyze past patterns of seismic activity to estimate the probability gain in the likelihood of a sizeable earthquake occurring in a specified space–time window. This is a tractable computational task because drawing inferences from the study of spatial clusters is a mathematical forecaster's trade. Indeed, a mathematician[13] has shown that burglaries in Los Angeles cluster rather like earthquake aftershocks. The practical importance of cluster analysis was demonstrated on 22 February 2011, when Christchurch, New Zealand, was severely damaged by a M6.3 event following the M7.1 mainshock on 4 September 2010.

Progress has been made in developing so-called stochastic triggering models, which represent the short-term clustering behaviour of seismicity resulting from dynamical fault interactions.[14] Because of some similarity between the spatial spread of disease epidemics and the characteristic clustering of aftershock sequences, such models are associated with the acronym ETAS: Epidemic-Type Aftershock Sequence. Any other earthquake forecasting approach, whether using alternative complex statistical pattern recognition methods, non-seismological instrumental measurements or observations, animal behaviour, or whatever, must demonstrate superiority over this basic ETAS method, if it is not to be dismissed outright as irrelevant in practical terms, if not also unfounded scientifically.

In an ETAS model, the expected occurrence rate density of earthquakes with Magnitude M at any time t and location (x, y) is designated as $\lambda(x, y, t, M)$. This is represented as the sum of two contributions. The first is the spontaneous background activity following the Gutenberg–Richter relation, with the long-term average seismicity rate density being denoted by $\mu_0(x, y)$. The second is a triggered contribution from every previous event.

$$\lambda(x, y, t, M) = f_r \times \mu_0(x, y) \times \beta e^{-\beta(M - M_0)} + \sum_{i=1}^{N} H(t - t_i) \times \lambda_i(x, y, t, M)$$

In the second term, the Heaviside function $H(t)$ steps from 0 to 1 when the argument t becomes positive. The second term in the summation is decomposed into three factors:

$$\lambda_i(x, y, t, M) = K \times h(t - t_i) \times \beta e^{-\beta(M_i - M_0)} \times f(x - x_i, y - y_i)$$

For time dependence, a form of Omori's aftershock law is adopted: $h(t) = (t + c)^{-p}$. For spatial dependence, $f(x, y)$ is taken to be a radially symmetric smoothing function decreasing rapidly with radius.

Console et al.[15] have estimated the probability gains in retrospective forecasting of Magnitude 5 events in Italy for the period 1990–2006. They found a high probability gain of 625 for the M5.8 event which occurred 9 hours after the first M5.6 Umbria–Marche shock on 26 September 1997. This is of special human interest because of the tragedy that occurred at the church of St Francis in Assisi. Four surveyors of damage from the initial main shock were killed in the further progressive damage caused by the second Magnitude 5 event.

Following the M6.3 l'Aquila earthquake on 6 April 2009, daily aftershock forecasts were made which specified the expected rate of Magnitude 4 or greater events in prescribed geographical cells of a 0.01° x 0.01° grid. These forecasts were able to describe well the spatial evolution of seismicity. This encouraged Marzocchi *et al.* to examine retrospectively the capability of the model at forecasting the main event.[16] Applying the model just prior to the main shock yielded a probability gain, for a regional Magnitude 5.5 event or larger, of 25 times the daily background value of 1/50,000. A 1/2000 daily chance of a moderately damaging earthquake is far below any practical threshold for a major public alert. Indeed, the excess fatality risk for a local resident might have been comparable with the background daily accidental death rate for an Italian of about one in a million.

Despite the general unpredictability of earthquakes, in June 2010, the L'Aquila Prosecutor's office went as far as to name scientists and civil protection officials as suspects in the inquiry into the deaths of three hundred people. But given the low probability gain from the data on movements of the ground, the Italian scientists had acted fully in accord with the code of ethics concerning earthquake predictions.[17]

The earthquake peril remains an unpredictable public threat for which advance warning of any kind has generally been avoided by seismologists for fear of causing the kind of mass panic that blackened the reputation of earthquake prediction in the second half of the 20th century. But the 21st century has brought change in the global risk environment. In a post 9/11 world inured to a pervasive enduring international terrorist threat, the incapability of authorities to predict a hazard event is not an excuse for inaction or silence. Short of evacuation, there are commensurate risk management steps which can be taken to reduce the loss in the event of an earthquake arising.[18]

Amongst these measures are increasing public awareness and preparedness of a possible earthquake. A tragic L'Aquila fatality statistic is the significant proportion asphyxiated by dust. The inclusion of face masks in an emergency kit might have saved some lives. Advising on keeping such an emergency kit at home is just one of the numerous precautionary measures that might be taken in future, if there were a modest probability gain.

8.1.2 *Tsunamis generated by earthquakes*

Compared with the pitfalls of earthquake forecasting, the task of forecasting a tsunami generated by an earthquake is altogether more tractable a problem. Yet lives continue to be lost to such tsunamis along many coastlines of the world. Risk mitigation is so much easier for politicians to prioritize if a hypothetical danger has become a reality. On 1 April 1946, a tsunami generated by a great Aleutian Islands earthquake struck Hawaii and killed 165 people. As a result, the Pacific Tsunami Warning Center was established in Hawaii in 1948.

Seismological detection of large earthquakes has long been the principal monitoring endeavour, but earthquake Magnitude alone is insufficient for reliable coastal tsunami forecasting, and local tide gauge data may be all too late. It took another tsunami tragedy, the devastating Indian Ocean tsunami of 26 December 2004, to carry away an era of globally deficient tsunami observation. Post-2004 expansion of ocean monitoring and computer modelling of tsunamis launched a new data-enhanced era of tsunami forecasting.

For US coastlines, real-time sea bottom water pressure measurements from Deep-ocean Assessment and Reporting of Tsunami (DART) buoys are combined with tsunami numerical modelling computer codes to generate real-time forecasts of tsunami arrival time, heights, periods, and inundation.[19] Sea surface deformation is estimated using an elastic deformation model, which links the tsunami source functions with the underlying earthquake fault parameters. Each tsunami source function is equivalent to sea floor motion from a large earthquake with specified fault parameters of length, width, slip, etc..

Given the limited high Magnitude range of safety concern, the set of global tsunami source functions covering the Pacific, Atlantic, and Indian Oceans, can be pre-computed to expedite rapid real-time tsunami forecasting. Time series of deep ocean tsunami observations can then be decomposed as a best-fit linear combination of a set of these tsunami source functions, which then form the core basis of a tsunami forecast.

Each forecast models regional, intermediate, and near-shore areas. For modelling of the transformation of a tsunami from the open ocean to coastal areas, and wave runup and inundation, there is a practical need for digital elevation models constructed from high quality bathymetry and topography survey data. The solution sensitivity of the nonlinear shallow water wave equations to imprecision in such data, and the influences of breakwaters and other complex harbour structures, erode the accuracy of the prediction of the runup at specific locations.

A major test of post-2004 tsunami forecasting was presented by the M8.8 Offshore Maule, Chile, earthquake of 27 February 2010, which caused a Pacific-wide tsunami alert for the first time since 1964. The Pacific Tsunami Warning Center (PTWC) forecast one metre wave heights in most places in Hawaii, with two or three metres in Hilo and Kahului. The forecast turned out to be conservative by a factor of 50% or more, which was well justified by the preference to err on the side of caution, and avoid a repetition of the tsunami death toll of 1946. PTWC geophysicists had to allow not only for parameter uncertainties and data limitations, but also the well known resonance potential for Hilo Bay to amplify tsunami waves. Japanese forecasts of tsunami waves up to three metres in Northern Japan turned out also to be excessively conservative.

An indication that the Chile earthquake tsunami might only have been moderate in energy came from NASA research on a GPS-based method for improving the reliability of tsunami warning systems. If a tsunami is generated by seafloor movement which happens to be close to a coastal network of GPS stations, then the tsunami energy may be inferred by calculations based off the station measurements.

8.2   Verification

Accuracy is the first word that comes to mind with a hazard forecast: one expects forecasts to correspond well with observations. Yet quality in a forecast is not just about being correct most of the time. This is because, for rare events, one can be correct almost all the time with a simple null forecast – never saying an event will happen. This is clearly sub-optimal for storms as lethal as tornadoes, even if there is considerable uncertainty identifying those convective storms that would produce tornadoes. At the start of the 21st century, only one in four US tornado forecasts was verified, which is a worse ratio than for other types of weather event.[20]

Calculating Catastrophe

The basic issues concerning forecast verification emerged in the 1880s, through the publication of a paper on an experimental tornado forecasting programme. This seminal paper was written in 1884 by Sergeant Finlay of the US Army Signal Corps, which at that time banned the explicit use of the emotive word *tornado* in forecasts, for fear of causing panic, rather like the E-word 'earthquake'. Finlay's paper purported to show very high accuracy levels exceeding 95% for his forecasts of the occurrence or non-occurrence of tornadoes.

Finlay's forecasts were made for a number of districts in the Central and Eastern US, during the months of spring. The results of his forecasting experiments may be aggregated in space and time and are shown in the 2x2 contingency Table 8.1. Out of a total sample size of 2,803 forecasts, the table indicates that a tornado was correctly forecast 28 times but incorrectly forecast 72 times. The table further shows that the absence of any tornado was correctly forecast 2,680 times, but incorrectly forecast 23 times.

Table 8.1. Finlay's pooled experimental tornado forecasting results.

	Tornado occurred	*Tornado did not occur*	*Marginal Frequencies*
Tornado Forecast	$n_{11} = 28$	$n_{12} = 72$	$n_{11} + n_{12} = 100$
No Tornado Forecast	$n_{21} = 23$	$n_{22} = 2680$	$n_{21} + n_{22} = 2703$
Marginal Event Frequencies	$n_{11} + n_{21}$ $= 51$	$n_{12} + n_{22}$ $= 2752$	$n_{11} + n_{12} + n_{21} + n_{22}$ $= 2803$

A naive measure of forecast success is the fraction of correct forecasts, namely: $(n_{11} + n_{22}) / (n_{11} + n_{12} + n_{21} + n_{22})$, which is 0.966. This high success ratio seems impressive until it is pointed out, as Gilbert did,[21] that adoption of a null forecasting strategy, i.e. predicting no tornadoes at all, leads to an even higher success ratio of $2752 / 2803 = 0.982$! Gilbert made the observation which seems to have escaped Finlay, that, given the rarity of tornadoes, forecasting the occurrence or non-occurrence of tornadoes are tasks of very unequal difficulty.

As one measure of forecasting capability, Gilbert suggested a ratio of verification, which is defined as: $v = n_{11} / (n_{11} + n_{12} + n_{21})$, which is the ratio of the joint frequency of tornado forecasts and observations to the total frequency of tornado forecasts *or* observations. For Finlay's data, the value of this verification ratio is 0.228. Gilbert himself admitted weaknesses of this measure, but at least it thwarts the null forecasting strategist, who would earn a null score.

A second measure proposed by Gilbert defined a ratio of success which took account of the fortuitous occurrence of tornadoes as forecast. Given that the number of tornadoes forecast is $N_F = n_{11} + n_{12}$, and that the relative frequency of tornado occurrences is

$$f_T = (n_{11} + n_{21}) / (n_{11} + n_{12} + n_{21} + n_{22})$$

the expected number of correct tornado forecasts is $N_F . f_T$. Allowing for this expected number of chance successes, Gilbert's ratio of success is:

$$[n_{11} - N_F . f_T] \ / \ [n_{11} + n_{12} + n_{21} - N_F . f_T]$$

Using Finlay's data, the expected number of correct tornado forecasts $N_F . f_T$ is 1.8, and the ratio of success has the value 0.216. Apart from Gilbert's suggestions, a variety of alternative measures of forecasting performance have been proposed for the analysis of elementary 2x2 contingency tables. For the general problem of larger dimension contingency tables, satisfactory solutions are hard to find.

The possibility that there may be fortuitous coincidences between forecast and observed events, makes it necessary to distinguish between absolute accuracy and relative accuracy in forecasting. In assessing the relative accuracy of a forecast, a judgement of the forecaster's *skill* is involved; skill being an apposite term introduced by Gilbert, which is key to the modern perspective on forecast verification.[22]

Null forecasting, of course, makes no demands whatsoever on meteorological skill, but the identification of the degree of skill in other forecasting methods is rarely as transparent. Skill is a relative concept, and may be defined as the accuracy of forecasts relative to the accuracy produced by some reference method. The complication arises from the variety of reference methods against which skill may be measured. At the bottom end are naive methods, which are based on rules-of-thumb and require no specialist hazard knowledge nor expertise in data analysis; at the upper end are elaborate artificial intelligence techniques which are capable of extracting a significant amount of information from the mining of historical data, without any formal need for specialist hazard knowledge or training.

In meteorology, a naive method might involve a persistence rule, according to which the weather would be forecast in a guileless way to be the same tomorrow as today. This is a sufficiently general approach that it may be usefully applied to forecasts of severe space weather as to terrestrial weather.

A more elaborate weather forecasting method might introduce some climatological principles. For hurricane track forecasts, a statistical reference climatology and persistence model, containing no information about the current state of the atmosphere, is CLIPER5, which is a five-day version of the original three-day CLIPER. For intensity forecasts, there is an analogous model DSHIFOR5. In seismology, the stochastic triggering model described above may be taken as a benchmark.

Another class of reference methods are those rooted in the historical record, whereby forecasts might assume a repetition of past documented hazard sequences, subject to some degree of dynamic perturbation. Finlay's empirical forecasting system, which was advanced for the time, identified meteorological conditions under which tornadoes had occurred in the past. Then there are stochastic reference models, which assume some specific temporal pattern for event occurrence: in the simplest case, a random Poisson time distribution. At the sophisticated end of the spectrum of reference methods are those resorting to neural network and pattern recognition techniques.

Absolute measures of quality can be defined to apply to a generic forecast. The most obvious measures of accuracy are the mean error or mean square error in comparing forecasts with observations. These do not relate to, or reward, forecasting skill. The fractional improvement in forecast accuracy over that of a reference method can be gauged by a skill score. If, for observational data $x = (x_1, x_2, ..., x_n)$, the ratio of the mean square error for the forecast method to that of the reference method is denoted as $R(x)$, then a skill score may be defined most economically as $1 - R(x)$. For a perfect forecast, the skill score is unity, but if the mean square error for the forecast method is the same as that of the reference method, the skill score is zero. If, ignominiously, the mean square error for the forecast method is actually greater than that of the reference method, then the skill score becomes negative. Apart from this fairly elementary skill score, other scoring rules can be defined from the correspondence between forecasts and observations, and these may serve as a basis for performance assessment.

Other than accuracy and skill, there are further attributes that are sought in gauging the quality of a hazard forecast. For example, where probabilistic forecasts are quoted, *sharpness* is desirable. A sharp forecast is one where probability assignments are close either to zero or unity. Sharpness is increased where high and low probabilities tend to be quoted more often. Where a probability distribution is assigned to a forecast parameter, a narrow peaked distribution is more informative than a broad one. Of course, sharpness of forecasting is of little avail if the forecasts are not well calibrated; there is no merit in being confident, if that confidence is misplaced. A forecast may be said to possess *reliability* if the mean observation, given a particular forecast, is close to the forecast itself. The twin qualities of informativeness and good calibration, which are regarded as desirable virtues in a hazard forecaster, are no less desirable in any expert exercising judgement.

For reasons of computational and statistical facility, forecast verification has traditionally centred on a small number of key aspects of forecasting performance, such as those few outlined above. But ideally, from a theoretical viewpoint, verification might encompass all statistical aspects of the forecasts and observations. Rather than use simple measures for forecast verification, a more complete approach uses distributions. Suppose that the set of forecast values is $f = (f_1, f_2, ..., f_m)$, and that the set of observed values is: $x = (x_1, x_2, ..., x_n)$. Expressed succinctly, forecasting verification consists of characterizing the joint distribution of forecasts and observations $p(f, x)$.

Meteorological forecasts can be made on different time scales. Venturing beyond real-time hurricane tracking, seasonal hurricane forecasts, based on the identification of key predictor variables, have been made with significant skill in early June and early August. But to attempt at forecasting hurricane activity beyond one season requires much more than statistical analysis of historical experience. It requires the use of dynamical computer models.

Taking account of forcing by observed sea surface temperatures, climate models are capable of simulating interannual variations in Atlantic tropical storm frequency. Using a decadal prediction system based on global climate modelling, Smith *et al.* have managed to demonstrate skill in predicting hurricane numbers on seasonal to multi-year timescales.[23]

8.3 River Flows and Sea Waves

Forecasting any natural hazard can be a precarious occupation. Yet, compared with their geological counterparts, flood forecasters are more skilful, being secure in knowing that the physical parameters which they can monitor, e.g. rainfall and water levels, are more immediately related to the incipient threat, than, for example, low level tremor activity is to an impending earthquake. The challenge of earthquake forecasting in Italy has been cited; river flood forecasting is easier, even if more rain falls in a single night than in a month. When this happened in Rome in December 2008, the mayor described it as being like an earthquake, except that the causal link between the rain and rising water levels in the River Tiber was abundantly clear to all.

Successful flood forecasts can be made which depend on links established between an observable upstream variable and a forecast downstream variable. These links may be forged from historical experience, or may be determined from a physical understanding of the underlying hydrological processes, including models of the response of a basin or river system.

In the latter respect, because hydrodynamics is a classical branch of applied mathematics, flood forecasting has a more mature mathematical basis than geological hazard forecasting. This capability is especially needed in anticipating dangers associated with large amplitude flood waves. Such a hazard may be produced by a catastrophic failure, such as a breach of a natural or man-made dam, as much as from precipitation runoff, and the downstream prediction of the extent and time of flooding is often a matter of extreme urgency.

The most accurate method for short-term forecasting is dynamic routing.[24] This requires the solution of the full one-dimensional partial differential equations for unsteady flow in an open channel, developed by the French mathematician Barré de Saint-Venant. There is a simple fluid continuity equation of mass conservation:

$$\frac{\partial Q}{\partial x} + B \frac{\partial H}{\partial t} = q$$

In this first equation, Q is the discharge; H is the water level; B is the channel width; and q is the lateral inflow, or outflow, per unit distance. Secondly, there is a fluid momentum balance equation. This is rather more complicated, involving a phenomenological resistance law, which relates the conveyance capacity of the channel to its cross-sectional shape and longitudinal bed slope. In terms of the discharge Q, a resistance factor (the so-called boundary friction slope), $S_f(Q)$, is defined, the quadratic form of which compounds the nonlinearity of the flow description. The other variables in the following momentum balance equation are v the lateral flow velocity in the x (channel) direction, A the cross-sectional area of the flow, and g the acceleration due to gravity:

$$\frac{\partial Q}{\partial t} + \frac{\partial(Q^2 / A)}{\partial x} + g A \frac{\partial H}{\partial x} + g A S_f(Q) - qv = 0$$

For operational streamflow forecasting, use may be made of simplified methods of routing, which adopt an approximate form of the nonlinear momentum equation, or may only use the continuity equation. Such simplifications are more successful when the flood wave can be regarded as a steady progressive flow.

Whichever routing method is selected, it is essential that all the uncertainties in forecasting are explicitly taken into account. This requires an uncertainty audit of the various sources of error and bias that can affect the reliability of a forecast, and an assessment of the way in which the individual sources of uncertainty propagate through to a forecast delivered to the public. Because the uncertainty in flood discharge, or the time to peak water surge, may increase downstream, the treatment of uncertainty is an acute issue in deciding on alternative grades of public flood alert. Forecasts should be provided at differing confidence levels, so that decision-makers are aware of the degree of uncertainty in a forecast.

For the River Tiber in Rome, which has a catchment area of 16,000 sq. km., Calvo *et al.* have developed a real-time flood forecasting model, which includes confidence intervals for forecast water surface elevations.[25] Flooding is a prominent natural hazard in modern Rome as it was in ancient times, and there were significant floods in 1976, 1984, and 2005, which have been simulated quite accurately through numerical modelling.

Clearly, the shorter the lead time for forecasting, the more accurate the forecast should be. A viable early warning system weighs the need for sufficient lead time in which to take action, against the increasing uncertainty of the forecast at long lead times. A practical solution, such as adopted in Germany, is to have several warning stages. Low accuracy forecasts are directed only at low local administrative levels; with increasing certainty that a critical flood level will be exceeded, senior officials are notified; and when a high degree of confidence is reached that a flood is imminent, a public warning is issued by a regional executive administrator.

A feature of this multi-stage warning approach is the systematic way in which scientists can relay to decision-makers technical information, which also conveys a sense of uncertainty. Visual observations of river water levels, steadily rising with heavy rainfall, can provide a clear indication of increasing risk of the overflow of river banks. Where saturated river defences are almost certain to fail, the only forecasting technology required may be a means for transmitting information on water levels; horseback was used during the Ming Dynasty in China.

Far less clear is the subsequent performance of modern engineered river flood barriers, such as dikes. In the Dutch flood of 1995, an alarming prognosis was made early on of flooding. A mass evacuation of 250,000 was decided upon fearing the breaching of saturated dikes. As it turned out, theoretical estimates of geotechnical dike instability proved conservative: the dikes fared better than expected. Uncertainty over the failure of an engineered dike is somewhat akin to the uncertainty over the failure of rock, which might lead to an earthquake. Signs of increasing seismic activity may be monitored, but the ultimate moment of catastrophic energy release may not necessarily arrive.

8.3.1 Sea waves generated by extreme storms

The Gulf of Mexico oil spill catastrophe of 2010 was a protracted public reminder of the risky environment in which offshore oil and gas production takes place. Not only are the logistics of undertaking a complex offshore engineering operation difficult, risk managers have to cope with natural hazards, notably the impact of severe sea waves.

The forecasting of wind-driven sea waves is analytically supported by numerical wave models integrating a transport equation with a wind forcing function.[26] The value of such forecasting is clear from the offshore damage wrought, both in the North Sea, which is exposed to European winter storms, and particularly in the Gulf of Mexico.

In September 2004, Hurricane Ivan tracked through the Gulf of Mexico as a Category 4 storm, with waves and winds which equaled or exceeded the 100-year design criteria of many offshore installations. Seven fixed platforms were destroyed, and five drilling rigs suffered major damage. A weather buoy close to one of these, the Ensco 64, measured 83 foot waves. Even larger waves were generated: the US Naval Research Laboratory ocean-floor pressure sensors detected a wave

91 foot high. A wave of this height or even higher is feared by mariners as a *rogue wave*. In February 1995, the cruise liner Queen Elizabeth II encountered a rogue wave of this height in the North Atlantic. Such encounters here may be as disastrous as they are brief: the MS München was sunk by a rogue wave in December 1978.

The modelling of rogue waves excites the interest of physicists as much as oceanographers, because they share some of the fascinating nonlinear characteristics of coherent solitary waves, called solitons.[27] The observation of rogue waves has been advanced by the use of Synthetic Aperture Radar (SAR) satellite data from the European Space Agency, which has created an atlas of rogue waves, identifying where they have appeared in the past.[28] As with earthquake forecasting, for which SAR data also hold some promise, this type of historical map is a step towards a prospective rogue wave forecast.

8.4 Accelerating Approach to Criticality

The eruption on 8 May 1902 of Mt. Pelée on the Caribbean island of Martinique stands as one of the most notorious in volcano history. The first sign of change at Mt. Pelée was detected in February with the strong smell of sulphur. From then until the eruption, a series of precursory eruption indicators were observed. On 2 April, steam emission was observed. On 23 April, light aftershocks were noticed. On 24 April, a plume of black smoke rose, and the following day, a blanket of ash fell. On 28 April, there were ground rumblings and the vapour column rose higher. On 2 May, there were copious mudflows. Loud noises, a large pillar of black smoke, and a blanket of ash spread across the northern part of Martinique. On 5 May, a crater lake burst. The associated torrent of water turned into a lahar entraining 50 ton blocks, which destroyed a sugar cane plant, killing 30 workers. On 7 May, the residents of St Pierre were startled by an enormous roaring. The next day, Mt. Pelée erupted, killing all but two of the 30,000 islanders.

This catastrophic obliteration of human life was still a tragic memory on Martinique during the volcanic crisis of 1929, when inhabitants were evacuated as a precaution against incineration by lethal pyroclastic flows.

At the end of October, reference to this volcanic crisis was made in an editorial note of consolation to US newspaper readers suffering financially from the 1929 Great Crash: 'To comfort yourself, if you lost, think of the people living near Mt. Pelée, ordered to abandon their homes.' Thinking of volcanoes, or other natural hazards, is sound advice for investors, who need to be as prepared for extreme events as those who live within the shadow of a volcano. At the time of the Great Crash of 1929, investors would have been prescient and prudent to have pondered the connection between the approach to a cataclysmic volcanic eruption and a stock market crash. Catastrophe modellers have sought such a conceptual link through analysis of critical phenomena.

The critical temperature of an iron magnet is analogous with that critical moment in a stock market when the actions of independent traders, which at other times are disordered and subject to a significant random variation, suddenly and dramatically become aligned. The balance between buyers and sellers is broken. The consequence may be a market crash, or liquidity crisis, as selling panic takes hold. Mechanisms explaining the alignment of the actions of traders are not hard to find. Professional market makers, who make their profits from the spread between bid and asked prices, insure against volatility by *delta hedging*: as the market moves, the delta hedger moves the same way – buying and selling according to whether the price is rising or falling. There is also the herd instinct of mutual fund managers whose performance is assessed, not on an absolute basis, but relative to their peers. In normal times, managers may be prepared to follow a separate path, but, in a crisis, individual managers are under job pressure to stay with the herd.

The analogy with critical phenomena in physics may be taken to a quantitative level by developing a mathematical model for market crashes. The collective result of the interactions between market traders is represented succinctly by a hazard rate $h(t)$, which is assumed to evolve according to the following simple power-law rule: $h' = C h^{\delta}$, where C is a constant, and the index δ is greater than 2. This constraint on δ reflects the effective number of interactions experienced by a trader, which is $\delta - 1$. For a meaningful theory, there should be at least one interaction per typical trader.

Integration yields: $h(t) = B / (t_c - t)^{1/(\delta-1)}$, where t_c is the most probable time of a market crash. Even if the latter parameter remains notoriously hard to pin down from statistical data analysis beforehand, (but inevitably simpler afterwards with hindsight), this formula does give a general mathematical sense of the acceleration towards a market crash. Outside the stock market, the housing market crash of 2008 is a 'subprime' example, where the relationship between US house prices and rents soared spectacularly before peaking and crashing.[29]

This very same type of analysis, appearing with different mathematical symbols, was earlier proposed by Voight *et al.* as a predictive model for volcanic eruptions.[30] The hope is that, by drawing an inverse rate plot of $1/h(t)$ against time, the extrapolated intercept may be interpreted in terms of the time to failure of the eruptive system. The term *hazard rate* is apposite in this context, since the variable $h(t)$ is an observable quantity, (e.g. rate of ground deformation, seismicity, or gas emission flux), which may be indicative of the time to eruption. For their inspiration source, Voight *et al.* reference the science of materials, from which the simple power-law rule represents a law of material failure.

A number of simple volcanological applications of the material failure equation have been attempted, with the aim of forecasting the time of occurrence of volcanic eruptions. There have been some rather modest successes. However, the correspondence between the hazard rate and events interior to the volcano may be very complex. This happens when the nonlinear dynamics of multi-phase flow play a significant role in eruptive behaviour, as demonstrated for the Soufrière Hills volcano on the Caribbean island of Montserrat. One of a number of other complicating factors is the network of sills within a volcano. As happened during the 2010 Eyjafjallajökull explosive eruptions in Iceland, magma intrusions may lead to eruptions not only when they reach the surface, but also when they reach magma in the roots of a volcano.[31]

Interesting to note, however, the evolution of water discharge in a pressurized subglacial channel during an Icelandic glacier burst *jökulhlaup* does exhibit the hyperbolic approach to criticality, as do outburst floods from glacier dammed lakes in general.[32] The dynamic feedback arises from the unstable growth of the pressurized channel, due to melting at the channel walls.

The universality of the principles of materials failure suggests one might additionally look for an application to the breakage of ice masses. From computational stress models of an ice mass breaking from a cliff, a hyperbolic relation between movement-rate and time might be expected to apply here also, and thus provide an estimate for the time to criticality for large ice masses to break off from steep alpine glaciers.[33]

This is far from an academic exercise. In 1819, a vast snow and ice avalanche emanating from a hanging glacier on the Weisshorn severely damaged the Swiss alpine village of Randa in Valais.[34] In 1972, the formation of a prominent crevasse on this glacier caused sufficient consternation for movement surveys to be undertaken. From the resulting data, the best fit for the movement rate was found to be a hyperbolic relation, the rate being proportional to: $1/(t_c - t)$. Using this model, a forecast was made of the date at which breakage would occur. An uncertainty band of ± 40 days was accorded to this forecast, which was well satisfied by the actual event, which occurred only 16 days adrift of the due date. In a later study for a hanging glacier in the Bernese Alps, another successful forecast was made of an icefall which was menacing tourist facilities. The error in this case was just three days, which was well within the uncertainty band of ± 6 days.

For the allied threat of a large rockfall, or *sturzstrom*, which is a giant landslide of shattered rock, Kilburn and Petley have shown that Voight's theory might have been able to forecast, almost a month in advance, the catastrophic collapse of Mt. Toc into the Vajont reservoir on 9 October 1963.[35] Engineers had hoped to control a potential massive landslide by altering the level of the reservoir. Instead, catastrophic failure occurred. During the filling of the reservoir, a vast block of about 270 million m^3 detached from one wall and slid into the lake generating a gigantic wave which overtopped the dam by about 250 m. In the most tragic of recorded European landslides, about 2,500 inhabitants were swept to their deaths in their obliterated Alpine villages. Their epitaph is a warning about catastrophic landslides in high Alpine regions of the world. Previous geological misinterpretation of some mountain landslides as glacial moraines suggests an underestimation of risk.[36]

8.5 Evidence-Based Diagnosis

The intrepid and outspoken volcanologist Haroun Tazieff drew a parallel between volcanology and medicine: 'Similarly to a medical doctor, a volcanologist has to give diagnoses deduced from a series of observations, measurements, and analyses. These diagnoses tell him what is happening in the patient's body.'[37] There is a human inclination to anthropomorphize volcanoes, so the notion of the volcano doctor is quite intuitive. This metaphor has also a quantitative expression in a procedure for updating diagnoses on the basis of evidence.

Evidence-based medicine involves the integration of research evidence with clinical expertise.[38] Consider a medical disorder for which a test has been devised. The *sensitivity* of the test reflects the proportion of patients with the disorder that have a positive result, out of the total number of patients with the disorder. The *specificity* of the test reflects the proportion of patients without the disorder that have a negative test result, out of the total number of patients that do not have the disorder. For a group of $A + B + C + D$ patients, test results are tabulated below:

Table 8.2. Generic diagnostic test results.

TEST RESULT	Disorder Present	Disorder Absent
Positive :	A	C
Negative:	B	D

The sensitivity is $A / (A + B)$ and the specificity is $D / (C + D)$. Suppose that a test result is positive. It is traditional in this context to use the terminology of *odds*: the ratio of the probability of an event to the probability of its negation under the same circumstances. The posterior odds that the patient has the disorder are given by the following formula:
Posterior odds = Prior odds $\times$ sensitivity $/ [1 - \text{specificity}]$.

As with most medical information, volcanological observations are indirect, and the detection of an impending eruption calls for a systematic evidence-based approach so that cognitive bias in hazard updating can be avoided. An active volcano which serves as an opportune laboratory for testing forecast technology is Galeras in Southwest Colombia. A very specific type of seismological observation linked with this South American volcano has a characteristic tapered seismogram trace visually resembling a screw (*tornillo* in Spanish).

Stanley Williams was amongst a party of volcanologists up in the crater on 14 January 1993, when an eruption occurred, inflicting horrific injuries on him and killing several colleagues. In his survival memoir, he wrote, 'Only after further eruptions in 1993 did we finally come to understand that small numbers of tornillos at Galeras – even as few as one or two per day – might presage an eruption.'[39] Since then, the sensitivity of tornillo recording as a diagnostic eruption test has proven to be high. However, there have been weeks of tornillo observations not associated with any culminating eruption, so the specificity of this diagnostic test has not been so good.

There is a tendency for the number of observed tornillos to increase with eruption size. However, the sensitivity of tornillo number as a diagnostic test for large eruptions is not ideal. Fifteen years after the crater tragedy, on 17 January 2008, a stronger sudden eruption occurred, presaged by only a handful of tornillos. Short-term eruption forecasting at Galeras is improved by incorporating other seismological precursory information, such as a tendency for the duration of the seismic signals to lengthen prior to an eruption.

More generally, eruption forecasting should be based on inferences from all available observational evidence: geochemical, geodetic, geological as well as geophysical. Such information is indirect, uncertain, vague and incomplete, but quantitative sense can be made of this sparse evidence provided that the causal relationship structure is maintained between the underlying dynamic variables and observables of the volcanic system. This may be achieved using a *Bayesian belief network* framework. This involves constructing an intuitive graphical model encoding probabilistic relationships amongst the variables in order to facilitate efficient inferences from the available observations.[40,41]

Apart from the detection of temporal clusters as a forecasting tool, diagnostic methods for spatial cluster detection exist which identify spatial sub-regions of some larger region where the occurrence count is higher than expected. In spatial event surveillance, a search is conducted for emerging patterns of occurrences in spatial sub-regions.

Spatial surveillance is needed to illuminate the panoply of hazards. For geological hazards, spatial analysis of clustering may shed early light on the physical origin of emergent dangerous phenomena. For infectious disease, the detection of emerging patterns of infectious disease through surveillance is a key feature of epidemiologic practice.[42]

In the 21st century, early detection of a hazard may be facilitated by online messaging and web searches. A US study of Google search queries on influenza revealed a high correlation with the percentage of influenza-related visits to a physician.[43] For a diverse range of perils, natural and man-made, the general population serves as a geographically dispersed self-organized dense social network of hazard sensors, linked by the internet. Through such spatially distributed network intelligence in hazard surveillance, citizens may become self-enlisted agents for combating emergence with emergence.

For analyzing less contagious but potentially more lethal infectious diseases than influenza, such as might be spread maliciously, Xia Jiang *et al.* have adopted the Bayesian belief network (BBN) approach,[44] which models the relationships between the events of interest, i.e. regional outbreaks of infectious disease, and the observable symptom status of the population. This is especially advantageous in detecting disease outbreaks, because observations are often indirect, being based on the symptoms of patients presenting at hospital emergency departments or doctor's surgeries, or purchasing particular medications, rather than on actual disease confirmation.

The Data entered into the BBN consists of the symptom status of all the individuals. Denote by $Data\,[i]$ the data obtained by the i th day of an outbreak. As the days pass, the accumulation of evidence may reach a threshold for health officials to declare an outbreak. The delay before notification of an outbreak is governed by $P(Outbreak \mid Data\,[i])$, which may be updated daily, using the BBN. A delay of some weeks may be prudent if there is a low tolerance of false alarms.

Chapter 9

Disaster Warning

No pen could describe it,
nor tongue express it, nor thought conceive it,
unless by one in the extremity of it.
Daniel Defoe,
The Storm

There is always risk associated with being on a maiden journey of any mode of public transportation. This is of course the Titanic syndrome. The first passenger to be killed on a railway was William Huskisson, on 15 September 1830, at the opening of the Liverpool and Manchester Railway. Stephenson's prize-winning *Rocket* locomotive was coming down the track. A warning was shouted. For all its capability of hauling a 20 ton load at 10 mph, *Rocket* had no brakes, and could only be stopped in an emergency with difficulty by putting the engine in reverse. Huskisson had been on the Duke of Wellington's train, which was halted, allowing passengers to stretch their legs. On hearing the warning, he panicked and stumbled across the line, where he was tragically run over by the *Rocket* locomotive. Huskisson's death may be a tragic footnote in transport history, but the saga of a runaway train lives on in moral philosophy as a classic dilemma of decision-making.

A runaway train is bearing down on five people, who will be crushed to death unless you find some means to change the train's course. You can choose to turn a switch that diverts the train onto another track, where a worker is carrying out repairs. If you do, the worker is likely to be killed, but five lives would be saved. What would you do? Consider the following variation of this moral dilemma. You are standing at a point overlooking the tracks, between the train and the five people. Near you stands a stranger; should he be pushed onto the track and struck by the train, the five people further down the track would be saved. What would you do in this case?

In the first formulation of the dilemma, 90% of people might be prepared, reluctantly, to divert the train. An aviation parallel can be drawn with the policy, adopted after 9/11, to shoot down a hijacked aircraft; the cold reckoning being that those on the aircraft are doomed anyway, and any casualties among street bystanders from falling debris should be far fewer than among those trapped in an impacted skyscraper.

By contrast, in the second formulation of the dilemma, 90% of people would balk at pushing a stranger into harm's way, even though more lives would be saved. The intentional killing of a particular individual is anathema to most people. The human decision-making process in coping with these two dilemmas was elucidated by Josh Greene *et al.*[1] in a brain functional Magnetic Resonance Imaging experiment: the contrasting decision response to the second dilemma is manifested by the activation of brain areas associated with social and emotional processing. Ironically, this seminal advance in neuroethics was published in the very same week as the World Trade Center and Pentagon attacks, masterminded by Khalid Sheikh Mohammed, known respectfully within Al Qaeda as *mukhtar*, which is Arabic for 'brain'. His terrorist brain was so inured to violence that the mass murder of thousands of strangers was perceived to be justified means to achieve political ends.

The prospect of impending catastrophe strains the nerves of any decision-maker. The difficulty of a decision is magnified by the uncertainty as to what may happen. Faced with a daunting decision under uncertainty, which is often considerable, decision support is clearly welcome. For a start, there is the guidance from ethics. A deontologist like the German philosopher Immanuel Kant would argue that one has an unconditional obligation to act morally: decisions are right or wrong, whatever the consequences. It is never right to put someone in harm's way just for the practical expedient of saving others. Other than out of patriotism, he would have disapproved of the deception played by British intelligence on the German *Luftwaffe* in 1944 to direct flying bombs away from the densely populated central areas of London to the less populated southern suburbs. By the same token, deontologists would not consider it right to save a city from flooding by diverting floodwater through a village, or save a town from incineration by diverting a lava flow through a villa.

Adopting deontological principles, a decision-maker should always act with caution in the presence of uncertainty, avoiding exposing people to danger. Risk analysts use the terminology of cautionary or precautionary principles. If a severe nuclear accident cannot be ruled out, and the safety of nuclear waste disposal remains in question, then a precautionary licensing attitude might be to suspend construction of nuclear installations. Indeed, adhering to these principles, many countries impose a moratorium on the development of nuclear power.

Where critical installations are constructed, the precautionary principle cedes ground to the more pragmatic ALARP principle, that risk should be 'As Low as Reasonably Practicable'. An example of a precautionary regulatory doctrine ceding to the ALARP principle is the no-fly zone around an erupting volcano. A pilot's nightmare is the complete loss of power of all four engines, which a British Airways Boeing 747 suffered in June 1982 when it penetrated an ash cloud 150 km from Galunggung volcano in Indonesia. 'The flying ashtray', as it was later dubbed, managed to regain power, after involuntarily breaking a gliding record.

Catastrophe analysts learn to appreciate the unfathomable depth of such dangerous predicaments. An even worse nightmare is the complete loss of power over high mountainous terrain, leaving only a few minutes to restart the engines. This happened on 15 December 1989, when a KLM Boeing 747 in Alaska flew into an ash cloud emanating from the Redoubt volcano.

The resulting international guidance for planes encountering volcanic ash was clearly precautionary: fly around ash clouds so jet engines have zero interaction with ash. This guidance tacitly assumes some viable alternative flight paths. This was not so for many European airports when the Iceland Eyjafjallajökull volcano erupted on 14 April 2010, producing a cloud of fine ash that covered much of Northwest European air space for a week. Grounding of planes for a few days was tolerable, but the accumulating economic losses and travel disruption became sufficiently staggering for a form of ALARP principle to be invoked.

Instead of a precautionary zero, a volcanic ash density tolerance level was agreed with engine and plane manufacturers, and was set by the UK Civil Aviation Authority. Although air space with a high ash concentration would still be a no-fly zone, this regulatory relaxation opened up apparently safe air corridors permitting a resumption of UK flights after five days. Accused of excess caution in adhering to the precautionary principle for so many days, the head of the Civil Aviation Authority retorted that he would never apologize for putting safety first.

A heavy moral burden rested on his shoulders in sanctioning the re-opening of UK air space, whilst the skies were still laden with some ash. This decision was made under significant uncertainty over the ash dispersion modelling, and the certification process for engines to operate safely in ash. There was also commercial pressure from the airlines and their stranded passengers to resume flying. Indeed, following further airspace closure, some airlines suggested that they should be left to decide on flying in a low density ash cloud on the balance between loss of passenger revenue and the cost of engine repairs.

Such utilitarianism was originally proposed by the English philosopher Jeremy Bentham and developed by John Stuart Mill, and later by eminent European social scientists, such as Vilfredo Pareto. It deems an action to be right if it yields the greatest net societal value. The mathematical expression of utilitarianism is the utility function, which embodies the relative importance to the decision-maker of a range of relevant factors that need to be traded off against each other.

Balancing economic, security, safety and other factors can be achieved within the framework of *Multi-Attribute Utility Theory*, whereby the decision-maker evaluates and takes into account the interests of all the various stakeholders, including corporations, the authorities, the general public, and environmental groups. An early application was to the siting of Mexico City airport, where the factors included cost, capacity, access time, safety, noise pollution, and social disruption. Such methods are capable of supporting risk informed decision-making in many diverse practical situations of civic importance, where the invidious comparison of apples with oranges is unavoidable.[2] In a catastrophe risk context, the decision reduces starkly to balancing the human benefits of personal safety against the economic costs of disruption.

9.1 Decision in the Balance

Sigmund Freud said that when making a decision of minor importance, he always found it advantageous to consider all the pros and cons. However, in vital matters, his psychoanalyst's view was that, 'The decision should come from the unconscious, from somewhere within.' Proponents of the unconscious thought theory argue that unconscious thought works bottom-up, and can integrate large amounts of information, whereas conscious thought is very limited in its capacity and works top-down. A period of distraction allowing the unconscious to work may therefore be advisable in decision-making.[3]

Another quirk of human decision-making is the divide between maximizers and satisficers.[4] *Maximizers* tend to check all available options to ensure they have picked the best one. By contrast, *satisficers* only look as far as finding something that fulfils their requirements. Klein analyzed the actual decision-making behaviour of many groups, and found that often simple strategies are taken.[5] Thus, under time pressure, satisficing is pragmatic: options may be evaluated one at a time until an acceptable one has been found. More generally, experienced people may be confident in their own ability to size up a crisis situation.

Reliance on instinctive gut feelings comes naturally for many, if not most, common decisions in life.[6] But beyond the use of intuition, there are specific public safety situations where the task of checking available options is preferable for reasons both of accountability and optimality. This may involve integration of large amounts of information.

In a letter written in London to Joseph Priestley in 1772, Benjamin Franklin described his version of this approach. This involved dividing a sheet of paper by a line into two columns, writing over one *pro*, and over the other *con*. Then, during three or four days of consideration, presumably allowing time for subconscious reflection, he put down under the two headings the different motives for and against the action. Of this method, he wrote, 'Though the weight of reason cannot be taken with the precision of algebraic quantities, yet, when each is thus considered, separately and comparatively, and the whole lies before me, I think I can judge better, and am less liable to make a rash step; and in fact I have found great advantage from this kind of equation, in what may be called moral or prudential algebra.'[7]

Benjamin Franklin's sheet of pros and cons has been extended in the 21st century to a computer spreadsheet of benefits and costs of an action. These are monetized to establish a common calculational basis for cost–benefit analysis. Consider a situation where a decision-maker has to choose between two actions: either (a) protect; or (b) do not protect. The cost of protection is C. In the absence of protection, the decision-maker incurs a loss L, which exceeds C, if an adverse hazard state arises. Let the probability of the adverse hazard state arising, within a specified time window, be denoted by P. If the expected expense is minimized, then the optimal policy is to protect, if $P > C / L$ and not to protect if $P < C / L$. The minimum expense is then the lesser of C and $P \times L$.

A straightforward application of cost–benefit analysis is the decision to fly out aircraft stationed near an active volcano during a volcanic crisis. During World War II, 88 B-25 Mitchell bombers on airfields near Mt. Vesuvius were scrapped, having been damaged by ashfall from the March 1944 eruption.[8] This costly misjudgement was not repeated by the US Air Force in June 1991: Clark Air Base, Philippines, was evacuated prior to the cataclysmic eruption of Mt. Pinatubo, which was less than 25 km distant. In April 2010, two highly valuable NATO AWACS radar planes were relocated from Germany to Sicily to avoid the Iceland volcanic ash cloud menace. The cost of potential engine damage from volcanic ash greatly exceeded the benefit of continuing surveillance operations based from Germany.

These aviation relocations are amongst many significant warning decisions that can be justified readily by straightforward cost–benefit arguments. One that caused public controversy as squandering taxpayers' money was the UK government's decision, at the height of the 2009 H1N1 crisis, to make plans to order enough influenza vaccine to give two doses to everyone in the UK. As it turned out, because of the eventual mildness of the outbreak, there was a massive surplus of millions of doses. Yet there had been a small chance of a much more lethal virus mutation, and a single dose may not have conferred full immunity. The cost of vaccination was patently very low in relation to the value of lives that might have been saved.

9.1.1 Hazard advisory

In daily life, the general public is commonly exposed to remote uncertain hazards, which would pose a threat to life and property if they were to materialize. Hazard advisories provided by authorities elicit a wide range of precautionary responses, many of which involve comparatively little cost. Air passengers buckle their safety belts during turbulence. Homeowners in the Caribbean board up their windows with the approach of a tropical storm, just in case it intensifies into a damaging hurricane. US citizens have bought duct tape to seal their homes for fear of a terrorist attack involving toxic aerosols.

Disaster preparedness is a highly nonlinear phenomenon: small measures adopted early can leverage disproportionate benefits in risk reduction. In the 17 January 1995 Kobe earthquake, independent emergency response organizations in Japan were unable to make a rapid transition to an emergency response system vital to saving lives in the first hours following the earthquake.[9] Putting first responders on special alert enables the rapid transition needed to save more lives. Deciding on the extent of such a civil protection alert, with the corresponding extra public cost burden, would depend on an evaluation of the probability gain associated with the monitoring of some possible earthquake precursors. A time of increased probability (TIP) of an earthquake might encourage some other basic earthquake risk mitigation measures, e.g. conducting earthquake drills and seismic safety checks, advancing inspection and retrofit schedules, and improving signposted warnings in areas prone to secondary perils such as tsunamis and landslides.

A lesson from the influential public policy discourse of Thaler and Sunstein is that citizens and organizations can be gently nudged into taking courses of safer action, without undue authoritarian pressure.[10] A compelling example from their book *Nudge* is that of public hygiene in men's urinals: those with embedded fly images as targets improve standards of cleanliness remarkably. Health and safety measures need not be mandatory or coercive; just voluntary. Through self-organization, an informed citizen can play a role as an individual decision-maker. Emergency management skill is a core competency for a citizen.

The optimal level of self-organization does depend on the peril, threat level, and warning capability. For most Australian bushfires, there is sound sense in the binary choice for households to (a) *prepare, stay and defend*, or (b) *leave early*. But for ferocious bushfires, such as claimed the lives of 173 in the state of Victoria on Black Saturday, 7 February 2009, a coordinated public evacuation plan was needed.[11]

9.2 Evacuation

One evening in early January 1982, a couple living at the base of a steep hillside in the San Francisco Bay area were watching the late news. They heard a story about local flooding from a heavy rainstorm, but nothing about mudslides. This news came to them in the most direct form of reality TV, when their home was struck by a debris flow, which crushed their three sleeping children. It often takes a tragedy for the urgency of a hazard warning system to be appreciated. After this storm, the US Geological Survey developed a debris flow warning system, based on estimating the critical amount of rainfall required to trigger debris flows on susceptible slopes.[12] The use of rainfall measurements to gauge the imminence of a landslide or debris flow has proven effective in many climatic and geological environments, even though torrential rain may develop suddenly before any warning can be given.

The three key components of a landslide or debris flow warning system are: [1] rainfall sensors and telemetry; [2] a rainfall threshold model to gauge when rainfall exceeds amounts that have triggered past landslides; and [3] an effective public communication system. The reliability of landslide and debris flow warnings may be improved with additional remote sensing observations of rainfall, but is worsened by the inadequacy of simple slope stability models to account for heterogeneity of hillslope materials and their hydrological characteristics.

In Hong Kong, which has steep terrain, intense seasonal rainfall, as well as extremely dense hillslope development, warnings are aimed at predicting the occurrence of numerous landslides, accepting that isolated landslides will occur without a warning being provided. With its high landslide vulnerability, the Hong Kong Observatory would be thankful that this Chinese territory is not situated also in a zone of significant seismic hazard. Not only is evacuation prior to an earthquake almost impossible, but even after an earthquake has occurred, evacuation from seismically-induced landslides may not be feasible, as exemplified by the Wenchuan earthquake of 12 May 2008, when disoriented survivors of ground shaking were mown down by giant boulders rolling down hills.

9.2.1 Landfalling hurricanes

For natural as with man-made perils, advances in hazard monitoring are vital in helping reduce false negatives and positives in evacuation calls. The most notorious historical hurricane false negative was in September 1900. Thousands died when a hurricane storm surge inundated the port of Galveston. At that time, the Texas section of the US Weather Bureau depended on cables from Washington DC headquarters for the issuance of storm warnings. Scant attention was paid to Cuban information. The failure of the Weather Bureau to predict and track the storm's approach to Galveston became the subject of acrimonious public debate.

In the absence of satellite monitoring and computational hurricane forecasting tools, the reliability of hurricane warnings in 1900 was poor. The reliability progressed significantly with the advent of weather satellites, the first of which was launched in 1960. Since then, the accuracy of hurricane track forecasting has improved enormously, even though intensity forecasting has lagged. Very rapid intensification from Category 1 up to 5, such as happened with the Florida Keys Labor Day hurricane of 1935, could pose an acute evacuation timing dilemma.

Decision lead times are critical to allow adequate time for effective evacuation. A century after Galveston, a four-figure death toll was tragically realized with the landfall of Hurricane Katrina on the US Gulf Coast early on Monday, 29 August 2005. At 10am the previous day, Mayor Ray Nagin had ordered the first mandatory evacuation of the city of New Orleans. Earlier, at 4pm on Saturday, 27 August, the Louisiana governor had given the sign to activate the traffic contraflow system. But the New Orleans mayor then remained reluctant to order a city evacuation for fear that the city would be sued for disruption to the tourist trade. The uncertainty was worrying. Sixty hours before the storm passed New Orleans, the official strike probability was 17%, and did not exceed 50% until less than 24 hours beforehand. With evacuation costing more than a million dollars per mile of coastline, deciding to evacuate early is a very tough call. Ultimately, it took President Bush to get the mayor to make the evacuation mandatory.[13]

Using a stochastic model of hurricane tracks, Regnier studied the connection between lead time and track uncertainty, and assessed the implications for evacuation decision-making.[14] In her Markov state model, a storm is defined by its centre and its travel direction. Storm motion is represented by state transitions at standard six hour intervals, with state transition probabilities based on historical hurricane track data.

For New Orleans, she found that unless evacuation times can be kept below 30 hours, civic officials intolerant of a 10% false negative probability of failing to evacuate, must be prepared to accept that three-quarters of evacuations may be false alarms. This would be close to the 2005 false alarm rate for US tornado warnings. Reduction in population risk lies in the deployment of improved monitoring and sensing technology, to capture key input data for atmospheric-oceanographic dynamic forecasting models.

9.2.2 Volcanic eruptions

In volcanic crises, the trade-off between human safety and economic loss is even more fraught, because of the greater physical danger posed by eruptions, and their long duration. There are no easy options. Accordingly, decision-makers need maximal support. For example, in October 1999, the population of the scenic tourist town of Baños, Ecuador, was evacuated in anticipation of a violent eruption of Mt. Tungurahua. Citing geological experts, who estimated an 80% probability of such an eruption, the president urged endangered citizens to flee. However, poor living conditions for the evacuees were compounded by an economic crisis in Ecuador, and after three months of activity with no major eruption, Baños community leaders organized a return even though the town remained under an evacuation order.

The economic hardship of Ecuador contrasts with the oil wealth of Saudi Arabia. In May 2009, Al-Ais, a town 550 km northeast of Jeddah, and on the fringe of a volcano field, suffered a series of tremors. When one attained the critical Magnitude threshold of 5, the Saudi government moved residents of Al-Ais and surrounding villages to neighbouring cities, where they stayed in apartments paid for by the state. The provincial governor, Prince Abdul Aziz, promised care for the evacuees, and families also received financial assistance. Three months later, after enduring further seismic alarms, the evacuees were allowed to return. In both of these crises, the volcanologists preferred to err on the side of giving an early alert leading to a temporary evacuation.

A false alarm inevitably subjects the evacuation decision to public scrutiny. But the trade-off between human life and economic loss arises in the absence of volcanologists: on Mt. Merapi in Indonesia, villagers balance the risk of personal volcanic harm against the risk of their livestock starving, if unattended during a period of evacuation.

Both of the above evacuation decisions intuitively struck the right balance between the human benefits of saving lives and the economic costs of evacuation: failure to call for an evacuation would have undervalued human life. This can be benchmarked by a cost–benefit analysis (CBA).

A quantitative CBA requires the evaluation of both costs and benefits in the same common unit, the most convenient being monetary value. When asked in a courtroom whether he had put a value on human life, the Harvard risk analyst, Dick Wilson, gave the proper response: 'No, I decline to do so. I recognize that a human life is priceless'.[15] However, he also cited an objective measure: the amount society has paid in the past to save a life. Where a trade-off is considered between human and economic loss, it is essentially the *minimum* value of life which is taken as a loss measure: delay in evacuation should not undervalue life.

The concept of Willingness to Pay for Life Saved (WPLS) offers another way of monetizing a life. WPLS represents the amount of money available to reduce a specific lethal risk per person. It is necessarily a bounded value because resources are finite, and risks cannot all be eliminated. Valuation is fundamental to comparing different risks and to prioritizing optimally the finite funds available for risk mitigation. In this way, it is possible to avoid inequitable differences between money spent to reduce one risk than another.

Let N be the size of the population who may be evacuees in the event of a volcanic crisis. The zone evacuated is typically cautiously drawn to be inclusive of all areas that might be threatened by a major eruption. In the absence of any evacuation call, an actual eruption event might only impact a sub-region, and a substantial part of the population in direct danger might manage to flee in time anyway. This would leave a proportion E of the N people at risk who would owe their lives to the evacuation call, should the adverse eruptive hazard state materialize: in the absence of an evacuation call, these would become fatality statistics. If the WPLS is denoted by V, then the event loss is the product: $L = E \times N \times V$.

Just as with all national civil emergencies, the state should bear its own logistical costs involved in the operational management of an evacuation involving the police and the military, and other public employees. For a government acting on behalf of, and in the interests of, its citizens at risk, the most relevant metric for the disruption cost C of an unnecessary evacuation is $N \times R$, where R is the average socio-economic loss per capita, for the duration of an evacuation. Then $C / L = (N \times R) / (E \times N \times V) = (R / V) / E$. This expression is independent of N, the population at risk.

For the 1999 Mt. Tungurahua crisis, the likelihood of a major eruption was high, estimated at 80%. Given a degree of natural protection for Baños provided by deep gorges, the proportion of the people at risk who would have owed their lives to the evacuation call might have been about 25%. WPLS then works out at a multiple of about five times the socio-economic loss per capita. Even a developing country, such as Ecuador, in the midst of an economic crisis, should be willing to pay this much for a life saved, as was indeed the case with the president's call for evacuation.

Regarding Al-Ais in Saudi Arabia, the ambient volcanic hazard has been historically quite low, apart from a moderate eruption in 1256, which was widely reported in Islamic chronicles. The likelihood of an imminent explosive eruption, contingent on the limited seismic monitoring data, would have been comparatively small, at most 1/20.

Given also the limited explosive potential of the volcano, the proportion of the people at risk who would have owed their lives to the evacuation call would also have been quite modest, perhaps at most 5%. Assuming a basic 3 month cost disruption of about $2,500 per evacuee, the WPLS works out to be about $1 million. The willingness of the provincial governor to pay this much for a life saved reflects his expressed keenness to ensure the safety and security of both Saudi citizens and expatriates.

The evacuation of potentially hundreds of thousands of inhabitants from a volcanic danger zone is a logistical challenge that dwarfs those for the above crises. Yet, this is the situation in the most densely populated major city in Italy, Naples, which is overshadowed by Vesuvius. The desirability of reducing the population exposure to volcano risk around Vesuvius brought about an initiative to encourage families to move away from the red hazard zone, which is the designated area for evacuation before an eruption. Called *VESUVIA*, (meaning away from Vesuvius), the amount on offer to a family to move away from the red hazard zone indicated an implicit WPLS value of about €860,000, which is broadly consistent with values used for risk studies in industrialized nations.[16]

In October 2006, an exercise, *MESIMEX*, was conducted to test and improve emergency procedures for dealing with a crisis at Vesuvius. In this exercise, the alarm level for evacuation from the red zone was considered justified when there were clear signs of rising magma, corresponding to a high eruption probability. Depending on the emergent complexity of actual evacuation logistics, a bolder decision might be needed in reality. Prioritizing safety in accord with the WPLS might warrant evacuation whilst there was still significant scientific uncertainty over the imminence of an eruption.

The deterministic ethos of scientists makes it very hard for them to call for an evacuation unless the perceived event probability is high. But this may not be optimal for saving life. Where effective evacuation logistics are in place, so that the marginal likelihood of incomplete evacuation is small, then a delay until the next volcano bulletin might well be warranted. But where, as around Naples, traffic might become gridlocked by emergent road blockages, a delay of a day or two might have a significant impact on the percentage remaining in danger.

9.2.3 River floods

Heavy rainfall is a highly visible and measurable precursor to river flooding. Often the flow discharge rates will provide sufficient warning time for an orderly evacuation, as exemplified by the mass evacuation of 250,000 in the Netherlands during the 1995 Rhine River flood. Mostly, river flood risk arises from the overtopping of river banks or flood barriers. A more severe and challenging situation arises where flood protection is provided by dikes, as in the Netherlands, which may not only be overtopped, but may also be physically breached. Evacuation decisions typically are based on a water height threshold criterion, as in 1995, but consideration in the Netherlands is given to a risk-based approach incorporating information on dike failure probabilities.

From the Australian perspective of the New South Wales flood management advisory committee, consideration has been given to the complex and interdependent evacuation issues. In particular, failure to address time management is reckoned likely to degrade response.[17] They note that the decision to evacuate should ideally be made when the flood prediction has a high level of confidence, so as to avoid unnecessary evacuations. Evacuations will always be costly to the community, and cost must be factored into a balanced flood risk assessment.

For the residents of the Hawkesbury-Nepean river valley on the western outskirts of Sydney, evacuation within a 24 hour time window requires the Australian Bureau of Meteorology to use 12 hours of forecast rainfall in their flood prediction model. This introduces a high level of uncertainty, that might encourage a decision delay. However, a late evacuation call might entail a massive flood rescue operation, swamping the capacity of available helicopter and boat rescue services.

Decision-making pressure has been alleviated by the construction of an evacuation bridge, opened in September 2007. Apart from easing regular traffic flow, the expense would have been amply justified by a safety cost–benefit analysis. Otherwise, under intense rainfall for several days, with river water flow restricted by narrow gorges, and with evacuation routes heavily congested, there was a high probability that 15,000 people might have been trapped and endangered by floodwater.

However diligent the flood planning, where an extreme amount of rain falls within a short period, decision-makers struggle with the uncertainty in the spatial–temporal resolution of precipitation forecasts, and the logistical difficulty of rapid evacuation. A sudden deluge impacts rather like an earthquake. At the end of July 2010, the Pakistan Meteorological Department reported 31 cm of monsoon rain falling in the northwest within 36 hours, causing worse flooding than a landmark historical flood in 1931. In the politically unstable Swat district, what transport infrastructure remained after sustained terrorist attacks was swept away by the flash floods, rendering evacuation impossible for the hundreds of thousands left stranded. The coupling between natural and man-made hazards aggravates in a highly nonlinear way the logistical challenge of post-disaster response.

9.2.4 Terrorist attacks

Protected by the Thames Barrier against flooding, London is fortunate to be mostly safe from the ravages of natural hazards. But as the political, economic, and tourist capital of Britain, it has long been exposed to sustained campaigns of political violence. Whereas most terrorist organizations would not inform the authorities of an impending attack, this was not so of the Irish Republican Army (IRA), whose community support would be eroded by mass killings. Accordingly, the IRA campaign offers a tutorial in evacuation under uncertainty.

A devious terrorist tactic favoured by the IRA was to give coded bomb warnings to alert the police services in Northern Ireland and Great Britain of an imminent explosion in a particular area. The use of code-words allowed warnings to be authenticated as coming from the IRA, but even if the source was genuine, there was no assurance that the threat would be carried out: the false alarm was a weapon of disruption in itself. A high proportion of bomb warnings turned out to be hoaxes, which nonetheless served the IRA's purpose of causing panic, mayhem, and economic disruption without an attack at all. The IRA recognized that once a coded warning had been given, the civic authorities would have to acknowledge threat credibility and be duty bound to evacuate.

One of the most notorious hoaxes, affording terrorists their craved oxygen of publicity, forced the evacuation in April 1997 of a crowd of 60,000 race-goers at Aintree, England, where the prestigious annual Grand National horse race was due to be held. With the evacuation disruption being limited in both spatial location and duration, and the evacuation process taking only an hour, a decision to evacuate made eminent common sense, once the threat was deemed to be credible.

Evacuation need not be an automatic response to a credible bomb warning. A contrary decision against evacuation might be made where the security staff could be extremely confident that the location was bomb-free. With the worldwide foreboding over the Y2K millennium computer bug, to make such a decision on millennium eve, 31 December 1999, would have been a civic official's nightmare. It was no coincidence that this date was chosen by the IRA to issue multiple coded bomb warnings. Furthermore, the target was inevitably the Millennium Dome arena in London, the focus of Britain's celebrations. No natural hazard could have been as predictable in timing and location as this.

On this singular occasion, the moral obligation not to put lives of dignitaries at risk was finely balanced against the economic and political cost of cancelling the grand celebration. A rigorous search by army engineers minimized the likelihood that a bomb actually had been planted, and tilted the decision for the show to go on. Although public safety is paramount in civil protection, it is not the only concern, else the precautionary principle would always be invoked where evacuation is logistically feasible as it was at the Millennium Dome.

These two contrasting case studies highlight key generic aspects of the evacuation decision process. The person authorized to make the decision does so on the basis of an independent assessment of risk. In the first case, the threat was deemed credible. In the second case, although the bomb sweep by army engineers could not be guaranteed to be error-free, the threat was not deemed credible enough to warrant evacuation. In practice, the balance between precaution and disruption is often a fine qualitative judgement of the decision-maker. However, such an individualized utilitarian analysis is unavoidably prone to behavioural biases, such as cognitive dissonance, especially where fresh evidence arises which may be at odds with a previous entrenched position.

9.3 The Wisdom of Experts

On public safety issues, decision-makers have been slow to follow a probabilistic approach; reticence which reflects the predominant deterministic training of administrators and civil engineers. In traditional engineering practice, a safety factor in a design ensures that a building is safe, in the absolute sense understood by the public. Deciding on a safety factor involves recourse to professional engineering judgement, which, despite the similarity of name, is distinct from the probabilistic concept of expert judgement. It is improper for a probabilistic judgement to be made without a facilitator upholding the laws of probability.

Public advice during a natural hazard crisis is usually solicited from a chief scientist. The offer of advice, rather than mere supply of information, has a strict legal connotation. The pressures on an individual may result in such advice being unduly influenced by his or her state of mind, or other factors extraneous to the actual state of knowledge. In particular, there is an outcome asymmetry in the personal consequences for an individual, which may lead to bias.

If a decision ultimately proves to be unduly cautious, there are unlikely to be major recriminations for the decision-maker, who can always plead that safety is paramount. However, should a less cautious decision be made and a disaster actually materialize, then the responsible decision-maker may be accused of putting economics or other considerations before safety, and jeopardize his career, if not livelihood, and even liberty. Individual accountability may potentially result in decisions serving the decision-maker's own personal self-interest more than might be desirable for the collective public good. The fear of being wrong may weigh unduly on scientific opinion.[18]

In outlining a route to more tractable expert advice, which circumvents this asymmetry issue, Aspinall has advocated the pooling of the opinions of a group of experts.[19] This accords with the philosophy of science perspective: 'History shows us clearly that science does not provide certainty. It does not provide proof. It only provides the consensus of experts, based on the organized accumulation and scrutiny of evidence.'[20]

As advocated by Surowiecki, there is much to be said for the wisdom of crowds, at least in pooling expertise for estimation under uncertainty.[21]   Francis Galton, a relative of Charles Darwin, and a voracious consumer of statistics, discovered this at an English country fair: the average of 787 guesses at the weight of an ox, the collective wisdom of the informed farming crowd, was correct to a single pound. The power of diversity in problem solving is generally established as an advantage of *crowdsourcing* multiple opinions.[22]

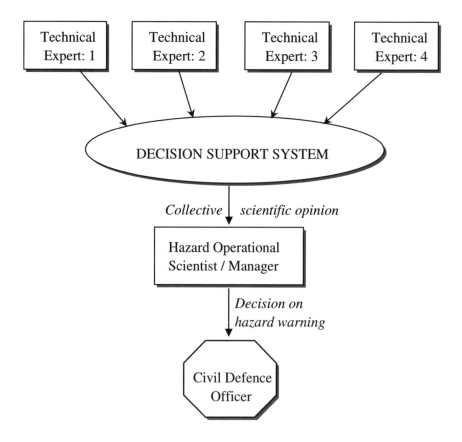

Figure 9.1.   Diagram of hazard warning communication links between individual technical experts, the hazard operational manager, and the civil defence officer.

Whatever differences there may be between individual scientists, a *single* collective opinion should be communicated to a civil defence officer. This is the task of a hazard operational manager, who should be scientifically knowledgeable, and capable of liaising with all the scientists involved in monitoring and data analysis. The hazard operational manager may well be one of the senior scientists, with a good overall grasp of all the hazard issues. This operational manager would be responsible for conveying the gravity of a hazard situation to a civil defence officer, and informing him of the collective opinion of the scientists. The civil defence officer would then have the responsibility of communicating any warning to the emergency services, the media, and the general public, as well as upper echelons of government.

9.3.1 Elicitation of expert judgement

The thought of convening an advisory group of combat-hardened military officers with doctorates from top-ranked universities might seem another fanciful but ill-conceived notion borrowed from a fantasy video game. But it was actual reality in Iraq in 2007, when General Petraeus assembled his stellar brains trust to find the smartest way of playing the abysmal hand he had been dealt by his predecessors.[23] His legendary Iraq success in overcoming the mother of all challenges obviously reflects well on one of America's greatest generals, but it also suggests to a risk analyst that more might be expected of the process of eliciting expert judgement in crisis situations. The Iraq War darkened the horizon of the western alliance in 2007, as did the menace of thermonuclear war half a century earlier. To assess this earlier dire global threat, a new technique of scenario analysis was devised to explore the range of possible events. In this Dr Strangelove doomsday setting, the formal elicitation of expert judgement was pioneered by the RAND Corporation as the optimal means of gauging informed opinions.

Like the study of Cold War threats, the study of natural hazards is an exercise in hypothesis based on partial observation, if not also paranoia and fear, and the accumulation of real data cannot be expedited by the conduct of experiments: the passage of time is required for hazard events to occur. Especially where the events are rare, the paucity of data creates significant ambiguity in scientific interpretation, which aggravates the uncertainty over decision-making.

One of the main avenues for reconciling diverse opinions is to allow for some degree of interaction between the group of experts. This could be organized by circulating to each expert the assessments of all other experts, perhaps with accompanying explanations. After several iterations, opinions may converge. This so-called Delphi method does not involve the experts actually meeting; a constraint which has its logistical and financial advantages, but limits the opportunity for open dialogue. An alternative is to hold group decision conferences, so that all the technical issues can be discussed by experts face to face. Such meetings need to be chaired by an experienced independent facilitator whose brief is to maintain the formal structure of a conference, and to prevent groupthink: the suppression of dissent in the interests of group harmony.[24] In the absence of such a facilitator, academic seniority and insistent eloquence might be rewarded over views expressed with less authority or clarity. Another feature of group decision-making of which a facilitator needs to be aware is the tendency for group polarization. Members of a deliberating group may end up at a more extreme position in the same general direction as their original inclinations.[25] This may happen over some factual matter, or with regard to some risk issue. There may be a risky shift, with members being disposed to taking risks.

9.3.2 *Informativeness and calibration*

The judgements of experts inevitably have a subjective element, but this does not mean that their different performance standards cannot be compared and recognized. Judgements may be compromised by a combination of bias, over-confidence, and uninformativeness. In order to evaluate a set of probability assessments, it is helpful to have a *scoring rule*, which is a function of the difference between actual outcomes and the assessed probability distribution. Various types of scoring rule have been proposed, one of the more widely used being based on the quadratic differences between the assessed probability of events and the proportion that actually occur. This has been used, for example, in evaluating meteorologists' capability in forecasting the probability of rain.

A mathematical approach for weighting expert judgements, with an explicit focus on informativeness and calibration, was devised by Roger Cooke.[26] This method overcomes some of the technical difficulties which have beset previous weighting attempts, while being convenient and efficient for practical use. In this approach, each expert is asked to assess the values of a range of quantiles for a chosen set of test parameters, as well as for the parameters of actual interest. On the basis of each expert's assessments of the test parameters, (which are selected for relevance to the issues of concern), a weight is assigned to the expert. Each weight is non-negative, and together, considering all experts, they sum to unity. However, they are not taken to be equal, *a priori*, as in elicitation procedures which regard as invidious the grading of experts.

The two key measures which need to be defined relate to the informativeness and accuracy of an expert. Considering informativeness, it is natural to adopt the formalism widely used in the statistical theory of communication. Suppose an expert's probability distribution $p = p_1, p_2, p_3, \ldots, p_n$ is defined over n alternatives. Then the entropy $H(p)$ is defined to indicate the lack of information in the distribution:

$$H(p) = -\sum_{i=1}^{n} p_i \, ln\,(p_i)$$

The maximal value of $ln\,(n)$ is attained when each p_i equals $1/n$. The minimum value of zero is obtained when all but one of the p_i are zero, and the other is unity. High values of entropy therefore indicate low informativeness, whereas low values indicate high informativeness. If $s = s_1, s_2, s_3, \ldots, s_n$ is a probability distribution over the same n values, and each p_i is positive, then the discrepancy between s and p can be measured by $I(s, p)$, the relative information of s with respect to p:

$$I(s, p) = \sum_{i=1}^{n} s_i \, ln\,(s_i / p_i)$$

$I(s, p)$ is always non-negative, and $I(s, p)$ is zero if and only if s is identically equal to p. $I(s, p)$ may be taken as a gauge of the information learned, or surprise, if an expert initially believes p, and later learns that s is correct; larger values correspond to a greater measure of surprise. It is then possible to devise a statistical calibration out of $I(s, p)$ which credits a higher score to those surprised less.

Indices of informativeness and calibration of an expert's assessments can be defined in terms of $H(p)$ and $I(s, p)$, and a commensurate weight calculated which is proportional to the calibration index, and inversely proportional to the informativeness index. In practical applications, the calibration index can vary over several orders of magnitude for a reasonably large group of experts, whereas the informativeness index varies much less.[27–29]

Experts tend not to flaunt their ignorance by being uninformative; the reverse is more the case, where experts may declare minimal uncertainty. The French philosopher, Charles Renouvier, remarked that, 'Properly speaking, there is no certainty; there are only people who are certain.'[30] Elicitations are undertaken recognizing there is no certainty in parameter estimation. However, they should not be biased by experts who are certain but poorly calibrated.

9.3.3 The mathematician as decision-maker

The French mathematician, Pierre Laplace, was interested in the process by which collective judgements are made, especially by juries. Foreseeing groupthink, he noted that complete accord can arise through human factors other than overwhelming evidence, and suggested that a majority of nine out of twelve would greatly reduce the error rate.[31]

Although there have been instances elsewhere, France is the nation where the mathematician has most often been entrusted with high political office. It was the exalted view of Napoleon that the advancement and perfection of mathematics were intimately connected with the prosperity of the state. Mainland France is fortunate not to be afflicted by notable natural perils, although there have been damaging windstorms and floods, and occasional strong earthquakes such as struck the Rivièra in 1887 and Provence in 1909. The overseas departments are more exposed, including the volcanically active islands of Guadeloupe, Martinique, and Réunion. In France, the responsibility for national emergency decisions rests with the Minister of the Interior. Over the handling of the eruption crisis of La Soufrière on Guadeloupe in 1976, which led to the evacuation of 70,000 inhabitants, the serving French Minister of the Interior came under criticism;[32] there was no major eruption which would have clearly vindicated the evacuation order.

Napoleon greatly admired scientists, and as illustrious a scientist as Laplace held an appointment as Minister of the Interior. As it turned out, his appointment lasted only six weeks. Of Laplace's indifferent display of diligence in his public duties, Napoleon noted with ironic wit: 'He had carried the spirit of the infinitesimal into the management of affairs.' Mathematicians should always have a role in the science of decision-making, in serving and advising civic officials, but great mathematicians need not be great public administrators. Nor regrettably, are public administrators necessarily acquainted or familiar with the rudiments of risk quantification, except perhaps in a popular betting context.

Ordinary language itself thus has to be used with particular care. In the context of UK Defence Intelligence, for example, the formal association of probability with qualifiers, such as probable or improbable, has been defined in an 'Uncertainty Yardstick'.[33] There are just six grades: remote/highly unlikely; improbable/unlikely; realistic possibility; probable/likely; highly likely/very probable; and almost certain. For the first grade, covering what is remote or highly unlikely, the associated probability range is coarsely defined as less than 10%. The limited human capacity to resolve very small probabilities is the rationale for the disaggregation of rare events into a logic-tree with branches corresponding to contingent sub-event sequences.

Words also matter in mathematical models. The eclectic Hungarian mathematician John von Neumann defined a mathematical model as 'a mathematical construct which, with the addition of certain verbal interpretations, describes observed phenomena.'[34] The underlying narrative element of a mathematical model needs to be elucidated explicitly wherever a mathematician advises, or serves as, a political decision-maker.

Chapter 10

Disaster Scenarios

It is the mark of an educated mind
to expect that amount of exactness in each kind
which the particular nature of the subject admits.
Aristotle
Nicomachean Ethics, Book 1

It was Tolkien, the author of *The Lord of the Rings*, who remarked that fairy tales are only associated with children by accident. They are an integral part of country folklore, which is a mixture of pagan beliefs, local history, and actual experience. It is a storyteller's prerogative to tell a strange and fanciful story without being obliged or able to explain it in rational, let alone scientific terms. This is just as well, because otherwise some important historical accounts of natural disaster would not have survived to warn the present and future generations of rare strange perils.

The crater lakes of the Cameroon Grassfields region of West Africa have furnished abundant material for storytellers. According to legend, the bottoms of Lake Nyos and Lake Oku provide occasional glimpses of villages of the dead. In historical times, through lack of direct scientific observation, the potential hazard of major lake gas discharges had not been recognized, nor was this catalogued specifically as a volcanic region. Scientific interpretation of legends of exploding lakes and villages of the dead might be dismissed as a rationalization of mythology, a style of thinking known as *euhemerism*, after a 4th century Sicilian philosopher.[1]

Yet, this was far from being just an academic issue; it was a matter of life and death. On the night of 21 August 1986, carbon dioxide gas that had collected at the bottom of Lake Nyos emerged from the crater, and formed a river of lethal fumes, 50 m thick and 16 km long, which engulfed and suffocated the nearby villages. The death toll of almost 2,000 people marks this as the greatest known gas poisoning tragedy associated with a volcanic crater lake. Hopefully it will be the last at Lake Nyos, where measures are in place to siphon off the carbon dioxide.

A much greater potential gas disaster scenario has lurked elsewhere in Africa around the densely populated shores of Lake Kivu, on the border of Rwanda and the Democratic Republic of Congo.[2] The lake contains a staggering quantity of dissolved carbon dioxide and methane. But a management strategist would recognize this threat as an opportunity for a multi-megawatt methane power plant. In the fairy tale of Hansel and Gretel, this would be like the witch being turned into gingerbread.

The core of any catastrophe calculation is the disaster scenario. It may reflect poorly on the limited vision and imagination of catastrophe analysts that the more bizarre and unfamiliar scenarios, such as exploding lakes, may sound like fairy tales of the unknown unknowns, rather than life-saving wisdom handed down from a pre-scientific age.

More familiar are the scenarios which relate to specific questions. What if this fault were to rupture downtown? Contingent on a specific event occurring, what is the human and economic loss? An extreme hazard event, such as a Magnitude 8 earthquake, might occur in an uninhabited wilderness and cause minimal damage. It would be a curiosity for seismologists to study, and alarm the snakes, but be of little concern for society. By contrast, a Magnitude 6 earthquake epicentred under a densely populated urban area of a developing country could be highly lethal and destructive and make headline international news.

The wide variability in loss potential is illustrated by the death tolls from two earthquakes of similar size, which struck in 2010. The M7.0 Haiti earthquake of 12 January resulted from a fault rupture close to the capital Port-au-Prince, which was woefully unprepared, even though it was in a recognized seismic region. The M7.2 Baja California, Mexico, earthquake was epicentred in a lightly populated area near the Mexican border with the USA. Around a quarter of a million died in the Haiti earthquake, yet only a few lives were lost in the larger earthquake, which occurred on Easter Sunday afternoon, when most people were outdoors.

10.1 Scenario Simulation

Diligence, foresight, and preparedness are virtues expected to be displayed by disaster risk managers, whether working on emergency planning for civic authorities or NGOs, hazard mitigation for engineering firms, or financial loss control for insurers and banks. Lack of foresight and ill-preparedness can put lives at greater risk, and waste resources.

To minimize surprise at what may happen, risk managers have a duty of care to explore and understand the broad spectrum of potential future scenarios. They should be as well informed as possible not just about disasters that have occurred historically, but also appreciate what might have occurred in the past, and be imaginative about disasters waiting to happen in the future.

10.1.1 Counterfactual history

It is because disasters are comparatively rare occurrences that a historical perspective on catastrophes is so crucial for their quantitative understanding.   Far more can be gleaned from history than just knowledge of the specific events that actually occurred. The historical record of events is just one particular realization of what might potentially have happened in a stochastic world.   Exploring counterfactual history, events that might have occurred – but did not – is a useful exercise for expanding imagination in scenario simulation.

Whenever an event occurs which is the cause of regret and recrimination, history may be revisited and reconstructed. After Aldrich Ames was arrested as a Russian spy in 1994, with a tip-off from a KGB defector code-named 'Avenger', the CIA convened a meeting of counter-intelligence experts to explore how this duplicitous staff member might have been arrested earlier. The experts considered a range of alternative security measures, and the extent to which they might have tripped up the double-agent had they been in place earlier.

In his review of counterfactuals and international relations, Lebow has noted the fractal-like structure of counterfactuals, with the chain of connections being extended further and further.[3] Event sequences have a self-similar tree-like branching structure. There is no shortage of historical examples, with branches stretching back to antiquity. Consider the dependence of Western civilization on its common Christian heritage. Had Emperor Constantine not been so successful militarily, it is much less likely that Christianity would have become dominant in the Roman Empire, and Europe a cohesive power in the world.

More fanciful, consider what would have happened had Mozart not died in 1791 at the age of 35, but lived to develop the postclassical musical tradition at the detriment of romanticism, which, some historians may contend, was a cultural source of inspiration in the adoption of violence to achieve political goals. How much different would the political landscape of Europe have been? As the string of counterfactuals from antecedent to consequent lengthens, the likelihood of the outcome progressively decreases. Thought experiments with counterfactuals provide a means of exploring the domain of improbability, which is the catastrophe realm. Mozart's early death was a catastrophe for music, but might it also have been a catastrophe in other ways for Europe?

Lebow has scripted a fictional narrative of two Berliners returning from a performance of a hypothetical opera *Oedipus* by a middle-aged Mozart. Over drinks in a café, they discuss a tragic counterfactual based on Mozart dying prematurely at 35, and speculate on subsequent political upheavals spawned by the spirit of romantic nationalism. In reflecting on how unlikely this would seem, hindsight bias is raised. As noted by Baruch Fischhoff, an astute observer of behavioural risk, once an event occurs, people upgrade their prior estimate of its probability.

Following a similar exercise, a counterfactual café narrative might be constructed about a supposedly hypothetical hurricane, named Katrina, which struck the Gulf coast, causing levee failure, widespread flooding, more than a thousand deaths, and severe environmental consequences. Major catastrophes seem so much more likely afterwards than before. For café dreamers of possible nightmare scenarios, Hurricane Katrina was a wake-up call in 2005. Unlike historians, catastrophe risk analysts use substantial computer resources to trawl through vast numbers of counterfactuals, portending future disasters. But even with these resources, an informed and lively imagination is still a prerequisite for simulating an adequately comprehensive set of future scenarios.

10.1.2 Stochastic event sets

The historical record, to the best that it may be known, is the foundation
of any procedure for constructing a stochastic event set comprising a
broad spectrum of possible scenarios. An actual historical event is just
one realization of what is dynamically feasible. On 28 July 1945, a
cloudy day in Manhattan, a B-25 bomber flew into the 79th floor of the
Empire State Building.[4] The so-called 'Miracle on Thirty-Fourth Street'
was that the consequent loss was remarkably limited. But had the plane
impacted a bit higher or lower, a column might have been bent, with
potentially grave structural consequences. For every man-made hazard
near-miss or moderate disaster, there might have been an actual loss
event or great disaster.   Alternative wind and rain conditions at
Chernobyl would have led to Kiev suffering severe radioactive
contamination; stormy weather when the Exxon Valdez was grounded
would have exacerbated coastal oil pollution.

In respect of natural hazards, supplementary events may be inferred
from the archaeological and palaeological records preserved from pre-
historical and geological times. Other physically plausible events might
be constructed from dynamical perturbations to the crustal, atmospheric,
or oceanic state. Taking a seismological example, in intraplate tectonic
environments, such as Northwest Europe, the epicentres of historical
earthquakes from a long historical catalogue can be spatially smoothed to
generate a 2-D map of potential earthquake locations.[5] This allows for
earthquakes to occur where they are not known to have occurred before.

A meteorological example might also be drawn from Northwest
Europe. The historical record covers centuries of windstorm disasters.
One such great storm in November 1703 cut a swath of destruction
across Britain. The English navy lost more ships in this storm than in
any enemy encounter. Heedless of national frontiers, the storm badly
damaged Utrecht Cathedral in Holland, as well as many houses and
churches in Denmark, and blew down church spires in some North
German towns. The windfields from major historical events such as this
can be replicated by numerical weather forecasting computer simulation,
which can generate large ensembles of possible future windstorms,
forming a stochastic event set.

Whatever the peril, whether meteorological, hydrological, or geological, counterfactual historical records can replay former events with modern updated building construction standards. Vitelmo Bertero has recounted how the national development of earthquake engineering has often followed major damaging earthquakes:[6] Chile and California in 1906, New Zealand in 1931, India in 1935, and Argentina in 1944. Repetitions of such seminal seismic events would generate different patterns of damage now because of the adoption and enforcement of national earthquake building codes.

10.2 Footprints and Vulnerability

There are three pillars of scenario loss estimation. The first is a spatial footprint marking the geographical area impacted by a hazard event. Within this footprint, the severity of the hazard varies, tapering to the background level at the perimeter. The second is the human and economic exposure within the footprint. The population, property, and other economic assets located within the footprint at the time of the hazard event are exposed to harm and damage. The third is the vulnerability of the exposure within the hazard footprint. This varies according to the health and safety provisions for individuals and the local standards of engineering design, construction, and maintenance. With the vulnerability prescribed, overlay of the hazard footprint onto the exposure allows loss to be mapped for the scenario.

A scenario event causes a regional disturbance from the norm, which may be characterized by a hazard severity field $I(x, y)$, where (x, y) is a position on the Earth's surface. For windstorm, the hazard severity might be peak wind speed; for flood it might be depth of water; for earthquake, it might be ground shaking Intensity; for a volcanic eruption, it might be thickness of ashfall.

For a major meteorite impact, the indirect effects might be truly global, but for terrestrial hazards, there is a finite bounded surface area over which $I(x, y)$ is potentially damaging. This finite area defines a spatial template, which is figuratively called a *footprint*. This physiological metaphor is not merely quaint: footprints differ in absolute scale, but have a similar shape (up to left–right symmetry) which can be characterized using geometrical statistics.[7]

The footprint is an apt graphic metaphor to use because, for a given type of hazard, the disturbed areas will encompass a wide range of spatial scales, but bear some basic similarity in geometrical shape, which may be distorted by local topographic or dynamic effects. For tropical cyclones, footprints are defined by elongated corridors around tracks; for extra-tropical storms, footprints are defined by areas of high wind speed enclosing atmospheric depressions; for tornadoes, footprints are defined by isovel lines around travel paths; for earthquakes, footprints are defined by elliptical isoseismal lines around fault ruptures.

For volcanic eruptions, footprints are defined by zones of pyroclastic, lava and lahar flows which descend under gravity following terrain topography. In addition there are footprints associated with airborne ejecta of volcanic projectiles and wind-dispersed ashfall.

For a variety of sporadic hazards, such as hailstorms, the associated footprints have the characteristics of a stochastic random field, where the hazard severity is spatially clustered and extremely inhomogeneous, being significant only in a sparse set of locations.

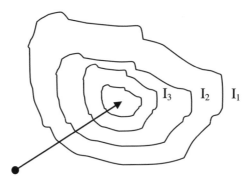

Hazard severity $I(x, y)$ decreases outwards towards the extremities of the footprint

Figure 10.1. Overhead view of a schematic hazard event footprint, showing curves of equal severity having broadly similar shapes.

10.2.1 *Footprint uncertainty*

Such is the medical progress made in tackling disease and degeneration, a leader of the UK actuarial profession has speculated that a day may come when death will only happen by accident. Randomness plays a large, yet underestimated, part in daily life; this is especially true of accidents. Indeed, according to Charles Perrow's normal accident theory,[8] minor factors may haphazardly cause serious accidents.

In the shadow of a major hazard event, randomness can be the difference between life and death. Should there be a large airborne release of a toxic plume, the erratic drift of the plume may decide which communities will lie within the footprint of dangerously high pollution.

Randomness plays a significant part in natural hazard footprints, not least in regard to earthquake risk. Because of their vital societal role in disaster response, seismic design requirements for hospitals are more stringent than for ordinary buildings. So those in hospital when a large earthquake strikes may be grateful to be in a place of comparative safety. But hospitals can still be vulnerable to major earthquakes.

Imagine a situation where you are a patient in a hospital, when a large earthquake strikes. Being close to the epicentre, the hospital suffers significant damage and incident managers decide to evacuate patients to another hospital 20 miles away, much farther from the epicentre. On journeying down to this receiving hospital, it turns out also to be condemned due to earthquake damage, and you have to be moved on to another hospital. Such an earthquake scenario, you might think, would be a nightmare associated only with developing countries. Surely it wouldn't happen in the USA, let alone the high-tech state of California? But so it did during the Northridge earthquake of 17 January 1994.[9]

The severity of ground shaking at a given distance from the epicentre of an earthquake of a specific Magnitude is highly variable. Differences in ground acceleration can be a factor of two or three. For one reason, there may be marked directionality in the propagation of seismic energy away from the epicentre: the shaking in one direction may be more intense than another. This was the case in the Northridge earthquake. Thus two hospitals equidistant from the epicentre can be subject to significantly different shaking.

The spatial pattern of the hazard severity of an event footprint has a complex uncertainty structure, which scientific observation and analysis are continuing to unravel with the prospect of addressing practical questions of the following kind. During a large earthquake, what is the chance that the only two hospitals in a town would both experience levels of ground shaking exceeding their design basis? Given the ambiguity in answering this question, decentralizing critical medical infrastructure makes eminent sense. Indeed, this planning strategy was adopted in the aftermath of the destructive Kobe earthquake in Japan, which occurred exactly a year to the day after the Northridge earthquake.

For any hazard, the conceptual framework for modelling an event footprint is typically based on the underlying scientific understanding of what may happen when an event occurs. Historical reconstructions of event footprints, using both instrumental measurements and qualitative human observations of hazard severity, then establish an empirical footprint library which can be used to support the parameterization of a footprint model.

10.2.2 *Vulnerability*

To allow for uncertainty in quantifying the damage that might be inflicted on a specific type of building, the concept of *vulnerability* is introduced. Subject to a prescribed level of ground shaking, the damage to a building is not determinate, but is a random variable describable by a probability distribution. As a function of ground shaking, the vulnerability of a building is the relative likelihood of the building suffering degrees of damage ranging from none to total.

The most direct and compact representation of vulnerability is provided by a *vulnerability matrix*, which is specific to seismic region and building type. Appropriate to a given region, and its vernacular architecture, will be an Intensity scale most suited for categorizing different levels of earthquake damage observed there. For each building type, a vulnerability matrix is defined by estimating, at each Intensity level, the percentages of buildings falling within each of a number of alternative damage states. The number of damage states depends on the practical resolution of damage observations: e.g. none; slight; moderate; extensive; and complete. Because of regional differences in building practices, styles, and materials, the loss ratios associated with these states need to be defined.

As a concept emerging from Allin Cornell's probabilistic thinking on seismic hazard, a vulnerability matrix can be used directly to estimate the expected annual economic loss L at a site, of value V, resulting from seismic activity. Let $F(I)$ be the frequency of Intensity I shaking at the site. When exposed to this Intensity, the site experiences damage in category K with relative likelihood $P(D_K | I)$. Let $R(K)$ be the mean loss ratio to the site if it suffers damage in category K. Then the expected annual economic loss L to the site, which may include casualties on site, can be estimated by the following double summation over Intensity and damage category:

$$L = \sum_I F(I) \sum_K P(D_K | I) . R(K) . V$$

The concept of a vulnerability matrix is universal, but empirical data on damage percentages exist only for a limited range of Intensities and building types. Useful as they are in countries of the Old World where there are centuries of Intensity data, the sheer dimension of vulnerability matrix tables can make them impractical to parameterize. Earthquake engineers therefore replace multiple rank vulnerability matrices with continuous vulnerability functions, in which damage variability is associated with a simple parametric probability distribution, such as a beta distribution. This may be modified with discrete probability masses at zero and unity, to reflect the proportion of buildings either entirely undamaged or completely wrecked. Even at high Intensity, a significant proportion of resilient wooden buildings may emerge unscathed.

Invaluable in charting earthquake felt effects, Intensity nevertheless remains a qualitative measure of the severity of ground shaking. A remedy is found in the steady global accumulation of instrumental recordings of strong earthquake motion, which have established a more quantitative route to defining earthquake loss potential, which is much needed for modern construction.

In architecture as in civil engineering, sustained practical experience is a prerequisite for dependable seismic design. Few architects have had longer experience than the nonagenarian I.M. Pei, who learned through many decades of experience that breakthroughs in architecture are rare, and come with technology.[10] For buildings adopting technological advances, the task of assessing earthquake vulnerability poses an obvious challenge. Assessment cannot be based on past performance history, but has to involve engineering dynamic analysis.

From the formation of small cracks to the crumpling of columns, the inter-relation between force and deflection governs the damage state of a building. The capacity of a building to withstand earthquake shaking is defined by a force-deflection plot, which is essentially a 'push-over' curve tracking the dependence of lateral load resistance on lateral displacement. A convenient and instructive way of representing building capacity is to convert the force axis to *spectral acceleration* and the displacement axis to *spectral displacement*. A generic capacity curve converted in this way is illustrated below.

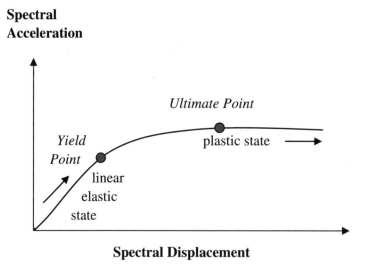

Figure 10.2. Building capacity curve showing the yield point, marking a transition from a linear elastic state, and the ultimate point leading to a plastic state.

In accordance with Hooke's Law, the capacity curve is initially linear. At this stage, much of the energy imparted to the building by an earthquake is stored temporarily in elastic strain energy and kinetic energy. However, with strong earthquake excitation, the elastic yield point is exceeded in some parts of the building. For construction with brittle material, like unreinforced masonry, this can lead to cracking. A brittle structure may only withstand minor deformations before failure.

For a building of ductile material, like timber, steel, or reinforced masonry, strong earthquake excitation causes further deformation to take place beyond the yield point, whereupon permanent energy dissipation of inelastic strain energy begins. The process of energy absorption during post-elastic deformation of a building results in progressive damage. From the yield point until the ultimate point, there is a ductile transition from an elastic to plastic state. Significant levels of building damage can arise through ductility. Rather like vehicle crumple zones which absorb crash impact energy, ductility design has traditionally been accepted in building codes, which have prioritized the saving of life. However, the additional desire to minimize building damage and reduce economic loss motivates innovative *performance-based* seismic design. Essential facilities may have a continued operations performance objective.

Wind vulnerability

Palm trees can be blown down in very severe tropical cyclones, but the evolutionary process has adapted them to the force of strong tropical winds. The aerodynamic furl of their branches tends to reduce drag, and the fan action of their branches tends to dampen swaying motion of the trunk. In temperate zones, the autumn shedding of broad leaves increases the natural vibration frequency of trees above the predominant frequency range of wind energy, so enabling trees to withstand strong winds better. But whilst in leaf, such trees are highly vulnerable to strong winds. On 29 September 2003, Hurricane Juan tracked up the US Atlantic coast and struck Nova Scotia as a rare Canadian Category 2 hurricane: 100 million trees, including many maples, were brought down.

A form of evolutionary stochastic process applies to buildings exposed to windstorms, except there is no irrevocable extinction. Even if all the poorly connected buildings in a village are blown away, they may be rebuilt in the same defective style unless building codes demand otherwise. Where there is a regulatory vacuum, nails may continue to be used to anchor walls to foundations, leaving wood frame houses vulnerable to being blown off their foundations in only a 35 m/s wind.

Heavy damage may of course be anticipated at high wind speeds. But a significant amount of damage is inflicted at moderate wind speeds. Indeed, the inadequacy of roof, wall, and floor connections in non-engineered, or partially engineered light-frame construction has been the most common cause of failure.[11] This was borne out by the damage to tens of thousands of homes inflicted by Hurricane Andrew in 1992.

Whether the winds are due to tornadoes, hurricanes, or straight winds, local damage to walls and roofs, as well as structural failure, are caused by pressure loading, which is essentially proportional to the square of the wind speed. Let A be a reference area of a given structure; U be the reference mean wind speed at the top of the structure; and ρ be the air density. Then the reference mean velocity pressure is: $q = \rho U^2 / 2$, and the corresponding reference mean force is $q\, C_F\, A$, where C_F is the force pressure coefficient.

The vulnerability of a building to strong winds depends to a large extent on the ruggedness of its structural frame, and the strength of its components and peripheral cladding. Structural failure of the frame is serious, and can result in a complete loss. But if the frame remains intact, damage should be contained. However, failure of components or cladding can result in the breach of a building, which would then open the interior and its contents to the secondary loss of wind and water damage. Missile impact from flying debris is another source of secondary hazard.

Subject to a sustained battering by hurricane wind and rain, a building can transition progressively between sequential states of decreasing hazard protection. Thus an asphalt roof covering might be displaced or deflected, so exposing wooden roof layers to driving rain. With water permeating hitherto water-tight spaces, rainwater may then flow into the building interior. Through such a damage state transition mechanism, significant loss may occur, potentially even in fairly light winds with gusts less than 40 m/s. Such heightened vulnerability of roof coverings was revealed by Hurricane Ike in September 2008.

For a windward surface of a building, gusts are directly related to peak loads. However, wind loads which damage structures are only partially related to short duration maximum wind speeds. Dynamic flow patterns, such as the separation and re-attachment of flow around a building, can lead to severe local wind loads. The duration of winds above a high threshold may be one of several factors which may jointly yield a better correlation with damage than peak wind speed alone. However, it is often expedient to define vulnerability in terms of just peak wind speed, albeit recognizing a substantial variation in damage potential for a given type of building construction.

The simplicity of the peak wind speed descriptor of hazard is one of the numerous sources of uncertainty in characterizing building vulnerability to wind loading. A probabilistic representation of vulnerability should allow for air flow uncertainties in wind pressure, including the presence of local gust factors and the shielding and funnelling effects of neighbouring structures. In addition, there should be an allowance for the uncertainty associated with the pressure coefficient which relates maximum wind speed to induced pressure on the surfaces of a building. Contributing to the epistemic uncertainty are factors such as ignorance of anchorage detailing, which governs the potential for roof uplift and wall collapse, and ignorance of interior layout, which influences the stability of framing systems. Furthermore, there is uncertainty over design strengths for building materials such as concrete and steel, and over the degree of building code non-compliance, which would debase the national standard of wind engineering design.

10.2.3 Murphy's Law

It is instructive also to study the aleatory aspects of windstorm damage. After a severe English windstorm, one sleeping resident ended the stormy night on the ground floor ruins of his home. The force of the wind had toppled the house chimney, which fell through the roof, which partially collapsed onto the bedroom floor, which in turn collapsed onto the floor below. This progressive compounding of damage would suggest a long-tailed distribution for building vulnerability.

The principle that, if something goes wrong, then other (if not all) things will also go wrong, is known colloquially as *Murphy's Law*. Some freak accidents are so bizarre and hard to comprehend that an invocation of Murphy's Law provides a human psychological coping mechanism; one that appeals to a higher authority as partly responsible for matters going from bad to worse.

In April 1992, construction workers rehabilitating a bridge across the Chicago River drove a piling into the bottom of the river alongside an old rail tunnel. This cracked the tunnel wall, allowing mud to ooze in. After the mud passed through, water began to gush through the hole. The tunnel rapidly flooded, sending river water into the basements of buildings and retail stores. Utility supplies to the business district were then curtailed, leaving thousands of major offices no option but to shut down for half a week. Losses amounted to several billion dollars.[12] Save for the accidental rather than intentional act of cracking the tunnel wall, this kind of induced flooding scenario has been a terrorism worry to city authorities in the USA and UK. Indeed, some post 9/11 plots have considered exploiting this specific urban vulnerability. Murphy's Law exacerbates loss, ramping up leverage to the levels that so characterize the menace of asymmetric warfare.[13]

Potentially even more dangerous than a flood trigger of business interruption to city centre offices is a trigger of a major technological accident by flood, earthquake, tsunami, hurricane, or lightning. These domino hazard sequences are significant enough to merit special designation as *Natech* (Natural-Technological) events. With numerous industrial installations being sited close to rivers, seas or oceans, the global exposure to such combination events is massive.

Explosion accidents are a leading cause of fatalities in the chemical process industry, because they occur without warning time for evacuation or other mitigating action. Explosives are normally stored underground. It requires imagination to think of plausible routes by which a flood could cause severe damage to an underground storage facility. But they exist.[14] Some explosives are sensitive to shock; others react chemically with water. Furthermore, a flood might trigger pipe breaks or tank breaches, resulting in the release of hazardous materials. Murphy's Law will not be repealed any time soon.

10.3 Fermi Problems

The model statistician George Box famously wrote, 'Remember that all models are wrong; the practical question is how wrong do they have to be to not be useful.'[15] This concurs with a contemporary line of thinking of philosophers of science that, rather than attempting to validate or verify models, we should aim to confirm models, not in generality, but rather in their adequacy for particular purposes. Stress tests then may be considered to assess a model for inadequacy for its intended purposes.

This pragmatic approach of being fit for purpose underlies the calculation of catastrophe, and accords with the maxim of the economist John Maynard Keynes that it is better to be approximately correct than precisely wrong. The Bank of England heeds this wisdom in its forecasts of GDP growth, which are not deterministic, but are presented visually as broad fan charts representing a diverse range of alternative possibilities.

In a similar vein of thought on facing uncertainty is the advice of the statistician, John Tukey: 'Far better an approximate answer to the *right* question, which is often vague, than an *exact* answer to the wrong question, which can always be made precise.'[16] Analysis progresses by way of approximate answers.

Irrespective of the area of application, judicious approximations lie at the heart of a useful calculational model. Some are gifted with special intuition, but through apprenticeship and professional experience, modellers progressively learn to improve their capability at making approximations, albeit belatedly after actual disasters.

Theoretical physicists, who are inveterate modellers, have been described as artists of the approximation. Whereas mathematical physicists adhere to a very strict professional code of mathematical rigour, which may be perfectly justified as a worthy end in itself, their theorist colleagues are prepared to take bold leaps in their calculations in their quest to explain puzzling experiments, anomalies and other curious observations of the physical world. Rough calculations can be sketched on pads, wall-boards, coffee table tops, even napkins, and of course in the head – the only option for Stephen Hawking. Each calculation captures enough of the problem at hand to be useful as a stepping stone towards a more elaborate model.

One who epitomized a commando spirit of calculational adventure is Enrico Fermi. As one of the leading nuclear scientists in the USA during World War II, Enrico Fermi was involved in the Manhattan Project, and observed the first test of an atomic bomb in the summer of 1945. He wrote, 'On the morning of the 16th of July, I was stationed at the Base Camp at Trinity in a position about ten miles from the site of the explosion. The explosion took place at about 5.30 a.m.. About 40 seconds after the explosion, the air blast reached me. I tried to estimate its strength by dropping, from about six feet, small pieces of paper before, during and after the passage of the blast wave. Since at the time, there was no wind, I could observe very distinctly and actually measure the displacement of the pieces of paper that were in the process of falling while the blast was passing. The shift was about 2 1/2 meters, which, at the time, I estimated to correspond to the blast that would be produced by ten thousand tons of TNT.'[17]

The actual TNT yield was about 20 kilotons, just twice Fermi's estimate, which was based on a simple indirect measure of the blast. Given the power-law character of catastrophe events, a factor of two error for a rapid calculation is quite commendable. The capacity to make approximate, yet adequately accurate, calculations with scant information was one of Fermi's many intellectual gifts. Estimating a parameter sensibly with sparse information is called a Fermi problem. Considerable ingenuity and mental agility are often needed to think of benchmarks by which a complicated parameter can be calculated. No wonder that Fermi problems are posed in job interviews.

Disaster scenario loss estimation is a characteristic Fermi problem. After the London transport terrorist attack of 7 July 2005, when three Underground trains and a bus were bombed during the height of the morning rush hour, hospitals were on standby to receive an unknown number of casualties ranging widely from hundreds to thousands. Fortunately, the actual number was not near the upper end of the range.

In the immediate aftermath of any hazard event, there are many stakeholders in the public and private sectors with an interest in estimating casualties and damage. Accident and emergency rooms in hospitals need some idea of the serious casualty count so that the maximum number of those with life-threatening injuries can be treated within the vital 'golden hour'. The fire and police departments need some sense of how many fires may break out, and how many people might need to be rescued. Aid agencies and NGOs need to assess short-term aid requirements, and insurers need an estimate of what claims to expect. If there were only a few types of disaster to expect, highly specific preparedness measures might be adopted. But the possible crisis situations are numerous, and action has often to be decided rapidly under time pressure and limited information.

To guide general intuition across perils, a wide selection of Fermi problems is presented, illustrating the power of simple approximate calculations in developing basic understanding, and shedding light on some of the diverse facets of catastrophe risk.

10.3.1 The Fermi paradox

While working at the Los Alamos National Laboratory in New Mexico, Fermi stumbled across a paradox, which bears his name. In 1950, there had been a number of UFO sightings, which prompted conversation amongst Fermi's colleagues as to the prospect of the Earth being visited by extra-terrestrials. This was a classic Fermi problem. He did some quick calculations and figured that the Earth should already have been visited many times. But if this were true, Fermi then wondered, 'Where is everybody?' A decade later, astronomer Frank Drake formalized the discussion of extra-terrestrial intelligence through his equation:[18]

$$N = R . f_p . n_e . f_l . f_i . f_c . L$$

N is the number of civilizations in our galaxy that can communicate.

R is the average rate of star formation per year in our galaxy.

f_p is the fraction of those stars that have planets.

n_e is the average number of planets that can support life, per star that has planets.

f_l is the fraction of the above that eventually develop life.

f_i is the fraction of the above that eventually develop intelligent life.

f_c is the fraction of civilizations that develop technology that signals existence into space.

L is the length of time such civilizations release detectable signals into space (before dying).

The product of all but the last factor L is the number of new communicating civilizations born each year. Multiplying this by the average lifetime of such a civilization then yields the average number existing at a given time. Drake's original calculation gave a number of 10, this being the product of the seven terms: 10, 0.5, 2, 1, 0.01, 0.01, and 10,000. As simple as it is uncertain, this arithmetic nevertheless suggests that N may well be at least one, which opens an astrobiological window for thinking about extra-terrestrials.

Einstein said, 'Intellectuals solve problems, geniuses prevent them.' To the extraordinary mind of Stephen Hawking, this kind of calculation makes thinking about extra-terrestrials perfectly rational, the challenge being what to expect. On this subject of intensive astrobiological research, he has speculated, 'If aliens ever visit us, I think the outcome would be much as when Christopher Columbus first landed in America, which didn't turn out very well for the Native Americans.'[19] This characteristically British understatement of colonial history challenges the world to consider extra-terrestrial intelligence not just as an esoteric scientific issue, but also as a source of catastrophe risk, with the arrival of extra-terrestrials being a potential global disaster scenario.

Whilst some astrobiologists might dispute Hawking's colonial analogy, all should endorse efforts to parameterize Drake's equation using improved astronomical observations; particularly, to estimate better the average number n_e of life-supporting planets in a star. This is a key objective of the Kepler mission to survey *Goldilocks* planets that lie within the habitable zone of a star. Within a couple years of launch in March 2009, the Kepler space telescope found a Sun-like star with as many as six tightly orbiting planets.[20] Hawking's worry over the galactic horizon would be this: where the Goldilocks criterion is shown to be satisfied, can the three bears be far away?

Natural philosophers need not wait for one problem to be solved before posing another. Marcelo Gleiser has dared to contemplate the Drake equation for the multiverse of parallel universes, such as inspired by the anthropic landscape of string theory.[21] How many civilizations might exist in the multiverse? Information from extra-terrestrials would help to answer this question.

10.3.2 Earth impacts of a meteorite strike

Consider the disaster scenario of a meteorite hurtling towards Earth. You specify the impactor diameter, density, and velocity before atmospheric entry, together with the impact angle, and whether the impact target is sedimentary or crystalline rock, or a water layer above rock. Suppose you are interested in the environmental effects at a particular distance from the target, and want instant web-based results. This is clearly a Fermi problem of a high order, requiring a variety of necessary approximations, including the use of compact parametric formulae to characterize complicated physical phenomena demanding supercomputer facilities to analyze in detail.

Fortunately, one of the world's foremost experts on meteorite impact happens to have an agility at making approximations that comes with his Caltech Ph.D. in theoretical physics: Jay Melosh. Together with colleagues Gareth Collins and Robert Marcus, he devised a web-based computer program for calculating the regional environmental consequences of a meteoroid impact on Earth.[22] With the thickness of ejecta deposits and air-blast pressure decaying more rapidly with distance, they found that seismic ground shaking has the most wide-reaching effects.

To gauge the style of Fermi approximations made, the treatment of the seismic effects provides a good illustration. From the meteorite input values, the kinetic energy of the impact can be calculated. The fraction of the impact kinetic energy that is dissipated as seismic waves is approximately 1/10,000, based on experimental data. The standard seismologist's energy conversion rule, that a unit increase in earthquake Magnitude corresponds to a 30-fold increase in seismic energy release, can then be used to estimate an equivalent Magnitude for the impact seismic energy. This Magnitude then governs the consequent attenuation of seismic wave energy with distance, and the felt effects at a designated distance can be estimated with reference to the Modified Mercalli Intensity Scale.

Among other scenarios, Melosh *et al.* consider what would happen if a 1.75 km diameter stony asteroid were to impact at 20 km/s into Los Angeles. This corresponds to an impact event that formed the Ries crater in Southern Germany about 14 million years ago. The seismic energy generated would be that of a Magnitude 8 earthquake epicentred in Los Angeles, being capable of causing some shaking damage in San Diego, but hardly any in San Francisco. Residents of San Diego living in wood-framed buildings should manage to ride out the seismic shaking, but would be advised to guard against complacency – the peak air-blast overpressures resulting from the impact shock wave might cause such buildings to collapse.

10.3.3 Solar storm impact on satellite orbit decay

Satellites in Low Earth Orbits, between 300 km and 1,000 km above the Earth, eventually experience enough frictional drag from the atmosphere for their orbits to decay, and at altitudes below 300 km they fall back to Earth and burn up. One of the serious ways that a major solar storm might affect satellites is to increase the density of the atmosphere, and cause satellites in Low Earth Orbits to lose altitude. There is a clear correlation between sunspot counts and the number of satellite re-entries: as many as 45 re-entered in 1989, when there were 162 sunspots.

Odenwald *et al.* have developed a simple model for satellite orbit decay.[23] Denoting the closest point on the elliptical orbit to the Earth, i.e. the perigee, as $P(t)$, then $P(t) = P_0 - A(t).t^\alpha$, where P_0 is the initial perigee, and $A(t)$ is a sinusoidal function of time with 11 year solar cycle periodicity. This Fermi problem formula is handy for estimating premature re-entries of satellites in the decades ahead. This depends on the way a future major solar storm increases the atmospheric drag for the satellites in the lower orbits.

10.3.4 Building resonance under earthquake excitation

Wherever buildings are situated, they should be designed to cope with the dynamic loading which they may reasonably experience during their lifetime. Although complex dynamic analysis is undertaken for critical installations and major structures, for ordinary buildings, simple Fermi approximations suffice. A standard earthquake engineering procedure, popular for its simplicity, is to specify earthquake loading in terms of the response of the core unit of a dynamic vibrational system: a single-degree-of-freedom oscillator, with some viscous damping.

The equation of motion for the displacement Δ of a simple system of mass M with natural frequency ω and damping parameter ζ, subject to a harmonic forcing term $F \sin \Omega t$, can be written as:[24]

$$\ddot{\Delta} + 2\zeta\omega\dot{\Delta} + \omega^2\Delta = (F/M)\sin\Omega t$$

Let $R = \Omega/\omega$, the ratio of the frequency of the forcing function to that of the system. Compared with the static forcing case, the dynamic amplification factor for the system displacement is:

$$\frac{1}{\sqrt{(1-R^2)^2 + (2\zeta R)^2}}$$

When the external forcing frequency equals the system frequency, then this dynamic amplification becomes $1/2\zeta$, which is very large when the damping ζ is small, e.g. a few per cent. Resonance is one of the universal phenomena in physics. As in the diagnostic use of magnetic resonance imaging, resonance can save lives. But where a building of low damping is excited by external forcing which includes a significant component of similar frequency, resonance can be hazardous. The swaying of tall buildings in response to a distant large earthquake is typically not dangerous where adequate allowances have been made within building codes. However, on soft soil sites, the exceedance of design ground motions from great earthquakes is possible, and might cause consternation in a state such as Singapore, where the ambient threat from earthquakes is otherwise low.[25]

10.3.5 *Real-time earthquake casualty estimation*

Rapid approximate estimation of the toll of casualties following a large earthquake is crucial for the effective organization of prompt humanitarian response. Real-time Fermi casualty estimates can be made by performing the following four-step analysis: [1] Obtain the earthquake hypocentre and Magnitude from the USGS National Earthquake Information Center (NEIC); [2] Calculate the strength of ground shaking as a function of epicentral distance; [3] Estimate the damage inflicted on the regional building stock by the ground shaking; [4] Estimate the casualty impact of damaged buildings.[26]

The first step can be accomplished within a matter of minutes, with a degree of accuracy that improves with the density of regional seismological instrumentation. The second step can also be undertaken quite quickly, using standard off-the-shelf ground motion attenuation relations, augmented by actual measurements of strong motion, where regional instrumental networks are deployed.[27] The third step ideally involves engineering surveys of building stock, which might take several man-weeks per city. More expedient, if maybe less pertinent, is the engineering data on buildings accumulated by the Earthquake Engineering Research Institute (EERI) in its world housing encyclopaedia. Deficiencies can be remedied by using satellite images to build 3-D models of cities, and then remotely classifying building stock according to soil conditions and vulnerability. The fourth step is crucially dependent on the third, and also requires a global population database with very fine geographical resolution.

Even to achieve order of magnitude estimates of casualties, good quality of information is required on the current standard of construction, soil properties, and local demographics. The Canterbury, New Zealand, earthquake of 4 September 2010 had the seismological makings of a high casualty event, with strong levels of ground shaking generated by a local Magnitude 7.1 shallow fault rupture. Thankfully, with the earthquake occurring before dawn, there were no earthquake fatalities. By contrast, the subsequent regional M6.3 earthquake on 22 February 2011 occurred at lunch time, and caused several hundred deaths in Christchurch, where some extremely high levels of ground shaking were recorded.

10.3.6 Tsunami travel time

An understanding of the ocean propagation of a tsunami may be a lifeguard for those visiting the coast. For a large earthquake, a tsunami may be tens of kilometers wide and of the order of 100 km long. Given that the ocean water depth d is generally not more than a few kilometres, use is justified of shallow-water (long wave) fluid dynamical theory as a first-order approximation. This yields a tsunami propagation speed, at longitude-latitude location (x, y), of $v(x, y) = \sqrt{g(y) . d(x, y)}$, where $g(y)$ is the gravitational acceleration at latitude y, and $d(x, y)$ is the water depth. The travel times from the earthquake epicentre can be calculated using a time minimization approach based on Huygens' principle, which is a classic method for constructing the position of a wave at successive times.

Avoiding the complication of constructing tsunami wave propagation and diffraction patterns, a Fermi solution to estimating tsunami travel time is to assume an average ocean depth of five kilometres, and a geographically uniform value of gravitational acceleration of 9.81 m/s^2. This yields a tsunami travel speed of approximately 500 miles per hour, which is around the cruising speed of a passenger jet.

The great Indian Ocean earthquake of 26 December 2004 generated a destructive tsunami on surrounding coastlines. This was the first time that a tsunami caused by an earthquake had affected Sri Lanka, and no contingency plans had been prepared.[28] Tragically, along the south and east coasts of Sri Lanka, about 50,000 lives were lost to the tsunami.

Batticaloa was one of the east coast districts severely affected by the tsunami. Almost 4,000 people there were reported dead or missing, and 16,000 houses were completely damaged. The distance from Batticaloa to the earthquake epicentre was about 1,000 miles, which would yield a Fermi estimate of about two hours for the travel time. This is consistent with the first arrival time of 8.30 a.m. given by local eye witnesses. Elsewhere along the south and west coast, the accuracy of the Fermi estimate is eroded by diffraction effects, which delayed the arrival times up to an hour. With access to some hazard event communication, rapid Fermi mental arithmetic might be a life-saver.

10.3.7 Gauging injury severity

An important medical challenge associated with disaster management is scoring the degree of critical illness of a victim. This is a Fermi problem because any method which reduces injury severity to a single figure can only be rather crude and approximate. There are inherent differences between patients, not least their medical history, which affect a victim's response to injuries sustained: information is always lost in a score. Many scoring systems have been proposed, and all have advantages and disadvantages.

The Abbreviated Injury Scale (AIS) is one such scoring system. Injuries are ranked on a scale of 1 to 6, corresponding to minor, moderate, serious, severe, critical, and non-survivable injury. Disasters, both natural and man-made, are especially harmful because of their ability, accidentally or intentionally, to cause multiple injuries. A scoring system that provides an overall score for patients with multiple injuries is the Injury Severity Score (ISS). Each injury is assigned an AIS score and is allocated to one of six body regions: head, face, chest, abdomen, extremities, and external. Only the highest AIS score in each body region is used. The three most severely injured body regions have their score squared and added together to produce the ISS score. The ISS score range is only from 0 to 75. The top figure is used if any injury is non-survivable and therefore assigned an AIS of 6.

The simple arithmetic basis for the ISS score, involving summing the squares of the three highest AIS values, has the appearance of a rough-and-ready calculation, but it makes basic sense as any Fermi problem solution should, and correlates with mortality, morbidity, hospital stay, and other measures of severity.

As a place and time for a practical application of the ISS scoring system, consider Madrid on the morning of 11 March 2004, three days before a Spanish general election. Ten backpack bombs were exploded by Islamist terrorists almost simultaneously in four commuter trains, killing 177 people instantly and injuring more than 2,000. Of 29 deemed to be in critical condition, two died almost immediately on arrival, leaving 27, all with multiple injuries, to be admitted to an Intensive Care Unit. Within 24 hours, the severity of their injuries was assessed using various measures, including the ISS system. The average ISS score was 34. Nine patients had ISS scores above 40. Just four of the 27 patients in intensive care had ISS scores exceeding 50. Of these, three, with ISS scores of 75, 57, and 57, failed to survive.[29] The outcome that the three deaths in intensive care were of patients with particularly high ISS scores, shows the predictive capability of ISS, simple as it may be, and the value of Fermi calculations in rapid disaster response.

10.3.8 H5N1 avian pandemic influenza

The World Health Organization (WHO) received reports in early 2004 that a new highly pathogenic strain of avian influenza, H5N1, was spreading across Asia, infecting both poultry and people. Given the potential of the virus for genetic reassortment, concern was raised over sustained human-to-human transmission, and the possible outbreak of an avian influenza pandemic. WHO issues statistics of laboratory-confirmed cases of human infection with H5N1. How can such data be used to gauge the likelihood of an H5N1 influenza pandemic?

In assessing the public health risk from avian H5N1, Ferguson *et al.* proposed a simple probabilistic analysis of the risk of a pandemic.[30] Let p be the probability that an individual who is infected with avian influenza is coinfected with human influenza. Approximately 10% of the population is infected with human influenza over the 12 weeks of a typical influenza season, and coinfection might be possible within a one-day time window in early infection. These disease assumptions yield an approximate figure of $1/840 \approx 0.0012$ for p.

If there are N cases of avian influenza, the probability that at least one person is co-infected is $c = 1 - (1 - p)^N$. Let q be the conditional probability that a coinfected person becomes the unfortunate host for a viral genetic reassortment event. Then the overall annual probability of a transmissible pathogenic avian influenza virus being created is $c \times q$. As Day *et al.* observe, the number of unreported or unconfirmed cases is likely to be large. This is supported by the high lethality rate of above 50% among the laboratory-confirmed cases.[31] Advances in theoretical biology may shed future light on q. But it is not well constrained observationally, so the overall annual probability of a transmissible pathogenic avian influenza virus is also rather poorly constrained. However, the trend in the values of c, the probability that at least one person is co-infected, is useful in providing general insight into the variation over time of the H5N1 pandemic threat level. The WHO count data of laboratory-confirmed cases for the period 2003 to 2010 are tabulated below, together with the corresponding values of c.

Table 10.1. Annual variation in the number of laboratory-confirmed cases of H5N1, and corresponding values of the probability that at least one person is co-infected.

Year	H5N1 Case Number N	Co-infection Probability c
2003	4	0.5%
2004	46	5%
2005	98	11%
2006	115	13%
2007	88	10%
2008	44	5%
2009	73	8%
2010	48	6%

10.3.9 Global temperature of the Earth

An increase in infectious disease is just one of the concerns about future climate change. A basic understanding of the physics governing the temperature of the Earth is helpful before addressing the complex meteorological issues of climate modelling. The zeroth order approximation for the average temperature of the Earth over the entire year is calculable simply by equating the rate of incoming solar radiation energy with the rate of radiated energy emitted by the Earth.

The solar constant S is defined as the quantity of solar energy at normal incidence outside the atmosphere at the mean Sun–Earth distance. Its mean value is 1367.7 W/m². Denoting the average Earth radius as R, and the fraction of the solar radiation reflected, i.e. the albedo, as α, the rate of incoming solar radiation energy is $(1-\alpha).(\pi R^2 S)$. The terrestrial albedo is approximately 30%.

According to the Stefan–Boltzmann Law, the total energy radiated per unit surface area of a black body in unit time is proportional to the fourth power of the temperature. Assuming the Earth is a black body radiator, then the rate of total energy radiated is $4\pi R^2 \sigma T^4$, where the proportionality constant σ is 5.67×10^{-8} W/m² per K⁴. Equating the incoming and radiated energy rates then yields an Earth black body temperature of about 255°K. Compared with the average Earth temperature of 288°K, this constitutes an error of about 10%, which is not bad for a simple Fermi problem hand calculation.

More significantly, this Fermi problem also provides a basic yet relevant tutorial in the treatment of model risk, which is the predicament for risk analysts that alternative models may yield contrasting views of risk. Mindful of George Box's adage that all models are wrong, how should risk ambiguity be treated?

Lenny Smith has rightly pointed out that no amount of parameter uncertainty modelling can compensate for the fundamental error in this elementary simplistic model for global Earth temperature.[32] Repeating the above calculation with perturbed albedo, solar constant, Earth geometry etc., would generate an array of alternative estimates of temperature, but would not expose the plain inadequacy of the underlying model. Risk output might be generated on the annual probability of heat wave temperatures in Siberia, but it would be grossly unreliable for practical decision-making. Before any attempt at quantitative uncertainty analysis would be gainful, the core of any risk model has to capture sufficient characteristics of the phenomena being modelled to reach a minimum credibility threshold. Omission of vital features, e.g. the greenhouse effect in the above example, needs to be remedied before any uncertainty analysis would be meaningful.

Chapter 11

Catastrophe Cover

Poverty is a threat to peace.
Mohammad Yunus,
Nobel Peace Lecture

Survivors of the 1906 San Francisco earthquake, who gathered at Lotta's Fountain at 5.12 a.m. on 18 April each year, might have included in their anniversary commemoration the name of a Lloyd's underwriter, Cuthbert Heath. On hearing news of the earthquake, Cuthbert Heath, living up to the Lloyd's motto of *utmost good faith*, telegrammed his local agent, 'Pay all our policy-holders in full, irrespective of the terms of their policies.' This telegram did much to assist in the reconstruction of San Francisco, and establish catastrophe insurance cover as a vital pillar of support enhancing the disaster resilience of a stricken city.

The decision to make claim payments in full, irrespective of terms, made practical business sense because fire, whether accidental or deliberate, ruined properties without specific earthquake coverage. 500 city blocks were consumed by fire following the earthquake, and 30,000 houses were destroyed. The 1906 earthquake cost Lloyd's underwriters an estimated £100 million, but the seismic shadow cast by the crustal stress release shielded them from further California earthquake catastrophe in the decades ahead.

A century later, after the terrorist attacks on Mumbai on 26 November 2008, in which 165 died, Lloyd's terrorism underwriters paid for hotel damage caused not just by the terrorists, but also by the response of the Indian National Security Guard.[1] Cuthbert Heath's expansive vision for underwriting catastrophe insurance lives on within the aggregation of syndicates that is the Lloyd's market in London.

In 1963, the economist Paul Samuelson proved what every Lloyd's underwriter knew intuitively, that the system of fractional participation in one risk is a more fundamental way of reducing risk than having replicates of identical independent risks: an insurance organization does not reduce its risk by doubling the number of properties it insures.[2] Each Lloyd's syndicate focuses on selecting its own preferred share of a risk, without knowing, or even needing to know, all the other participants in the risk. For a market with many syndicates, there is safety in numbers.

A competitive insurance market is one, like Lloyd's, with numerous buyers and sellers, who are well informed. Of all practical domains of application of catastrophe calculations, insurance is one of the most important, since these calculations are much needed to keep the market well informed about the catastrophe risks which are being underwritten.

For an insurance market to operate effectively, there has to be a reliable flow of information between the insurer and the policyholder. Without this, pricing distortions may occur which eventually can lead to market failure. One major problem is adverse selection. If inadequate information on a higher risk property is made available to an insurer by the buyer, a policy may be under-priced. A general consequence of under-pricing could be to over-weight a portfolio with poor risks.

In addition, insurers are also exposed to a moral hazard, where insured properties are not well maintained by policyholders, or where risk mitigation measures are poorly implemented. Furthermore, in the event of a loss, claims may be exaggerated either intentionally or through over-reporting errors. To minimize moral hazard, insurers need to enforce tight loss control, and to have available sufficient resources to monitor policyholder behaviour.

Adverse selection and moral hazard remain concerns even in developed insurance markets, where information asymmetry is comparatively low. However, for middle and low income countries, information asymmetry may well be high. The consequent greater uncertainty over losses forces insurers to set aside larger amounts of capital for underwriting risks in these countries, which implies higher premiums. But this pricing for lack of knowledge is reduced with improvements in the acquisition of reliable exposure data, and the greater use of catastrophe modelling tools for portfolio risk management.

11.1 Probable Maximum Loss

The requirement to gauge an upper limit to the loss arising from a fire, explosion, or other peril, has always been a core element of sound insurance practice. The insured will need to fix the ceiling on the cover required, and so will the insurer in deciding how much cover to grant or retain.   Loss arises from the occurrence of a hazard event, and vulnerability to this hazard. Therefore any definition of maximum loss should reflect the dual hazard and vulnerability aspects of loss. According to a dictionary of insurance, 'It should be the largest possible loss which it is estimated may occur, in regard to a particular risk, given the worst combination of circumstances.'[3]

The use of absolutes such as *largest possible loss* and *worst combination of circumstances* in the wording of this basic definition, reflects an understandable quest for clarity in the midst of ambiguity, and objectivity in the midst of subjectivity.   However, such clarity and objectivity are often illusory. Imagine the largest possible loss stemming from the Gulf of Mexico oil well fire and blow-out on 20 April 2010.

The notion that residual risk need not be quantified was engrained in the confident NASA assurance of Challenger shuttle safety: 'Since the shuttle is a manned vehicle, the probability of mission success is necessarily very close to 1.0.' This is a circular statement: prior to the 1986 disaster, no formal quantitative risk assessment had yet been carried out.   Post-disaster risk analysis revealed the shuttle failure probability to be greater than 1/100.

There is considerable uncertainty over the severity of loss that might arise under a broad variety of hazard event circumstances. Rather than endeavour to estimate the uncertainty, the determinist seeks a conservative loss bound; one that circumvents the need for risk quantification.   Scientific laws of Nature underpin the deterministic tradition: if a clear upper loss bound may be established from fundamental scientific principles, such as the physics of combustion governing the spread of fire, there should be no need to quantify risk.

Economy is one of the attractions of determinism.   Diligence in assessing the largest possible loss, and identifying the worst combination of circumstances, may absolve a determinist from the numerical burden of modelling vulnerability and hazard in order to quantify risk. Given the computational labour avoided, determinism was for long a compelling practical doctrine. Those unsure of the arguments against risk analysis would have been persuaded by the tedious hours of hand calculations. Needing a vast staff of clerks, Lewis Fry Richardson's pioneering plan for numerical weather forecasting was never viable in a pre-computer age, likewise for numerical risk assessment.

So it was that deterministic estimates of maximum insured loss prevailed more or less unchallenged into the last quarter of the 20th century. For an industry whose very business was risk, catastrophe insurance lacked for decades what might seem an essential tool: a workable quantitative risk index to measure catastrophic losses.

11.1.1 Deterministic estimates of maximum earthquake loss

Early practitioners of earthquake hazard adopted the creed of determinism. The professions directly concerned with this hazard were civil engineering and geology. Civil engineers traditionally followed deterministic construction practices and building code guidelines in the quest for absolute safety, and dealt with uncertainty not by quantifying it, but by incorporating explicit factors of safety in design procedures. Evaluating risk was not a traditional part of a civil engineer's education. Neither were concepts of risk evaluation in the standard working vocabulary or training manuals of field geologists. Given a site location, an engineering geologist would follow a prescriptive procedure to set a ground motion level for seismic design.

One of the main reference regions for deterministic assessments of Probable Maximum Loss (PML) has been California. The deterministic PML approach is implicit in the prescriptive language of the 1972 Alquist–Priolo Earthquake Fault Zoning Act, prohibiting the location of most occupied structures across traces of active faults. Within a deterministic approach, a very high loss potential might be assigned to a site, merely on the slim evidence of activity on a neighbouring fault. But no allowance is made for active faults that remain to be discovered.

On 4 September 2010, a M7.1 New Zealand earthquake occurred on a hitherto unknown fault near Christchurch, Canterbury. The fault was buried under glacially deposited gravels undisturbed for at least 16,000 years. If this was not surprise enough for determinists, more was to come. A consequent M6.3 earthquake, even closer to Christchurch, occurred within six months on another buried fault, and generated levels of ground shaking exceeding building code standards.

Allowing for the inevitable differences in geological opinion on the interpretation of partial evidence, instability and controversy have accompanied many a deterministic seismic ground motion assessment.[4] One of the most publicized cases featured the nuclear test reactor at Vallecitos, in Northern California, 35 miles from downtown San Francisco.[5] When the operating license came up for renewal, some additional geological investigation was carried out at the base of a hill behind the reactor. Specifically, two trenches were dug which appeared to indicate that the clay and gravel strata in the trench wall had been sheared at some time after their deposition in the geological past.

The fifteen feet discontinuity was so sharp that no irregularity in soil deposition or weathering could have produced it. Some geologists thought this discontinuity had been caused by earthquake movement on the Verona fault, one of many in the California Coast Ranges. But this inference was disputed by other geologists who used local topographical information to argue a non-seismotectonic landslide interpretation.

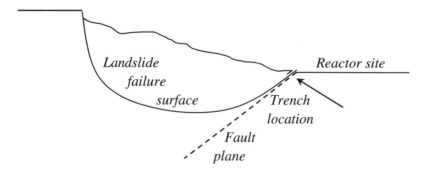

Figure 11.1. Cross-sectional diagram of regional terrain, showing how an ambiguity can arise in the geological interpretation of an observed trench displacement (Meehan, 1984).

The task of decision-making in an environment of contrasting geological opinion would seem well suited to probabilistic fault displacement hazard analysis. Indeed, this has been recognized in the nuclear installations seismic safety standards of the International Atomic Energy Agency.[6] Significant exceedance of seismic design ground motion at a nuclear plant is a serious concern, and did happen at the world's biggest facility. On 16 July 2007, during the M6.6 Niigata, Japan, earthquake, the Kashiwazaki-Kariwa plant experienced high levels of shaking, but still shut down safely.

11.1.2 *Rationale for a probabilistic approach*

As disquiet spread over deterministic assessments of seismic hazard, so risk-based methods emerged in the late 1960s. Probabilistic seismic hazard analyses began to be applied in the 1970s in studies for critical industrial installations such as nuclear facilities, petrochemical plants, liquefied natural gas plants, and dams. The rate of progress was slowed by the reluctance of regulators to countenance major innovation such as the introduction of probabilistic methods. Setting aside determinism, which found favour with lawyers, the rationale for the development of probabilistic risk assessment for such critical installations was clear. For an ordinary factory, the worst accident might destroy all the factory buildings and the workers within. But for a nuclear facility, the worst accident might transcend site boundaries, and lead to the deaths by irradiation of many people off site. Given that no nuclear facility, however well deterministically designed, can be entirely safe, the risk to the public has to be quantified. Acknowledging this necessity, the principles of probabilistic risk assessment were developed in the 1960s.

Maximum Credible Earthquake (MCE)

Earthquake risk studies for insurance applications began with important individual sites, such as industrial installations, exposed to seismic activity on nearby faults. Acknowledging that the neglect of fault activity rates was a serious weakness of the deterministic approach, seismic hazard consultants provided a risk-based definition for the expression *Maximum Credible Earthquake*, which had hitherto been used by geologists in a purely deterministic sense. The MCE for a fault was defined as the event with a 10% probability of exceedance in 50 years. Where earthquakes occur as a Poisson process on a fault, this is tantamount to a return period of about 475 years for the MCE, since: $1 - \exp(-50/474.6) = 0.1$.

This definition immediately resolved the deterministic conundrum of dealing with faults near an insured site which have not moved in many thousands of years. At the prescribed tolerance level, these can be ignored, and the attention focused on the more recently active faults. Once the MCE is specified for each threatening fault, the implications of this earthquake for a property portfolio remain to be assessed by structural engineers. The simplest option for these engineers is to estimate a conservative deterministic upper bound for the consequent portfolio loss, from a map of ground shaking generated by the MCE.

Where such conservatism might be deemed excessive, an alternative is to estimate a high (e.g. 90%) confidence bound on the portfolio loss from the MCE. This refinement would require a statistical analysis of building vulnerability. If such 90% loss bounds were estimated for each individual fault, then the overall PML for a portfolio would be taken as the highest 90% confidence portfolio loss from any fault, where the defining fault earthquake is the MCE with a 475 year return period.

The use of the risk-based MCE in defining PML was a notable improvement over the deterministic procedures which hitherto had held sway. Fortunately, such improvement came at a modest cost in terms of professional manpower and computing resources. In particular, no elaborate risk software was required. As a consequence, this pragmatic risk-based MCE method proved very popular with earthquake consultants. However, the use of 475 years as a reference return period for an earthquake on a fault is arbitrary; other long return periods might be chosen. Furthermore, regardless of return period, any PML definition which is based on fault-specific event recurrence neglects the diverse range of faults which collectively contribute to the earthquake risk to the portfolio. Not just one, but a sizeable number of faults may each generate 475 year return period earthquakes capable of causing major portfolio loss.

11.1.3 Hazard exceedance probability curves

A mathematical procedure to quantify seismic hazard would have been specious before the plate tectonics discoveries of the 1960s established the causal mechanism for earthquake generation. Seizing the moment to understand and enumerate the contribution of the earthquake sources that might affect a site, Allin Cornell laid out the standard computational framework for probabilistic seismic hazard evaluation.[7] In doing so, he spread the 1960s spirit of revolution from science to engineering. According to one upholder of determinism, 'The probabilistic approach is more of a thought process than it is physics'.[8] Indeed, this is why Cornell's contribution was so revolutionary.

The conceptual basis of this procedure was just the total probability theorem. Let $f(M, x)$ be the frequency of earthquakes of Magnitude M, epicentred at x, and let $P(Z \geq z \mid M, x)$ be the conditional probability that the site ground motion Z (e.g. peak acceleration) is greater or equal to z, given the occurrence of this event. The expected annual number of site exceedances of this ground motion level is obtained by integrating over all possible earthquake epicentres and Magnitudes:

$$v(z) = \int dM \, dx \; f(M, x) \; P(Z \geq z \mid M, x)$$

For a Poisson process, the annual probability of exceedance of ground motion Z is just $1 - \exp(-v(z))$. On the resulting hazard curve, a specific point of earthquake engineering interest is the exceedance probability of 1/475, corresponding to a 475 year return period for the site. This return period has often been used as a building code criterion for a seismic design basis. The Uniform Building Code intended that structures be designed for life-safety in the event of an earthquake with a 10% probability of being exceeded in 50 years. The problem with this design earthquake was that it did not provide adequate protection for the infrequent but very large seismic events which occur in the Central and Eastern USA. The International Building Code (IBC) intends design for collapse prevention and consequent safety of occupants, in a much larger earthquake, with a 2% probability of being exceeded in 50 years.[9,10]

Irrespective of the design basis, a site PML can be defined in terms of the ground motion with a specific site return period. As with the fault-based MCE, a conservative estimate of maximum site loss could be made deterministically, from knowledge of the construction on the site. Less conservatively, a 90% confidence loss estimate may be assigned by reference to vulnerability functions for structures of the type found on the site. The 90% figure reflects the wording of definitions, such as developed by the California Department of Insurance,[11] that PML should be the expected shake damage loss experienced by 9 out of 10 buildings.

In this PML procedure, hazard and damage are treated here in distinct ways, and not integrated within an overall systematic risk-based approach. On the one hand, seismic hazard is probabilistically quantified, with the hazard contribution of all earthquake event scenarios weighted according to their likelihood of occurrence. On the other hand, damage is estimated either deterministically, or statistically at a specified confidence level. This is a hybrid quasi-probabilistic approach.

This hybrid approach can also be used to estimate PML for a secondary earthquake hazard such as a tsunami. Dominey-Howes *et al.* carried out a PML study for the US Pacific Northwest, where the primary tsunami threat emanates from occasional great earthquakes on the Cascadia Subduction Zone.[12] The loss potential to a coastal town in Oregon was evaluated, based on mapped tsunami water heights calculated to have an annual exceedance probability of 1/500. Cheerily named 'Seaside' after a summer resort built in the 1870s, it lacks a civic memory of the great tsunami of January 1700, unlike coastal areas across the Pacific Ocean in Japan. Oregon coast residents learning of the Japanese tsunami tragedy of 11 March 2011 should have been mindful of their own similar vulnerability.

11.1.4 Portfolio loss exceedance probability curves

Earthquake insurers have always ideally needed to construct an exceedance probability curve for loss to a portfolio covering multiple sites distributed over a wide geographical region. No specific fault would be singled out; this exceedance probability curve would implicitly encompass all conceivable hazard event scenarios, weighted according to their frequency of occurrence. The appropriate procedure to achieve this objective is essentially that of Cornell's seismic hazard analysis for ground motion exceedance at a single site. To extend this analysis to cover loss at a portfolio of sites, the same conceptual approach can be followed, except that instead of the exceedance parameter being ground motion at one site, it is the portfolio loss aggregated over all sites. The corresponding risk index for PML purposes is a high quantile of the portfolio annual exceedance probability (EP) curve.

Portfolio loss exceedance curves began to be developed in the late 1980s, when such analyses became numerically feasible on a desktop computer. However, available portfolio property data were sketchy in geographical coverage and building detail, and due to limited PC power, the early portfolio risk models were rather skeletal in the resolution of event scenarios. For as long as catastrophe risks could be readily placed in the insurance market with scant exposure information and limited risk analysis, the biggest impetus for significant model advancement would come in the wake of a major financial loss shock: 1992 for Hurricane Andrew, and 1994 for the Northridge earthquake.

Contributing to a turning point in catastrophe insurance management, the rating agency A.M. Best requested from insurers PMLs for high return periods. The establishment of insurance limits by reference to a loss return period has the merit of industry uniformity and the virtue of transparency, besides which the concept of a return period is readily understandable across tiers of insurance management.

As computer performance has been enhanced in the 21st century, so also has model resolution, and the elaborate complexity of the insurance and reinsurance contracts for which probabilistic loss results are computed. Apart from refinements in risk modelling, increasing computing performance has made practical and gainful high resolution portfolio data capture on building location and construction.

For those perils and territories for which catastrophe modelling software has been developed, the quantile index has largely superseded its less methodical and sophisticated predecessors as a PML measure, except that deterministic scenario methods continue to be used for supplementary accumulation control.

11.1.5 Loss aggregation

Economical with both resources and rigour, loss aggregation using deterministic or quasi-probabilistic methods has often been achieved by naive addition of PMLs. This is a gross simplification that deftly side-steps the problem of calculating the geographical correlation of loss between different hazard events. Thus if the PML for a Southern California portfolio was based on a Los Angeles earthquake scenario, and the PML for a Northern California earthquake was based on a San Francisco Bay earthquake scenario, the overall California PML might be taken to be the sum, even though the event scenarios were quite distinct. The Los Angeles scenario might generate some loss in Northern California, but it would not cause the PML loss. Similarly, the San Francisco Bay earthquake scenario might cause some loss in Southern California, but not the PML loss.

The loss exceedance probability approach is more sophisticated than its deterministic or quasi-probabilistic counterparts, and can be used by a conscientious analyst to aggregate PMLs more methodically.[13] Thus if PMLs for Northern and Southern California were obtained from separate regional Exceedance Probability (EP) curves, then a PML for the whole state might be obtained from a state-wide EP curve. Through making the effort to pool the regional portfolios, some diversification benefit would be expected in the form of a joint PML smaller than the sum of the two regional PMLs. This benefit is realized with California earthquake hazard. But must this always happen?

The exceedance probability curve quantile has been widely adopted for PML purposes. Although this index has been well tried and tested over the years, its usage has been the source of confusion in the interpretation of some results, which has led on occasion to the false suspicion of numerical error or a programming bug. The problem is that apparent inconsistencies can arise which defy common sense, and thus are nigh impossible for insurance analysts to understand for themselves or explain to their managers. An illustration of inconsistency is given.

Consider two factories A and B which are sufficiently distant not to be affected by the same earthquake. Given that no earthquake could affect both factories, the earthquake PML for $A + B$ should be less than the sum of the PMLs for A and B. There should be some diversification benefit in pooling the two factories together into a joint portfolio. However, the quantile PML does not automatically satisfy this requirement, which would seem fundamental enough to be taken as axiomatic. If only earthquake loss distributions were Gaussian, then the quantile PML would comply with this axiom; but of course earthquake loss distributions are much heavier-tailed.[14]

To highlight this apparent paradox, consider two widely separated independent portfolios A and B. Each regional portfolio is exposed to a tectonic environment where moderate Magnitude earthquakes are quite frequent, but not particularly damaging; but large destructive events occur with a longer return period of, say, 200 years. Then the 100 year PML for both portfolio A and B would be small. However, the 100 year PML for the joint portfolio is large, because this takes into account the 200 year return period of destructive events striking either portfolio A or B. Examples of the discouragement of risk sharing between independent risks are all the more disquieting for being easy to contrive.

11.2 Coherent Risk Measures

The history of the development of risk indices has been an evolutionary process, with less well adapted methods falling into disuse, and the advent of new technology catalyzing the introduction of more elaborate computer-intensive risk definitions. From time to time, this history has been punctuated by episodes of accelerated progress. One such episode was linked with writing down the characteristics a measure of financial risk should have. Whatever earlier motivation there may have been to address this question, the development of derivatives trading turned this ostensibly academic question into one of acute practical interest in the banking world. It is from this commercial source that the initiative came to establish an answer, which introduced the essential concept of a coherent risk measure.

Artzner *et al.* presented four axioms which collectively define a coherent risk measure.[15,16] These axioms cover any financial position, but here, for illustrative purposes, these four axioms are restated in terms of PML for one peril, which might be earthquake, windstorm, flood, etc..

From the viewpoint of risk to a property portfolio, the set of states of nature of insurance concern is the set of possible regional peril event sequences during a year. For each such sequence, a random variable A is defined as the highest loss a particular portfolio sustains from an event happening during the year. The loss to the portfolio is the net loss, accounting for deductibles, coverage limits, reinsurance etc.. (For ease of notation, the portfolio is also labelled as A). One historical realization of this random variable might then be $\{0, 0, 0, 10, 0, 0, 5\}$, if the only net losses were in the 4th and 7th years, and the highest net losses in these years were 10 and 5, in a standard monetary unit.

The question is how to define a meaningful measure of maximum annual event net loss in terms of such a random variable. There are many possible choices. But the alternatives are greatly reduced in number if some algebraic constraints are imposed. Artzner *et al.* define a measure as coherent if it satisfies these four basic criteria.

(a)   *Translation Invariance:* $PML(A + c) = PML(A) + c$
If a constant loss amount c is applied to the portfolio loss for the worst annual event, then the PML is changed by the same amount.

(b)   *Positive Homogeneity:* $PML(k . A) = k . PML(A)$ $[k > 0]$
A change k in the monetary scale of the portfolio exposure (e.g. from a currency conversion) changes the PML by the same factor.

(c)   *Monotonicity: If* $A \geq B$ *then* $PML(A) \geq PML(B)$
Whatever peril events occur during the year, if the largest event loss to portfolio A is greater or equal to the largest event loss to portfolio B, then the PML for portfolio A must be greater or equal to that of B.

(d)   *Subadditivity:* $PML(A + B) \leq PML(A) + PML(B)$
There should be some diversification benefit in pooling risks. The PML for the joint A and B portfolios should not exceed the sum of the separate PMLs for A and B.

In the limiting case that portfolio losses are so strongly inter-dependent that they always move together in the same direction, i.e. they are *comonotonic*, there is no diversification benefit; instead there is comonotonic additivity.

11.2.1 *Expected shortfall*

It turns out that there is a PML definition which satisfies all these four criteria, and is relatively easy to compute. An obvious characteristic of the simple quantile definition of PML is that it ignores the tail of the loss distribution beyond the quantile point. There may be considerable variation in the heaviness of the tail. On the exceedance probability curve shown in Fig. 11.2, an alternative tail beyond the risk tolerance level α is extrapolated.

**Annual Probability
of Exceedance**

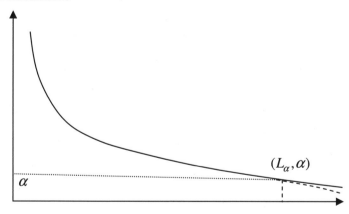

Portfolio Loss   L

Figure 11.2. Schematic portfolio loss exceedance probability plot, showing alternative tail behaviour beyond a specified risk tolerance level.

This deficiency can be rectified through introducing a coherent definition of PML. Of the possible candidates, the most natural and simplest definition in the present context is *Expected Shortfall.*[17] This is most conveniently explained using a Monte Carlo simulation. To start, set the risk tolerance level to be α. Suppose that N years of regional activity of a peril are simulated. These many random simulations are assumed to be equally probable. For each year, the worst (net) portfolio peril loss is identified. Rank these N losses in descending order. Let M be $N\alpha$, rounded up to the nearest integer. Then the Expected Shortfall is estimated simply as the average of the top M losses. Note that, even if the M th loss is shared by further years, it is only the top M losses which are averaged. It is easy to see that the Expected Shortfall is subadditive: the set of top M losses to a joint portfolio is, at worst, the same as the set of top M losses to the individual portfolios.

As an elementary example, suppose that 1,000 years of regional peril activity are simulated, and that the risk tolerance level is 1/200. Then M is 5. Suppose the top five losses (in a standard monetary unit) are: 5, 6, 8, 9, 12. Then the Expected Shortfall = 40/5 = 8. By comparison, a quantile-based estimate L_α would be the fifth largest loss, which is 5. Suppose that the top sixth loss happens also to be 5. This makes no difference to the Expected Shortfall. However, it would dilute a risk index based on the average over all losses of size L_α or above.

This observation leads on to a somewhat less conservative risk measure than Expected Shortfall: the Tail Conditional Expectation (TCE). This is defined as the conditional expectation of the losses greater or equal to L_α. The inclusion of a potentially large probability weight for a loss equal to L_α, may reduce the conditional expectation below that of Expected Shortfall. This dilution of loss has the effect that TCE is not always subadditive. For a continuous loss distribution, the conditional expected loss over the tail is:

$$(1/\alpha) \int_{L_\alpha}^{\infty} dL \, L \, \frac{dP(Loss \le L)}{dL}$$

Acerbi and Tasche have shown through introduction of a generalized inverse function of the cumulative loss distribution that this tail integral defines the Expected Shortfall where the loss distribution is discrete. The idea of using the conditional expectation of tail losses as a PML index is far from novel. From time to time, commercial studies for insurers have been undertaken in which this index has been computed. Furthermore, in other areas of insurance interest, such as capital allocation and dynamic financial analysis, the significance of expected deficit as a risk index has been long recognized.

What makes a difference is the existence of a sound mathematical reason for preferring this PML index to one based on a loss quantile. Until the work of Artzner *et al.*, there was no imperative rationale for switching PML indices. Now there is such a rationale: to uphold the principle of subadditivity of risks.

The breakdown of subadditivity is not a mere mathematical nicety; it may lead to misconceived schemes for risk management. Suppose that an insurer accepts the premise that the PML for joint portfolios $A + B$ exceeds the sum of the separate PMLs for portfolios A and B. Then by ceding a proportion λ of business, he would imagine he might reduce the PML by an even larger proportion. In reality, the PML might actually be reduced by a lesser proportion than λ. It is clear that this kind of misunderstanding could result in risk mismanagement.

For a prescribed risk tolerance level α, it is evident that allowing for large excess losses in the tail of the loss distribution will yield a higher risk metric than the basic quantile. Diers has used an explicit European windstorm example to show the possible implications for the risk capital requirements of a European insurer.[18]

Set against all the quantitative ways in which catastrophe tail risk can be managed, in parts of the developing world a resigned sense of fatalism still passes for risk management. Hope for the best; fear the worst, and if this should come to pass, then seek financial aid. But the amount raised may not necessarily satisfy the subadditivity criterion, due to the nonlinearity of the cooperative behavioural response to disasters. As shown by the 2004 Indian Ocean tsunami appeal, separate pleas for assistance from two territories may not raise more jointly than a single plea for the two territories combined.

11.3 The Samaritan's Dilemma

The world's first humanitarian organization, The Red Cross, was founded in 1863 by Henry Dunant, who was known as the 'Samaritan of Solferino', for his work in tending to the wounded after the battle of Solferino in Northern Italy. The parable of the Good Samaritan, which symbolizes the work of the Red Cross, is one of the abiding New Testament passages, and has continued in figurative English usage from the 17th century into the modern secular age.

The Samaritan's Dilemma is the title of an essay written by the Economics Nobel laureate, John Buchanan,[19] on the potential exploitation of altruistic donors by overly dependent recipients of aid. The most familiar paradigm is of well-intentioned food donors depriving African farmers of a meaningful incentive to grow their own food. This pattern of international economic behaviour has a simple game-theoretic interpretation. The donor has two options: to give or not to give. Being a benevolent soul, she would much rather give to the hungry, than not. The recipient also has two options: to grow his own food, or not. Being only human, he would rather choose not to toil under a hot sun. The equilibrium solution to this two-person game, noted by Buchanan, is simply for the donor to supply food to a dependent ex-farmer.

A catastrophe risk version of the Samaritan's dilemma exists in relation to post-disaster relief in hazard-prone developing countries. The custom of the international community to offer money and supplies for post-disaster relief can discourage *ex-ante*, i.e. advance, risk management in these countries. Ex-post disaster aid delivers financial assistance, but where it is perceived as an entitlement, it discourages more sustainable financial solutions, which may be viewed perversely as an implicit form of extortion. Isn't the Samaritan always unpaid?

Cummins and Mahul have pointed out the high opportunity costs for developing countries of post-disaster financing strategies.[20] When a disaster occurs, budget allocations are often diverted from essential development projects to fund emergency and recovery needs. In recent times, the World Bank has reallocated funds for around several dozen projects a year. The significance of reallocation is reflected in the World Bank's experience over several decades, when it made $3 billion available for natural disaster response through loan reallocations, while dedicating \$9 billion towards disasters through emergency recovery loans. For example, following the 26 January 2001 earthquake disaster in Gujarat, India, twelve projects were restructured, providing a total of more than \$400 million for immediate reconstruction.

International financial institutions, such as the World Bank, are encouraging the less impoverished developing countries, in their own interest, to embrace a comprehensive disaster risk management framework, involving improved emergency preparedness, risk mitigation to protect critical infrastructure, and the greater adoption of insurance for the transfer of catastrophe risk.

Less than 10% of losses in middle-income countries are covered by insurance. But progress is being made. Galvanized by the Izmit earthquake of 17 August 1999, which severely damaged more than 100,000 buildings, the Turkish government established the Turkish Catastrophe Insurance Pool (TCIP), with the assistance of the World Bank. TCIP offers homeowners efficiently priced earthquake insurance, while diminishing the Turkish government's moral obligation to provide housing subsidies in the aftermath of a potentially worse earthquake disaster, such as seismologists warn may befall Istanbul.

11.3.1 Earthquake risk transfer in Tehran

Tehran, the capital of Iran, has a picturesque location at the southern edge of the Alborz Mountains. However, a large fault is also located in this mountain range and there are several faults in the plains south of the city of Tehran. Virtually surrounded by faults, Tehran has often suffered large earthquake disasters. According to Ambraseys and Melville's authoritative history of Persian earthquakes, on 27 March 1830, an earthquake struck Tehran, leaving not a single house undamaged.[21] There may be a hundred times more inhabitants of Tehran now than in 1830. The expansion of Iran's largest city, mostly unplanned during the second half of the 20th century, has enormously increased its exposure to a destructive earthquake.

Tehran has expanded without experiencing a significant earthquake. This extended run of good fortune might have been seized as an opportunity for extensive seismic risk mitigation. Instead, there is inadequate urgency in reducing earthquake risk, and limited practical opportunity for local earthquake engineers to hone their skills by learning from actual damage occurrence.

The insurance affordability and premium sensitivity issues have been examined within the context of a probabilistic seismic risk study for a particular district in Northeastern Tehran.[22] Some results are tabulated below, expressed in terms of the annual average loss (AAL), and the loss with a return period of 250 years, i.e. an annual exceedance probability of 1/250. Even allowing for model risk in these results, some basic points can be made. By raising the deductible, which is the amount the policyholder is responsible for before the insurer pays, the insurance risk can be reduced quite substantially. Similarly, the insurance risk can also be reduced by lowering the limit of insurance cover.

Where a property has been seismically well designed and constructed, the policyholder may be sanguine about raising the deductible level and/or lowering the policy limit, so meriting a reduction in the earthquake risk premium. Earthquake insurance thus enhances societal resilience by promoting risk mitigation and seismic code compliance. These are prerequisites for controlling risk in a megacity where a major earthquake catastrophe looms.

Table 11.1. Dependence of Annual Average Loss (AAL) and 250 year return period loss on deductible and limit, for residential buildings in a Tehran district (Zolfaghari, 2010).

Deductible	Limit	AAL	250yr loss
0%	100%	0.23%	13.05%
5%	80%	0.16%	9.71%
5%	50%	0.14%	8.97%
10%	100%	0.14%	7.93%

11.3.2 *Diaspora disaster insurance*

Observing the destruction of the Chilean town of Concepción in February 1835, Charles Darwin remarked, 'Earthquakes alone are sufficient to destroy the prosperity of any country.' The atlas of natural disasters explains in part the unsustained prosperity of many developing countries, the fragile economies of which are disproportionately disrupted by destructive natural perils.

The mechanics of charitable fund-raising to assist hazard-prone countries have changed substantially since Victorian times, but the underlying ethos of soliciting charitable donations after an apparently unforeseeable tragedy of Nature is one that Darwin would recognize today. More astonishing to Victorians would be the significant presence in 21st century Europe of citizens with family links stretching across the globe. This growing diaspora can play a greater role in shouldering the disaster burden in developing countries.[23]

On Millennium Eve, London street collections were taken for victims of the Orissa cyclone who were still dying from disease and exposure two months after the cyclone had ravaged coastal areas of Northeastern India. This Dickensian scene of coins rattling in collecting tins for the destitute contrasts with the silent bustle of electronic trading in the City of London. How can a post-Victorian financial risk transfer solution be engineered to immunize developing countries better against natural catastrophes, and avoid the Samaritan's dilemma?

Public investment in disaster risk mitigation is a master key to reducing future tropical cyclone and flood losses. Such investment falls within a category of social finance which generates a good return by reducing future government liability. As with the financing of training for the unemployed, and rehabilitation for prisoners, current investment expenditure can save substantially greater monetary and human costs later. Recognizing that timely investment pays off, charitable financing of such social initiatives may involve the issuance of charity bonds, whereby an investor provides not a gift, but a loan, which is repaid after a set term, possibly with a return geared to the social benefits achieved. Charity bonds have been issued for some social needs, and may provide an additional source of finance for disaster risk mitigation.

Even without the 21st century spectre of global warming, population growth and increasing urbanization in developing countries are escalating the risk of human and financial loss from natural disasters, and hastening the urgency to find innovative financial risk management solutions. By and large, ordinary citizens of these countries simply do not have the financial means to pay themselves for this financial risk transfer. With the opportunity cost of cash being exceedingly high in poor countries, it is difficult to envisage how many impoverished people would choose to pay cash for insurance premiums. Hence disaster insurance penetration remains very low.

As president of the World Bank, James Wolfensohn campaigned to help the world's poor forge better lives. His mantra, 'Poverty anywhere is poverty everywhere', might be paraphrased here as 'Risk anywhere is risk everywhere'. Those made homeless by a natural disaster in one country, may become refugees in another. Migration is a major concern, especially to traditionally open welcoming countries, such as Canada. Risk in one country is also risk to expatriates living abroad. Diaspora communities share strong ties of kinship that transcend national borders: a disaster back home is their own disaster.

Acting individually or collectively, expatriates dispersed over the affluent nations could help spread a financial safety net over much of the developing world. Strong financial ties linking distant populations are a positive outcome of globalization, and motivate the concept of diaspora disaster insurance. The generosity of public response to the 2004 Indian Ocean tsunami relief campaign was remarkable in those European countries which lost its own citizens in the disaster. But such is the dense web of diaspora connections with the developing world that any major disaster would cause loss to European citizens or their relatives.

Remittances are a vital source of income for many developing countries, and form a substantial part of national GDP. They are used to meet a diverse array of needs. An ever important function of remittances is to provide a financial relief buffer following disasters of all kinds, economic and monetary crises, as well as natural perils. This crucial role is well appreciated at government level: remittances from expatriates working in the Gulf States were vital to the economic stability of the Philippines during the Asian currency crisis of 1998.

Other than rely on erratic post-disaster state assistance, households in developing countries may essentially self-insure through reliance on remittances from abroad. Records show that remittances typically soar after disasters. In January 2001, after the Gujarat earthquake, expatriate Gujaratis contributed hundreds of millions of dollars above their normal remittances. But although increased remittances over a short-term may cover moderate damage, they may be insufficient to pay for catastrophic loss. Rather than increase remittances over a prolonged period of time to cover catastrophic loss, remitters would benefit from risk pooling, as envisaged in diaspora disaster insurance.

Interviews conducted within the Indian diaspora community in England indicate a supportive attitude; one that might merit a government 'nudge', such as contemplated to facilitate other charitable donations. The Indian government has raised billions of dollars from its diaspora since 1991, and other governments have tapped into a foreign reserve of patriotism by issuing diaspora bonds to relieve debt.

In his essay on the *Samaritan's Dilemma*, Buchanan observed that modern man has become incapable of making the choices that are required to prevent his exploitation by predators of his own species. Aid agencies shipping equipment to Haiti after the earthquake of 12 January 2010 were confronted with the uncharitable choice of paying customs charges or customs officers. Being person-to-person transactions, remittances avoid the pitfall of misappropriation by government officials or unaccountable NGOs. Negative experience of the 2005 Kashmir earthquake slowed the response to the monsoon Pakistan floods of August 2010, which affected a fifth of the country. Yet the response of the Pakistani diaspora was swift and generous.

In his survey of insurance for the poor, Craig Churchill has likened microinsurance, (which is insurance protection for low-income people), with Janus, the Roman god with two faces.[24] Looking in one direction is the face of humanitarianism, with its focus on providing financial security for the under-privileged. Looking in the other direction is the face of the marketplace, with its focus on the commercial opportunity in serving the needs of billions at the bottom of the economic pyramid. As personified by the visionary C.K. Prahalad, there is a belief within the business community that poverty may be eradicated with profits.[25]

Chapter 12

Catastrophe Risk Securitization

FIFA is delighted with the positive response
from the international capital markets.
Sepp Blatter, FIFA president

High upon a wall in the Court Room of the Bank of England is a compass attached to a weathervane, installed on the roof in 1805, which informed bankers of the wind direction. A strong wind from the east indicated that ships would be sailing up the Thames into the city of London, where extra currency would be required for trading. Two centuries later, shipping remains a major business in London, and bankers still need to know about the weather, which has become itself an actively traded commodity, along with other catastrophe risks.

The geographical concentration of international commerce in a metropolis, such as London, is a manifestation of urban growth, which can be represented within a mathematical theory of urban living.[1] In the 19th century, the population of London expanded rapidly under industrialization from 1 million to 6.5 million. In 1950, only 30% of the world's population was urbanized; by 2010 the 50% milestone had been attained; and by 2050, this figure may reach 80%.

If there is a single invariance principle underlying the behaviour of individuals in society, it is that individual citizens make decisions according to their own preferences, but subject to the decisions of others. This leads to Zipf's law for the distribution of urban populations. As a result, substantial concentrations of asset value are exposed to loss in a single hazard event. With human populations doubling in some countries in just a few decades, the current environmental state is remote from equilibrium, with people clustering in areas of high hazard exposure.

Prudent insurance portfolio risk management dictates that the potential accumulation of loss in every hazardous region is subject to tight control. High urban concentrations of property strain the capacity of the insurance and reinsurance industry to provide adequate cover at a reasonable price. The greater the loss potential of a single catastrophe is, the larger the capital required. The extra cost of capital needs to be reflected in the insurance premium.

An urgent message establishing the need to extend reinsurance coverage for urban catastrophes was delivered in Florida by Hurricane Andrew in August 1992. The rationale for securitizing catastrophe insurance risks, and transferring them to capital market investors, made practical sense after this insurance loss of $17 billion – which might have more than doubled had the track been a little further north. Prior to 1992, there seemed less sense and little urgency in seeking alternative risk transfer to the capital markets, when the largest previous historical insurance loss, inflicted by Hurricane Hugo in 1989, had been a much more manageable $3.5 billion.

In 1994, shortly after Hurricane Andrew, the first 'Act of God' bond appeared. Unlike other bonds that an investor might hold, human action alone could not directly cause a default. As reported in the *New York Times*, an investor betting against the occurrence of a natural catastrophe was 'rolling the dice with God'. Many insurance-linked securities have been issued since. The monetary loss from many types of catastrophe can now be spread beyond the insurance world amongst the global capital markets. Damage repair for a Miami hurricane can be partly paid by an international network of investors in Zürich, Tokyo, London, and New York. It is as if a tsunami which devastated a single shoreline caused minor waves in all the oceans of the world.

In the capital markets, there is a keen appreciation of the commercial advantages of novel risk-shifting systems; progress in risk management which the economist Kenneth Arrow foresaw well before the era of financial engineering.[2] Although the markets for risk transfer are far from Arrow's concept of completeness, ever innovative catastrophe risk securitization deals are continually being financially engineered. These cover a range of natural catastrophes, life and health risks, and even destructive 'Acts of Man', some inspired by religion.

12.1 Catastrophe Bonds

Dating back to the second millennium BC, the Babylonian code of Hammurabi was the earliest earthquake building code in the world; the shortest; and the most brutal: the builder of a house which collapsed and killed an occupant was liable for the death penalty. If earthquakes were an impediment to the pursuit of commerce, so was highway robbery, and the code of Hammurabi introduced an early form of insurance contract whereby money lent for trading purposes was forfeited if the trader was mugged on his travels. As a testament to unchanging human nature, convoys from Basra to Baghdad have also needed such insurance in the third millennium AD.

The ancient Babylonian contract was adopted by the peripatetic Phoenicians, whence a maritime agreement *foenus nauticum* was introduced by the Romans.[3] Under this agreement, the insurer lent a sea-faring merchant the cost of his voyage. If the ship was lost, the debt would be cancelled, otherwise it would be repaid with a bonus. Several millennia later, this concept flourishes in the modern guise of the catastrophe bond – not for shipping but for property. The trader is typically a large insurer or corporation, with a sizeable natural catastrophe exposure. Through a bond issue, specific to peril and territory, financial provision can be made against a potential major loss.

A purchaser of a catastrophe bond runs the risk of losing part or all of the investment should a catastrophe occur, but otherwise earns a coupon (rate of return), the size of which reflects the risk of default. An investor may be attracted by the risk premium of bond coupons, but there are also strategic diversification reasons why the inclusion of catastrophe bonds within a large investment portfolio makes financial sense. In an era of global market correlation, catastrophe bonds form an asset class largely uncorrelated with others. Those authorized to change interest rates are not empowered to cause natural catastrophes.

Government institutions may also be advised to consider issuing catastrophe bonds to manage the risk of a negative impact on public finances of post-disaster emergency, relief and construction work.[4] For hazard-prone developing countries, fiscal budgets are often inadequate to meet excessive costs arising sporadically from natural disasters. On call to assist such countries in catastrophe risk financing, the World Bank developed a catastrophe bond issuance platform: MultiCat. Within this programme, the Mexican Ministry of Finance issued in 2009 a \$290 million bond covering both earthquake and hurricane risk, which was distributed to investors worldwide, thus spreading Mexican risk globally. Key to the issue being well received by the market was the capacity to construct credible models of earthquake and hurricane risk.

A devastating sequence of natural disasters is just one of the myriad possible pathways contributing to the default of sovereign bonds. Every sovereign bond investor will have some kind of valuation model, ranging from speculation about forthcoming events to a model of the global economy.[5] By contrast, for the peril-specific catastrophe bonds, pricing is considerably more transparent, detailed, and analytical, whilst still being subject to epistemic uncertainty.

12.1.1 Bond pricing

The financial structure underlying catastrophe bonds is explained by the following simple insurance illustration.[6] A primary insurer, Temblor Insurance Inc., writes a substantial amount of earthquake business in California. It is happy to retain most of this risk itself, but needs some protection in the event of a Californian earthquake of Magnitude 7 or more. Suppose that a reinsurance company, Cassandra Re, enters into a one-year reinsurance contract with Temblor Insurance Inc., whereby, at the end of the year, it will pay L dollars if a Magnitude 7 earthquake occurs in California during the year, otherwise it will pay nothing.

Because of epistemic uncertainty, there is no absolute scientific probability of a Magnitude 7 earthquake in California during the year. But if P_I is the probability as perceived by the insurance market, then the fair price for the contract, V_I, (ignoring expenses and profit), is obtained by equating the expected loss at the end of the year, $P_I L$, with the value of the premium at the end of the year, presuming it has been invested in risk-free US Treasury bills paying an interest rate of r: $V_I(1+r) = P_I L$.

One way that Cassandra Re can guarantee being able to pay L, in the event of a Californian Magnitude 7 earthquake, is to raise a capital sum C through the issue of a catastrophe bond. This defaults if there is such an event, otherwise it pays a coupon rate c per dollar to the investor and returns his or her principal. For the whole bond issue, if there is no such event during the year, Cassandra Re will pay collectively to the investors a total of $C(1+c) = L$, which is what it would have had to pay Temblor Insurance Inc. had there been an event.

Let P_B be the bondholders' assessment of default probability, i.e. their view of the probability that a Magnitude 7 earthquake will occur in California during the year. The coupon rate c is determined so that an investor pays one dollar to receive $1+c$ dollars a year later, if the Magnitude 7 event does not materialize: $1+r = (1+c)(1-P_B)$.

Let us define $V_B = P_B L / (1+r)$, which is the fair price for the reinsurance contract from the bond market perspective. Then using the above equation, we find that: $(V_B + C)(1+r) = L$.

Provided $P_I \geq P_B$, i.e. that the earthquake likelihood is perceived to be as high or higher by the reinsurance market than the bond market, then $V_I \geq V_B$, and hence $(V_I + C)(1+r) \geq L$. This inequality would allow Cassandra Re to collect the reinsurance premium V_I and cash C from the bond market, invest them at the risk-free rate r, and have enough to pay off any future Magnitude 7 earthquake loss L, as well as pay the coupon and return the principal to bondholders, if no such event were to happen. On the other hand, if $P_I < P_B$, i.e. the bond market is more pessimistic than the reinsurance market about an imminent large Californian earthquake, then $V_I < V_B$, and hence $(V_I + C)(1+r) < L$.

In this case, the coupon payment required to attract bond investors may be deemed too high, except if there are other commercial motives, e.g. credit risk concern about the financial strength of reinsurers, following a sequence of major catastrophes. In the latter regard, the remarkable demise of Lehman Brothers in 2008 tarnished the otherwise solid reputation of catastrophe bonds as being unexposed to credit risk. Funds from bond issuance are placed in Special Purpose Vehicles, which should be essentially risk-free.

Reinsurance market rates have historically exhibited quasi-cyclic behaviour: rates have tended to rise sharply immediately after a catastrophic loss, and fall gradually thereafter until the next major loss. The temporal fluctuation in rates can be very significant. During the hard phase of the market, a rate may rise to a level several times the true technical rate; whereas, during the soft phase of the market, a rate may well lapse below the true technical rate. These fluctuations might be justifiable scientifically if event clustering were favoured as a theory of hazard recurrence. But the violent market lurches of the past reflect more a desire by insurers to have some early pay-back in order to recoup their losses. In other words, there is some tacit element of re-financing involved in the cover provided.

When reinsurance prices are high, bond issues can exploit sizeable discrepancies between reinsurance market hazard rates and scientifically-based technical rates. However, when reinsurance is cheap, little margin remains for exploitation. If a catastrophe bond issue appears over-priced, then an opportunity would exist for a reinsurer to step in to undercut the issue, as has happened with the California Earthquake Authority.

The existence of an alternative financial means to transfer the risk of natural catastrophe helps stabilize the market, and reduce the volatility in rate fluctuations. But a question remains about differential rates for hazard events. There is no arbitrage principle establishing an absolute fair price for a catastrophe bond. Inevitably, there is a degree of volatility associated with quantitative risk modelling, as well illustrated by the WinCAT bond, the first such bond to be publicly placed.[7]

12.1.2 The WinCAT bond

On 22 March 2010, after a long dry spell, a severe hailstorm struck Perth, Western Australia. The storm produced the largest hail (some golf ball-sized) known to have occurred in Perth. Over 40,000 motor vehicles were damaged, including expensive luxury cars in dealerships lacking adequate covered garage space. Motor vehicle insurance losses reached catastrophe levels, being inflated by the need to fly in specialist hail repairers from around the world; a claims amplifier called *demand surge*.

The occurrence of a motor vehicle hailstorm loss amounting to hundreds of millons of Australian dollars had traders in insurance-linked securities checking the deal archive for the 1997 WinCAT bond.[8] A Swiss insurance company had a significant book of domestic motor vehicle business, exposed to potential catastrophic loss from the impact of hail or strong winds. In a $280 million risk transfer, a three-year convertible bond was issued at a face value of 4,700 Swiss francs. The bond was convertible into five registered shares of the insurance company at maturity, giving it the aspect of a European-style option.

Given the issue price of the bond and this option, had the bond been issued to pay a fixed annual coupon, the annual coupon rate would have been about 1.49%. However, as the name suggests, WinCAT was no ordinary fixed-rate bond. The annual coupon rate was set higher at 2.25%, but its payment was contingent on the absence of catastrophic hail or windstorm loss to their motor vehicle account. Specifically, there would be no coupon payment if, on any one calendar day during the corresponding observation period, more than 6,000 of their insured motor vehicles were damaged in this way. For this pioneering transaction, the capital of wary investors was protected in exchange for receiving a comparatively modest risk coupon.

Much is now known about the physics of the formation and particle growth of hail, but the forecasting of hailstorms is complicated by difficulty in distinguishing hail-producing storms from severe thunderstorms. If timely and reliable hailstorm warnings were available, motorists would of course have the opportunity to find shelter for their vehicles, and so save them, and their insurers, from hail loss. Modern motor vehicles are especially prone to hail impact damage, because their crashworthiness depends on their ability to absorb impact energy.

In common with mid-latitude areas of North America, China, Australia, and the Indian subcontinent, Central Europe is afflicted by large hailstones, which are typically associated with summer thunderstorms. Unlike large raindrops, which break up under air resistance if they grow beyond a certain size, there is no aerodynamic limit for hail. The limiting factor is the speed and duration of the updraught needed to keep a hailstone aloft. In extreme cases, hailstones can be large enough to cause human injuries, and even fatalities. In

1888, 250 people were killed in Northern India by a bombardment of hailstones. In 1986, 92 people in Bangladesh were killed by enormous hailstones, one of which weighed as much as a kilogram.

In countries with few unsheltered inhabitants, the primary loss from hailstorms arises from damage to material assets, including vineyards, greenhouses, buildings, aircraft, and motor vehicles. A total loss in excess of 1 billion US dollars was suffered in a summer hailstorm on 12 July 1984, which struck Southern Germany, particularly the southern half of Munich. As many as 70,000 homes, and 200,000 motor vehicles were damaged by hailstones, which were typically a few centimetres in diameter, although one had a diameter of 9.5 cm, (grapefruit size on the National Weather Service scale), and weighed as much as 300 grams. At the airport many small aircraft were damaged.

If the insurance concern were agricultural loss, it might at least be possible to identify the crops at risk reasonably precisely. However, even this is not achievable for motor risk, because the assets are mobile. The geographical variability of the exposed assets, combined with the coarse resolution of the hailstorm hazard, together beg the question: how does one estimate the likelihood of 6,000 motor vehicle claims from a hailstorm or windstorm?

In the absence of a dynamical model of hail loss, reliance tends to be placed by insurance companies on historical loss experience, in this instance, on a brief ten-year record of the aggregate number of motor claims from hailstorms and windstorms. During this period, fifteen hailstorms generated claim numbers exceeding 1,000, of which two, on 21 July 1992 and on 5 July 1993, resulted in claim numbers exceeding 6,000. The former event was a veritable hail catastrophe, generating claims exceeding this threshold by about 50%.

Given the rather meagre data, it is inevitable that there should be considerable uncertainty in attempting to estimate the probability of the 6,000 claim threshold being breached. This has been demonstrated by Schmock, who considered a variety of alternative statistical models for his analysis. From the theoretical perspective outlined already, the generalized Pareto distribution might be justified as particularly appropriate in the current context. Let the number of claims from an event be denoted by X. Financial interest here is restricted to claim numbers exceeding a threshold of u (i.e. 1,000), and the likelihood that an event giving rise to this many claims might give rise to as many as 6,000 or more. In order to proceed, we need to characterize the excess distribution function of X. Let the excess number of claims over 1,000 be denoted by Y. Then the distribution of Y is defined by:

$$F_u(y) = P(X - u \le y \mid X > u) = P(Y \le y \mid X > u)$$

This distribution $F_u(y)$ may be approximated by the generalized Pareto distribution: $G(y; \sigma(u) : \xi) = 1 - (1 + \xi y / \sigma(u))^{-1/\xi}$ where ξ is a parameter greater than zero, and σ depends on the threshold u. Schmock parameterized the generalized Pareto distribution from what data were available, and arrived at an estimate of 0.08 for the conditional probability of more than 6,000 claims, given that there are 1,000 claims. As might be expected, the approximate 68% confidence interval for this conditional probability is broad: [0.022, 0.187].

There are various major sources of uncertainty in estimating loss probability. Where statistical analysis of loss data forms an important part of the estimation procedure, the potential error due to the limited historical sample may be gauged by following the bootstrapping method, which involves multiple resampling of the dataset, with replacement. For this hailstorm bond, statistical analysis of past loss experience obviated the need for construction of a meteorological model of the process of hailstorm occurrence and damage in Switzerland.

Another European catastrophe bond deploying extreme value analysis was Mediterranean Re, issued in 2000, which covered the twin perils of French windstorm and Monaco earthquake. Actual windstorm losses experienced by a French insurer were fitted to a generalized Pareto distribution. The robustness of such a statistical approach depends on having some catastrophic tail events in the experience dataset. In the French windstorm dataset, there were the windstorms Lothar and Martin in late December 1999 which caused €6.5 billion insured loss; in the WinCAT hailstorm dataset, there was the hailstorm of July 1992. In both cases, the recent occurrence of major losses not only motivated the transactions, but also provided key data for extreme value analysis.

12.2 The Price of Innovation

In general, catastrophe bonds contingent on natural hazards are priced according to the output from computerized scientific catastrophe models. For Mediterranean Re, the Monaco earthquake risk was evaluated not from actual insurance loss experience, of which there was none, but from a seismic hazard analysis based on instrumental monitoring of Mediterranean seismicity, augmented by centuries of documentation of historically felt earthquakes around Monaco. One of these, in 1564, was described in a history of Provence, written by César Nostradamus, son of the legendary prophet of doom. Even the elder Nostradamus might be surprised at the scale of development on the slopes of Monte Carlo: the concentration of property value gives rise to a massive aggregation of risk from an occasional Magnitude 6 earthquake.

In all catastrophe bond risk analysis, there is a residual element of epistemic uncertainty involved in estimating the likelihood of an event that would result in default. Reflecting the parameter range of physical models, different experts may legitimately hold contrasting opinions on the likelihood, severity, and consequence of a hazard event. A systematic method for treating epistemic uncertainty is the logic-tree approach well established in seismic hazard analysis.

The initial step is to identify an ensemble of alternative plausible models, and assign a probabilistic weight to each according to the perceived likelihood of the model actually being realized. By weighting appropriately the coupon value associated with each model, an expected coupon value can be found. The spread of coupon values, obtained for the ensemble of alternative models, is a measure of volatility. Where only a single model is used, the degree of volatility in the resultant coupon value should emerge from systematic model stress-testing.

Ken Froot *et al.* pointed out that, provided a risk analysis is unbiased, the fact that there may be epistemic uncertainty in the results does not in itself merit special compensation for an investor, since the higher moments of the excess return distribution are unaffected.[9] The due diligence process is an effective means of eliminating any unwitting bias against the investor. So also is the scrutiny of rating agencies. But of course, investors cannot themselves be sure the risk analysis is bias-free.

Unfamiliarity with an innovative catastrophe bond is often cited as grounds for cautious investors to be especially wary, and to expect a higher coupon spread. However, with the introduction of a new peril or territory, an investor's anxiety over an unfamiliar risk analysis may be more than compensated by the positive prospect of taking on a risk uncorrelated (or weakly correlated) with other portfolio catastrophe risk holdings. A perfect example of this was Mediterranean Re, the only catastrophe bond to include the peril of earthquake around Monaco. The comparatively low Sharpe (reward-to-volatility) ratio for this transaction indicated that investors were much more attracted by the potential portfolio diversification benefits than disconcerted by a novel risk.

Since then, earthquake risk for other Mediterranean countries and other continents has been transferred to the capital markets. Indeed, most common types of natural catastrophe have become securitizable. More than a decade after Swiss hailstorm, there was a transfer of US thunderstorm risk alone in 2010.

One of the first earthquake catastrophe bonds, Concentric Re, gave protection to Tokyo Disneyland in 1999 against business interruption consequent on a major Tokyo earthquake. In Japanese folklore, the Disney-like image of thrashing of a giant catfish (*Namazu* in Japanese) is blamed for seismic activity. The 1999 Namazu Re securitization of Japanese earthquake risk introduced the novel idea of including, as part of the trigger mechanism, records of strong ground motion data. This was just becoming viable because of the establishment, after the 1995 Kobe earthquake, of the Kyoshin-Net strong-motion monitoring system. Prior to this transaction, earthquake Magnitude alone had been used to define parametric earthquake triggers, as for Tokyo Disneyland.

The innovation of using ground motion data was deemed desirable to reduce *basis risk*: the difference between the actual property loss and the bond payout. This could be lowered by recognizing measured spatial variations in ground shaking within the region affected. Much effort was spent explaining the novel complex trigger to rating agencies as well as investors, and gaining their confidence. This was successfully achieved, and the notion of a spatially refined trigger has since gained in popularity. Indeed, the appellation *second-generation* describes all triggers which depend on local recordings of hazard variables.

Earthquake strong-motion monitoring systems can function even under severe ground shaking, but anemometers are prone to malfunction under severe wind loading. With the development of a US coastal network of hardened weather stations for the instrumental recording of high wind speeds, the Paradex US Hurricane Index was established to facilitate hurricane risk transactions, where payout is triggered according to a zip code dependent function of wind speed recordings.[10]

12.2.1 Golden Goal Finance Ltd.

Before 9/11, an Egyptian operative, Abu Al Hasan, recounted to Osama bin Laden, 'I saw in a dream, that we were playing a soccer game against the Americans. When our team showed up on the field, they were all pilots.' In this single dream, Abu Al Hasan anticipated not just the terror of Jihadi suicide pilots, but the first securitization of terrorism risk, which was for the cancellation of the 2006 FIFA World Cup.

In soccer, a golden goal is one which wins a tied match in extra time. Whilst something is known of the early goalkeeping career of the tall Saudi, Osama bin Laden, and his support for the Arsenal football club in North London, it is not known if he let in any golden goals. But there were other reasons for this transaction to be named Golden Goal Finance Ltd.. As much as for any other transaction, default of the bond would have been a global catastrophe, given the male despondency if the world's most popular sports event were cancelled.

Prior to 9/11, terrorism was not perceived as a catastrophe insurance risk. With terrorism cover being comparatively scarce and expensive, the idea of a terrorism catastrophe bond was proposed in academic circles shortly after 9/11. Although conceptually such a financial instrument would appear to provide a viable alternative to insurance, risk ambiguity was considered too great an obstacle to be palatable for the rating agencies and investors.[11]

As with all new asset classes, the right opportunity would have to arise for initial implementation: one where the bond was price-competitive with insurance, and where investors could have confidence in the risk analysis, allowing for the risk ambiguity. Such an opportunity arose with the securitization of the cancellation risk of the 18th World Cup, hosted by Germany. FIFA had experienced difficulties in finding coverage for the 2002 World Cup in Korea/Japan, which was held within a year of 9/11. Warren Buffett stepped up to the penalty spot as the insurer of last resort. To open other avenues, early provision for coverage was made for the following World Cup in 2006.

The securitization of cancellation risk was especially resilient since the World Cup could be relocated elsewhere, and postponed for a year, if need be. The latter flexibility essentially made this a second event transaction, because if any event were to occur in 2006 preventing tournament completion, it might be rescheduled for 2007. Second event natural hazard transactions require at least two hazard events, e.g. two hurricanes or earthquakes, to occur for principal to be eroded, and correspondingly have lower risk.

Regarding terrorism, a postponement precedent had been set in golf with the 2001 Ryder Cup delayed to 2002, because of the understandable reluctance of US golfers to fly so soon after 9/11. Both relocation and postponement were FIFA options exercised previously. The FIFA women's world cup in 2003 was relocated from China to the USA because of SARS, and the FIFA youth world cup in 2003 was postponed from spring to autumn because of the proximity of the Iraq War to the host nation, the United Arab Emirates.

The resilience of the Golden Goal Finance Ltd. transaction was reflected in the risk analysis. Acknowledging the non-uniqueness of any individual risk model, alternative plausible models and parameterizations were considered. Rigour in the treatment of epistemic uncertainty was manifest in the construction of the logic-tree, the branches of which reflected the diversity in modelling the key factors such as target attractiveness; weapon capability; level of security; interdiction by intelligence services; and tournament curtailment after an attack.

German diligence in crowd protection and emergency preparedness was also recognized in the risk analysis. Security was organized at a military level, and medical plans were in place to treat up to 2% of spectators.[12] Hundreds of spectators might have been injured by a successful repetition of a plan hatched by the Algerian Islamic terrorist organization (GIA) to launch an armed attack during the 1998 World

Cup in France. This plot was thwarted by the capable French security service, with its well-trained team of Algerian informants.

For Golden Goal Finance Ltd., a conservative best estimate of about 5 basis points (0.05%) was obtained for the terrorism cancellation risk, and the range of logic-tree possibilities yielded terrorism risk results as high as 37 basis points. The risk ambiguity was made transparent in the bond offering circular, in that the calculational framework was explicitly described in sufficient detail to permit the investor the opportunity to perform an alternative assessment.[13]

An investment grade rating of A3 was given by Moody's Investor Service, following four meetings in London and New York addressing all aspects of the risk analysis. The willingness of Moody's to consider rating Golden Goal Finance Ltd. reflected a critical but open attitude towards terrorism risk assessment, consistent with their preparedness to down-rate some commercial mortgage-backed securities, heavily exposed to city centre terrorism. Standard and Poor's did not alter their rating on these CMBS deals, but ensured that investors knew what insurance provisions were in place on the buildings backing the transactions. Consistent with this perspective, and general reluctance to rate transactions perceived as unduly dependent on human behaviour, S&P declined to consider rating the FIFA cancellation risk bond, but did assign an A rating to FIFA's subsequent securitization of its World Cup sponsorship earnings, protected by this event cancellation bond.

A successful placement of the $260 million issue was made. The bonds were sold at a coupon of 1.5% above LIBOR. A factor in the bond pricing was investor confidence that the German government would take steps to maintain tight security. Indeed, as early as November 2004, preparations included the drafting of a National Concept for Staging the 2006 World Cup (NaSiKo), that covered the possible use of chemical, biological, and radiological weapons. But the ultimate decision on any event cancellation rested with FIFA, not the German government.

80% of the bonds were sold in Europe, reflecting greater familiarity with the World Cup there than in the USA, where the Superbowl is the football world championship. This transaction was the first to involve transfer of event risk, and the first to transfer the risk of man-made catastrophe to the capital markets. FIFA President Joseph S. Blatter welcomed the successful launch: 'This serves as yet another indication of the excellent reputation our organization enjoys throughout the world.'[14]

Game theory analysis suggests that high security at sports stadiums may deflect attacks elsewhere in the country holding a major tournament, or delay attacks until country-wide security levels decline. So it turned out in Germany at the end of July 2006, three weeks after the World Cup Final. Two bombs were found on trains in Dortmund and Koblenz in Germany. Because of a construction flaw, the propane gas tank bombs, which used designs found on the internet, failed to detonate. Two Lebanese men, in Germany to study, were caught on CCTV placing the suitcase bombs on the trains in Cologne station, and were later convicted.

Four years later, when the 2010 FIFA World Cup was staged in South Africa, game theorists might have predicted the international target substitution involved during the World Cup final. Elsewhere in Africa, there was terrorist slaughter of television viewers in an Ethiopian restaurant and a rugby club in Kampala, Uganda. Security in the host nation of South Africa was intensive throughout the tournament, making the Ugandan capital a more attractive softer regional target for Somali Islamist militants. Al-Shabab claimed responsibility for this Plan B attack, as part of its Jihad campaign in the Horn of Africa.

There was no need for a securitization of the cancellation risk for the 2010 FIFA World Cup because there was ample terrorism insurance coverage available for this event. Further opportunities for terrorism risk securitization would arise with future market failures.

12.2.2 *Mortality securitization*

Apart from spectacularly lethal terrorist attacks, the 2002/2003 winter deadly outbreak of SARS emanating from China concentrated the minds of life actuaries on the potential for catastrophic life insurance loss across continents, and motivated the first transfer of excess mortality risk to the capital markets: Vita Capital. Excess mortality was measured by a mortality risk index, weighted by the international issuer's exposure, segmented by gender and country. The trigger threshold was 30% higher than the average index level, based on 2002 mortality in these countries.

Concern over SARS as an infectious disease was superseded in 2006 by pandemic influenza strain H5N1. In November 2006, Osiris Capital was issued by a leading French insurer, needing to manage the explicit exclusion of pandemics in most of its catastrophe reinsurance treaties.[15]

Investor sales presentations for windstorm catastrophe bonds have been delayed by raging windstorms; a fallen tree on the track once halted a Eurostar train carrying French issuers to a windstorm road show meeting in London. But no windstorm bond is ever bought with the certain knowledge that, at the later time of issuance, a major windstorm will be happening, or be on its way. During the spring of 2009, an outbreak of swine flu H1N1 originated in Mexico and spread across continents to become a global pandemic. Whilst the pandemic was still spreading, Vita Capital was issued for the fourth time. Given the limitations of a purely statistical analysis of pandemic risk in dealing with a live event, the risk analysis for Vita IV was epidemiologically based, with an ensemble of scenarios capturing the range of possible outcomes of the H1N1 event itself, and others that might develop.

The control of infectious disease has contributed to a marked downturn in mortality in the 20th century. Just as drought is a risk like excess rainfall, so increasing longevity is a financial risk like excess mortality. Advancements in *geroscience*, which is the study of the interface between normal ageing and age-related diseases, may yield significant increases in lifespan in the 21st century. Such advancements form a stochastic process underpinning a prospective model of longevity, leading towards the securitization of longevity risk.[16]

12.2.3 *Counterfactual correlations*

Excess mortality bonds are particularly attractive to investors because of their low risk correlation with natural hazard catastrophe bonds, which might be held within the same insurance-linked securities portfolio. A virulent infectious disease cannot cause a large earthquake. But after the subprime mortgage meltdown, investors should be wary over lurking Black Swan correlations. What kind of obscure causal linkages might there be between natural hazards and infectious disease?

The outbreak of disease after a major earthquake is a public health concern. This is a particular problem in the Western Chinese province of Qinghai, where plague is endemic. After the M6.9 earthquake in Southeastern Qinghai on 13 April 2010, which killed several thousand, there were fears that flea-infested marmots might be prematurely awakened from their hibernation, and spread plague to the 100,000 homeless earthquake survivors. The marmot calendar earmarks the end of April for the end of hibernation, and September for the start of winter hibernation. So there was a better chance than one in three that the earthquake struck when the marmots were active in spreading plague.

Conversely, it is possible for the death toll from a pandemic to be aggravated by a natural disaster. The influenza pandemic of 1781–1782 swept across Europe, infecting most of the European population. The lethality rate was low, except for those with respiratory problems. As an exercise in counterfactual history, one might consider what the lethality rate might have been in Northwest Europe had the pandemic occurred two years later. It then would have coincided with the Laki eruption in Iceland, which released several hundred million tons of sulphuric acid aerosol into the atmosphere over eight months. The acid fog caused much illness, and many died in Britain and France. Benjamin Franklin wrote, 'This fog was of a permanent nature; it was dry, and the rays of the sun seemed to have little effect towards dissipating it.' For many influenza victims, breaths of acid fog would have been their last.

All stakeholders in catastrophe risk should appreciate the broadening of risk perspective that comes with counterfactual analysis. Investors in Vita IV kept watch on the growing count of the many thousand victims of the 11 March 2011 Japanese tsunami. More than a century earlier, in June 1896, another giant Japanese tsunami killed almost 30,000 people. Had this event occurred a few years earlier, it would have coincided with the pandemic of 1889–1890, which would have taken an especially high toll among the homeless. Historical precedent, rather than what might have happened, tends to guide human perception. Catastrophes are rare, and super-catastrophes are rarer still. Insight into the extreme tail of loss distributions can be gained by compounding hazardous situations which might potentially be concurrent, even if there is no known precedent for their previous conjunction in a perfect storm.

Chapter 13

Risk Horizons

The empires of the future
are the empires of the mind.
Winston Churchill,
Harvard University, 1943

As the founder of modern scientific intelligence, the physicist R.V. Jones trusted in Occam's Razor, that observations should be explained with the minimum number of assumptions. As a caution to intelligence officers, he contrived *Crabtree's Bludgeon*: 'No set of mutually inconsistent observations can exist for which some human intellect cannot conceive a coherent explanation, however complicated.' Like the Rorschach inkblot test, any explanation may reflect the human psyche as much as intellect.

In the spring of 2002, months after the intelligence failure of 9/11, US Defense Secretary Rumsfeld, wrote, 'Our challenge in this new century is a difficult one: to defend our nation against the unknown, the uncertain, the unseen, and the unexpected. That may seem an impossible task. It is not. But to accomplish it, we must put aside comfortable ways of thinking and planning – take risks and try new things.'[1]

The philosopher of war, Christopher Coker, has written of war in an age of risk, and argued that, in the early 21st century, war can be considered as an instrument of risk management, not order.[2] Writing from extensive Whitehall experience, David Omand has also argued the eminent sense of applying the principles of risk management to national security, noting that a bold move may reduce risk, and that risk management is about taking managed risks. He cited the example of the successful 1982 UK naval campaign to retake the Falklands, with the likelihood of naval losses as a risk accepted for their recovery.[3]

Unlike the Falklands War, some conflicts do not lend themselves to a clear declaration of victory, and continue even when the fighting stops. There are inhospitable ungoverned terrains, such as in Afghanistan, which have denied victory to invading forces across the ages. Control of this territory was part of the Great Game played between Britain and Russia in the 19th century. As a young British army officer, Winston Churchill served on the North-West Frontier. He wrote of the ferocious tribes straddling Afghanistan and Pakistan, 'Except at harvest time, when self-preservation enjoins a temporary truce, the Pathan tribes are always engaged in private or public war. Every man is a warrior, a politician, and a theologian.'[4]

Established in November 1893 as a buffer between the British Raj and Afghanistan, the 2,500 km Afghan–Pakistan border, known as the Durand Line, remains a source of conflict in the 21st century. Under the Durand agreement establishing the long porous border, belligerent tribes living either side of the border have freedom of travel into other areas. The security problems this agreement causes would not have surprised Lewis Fry Richardson, the meteorologist turned conflict theorist, who discovered fractal geometry in the course of analyzing the link between frontier length and the propensity for conflict.

Coker quotes the German sociologist, Ulrich Beck: 'Risk problems are characterized by having no unambiguous solutions; rather they are distinguished by a fundamental ambivalence which can be grasped by calculations of probability, but not removed that way.'[5] The absence of unambiguous solutions characterizes all the major societal issues of our time, including ecology, climate change, demographics, as well as conflict resolution. Ambivalence makes such risk problems so much harder to address and decide than problems of order.

In scanning the distant risk horizon, decades ahead, urban planners have the onerous responsibility of accommodating within their vision of the future, and civic financial budgets, rising population densities, resource shortages, and climate change. Natural disasters mock those planners lacking humility and wisdom in addressing this challenge. Hurricane Katrina stands as a tragic reminder of the costly failure which can befall even the most prosperous and technically advanced societies.

As an urban planner, Horst Rittel found traditional methods inadequate for the poorly structured problems he encountered. One might call them tricky; he called them *wicked*. He listed ten dire characteristics of such planning problems.[6] There is no definitive formulation of a wicked problem. Wicked problems have no stopping rule. Solutions to wicked problems are not true or false, but good or bad. There is no immediate and no ultimate test of a solution to a wicked problem. Every solution to a wicked problem is a one-shot operation. Wicked problems do not have an enumerable set of potential solutions. Every wicked problem is essentially unique. Every wicked problem can be considered to be a symptom of another problem. A discrepancy in a wicked problem can be explained in numerous ways. The planner has no right to be wrong.

To a scientist striving to discern the structure of Nature, the disordered working environment of a planner, filled with its panoply of wicked problems, brings to mind discomforting images from the writing of Franz Kafka. No planning problem is what it seems, can be, or ought to be. Scientists may be thankful not to be professionally engaged directly in planning issues, but their expert opinions are nevertheless sought in the planning of major safety-critical installations requiring elaborate risk assessments. This can be a harrowing Kafkaesque experience for a senior scientist unused to endless interrogation. An eminent professor of seismology suffered a heart attack after cross-examination in a judicial inquiry into the seismic safety of a nuclear plant in Northwest Germany.

Whatever the risks associated with other types of industrial installation, those associated with the long-term disposal of radioactive waste are of heightened concern because of the involuntary imposed risk burden on many future generations. In the political debate over the choice of Yucca Mountain, New Mexico, as a US nuclear waste repository site, considerable attention was paid to the hazard posed by a volcanic vent intruding into the site within 10,000 years. Perhaps as important as debate over long-term volcanism or seismicity has been contemplation by industrial archaeologists of the long-term integrity of nuclear waste repositories against accidental or malicious human intrusion.[7] Across the range of hazards, there is a degree of relativity in all risk assessment. The capacity to understand all perils enhances understanding of the risk contribution of any one peril.

13.1 Ecological Catastrophe

The ecological stability of the environment is easier lost than regained. Coral reefs, lakes, and woodlands are important environmental assets, which would be very costly and difficult to restore if they were to go. Of all the ecological hazards, desertification is especially detrimental to the global economy because of the reduction in the capacity of arid ecosystems to support sizeable populations. An arid area may exist in two states, one desertified, the other with perennial vegetation. The latter state is one where precipitation can be absorbed by the topsoil and be available for plant uptake. However, this capability disappears when vegetation cover is lost. Consequently, perennial plants struggle to recolonize an arid area which has fallen into a desert state. Such a stark realization of danger ahead ensures that desertification is recognized as a key factor affecting African development.

The loss of woodlands to herbivores is another example of an ecological crisis with particular African relevance. Unlike adult trees, younger trees are vulnerable to grazing herbivores. Once destroyed, woodlands can only be regenerated if the number of herbivores is kept firmly in check, which is not a policy which fits well with a national parks mandate to boost elephant numbers for the eyes and cameras of tourists. But elephants are not only to blame. Even in the absence of herbivores, lack of shelter by adult trees can jeopardize seedling survival in the heat, and worsen the prospect of an ecological transition from an open to woodland landscape.

Examples such as these motivate the development of theoretical models which provide quantitative insight into the underlying ecological dynamics. These models help to raise awareness that the response to environmental change has catastrophic potential if the ecosystem has alternative stable states. Wells of energy minima are termed *basins of attraction*. As the American mathematician, David Mumford, has heralded, the third millennium is the dawning of the age of stochasticity.[8] Catastrophes are the outcome of stochastic processes, which are quintessentially time-dependent random variables. The dynamics of the ecological environment preclude static deterministic thinking.

Environmental conditions are inherently stochastic, and change with weather, fires, pest outbreaks etc..

Suppose an ecosystem is in a state marked with a star on the upper branch of Fig. 13.1. Environmental conditions may change enough for the ecosystem state to pass the bifurcation point F, and make an abrupt transition to the lower branch. Once on this branch, it is harder to return to the upper branch, because the environmental conditions have to be restored not just to where they were, but all the way back to the bifurcation point B, from where the ecosystem can flip back to the upper branch. The curve section directly joining B and F represents the border between the basins of attraction of the two stable states on the upper and lower branches.

Ecosystem state

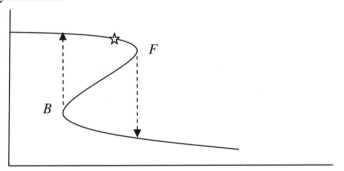

Environmental Conditions

Figure 13.1. System shifting between two alternative stable states (Scheffer *et al.*, 2001).

A simple mathematical model exhibiting this dynamic behaviour, known as *hysteresis*, is defined by the differential equation:[9]

$$\frac{dX}{dt} = a - b X + r f(X)$$

X is a key ecosystem property; a is a parameter representing an environmental factor driving X; b is the rate that X decays; and r is the rate at which X recovers as a nonlinear function f of X.

13.1.1 Early warning for tipping points

The dynamics of many complex systems approaching a tipping point share some generic properties which may, in some situations, provide early warning for critical state transitions. Indications of an impending transition may be inferred from observations of critical slowing down.[10] As a bifurcation like F or B is approached, an ecosystem becomes increasingly slow to recover from small perturbations. With shock impacts taking longer to be absorbed, the variance in the state variable increases. Furthermore, the slowing down process retards the intrinsic rates of change in a system, and enhances the system memory of a recent state, and hence its autocorrelation. This system behaviour near a tipping point can be represented mathematically in a simple way.

Writing y for the deviation of the state variable from equilibrium, sequential deviations are represented by a first-order autoregressive process model: $y_{n+1} = \alpha \, y_n + \sigma \, \varepsilon_n$, where α is the autocorrelation, ε_n is a random number from a standard Normal distribution, and σ is the standard deviation. As the autocorrelation α is enhanced, so is the variance:

$$Var\,(y_{n+1}) = \frac{\sigma^2}{1 - \alpha^2}$$

An example of this type of interesting dynamic system behaviour has been observed in a laboratory population of zooplankton,[11] which was given diminishing quantities of nutrients. In any animal population, the size oscillates. If there is an increase in births, there is extra strain on resources which can lead to extra deaths or a fall in births, which makes available resources for the population to grow once more. However, as a tipping point is approached, a system takes ever longer to recover its balance, until recovery no longer becomes possible, and a species may be headed towards extinction.

Apart from temporal indicators, changing spatial patterns may also be recognized as early-warning signals. Thus as a tipping point to a barren state approaches, vegetation changes from being patchy to displaying more regular spotty patterns.

13.1.2 Ecological resilience

The management of diversified financial asset portfolios owes much to Harry Markowitz's efficient frontier analysis. Suppose a portfolio contains n assets. Let the covariance between the rates of return of assets i and j be σ_{ij}. In deciding the weight w_i to give each asset, an investor can trade off the expected rate of return against the variance of the rate of return. Keeping the expected rate of return fixed, the method of Lagrange multipliers can be used to find the weights which define the efficient risk frontier by minimizing the sum $\sum_{i,j} w_i w_j \sigma_{ij}$.

The linkage between ecosystem diversity and stability is complex and subtle, but both the diversity between different species, and within individual species, seem to be practically important. As an example of the latter, population diversity has reduced the temporal variability of Alaskan sockeye salmon fisheries within a region which includes a number of rivers. Variance damping within communities lowers the probability of fishery closure. Using the language of prudent financial management, this is called the *portfolio effect*.[12]

As temporary stewards of the planet, every human generation has a responsibility to manage the global portfolio of planetary resources in a sustainable manner for future generations. This global sustainability problem, exemplified by the preservation of Alaskan salmon fisheries, is challenging because the social–ecological system formed by human contact with the environment has an extremely large number of interacting variables. Anderies and Norberg[13] have reviewed from a complex adaptive system perspective the challenges that mankind faces, illustrating the tough choices about resource consumption that lie ahead.

For an ecological system consisting of many interacting species, consider a simple one-dimensional projection, which might be the biomass of one particular species. In Fig. 13.2, the X-axis charts the 1-D projection, and the Y-axis charts the level of social welfare derived from usage. Points A and B correspond to stable equilibrium states, and the point T represents the location of the boundary between the respective basins of attraction of the stable equilibria. The significance of this terminology is explained as follows.

The social welfare level S is available to society provided the system remains within the basin of attraction of the steady state A. Even if the state variable is moderately perturbed from equilibrium, this level of social welfare remains sustainable. However, if the system is perturbed still further beyond the boundary T, ecological catastrophe awaits: the system falls into the domain of attraction of the equilibrium point B, and the social welfare dwindles to zero.

Social Welfare

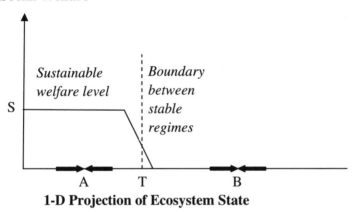

Figure 13.2. Collapse of social welfare level if the ecosystem falls into the domain of attractor of point B (Anderies & Norberg, 2008).

Suppose now that there is commercial intensification to increase the level of social welfare. For example, biological diversity may be reduced so as to favour one particular species of economic value. Whilst this intensification may benefit society, the system may be less tolerant to perturbations, and the domain of attraction of point A may shrink. As a consequence, the system may become more susceptible to falling within the domain of attraction of the point B, where the benefits lapse completely. Furthermore, if actions are taken to increase resilience and expand the basin of attraction of point A, heightened vulnerability to fluctuations in neglected variables may be an unintended consequence. Fragility may be adjusted within a system, but not completely removed.

13.1.3 Environmental impact assessment

Environmental impact assessments are undertaken to gauge the potential deleterious consequences of environmental pollution, resulting from human action. These consequences may span all time scales extending from hours, where rapid clean-up is possible, to eternity, if an Earth system change is irreversible. Environmental disasters are amongst the most feared and regretted catastrophes, because of their negative legacy to future generations. They are also amongst the hardest to enumerate and calculate, because of the complexity of the coupled social–ecological environment, and the protracted timescales and extended regions over which damage effects need to be assessed.

Were it not for the societal importance of quantifying environmental impacts, scientists might be deterred from entering this field by the observational data limitations and the inherent modelling uncertainty which expands over time, shortening the predictability horizon. But society needs to be informed about the pollution risk beyond this horizon, and expects assistance from the scientific community in making societal decisions under severe uncertainty, especially in providing some warning of a notable change in the environmental regime.

Realistically, timely warning may not be possible. Consider the problem of *eutrophication*, which is the over-enrichment of aquatic ecosystems with nutrients, notably phosphorus. Excess phosphorus is input into lakes from a variety of sources including sewage, industrial discharges, and agriculture. Assessing breakdowns in lake water quality, simulation studies suggest that decision-makers should have one to three years' advance notice, which unfortunately may not be sufficient for effective remedial action by a lake management system.[14]

The problem of determining whether a threshold is near is complicated by the proliferation of alternative models for many social–ecological systems. Public policy may be best served if decision-makers are provided with the entire posterior distribution of payoffs over the set of models, weighted by the posterior probability of each of the models, as fitted to the available data, and augmented by expert judgement. Appropriate actions can then be taken in accord with the particular preferences of the decision-makers.

13.2 Climate Change

One of the pioneering scientists of the 1920s was the German theoretical physicist Max Born. Holding court in Göttingen, with Heisenberg as his young assistant, he was a prominent figure in the heroic age of quantum mechanics, developing the statistical interpretation of the wave function of atomic particles, one of the most radical ideas in the history of science. He addressed a key question posed by Schrödinger's wave formulation of quantum mechanics: how is it possible to identify the position and velocity of a particle, when the wave function of the particle is known? Born's solution was that waves determine the probability of the measurements. In contrast with the determinism of classical mechanics, quantum mechanics gives only a statistical description.

His 1954 Nobel Prize citation offers a simple paradigm, 'When you shoot at a target it is possible in principle, according to the older conception, to aim the shot from the start so that it is certain to hit the target in the middle. Quantum mechanics teaches us to the contrary – that in principle we cannot predict where a single shot will hit the target. But we can achieve this much, that from a large number of shots the average point of impact will lie in the middle of the target.'[15]

Numerous atomic physics experiments over decades have repeatedly established the statistical interpretation of quantum mechanics, controversial and revolutionary though it once was. Addressing scepticism in his treatise on the natural philosophy of cause and chance, Max Born wrote of 'the vast communities of people ignorant of, or rejecting, the rule of science, among them the members of anti-vaccination societies and believers in astrology.'[16] In the 21st century, deniers of climate change might be added. Max Born lamented, 'It is useless to argue with them; I cannot compel them to accept the same criteria of valid induction in which I believe: the code of scientific rules.'

Through their formal education and training, professional scientists instinctively acknowledge and honour this code of scientific rules, and believe implicitly in valid induction. Theories may gather increasing support from empirical observations of the natural world, or may be falsified. Intuitive as it may seem to scientists, as a criterion demarcating science from pseudo-science, Born's 'valid induction' was criticized by

Karl Popper as somewhat of a myth: scientists make conjectures and tend to jump to conclusions, often after a single observation.[17] Most scientists pursue their careers without encountering philosophers of science, or having read any of their works, not even those of Popper. Yet the philosophy of science happens to be especially pertinent to climate change and the general public discourse on climate change.

A salient feature of the global climate system is the reabsorption of terrestrial infrared radiation, which gives rise to a natural greenhouse effect. As early in the industrial revolution as 1827, the French physicist Jean-Baptiste Fourier had envisaged climate change resulting from human modification of the energy budget. Considering incoming solar radiation and emitted thermal radiation, he pointed out the similarities between the glass of a greenhouse and the atmosphere. But whereas a gardener may measure the temperature of a greenhouse over a summer to confirm theoretical predictions of the greenhouse effect, it is not possible to confirm predictions of climate change decades ahead.

The effect of greenhouse emissions on global climate has been explored intensively using Global Circulation Models (GCM) to represent dynamical climate processes. These mathematical models have a dynamical core consisting of equations for the atmospheric state variables such as temperature, pressure, wind, and water vapour, dynamically coupled with component models of the oceans, land, and biosphere. These equations are driven by physical processes forcing the climate system. These include the absorption and radiation of solar energy, emission of terrestrial radiation, aerosols, cloud formation, ocean salinity, sea ice, soil moisture, land vegetation etc..

Any projection about the long-term future behaviour of a large complex nonlinear dynamical system is beset with uncertainty as to how the system will evolve. The climate system incorporates a host of important feedback mechanisms, which affect the sensitivity of the climate to temperature changes.[18] Clouds, for example, interfere with the transfer of radiation in the atmosphere. A warmer atmosphere results in more evaporation, and atmospheric release of more water vapour, which is a notable greenhouse gas. Ice melting increases the absorption of solar radiation, which leads to further warming. Rainfall changes alter ocean salinity and so interact with ocean circulation.

13.2.1 Climate model confirmation

John Houghton, the first chairman of the Physical Science Assessment Working Group of the Intergovernmental Panel on Climate Change (IPCC), has reviewed ways in which a climate model may be tested.[19] First, it can be run for a number of years of simulated time, and the climate generated compared in detail with the current climate. The average parameter distribution and seasonal variation have to compare well with observations.   Secondly, models can be compared with simulations of past climates, when key variables, such as the Earth's orbit, differed substantially from now.   Thirdly, climate predictions can be made of the effect of large perturbations, such as the cataclysmic Philippine volcanic eruption of Mt. Pinatubo in 1991, which injected about 20 megatons of sulphur dioxide into the lower stratosphere.

But even if all these comparisons are favourable, what inference about the value of a climate model is justified?   Models are inductive arguments, and since no inductive proposition can be proved absolutely, models can never be verified in a literal sense.   The tests listed above, indicating internal consistency, would offer partial validation, according to Houghton and other meteorologists.   However from the philosophy of science corner, Naomi Oreskes *et al.* argue that the agreement of a model with observations allows at best a model to be *confirmed*.[20] This critique led the IPCC to substitute the word *evaluation* for the terms verification and validation.   Another philosopher of science has proposed that we should aim to confirm the adequacy of models for particular purposes.[21]

With all this in mind, consider the problem of forecasting global average temperature as a function of the concentration of greenhouse gases.   This would seem to be a problem mired in Knightian uncertainty: a range of possible temperature increases might be estimated, but not the assignment of probabilities to various parts of this range.   This is a dread situation for political decision-makers.   In the aftermath of the banking catastrophe of 2008, the governor of the Bank of England, Mervyn King,[22] referred to John Maynard Keynes in assessing how people deal with situations lacking any scientific basis on which to form probability estimates: the prospect of future changes is largely ignored.   As Pielke has stressed, this is just political reality.[23]

To inform public policy, climate scientists are at least able to collate an ensemble of forecast models, with different versions and varying parameters. This ensemble may be viewed statistically as a sample from the underlying population of models.[24] If the relative likelihood of the various alternative models were assignable, then an overall estimate could be found of the probability that a critical threshold temperature increase, such as 5 °C, might be exceeded.

This is all very pragmatic. However, as long as the underlying climate models have shortcomings in representing future climate dynamics, the interpretation of ensemble-based probabilities is vague and their reliability is questionable.[25] Given the ambiguity aversion of the public, confidence in climate change communications is liable to suffer.

Returning to the paradigm of quantum mechanical shots at a target, Max Born's valid induction gives us confidence that from a large number of shots the average point of impact will lie in the middle of the target. Even though climate models are steadily improving, it is unclear when similarly high confidence could be placed in the mean projections of future climate trajectories.

13.2.2 Climate change impacts

Study of climate catastrophes that have occurred in the geological past seems to suggest sensitivity of the climate system to comparatively small changes in climate-forcing factors. Changes in the frequency of extreme weather events are a matter of heightened political as well as scientific sensitivity. Some areas hitherto free of tropical cyclones are likely to become exposed to such hazards, as increased areas of ocean attain the temperature threshold of 26 °C to 27 °C needed to sustain them. Changes in weather extremes may already be inferred by generating climate model simulations under conditions with and without greenhouse gas emissions. A probabilistic event attribution framework has quantified the anthropogenic contribution to flood risk in England and Wales in autumn 2000, the wettest since records began in 1766.[26]

Extremes of weather are perilous for mankind, but for some species they may challenge their Darwinian fitness. Reproductive success and species survival may be at far greater risk from these occasional extreme events than from average trends in climate change. On a Galapagos island, home to various species of finch studied by Charles Darwin himself, El Niño induces an approximate decadal oscillation between heavy rainfall and drought. A severe 1976–1977 drought diminished the supply of the cactus seeds on which Darwin's finches feed. With large hard seeds being in greater abundance, the long-beaked finch species dominated to a degree that a mathematical biologist could calculate using population persistence models.

Coupled with continued habitat disruption, spread of invasive species and disease, palaeontologists have warned that climate change might edge life on the planet gradually towards another mass extinction. Unlike the previous five mass extinctions, this might progress without the necessary intervention of asteroid impacts or supervolcanic eruptive activity. Major changes in climate state, known as tipping points, may be absolutely catastrophic in many ways. There remains considerable uncertainty over the potential trigger and timing of climate state changes. Among the most catastrophic scenarios for sea level rise are the irreversible melting of the Greenland ice sheet, and the disintegration of the West Antarctic Ice Sheet.

Even whilst the climate is in its untipped state, costly adaptation measures are needed to cope with progressive climate change. Here, the greatest economic uncertainty surrounds socio-economic responses to the impacts of climate change, such as conflict, migration, and the flight of capital investment. The nonlinear population dynamics associated with socio-economic and demographic shifts generate tipping points in population behaviour. Where adaptation fails to cope with the worsening climate, rising population discontent may trigger a tipping point from adaptation towards migration.

With significant population growth anticipated in developing countries needing to adapt most, the prospect looms of a migration catastrophe. The economist of climate change, Nicholas Stern, has warned that large scale permanent migration would bring threats of global conflict.[27] With water becoming scarce for agriculture, livestock, as well as human populations, the fair apportionment of water resources may become a mainstay of conflict resolution.

13.3 War and Conflict Resolution

Anyone who has stayed at a hotel near San Francisco airport knows the local town of Burlingame, but few would know about the extraordinary 19th century American lawyer and diplomat, Anson Burlingame, after whom the town is named. In the archives of the Chinese legation in London, the earliest staff photograph shows a group of austere Chinese Mandarins. In their midst, sporting a Victorian handlebar moustache, stands a single Caucasian: Anson Burlingame. Having originally been appointed by President Lincoln as US minister to China, in 1867 he led a Chinese diplomatic mission to the USA and Europe. Underlying this diplomatic gamesmanship and finesse is an essential principle that psychologists appreciate well: failure to understand the mind of another is a grave weakness in political negotiation.

At the time of the Tiananmen Square protests in 1989, the violent outcome was foreseen by former Chinese diplomats, but came as a surprise to many who had expected China to be swept up in the momentum of change in the communist world. One American political scientist who predicted the outcome months ahead was Bruce de Mesquita, whose affiliation with the Hoover Institution at Stanford University would have made him familiar with the Bay area town of Burlingame, if not the Chinese legend behind the name.

The role of mathematicians in war is usually perceived to be in the technical domain of cryptography or communications. If Alan Turing was the archetypical code-breaker mathematician, not fitting the traditional stereotype at all was the multi-talented Hollywood star, Hedy Lamarr, who co-invented a form of frequency-hopping communications technology. As David Hilbert noted, to be a mathematician requires imagination, which is a prized virtue for political conflict strategists.

Bruce de Mesquita advocated a shift towards quantitative models, and built a reputation for forecasting political events using game theory arguments founded on a specific narrow definition of rationality: politicians do what they believe is in their own best interest. De Mesquita's political logic of brazen self-interest may seem rather cynical, but is evidenced by an international gallery of leaders, on all continents, desperate to cling to domestic political power, prepared to rig elections, and refuse to accept an unfavourable outcome. Before WikiLeaks' exposure of diplomatic cables in 2010, the 19th century English politician, Lord Palmerston, had been a straight talker, 'We have no eternal allies and no perpetual enemies. Our interests are eternal and perpetual, and those interests it is our duty to follow.' This is a cold and ruthless foreign policy principle to endear itself at least to game theorists.

The usefulness of quantitative analysis in forecasting political events is illustrated at the simplest level by the application of arithmetic calculations in gauging the outcome of complex multi-lateral political decisions, such as limiting the nuclear weapons capability of North Korea or advancing the Israel-Palestine peace process. Some elementary arithmetic can clarify the key components of a decision-making process.

Consider a decision involving a number of interested parties, whose preferences may span a broad range of options. The impact of any individual depends not just on his or her preference P, but also on the individual's degree of influence I, and the extent S to which the issue being decided is salient or important for that individual. The product of the degree of influence and the salience is defined by de Mesquita as the individual's power:[28] $I \times S$. If either an individual is not influential, or if he or she is disinterested in the policy issue concerned, then the corresponding power is low compared with the power of one who is both influential and highly motivated about the issue. Weighting preferences according to an individual's power seems to yield a useful and convenient predictor of decisions. Lobbying the most influential of political decision-makers is an effective means of swaying policy.

13.3.1 *The logic of non-violence*

Sun Tzu, the master of war strategy, stated a preference for non-violence. In seeking to resolve political conflicts through non-violence, NGOs have an influential role in supporting polling organizations to sound out directly and democratically the opinions of the populations in conflict.

Consider a territory with a population aggrieved at denial of rights by an external ruling authority. This situation could arise through colonialism, racism, land occupation, or water or other natural resource appropriation.   If negotiation fails, politics may become stuck at an apparently intractable equilibrium point of mutual violence.   For as long as a campaign of violent protest by the aggrieved is waged and civilians are killed, public opinion amongst the ruling authority's own population may sanction a tough violent repressive response.   Conversely, for as long as action by the ruling authority is violent and brutal, public opinion amongst the aggrieved population may greatly favour active continuation of the armed struggle.

In an endeavour to search for common ground, it will be worthwhile to search for an alternative equilibrium point: one of non-violence, that can be supported strongly by both populations.   Where talking fails, there is a range of strategies that an aggrieved population could pursue, other than inaction.   In broad terms, these include a campaign of political violence, and various forms of soft and hard Alternative Resistance (AR).   The latter AR actions are distinguished by allowance of a limited degree of non-lethal force, e.g. stone throwing.

For each of these strategies, opinion polls would seek to ascertain attitudes of the ruling population towards a policy which was:

[a]   **Non-violent**, which may involve intimidation, but no actual physical pressure against the aggrieved population;

[b]   **Aggressive**, with sufficient physical pressure as to cause physical injuries, but not fatalities;

[c]   **Violent**, leading to a number of fatalities.

Correspondingly, given a specified ruling authority strategy (e.g. Non-violent, Aggressive, Violent), opinion polls would seek to ascertain attitudes of the aggrieved population towards a course of action which involved:

[1]   Inaction   [2]   Violence

[3]   Soft AR   [4]   Hard AR

The results of opinion polling would allow parameterization of the bilateral public opinion matrix, shown in Table 13.1.   Each box relates to

a pair of actions by the authority and the aggrieved. The first box entry
(**bold-type**) is the % support by the population of the ruling authority,
and the second entry is the % support by the aggrieved population. Thus,
for the box in the top right-hand corner, 50% of the population of the
ruling authority would support a non-violent response to hard alternative
resistance, whilst 65% of the aggrieved population would support hard
alternative resistance if the authority were non-violent.

Table 13.1. Matrix of possible actions supported by a sector of public opinion.

	Aggrieved: Inaction	Aggrieved: Violence	Aggrieved: Soft AR	Aggrieved: Hard AR
Authority: Non-violent	[**80%**, 30%]	[**0%**, 60%]	[**70%**, 80%]	[**50%**, 65%]
Authority: Aggressive	[**30%**, 20%]	[**80%**, 70%]	[**40%**, 50%]	[**60%**, 60%]
Authority: Violent	[**15%**, 5%]	[**95%**, 95%]	[**20%**, 30%]	[**40%**, 40%]

In the strategic game between the aggrieved and the ruling authority,
there is an obvious deplorable equilibrium state of tit-for-tat violence. If
the ruling authority is violent, then the action supported by 95% of the
aggrieved population is to adopt a campaign of violence. Similarly, if
the aggrieved embark on such a campaign, then the best supported action
of the ruling authority is violent. However, in this illustrative case, an
alternative peaceful equilibrium happens to exist with the aggrieved
adopting some form of soft AR, and with the ruling authority responding
in a non-violent manner. This equilibrium exists because, given the
choice of one protagonist, the other protagonist's best supported choice

is to follow the equilibrium choice: 80% of the aggrieved population support this strategy, and 70% of the population of the ruling authority support a non-violent response.

Of course, the ruling authority may choose to override the strength of its own public opinion and adopt a much less popular stance, such as aggression, or even a very unpopular stance, such as violence. By so doing, political hawks can perpetuate a cycle of violence, as has happened all too often in longstanding conflicts. But for states answerable to the court of international opinion, the game theory logic of non-violence points towards the prospect of political change. This logic is implicit in Mahatma Gandhi's plea, 'Bring your opponent to his senses, not to his knees.' But non-violence requires great discipline. Gandhi warned, 'It takes a fairly strenuous course of training to attain to a mental state of non-violence.' Maybe this state will be attained some day in Palestine.[29] There is no easy road to conflict resolution, but after war, violence, and malice have been released from Pandora's Box, there remains the gift of hope.

The strategic folly of fighting violence with violence applies also to dictatorships. After years of unpopular authoritarian rule, the hope for democracy among oppressed populations can be best realized through non-violent revolution. For decades, the foremost expert on this subject has been Gene Sharp, known as the Clausewitz of non-violent warfare. Albert Einstein himself wrote the foreword to his book about Gandhi. Dissidents around the world have been inspired by Sharp's books, notably *From Dictatorship to Democracy*.[30] The compelling game theory logic of non-violence, which attacks the weakness of dictators, underpins his strategy for toppling authoritarian regimes.

The chaotic windstorm of political change triggered in January 2011 in Tunisia should not have come as a surprise to students of complex systems. Public protest may be disrupted by tough police action. But the visible success elsewhere of non-violent popular uprisings against loathed dictators encourages perseverance of protest despite increasingly violent repression. Beyond a certain level of state violence, a tipping point may be reached where domestic and international tolerance of such brutal action wanes in the face of sustained non-violent protest. This establishes the conditions for political reform.

Epilogue

Black and Red Swans

The *Song of Hiawatha* by Henry Wadsworth Longfellow immortalized the Indian legend of the beautiful red swan,[1] whose plumage glittered in the sun. Yet there was never a confirmed sighting. The snow-capped beauty of Mt. St. Helens was admired in Indian folk tales of the fire mountain. When farmers and missionaries saw clouds of steam over the mountain in the 1830s, they considered the event just a curiosity.[2] The truth of the Indian legend was confirmed by the explosive volcanic eruption of 18 May 1980.

Disaster occurrence is a timeless historical experiment with the sporadic accumulation of data in dynamic risk environments. Striving to ensnare a rare Black Swan, catastrophe risk analysts are at liberty to posit copious *red swans*: plausible, attractive, and perhaps supported by limited circumstantial evidence, albeit of questionable reliability. But ultimately they may be as unreal as the red swans of Indian legend.

In an anthology of technology accidents reprinted in 1999,[3] Y2K was described as the quintessential inevitable system accident straddling both the 20th and 21st centuries. With hindsight, this foreboding was unduly pessimistic – the accident was far from inevitable. Fear mongering about hundreds of millions of deaths from war, pestilence, and famine leading up to the third millennium has also proved totally wrong.[4,5]

In Greek mythology, it was Cassandra's curse to have the gift of prophecy, but not to be believed. She foresaw the destruction of Troy, but lacking the gift of persuasion, she was unable to forestall it. Her pronouncements were dismissed as utterances of the insane. In 1939, Lewis Fry Richardson sent a paper on arms races to a journal with a forlorn plea that its rapid publication might help to avert World War II. The paper was rejected by the editors.[6]

The age-old challenge persists in the 21st century of telling Nostradamus apart from Cassandra; distinguishing a plausible but fictitious catastrophe scenario from one which seems implausible but turns out actually to be real. Movie simulation of a hypothetical eruption of a supervolcano like Yellowstone has yet to match the astonishing haunting images of the cataclysmic eruption of Krakatau in 1883. No Hollywood simulation of a tsunami has caught the actual frightfulness of the March 2011 Japanese experience, captured on many amateur videos. The alien attack scenes in the 1996 *Independence Day* movie were pure escapist science fiction, but they inspired the Al Qaeda leadership to create their own cinematic skyscraper attack horror, which destroyed the World Trade Center five years later on 9/11.

Analysts whose expectation of the future is rooted firmly in confirmed observations of the past, or in highly rigid Procrustean models of the future,[7] are destined to live a life of potentially catastrophic surprise. But even for horizon scanning analysts, some surprise is unavoidable. Named after Sir Michael Quinlan, the leading post-war UK defence intellectual, Quinlan's game-theoretic law states that in matters of military contingency, 'The expected, precisely because it is expected, is not to be expected'.[8] For analysts eyeing the scientific future, surprise is also inevitable. This is because all scientific progress involves a process of heuristic search and an element of serendipity, which has been defined as 'The art of finding what we are not looking for by looking for what we are not finding'.[9] A slip of the tongue in 1952 provided Murray Gell-Mann with key insight into understanding the newly observed *strange* sub-atomic particles.[10]

Theoretical physicists, like Gell-Mann, are at the other end of the research spectrum to statisticians bound by precedent. Theorists are liberated from past experience in thinking about the unknown; they use mathematics as a probe and license to explore unknown unknowns, discovering an occasional Black Swan, but leaving a long trail of forgotten red swans. In particle physics, if not in biology, if a white swan exists, it is natural to posit the existence of swans of other colours. Theorems about black hole singularities, the ultimate catastrophes of the universe, have been vindicated by indirect astronomical evidence. Other ideas may not be matched with observations for years, if ever. The prodigious Viennese calculator, Wolfgang Pauli, famously dismissed an excessively hypothetical paper as 'not even wrong'.

A hallmark of theoretical physics is the power to refute hypothetical catastrophes by sheer force of analytical calculations. Before the first atomic bomb tests, the fear was raised that an atomic bomb might trigger a catastrophic chain reaction in the oceans or atmosphere. In the 21st century, a so-called *killer strangelet* scenario was proposed, envisaging that a runaway reaction might be initiated from within a high-energy physics laboratory, or even that large earthquakes might be triggered. Neither of these global Armageddon catastrophes has any scientific merit. This is just as well. Bearing in mind the entire world population potentially at risk, even a doubt of homeopathic imperceptibility might justify abandoning chain reaction experiments.[11]

Alas, the great majority of catastrophe hypotheses cannot be resolved by force of scientific argument. However, most natural and man-made catastrophes can be better understood and explained in terms of the underlying principles of complexity, self-organization, phase transitions, and fractal scaling. Explanation serves to dispel ignorance, but there remains an irreducible level of uncertainty intrinsic to complex dynamic systems, and epistemic uncertainty associated with lack of knowledge.

Perfect clarity of vision, such as afforded by adequate reliable observational data and abundant statistics, is a dangerous and misleading illusion. With failing deterministic vision to anticipate, forecast, or prevent disasters, and with cognitive dissonance and other behavioural impediments to unbiased judgement, adoption of some mode of probabilistic reasoning helps decision-makers to see farther in identifying and tracking potential Black Swans, in managing extreme risks, and calculating catastrophe. To quote the 17th century empiricist philosopher John Locke, who took part in a scientific exercise extending the coverage of weather observations, we are afforded only the *twilight of probability.*

As anyone would know who has practical experience of probabilistic risk assessment, an intuitive sense of relative risk is important for balanced judgement. This survey of catastrophe science has covered a diverse range of natural and man-made risks, in the belief that the broader the knowledge and understanding gained about many types of risk, the deeper insights there will be into any specific catastrophe.

Bibliography

Prologue

1. Einstein A. (1938) Letter to President Franklin D. Roosevelt. *Frontiers: research highlights 1946–1996.* Argonne National Laboratory, Argonne, Il.
2. Pessl M. (2006) *Special topics in calamity physics.* Viking Press, London.
3. Levenson T. (2009) *Newton and the counterfeiter.* Faber and Faber, London.
4. Feynman R.P. (1993) *What do you care what other people think?* HarperCollins, New York.
5. Nebeker F. (1995) *Calculating the weather.* Academic Press, San Diego.

Chapter 1

1. Wilson K.G. (1993) The renormalization group and critical phenomena. In: *Nobel lectures 1981–1990.* World Scientific, Singapore.
2. Bramwell S.T., Holdsworth P.C.W., Pinton J.-F. (1998) Universality of rare fluctuations in turbulence and critical phenomena. *Nature,* **396**, 552–554.
3. Shelley M. (1818) *Frankenstein.* Lackington, Hughes, Harding, Mayor & Jones, London.
4. Stewart S. (1986) *Air disasters.* Ian Allen, London.
5. Spirtes P., Glymour C., Scheines R. (2000) *Causation, prediction and search.* MIT Press, Cambridge, MA.
6. Hacking I. (1983) *Representing and intervening.* Cambridge University Press, Cambridge.
7. Suppes P. (1970) *A probabilistic theory of causality.* North Holland Publishing Co., Amsterdam.
8. Davis W.A. (1988) Probabilistic theories of causation. In: *Probability and causality* (J.H. Fetzer, Ed.). D. Reidel, Dordrecht.
9. Schum D.A. (1994) *Evidential foundations of probabilistic reasoning.* John Wiley & Sons, New York.
10. Cox D.R. (1992) Causality: some statistical aspects. *J. Royal Stat. Soc.,* **155**, 291–302.

11. Alvarez W. (1997) *T.rex and the crater of doom.* Princeton University Press, Princeton, N.J.

12. Melosh H.J. (1989) *Impact cratering: a geological process.* Oxford University Press, Oxford.

13. Steel D.I., Asher D.J., Napier W.M., Clube S.V.M. (1994) Are impacts correlated in time? In: *Hazards due to comets and asteroids* (T. Gehrels, Ed.). University of Arizona Press, Tucson.

14. Tandberg-Hanssen E., Emslie A.G. (1988) *The physics of solar flares.* Cambridge University Press, Cambridge.

15. National Research Council (2008) Severe space weather events. *Workshop Report.* National Academies Press, Washington D.C.

16. Bridgman H.A., Oliver J.E. (2006) *The global climate system.* Cambridge University Press, Cambridge.

17. Elsner J.B., Murnane R.J., Jagger T.H. (2006) Forecasting US hurricanes 6 months in advance. *Geophys. Res. Lett.*, **33**, L10704, doi:10.1029/2006GL025693.

18. McCaul E.W. (1993) Observations and simulations of hurricane-spawned tornadic storms. In: *The tornado* (C. Church *et al.*, Eds.). *AGU Geophys. Monograph*, **79**, Washington D.C.

19. Fink A.H., Brücher T., Ermert V., Krüger A., Pinto J.G. (2009) The European storm Kyrill in January 2007: synoptic evolution, meteorological impacts and some considerations with respect to climate change. *Nat. Haz. Earth Sci. Sci.*, **9**, 405 –423.

20. Scholz C.H. (1992) Paradigms or small changes in earthquake mechanics. In: *Fault mechanics and transport properties of rocks* (B. Evans, T-F. Wong, Eds.). Academic Press, London.

21. Lomnitz C. (1996) Search of a worldwide catalog for earthquakes triggered at intermediate distances. *Bull. Seism. Soc. Amer.*, **86**, 293–298.

22. Harris R.A. (1998) Special triggers, stress shadows, and implications for seismic hazard. *J. Geophys. Res.*, **103**, 24347–24358.

23. Linde A.T., Sacks S. (1998) Triggering of volcanic eruptions. *Nature*, **395**, 888–890.

24. Walter T.R., Amelung F. (2007) Volcanic eruptions following (M ≥ 9) megathrust earthquakes: implications for the Sumatra Andaman volcanoes. *Geology*, **35**, 539–542.

25. Kienholz H. (1998) Early warning systems related to mountain hazards. In *Proc. IDNDR-conf. on early warnings for the reduction of natural disasters*, Potsdam.

26. Iverson R.M. (1997) Physics of debris flow. *Rev. Geophys.*, **35**, 245–296.

27. Kramer S.L. (1996) *Geotechnical earthquake engineering.* Prentice-Hall, N.J.

28. Smith K., Ward R. (1998) *Floods: physical processes and human impacts.* John Wiley & Sons, Chichester.

29. Gudmundsson A.T., Sigurdsson R.T. (1996) *Vatnajökull: ice on fire.* Arctic Books, Reykjavik.

30. Dube S.K., Jain I., Rao A.D., Murty T.S. (2009) Storm surge modeling for the Bay of Bengal and Arabian Sea. *Natural Hazards*, **51**, 3–27.
31. Goodman-Tchernov B.N., Dey H.W., Reinhardt E.G., McCoy F., Mart Y. (2009) Tsunami waves generated by the Santorini eruption reached Eastern Mediterranean shores. *Geology*, **37**, 943–946.
32. Lander J.F., Lockridge P.A. (1989) *United States tsunamis 1690–1988*. National Geophysical Data Center, Boulder, CO.
33. Harbitz C.B. (1992) Model simulations of tsunamis generated by the Storegga slides. *Marine Geol.*, **105**, 1–21.
34. Masson D.G. (1996) Catastrophic collapse of the volcanic island of Hierro 15 ka ago and the history of landslides in the Canary islands. *Geology*, **24**, 231–234.

Chapter 2

1. Gibbon E. (1776) *The rise and fall of the Roman Empire*. Strahan & Cadell, London.
2. Nye J.S. (1993) *Understanding international conflicts: an introduction to theory and history*. Harper Collins, New York.
3. Platias A.G., Koliopoulis C. (2010) *Thucydides on strategy*. C. Hurst & Co., London.
4. Kilcullen D. (2010) *Counterinsurgency*. C. Hurst & Co., London.
5. Guevara C. (1961) *Guerilla warfare*. Monthly Review Press. Reprinted by University of Nebraska Press, Lincoln.
6. Sharpe M.E. Inc. (1997) *International encyclopaedia of terrorism*. Fitzroy Dearborn Publishers, London.
7. Cronin A.K. (2009) *How terrorism ends*. Princeton University Press, Princeton, N.J.
8. Prechter R.R. Jr. (1995) *At the crest of the tidal wave*. John Wiley & Sons, New York.
9. Kuhn T. (1962) *The structure of scientific revolutions*. University of Chicago Press, Chicago.
10. Dodge T. (2010) The ideological roots of failure: the application of kinetic neo-liberalism to Iraq. *International Affairs*, **86**, 1269–1286.
11. Rapoport D.C. (2004) Modern terror: the four waves. In: *Attacking terrorism: elements of a grand strategy* (A. Cronin, J. Ludes, Eds.). Georgetown Univ. Press, Washington D.C.
12. Hoffman B. (2006) *Inside terrorism*. Columbia University Press, New York.
13. Davis J. (2007) Web War One. *Wired*, September.
14. McKenzie F.E., Samba E.M. (2004) The role of mathematical modeling in evidence-based malaria control. *Am. J. Trop. Med. Hyg.*, **71**, 94–96.

15. Jones K.R., Patel N.G., Levy M.A., Storeygard A., Balk D., Gittleman J.L., Daszak P. (2008) Global trends in emerging infectious diseases. *Nature*, **451**, 990–994.
16. Smith D. (2006) Predictability and preparedness in influenza control. *Science*, **312**, 392–394.
17. Stöhr K. (2010) Vaccinate before the next pandemic? *Nature*, **465**, 161.
18. Körner T.W. (2008) *Naïve decision making*. Cambridge University Press, Cambridge.
19. Fraser C., Riley S., Anderson R.M., Ferguson N.M. (2004) Factors that make an infectious disease outbreak controllable. *PNAS*, **101**, 6146–6151.
20. Kuecker G.D. (2004) The greatest and the worst: dominant and subaltern memories of the Dos Bocas well fire of 1908. In: *Memory of catastrophe* (P. Gray, K. Oliver, Eds.). Manchester University Press, Manchester.
21. Lancaster J. (2005) *Engineering catastrophes*. Woodhead Publishing, Cambridge.
22. Reason J. (2008) *The human contribution*. Ashgate, Farnham.
23. CSB (2007) BP America refinery explosion. *Final investigation report*. No. 2005-04-I-TX.
24. Dekker S. (2007) *Just culture*. Ashgate, London.
25. Reason J. (1998) Achieving a safe culture: theory and practice. *Work & Stress*, **12**, 293–306.
26. Thorogood J.L., Tourney F.G., Crawley F.K., Woo G. (1990) Quantitative risk assessment of subsurface well collisions. *Proc. Europec 90,* SPE20908, Hague, Netherlands.
27. BP (2010) *Deepwater Horizon accident investigation report*. BP, 8 September.
28. Barton L. (2004) *Crisis management*. Harvard Business Press, Boston, MA.
29. Perrow C. (1999) *Normal accidents*. Princeton University Press, Princeton, N.J.
30. Duffey R.B., Saull J.W. (2003) *Know the risk*. Butterworth Heinemann, Burlington, MA.
31. Mackay C. (1841) *Memoirs of extraordinary popular delusions*. Richard Bentley, London.
32. Epstein R.A. (1977) *The theory of gambling and statistical logic*. Academic Press, San Diego.
33. Iguchi T. (2004) *My billion dollar education*. JoNa books, Bedford, IN.
34. Leeson N. (1996) *Rogue trader*. Little, Brown and Company, London.
35. Lewis M. (2009) *Panic*. W.W. Norton & Co. Ltd., New York.
36. Lebor A. (2009) *The believers*. Weidenfeld & Nicolson, London.
37. Artzrouni M. (2009) The mathematics of Ponzi schemes. *Mathematical Social Sciences*, **58**, 190–201.
38. Henriques D.B., Healy J. (2009) Madoff goes to jail after guilty pleas. *New York Times*, 12 March.
39. Pézier J. (2003) A constructive review of the Basel proposals on operational risk. In: *Operational risk* (C. Alexander, Ed.). Prentice Hall, London.
40. Kerviel J. (2010) *L'Engrenage*. Flammarion, Paris.

41. Taleb N.N. (2004) *Fooled by randomness*. Random House, New York.

Chapter 3

1. Feynman R.P. (1968) What is science? *The Physics Teacher*, **7**, 313–320.
2. Taleb N.N. (2007) *The black swan*. Random House Publishing Group, New York.
3. Johnston A.C. (1990) An earthquake strength scale for the media and the public. *Earthquakes & Volcanoes*, **22**, 214–216.
4. Holland G.J. (1982) An analytical model of the wind and pressure profile in hurricanes. *Month. Weath. Rev.*, **108**, 1212–1218.
5. Wind Science and Engineering Center (2006) *Enhanced Fujita Scale*. Report for National Weather Service, Texas Tech University, Lubbock.
6. Doswell C.A., Brooks H.E., Dotzek N. (2009) On the enhancement of the Fujita scale in the USA, *Atmospheric Research*, **93**, 554–563.
7. Newhall C.G., Self S. (1982) The volcanic explosivity index (VEI): an estimate of explosive magnitude for historical volcanism. *J. Geophys. Res.*, **87**, 1231–1238.
8. Pyle D.M. (2000) Sizes of volcanic eruptions. In: *Encyclopaedia of volcanoes* (H. Sigurdsson, Ed.). Academic Press, San Diego.
9. Simkin T., Siebert L. (1994) *Volcanoes of the world*. Geoscience Press, Tucson.
10. Abe K. (1995) Modeling of the runup heights of the Hokkaido-Nansei-Oki tsunami of 12 July 1993. *Pageoph*, **144**, 735–745.
11. Song Y.T. (2007) Detecting tsunami genesis and scales directly from GPS stations. *Geophys. Res. Lett.*, **34**, LI9602, doi:10.1029/2007/ GL0301681.
12. Feng L., Luo G. (2010) Proposal for a quantitative index of flood disasters. *Disasters*, **34**, 695–704.
13. De Arcangelis L., Godano C., Lippiello E., Nicodemi M. (2006) Universality in solar flare and earthquake occurrence. *Phys. Rev. Lett.*, **96**, 051102.
14. Poppe B.B. (2000) New scales help public, technicians understand space weather. *EOS*, **81**, 322, 328.
15. Ruskin J. (1843) *Modern painters: their superiority in the art of landscape painting to all the ancient masters*. Smith, Elder & Co., London.
16. Mandelbrot B. (1977) *The fractal geometry of Nature*. W.H. Freeman, New York.
17. Richardson L.F. (1961) The problem of contiguity. Appendix to: Statistics of deadly quarrels. *Gen. Syst. Yearbook*, **6**, 139–187.
18. Hunt J.C.R. (1998) Lewis Fry Richardson and his contributions to mathematics, meteorology and models of conflict. *Annu. Rev. Fluid Mech.*, **30**, xiii–xxxvi.
19. Korvin G. (1992) *Fractal models in the Earth sciences*. Elsevier, Amsterdam.
20. Tufte E.R. (1997) *Visual explanations*. Graphics Press, Cheshire, CT.
21. Heffer K.J., Bevan T.G. (1990) Scaling relationships in natural fractures: data, theory, and application. *Proc. Eur. Pet. Conf.*, **2**, 367–376, SPE 20981, Hague.
22. Scholz C.H. (1998) A further note on earthquake size distributions. *Bull. Seism. Soc. Amer.*, **88**, 1325–1326.

23. Sparks R.S.J., Bursik M.I., Carey S.N., Gilbert J.S., Glaze L.S., Sigurdsson H., Woods A.W. (1997) *Volcanic plumes*. John Wiley & Sons, Chichester.

24. Pyle D.M. (1989) The thickness, volume and grain size of tephra fall deposits. *Bull. Volc.*, **51**, 1–15.

25. Costa A., Folch A., Macedonio G. (2010) A model for wet aggregation of ash particles in volcanic plumes and clouds: I. Theoretical formulation. *J. Geophys. Res.*, **115**, B09201, doi:10.1029/2009JB007175.

26. Self S. (2006) The effects and consequences of very large explosive volcanic eruptions. *Phil. Trans. Royal Soc. A.*, **364**, 2073–2097.

27. Salvadori G., Ratti S.P., Belli G. (1997) Fractal and multifractal approach to environmental pollution. *Environ. Sci. Pollut. Res.*, **4**, 91–98.

28. Ratti S.P., Belli G. (2008) Seveso 1976, Chernobyl 1986: fractal description of two ecological disasters. *Scientifica Acta*, **2**, 77–92.

29. Johnson P.A., McCuen R.H. (1996) Mud and debris flows. In: *Hydrology of disasters* (V.P. Singh, Ed.). Kluwer Academic Publishers, Dordrecht.

30. Yokoi Y., Carr J.R., Watters R.J. (1995) Fractal character of landslides. *Env. & Eng. Geoscience*, **1**, 75–81.

31. Yang Z.Y., Lee Y.H. (2006) The fractal characteristics of landslides induced by earthquakes and rainfall in central Taiwan. *10 IAEG Int. Congress*, No. 48, Nottingham.

32. Hergarten S., Neugebauer H.J. (1998) Self-organized criticality in a landslide model. *Geophys. Res. Lett.*, **25**, 801–804.

33. Bak P. (1997) *How Nature works*. Oxford University Press, Oxford.

34. Okal E.A., Synolakis C.E. (2008) Far-field tsunami hazard from mega-thrust earthquakes. *Geophys. J. Int.*, **172**, 995–1015.

35 . Lander J.F., Lockridge P.A. (1989) *United States tsunamis*. National Geophysical Data Center, Boulder, CO.

36. Rodríguez-Iturbe I., Rinaldo A. (1997) *Fractal river basins*. Cambridge University Press, Cambridge.

37. Melosh H.J. (1989) *Impact cratering: a geological process*. Oxford University Press, Oxford.

38. Maugham S. (1952) *Collected plays [inc. Sheppey]*. Heinemann, London.

39. Borhorquez J.C., Gourley S., Dixon A.R., Spagat M., Johnson N.F. (2009) Common ecology quantifies human insurgency. *Nature*, **462**, 911–914.

40. Clauset A., Young M., Gleditsch K.S. (2007) On the frequency of severe terrorist Events. *Journal of Conflict Resolution*, **51**, 58–88.

41. Brown A. (2005) *J.D. Bernal, the sage of science*. Oxford University Press, Oxford.

42. Wise R. (2004) *The luck factor*. Arrow Books, London.

43. Knopoff L., Sornette D. (1995) Earthquake death tolls. *J. Phys. De France I*, **5**, 1681–1688.

44. Pyle D.M. (1998) Forecasting sizes and repose times of future extreme volcanic events. *Geology*, **26**, 367–370.

45. Nateghi-Alahi F., Izadkhah Y. (2004) Earthquake mitigation in health facilities in mega city of Tehran. *Proc. 13th World Conf. Earthq. Eng.*, Vancouver, Canada.
46. Malthus T. (1798) *An essay on the principle of population.* T. Murray, London.
47. Bouthoul G. (1962) *Le phénomène-guerre.* Payot, Paris.
48. Garnsey P. (1992) Famine in history. In: *Understanding catastrophe* (J. Bourriau, Ed.). Cambridge University Press, Cambridge.
49. Newman M.E.J. (2005) Power laws, Pareto distributions and Zipf's law. *Contemporary Physics*, **46**, 323–351.
50. Dietrich W.E., Bellugi D.G., Sklar L.S., Stock J.D., Heimsath A.M., Roering J.J. (2003) Geomorphic transport laws for predicting landscape form and dynamics. In: *Prediction in geology.* Geophysical Monograph 135, AGU.
51. Cartwright N. (1983) *How the laws of physics lie.* Oxford University Press, Oxford.
52. Bass A.C.W. (2002) Chaos, fractals and self-organization in coastal geomorphology simulating dune landscapes in vegetated environments. *Geomorphology*, **48**, 309–328.
53. Clark K. (1949) *Landscape into art.* John Murray Ltd., London.
54. Pilkey O.H., Pilkey-Jarvis L. (2006) *Useless arithmetic: why environmental scientists can't predict the future.* Columbia University Press, New York.
55. Borges J. L. (1946) *On exactitude in science.* Los Annales de Buenos Aires, No.3.
56. Lamb H. (1991) *Historic storms of the North Sea, British Isles and Northwest Europe.* Cambridge University Press, Cambridge.
57. Woo G. (2002) Overlaying uncertainty on maps. *Proc. 12th Eur. Conf. Earthq. Eng.*, London.

Chapter 4

1. Greene G. (1980) *Dr. Fischer of Geneva or the bomb party.* Bodley Head, London.
2. Daston L. (1988) *Classical probability in the enlightenment.* Princeton University Press, Princeton, N.J.
3. Kolmogorov A.N. (1933) Foundations of the theory of probability. *Erg. Math.*, **2**. Springer-Verlag, Berlin.
4. Suppes P. (1994) Qualitative theory of subjective probability. In: *Subjective probability* (G. Wright, P. Ayton, Eds.) John Wiley & Sons, Chichester.
5. Ott E. (1993) *Chaos in dynamical systems.* Cambridge University Press, Cambridge.
6. Prigogine I. (1996) *The end of certainty.* The Free Press, New York.
7. Hacking I. (1975) *The emergence of probability.* Cambridge University Press, Cambridge.
8. Jeffreys H. (1939) *Theory of probability.* Oxford University Press, Oxford.
9. Laby Z. (2009) Weldon's dice, automated. *Chance*, **22**, 6–13.

10. Gray W.M., Landsea C.W., Mielke P.W., Berry K.J. (1994) Predicting Atlantic Basin seasonal tropical cyclone activity by 1 June. *Weather & Forecasting*, **9**, 103–115.

11. Lorenz E. N. (1993*) The essence of chaos.* University of Washington Press, Washington D.C.

12. Merz B., Thieken A. (2009) Flood risk curves and uncertainty bounds. *Natural Hazards*, **51**, 437–458.

13. Toro G.R., Abrahamson N.A., Schneider J.F. (1997) Model of ground motions from earthquakes in Central and Eastern North America: best estimates and uncertainties. *Seism. Res. Lett.*, **68**, 41–57.

14. Anderson J.G., Brune J.N. (1999) Probabilistic seismic hazard analysis without the ergodic assumption. *Seism. Res. Lett.*, **70**, 19–28.

15. Daubechies I. (1992) *Ten lectures on wavelets.* SIAM, Philadelphia.

16. Yomogida K. (1994) Detection of anomalous seismic phases by the wavelet transform. *Geophys. J. Int.*, **116**, 119–130.

17. David F.N. (1962) *Games, gods and gambling.* Hafner Publishing Co., New York.

18. Perrow C. (1999) *Normal accidents.* Princeton University Press, Princeton, N.J.

19. Knight F.H. (1921) *Risk, uncertainty and profit.* Beard books, Washington D.C.

20. Gillies D. (2000) *Philosophical theories of probability.* Routledge, London.

21. Calais E., Freed A., Mattioli G., Amelung F., Jónsson S., Jansma P., Hong S-H., Dixon T., Prépetit C., Momplaisir R. (2010) Transpressional rupture of an unmapped fault during the 2010 Haiti earthquake. *Nature Geoscience*, **3**, 794–799.

22. Ramsey F.P. (1931) *The foundations of mathematics and other logical essays.* Routledge and Kegan Paul, London.

23. De Finetti B. (1970) *Theory of probability.* John Wiley & Sons, Chichester.

24. Jeffrey R. (2004) *Subjective probability.* Cambridge University Press, Cambridge.

25. Winkler R.L., Murphy A.H. (1968) Good probability assessors. *J. Appl. Met.*, **7**, 751–758.

26. Allen C.R. (1995) Earthquake hazard assessment: has our approach been modified in the light of recent earthquakes? *Earthquake Spectra*, **11**, 357–366.

27. Aitken C.G.G. (1995*) Statistics and the evaluation of evidence for forensic scientists.* John Wiley & Sons, Chichester.

28. Woo G. (2008) Bayesian methods in seismic hazard analysis. *OECD workshop on recent findings and developments in probabilistic seismic hazard analysis (PSHA).* Lyon, France, 143–159.

29. Rumsfeld D. (2011) *Known and unknown: a memoir.* Sentinel HC, New York.

30. Binmore K. (2009) *Rational decisions.* Princeton University Press, Princeton, N.J.

31. Posner K.A. (2010) *Stalking the black swan.* Columbia University Press, New York.

32. Festinger L., Rieken H.W., Schachter S. (1956) *When prophecy fails: a social and psychological study of a modern group that predicted the destruction of the world.* University of Minnesota Press, Minneapolis.

33. Bovens L., Hartmann S. (2003) *Bayesian epistemology.* Oxford University Press, Oxford.

Chapter 5

1. Sloane N.J.A., Plouffe S. (1995) *The encyclopaedia of integer sequences.* Academic Press, San Diego.
2. Bakun W.H., Lindh A.G. (1985) The Parkfield, California earthquake prediction experiment. *Science, 229,* 619–624.
3. Lomnitz C. (1994) *Fundamentals of earthquake prediction.* John Wiley & Sons, New York.
4. Mlodinow L. (2008) *The drunkard's walk.* Penguin, London.
5. Gell-Mann M. (1994) *The quark and the jaguar.* Little, Brown and Company, London.
6. Scholz C. (2010) Large earthquake triggering, clustering, and the synchronization of faults. *Bull.Seism.Soc.Amer.,* **100,** 3, 901–909.
7. Rosenblum M., Pikovsky A. (2003) Synchronization: from pendulum clocks to chaotic lasers and chemical oscillators, *Contemporary Physics,* **44,** 5, 401–416.
8. Creager A.N.H., Lunbeck E., Norton Wise M. (2007) *Science without laws.* Duke University Press, Durham, N.C.
9. Strogatz S. (2003) *Sync.* Penguin, London.
10. Lisiecki L.E. (2010) Links between eccentricity forcing and the 100,000 year glacial cycle, *Nature Geoscience,* **3,** 349–352.
11. Yeates A.R., Nandy D., Mackay D.H. (2008) Exploring the physical basis of solar cycle predictions: flux transport dynamics and persistence of memory in advection-versus diffusion-dominated solar convection zones. *Astron. Journal,* **673,** 544–556.
12. Neuberg J. (2000) External modulation of volcanic activity. *Geophys. J. Int.,* **142,** 232–240.
13. Heaton T.H. (1975) Tidal triggering of earthquakes. *Geophys. J. R. Astron. Soc.,* **43,** 307–326.
14. Cochran E.S., Vidale J.E., Tanaka S. (2004) Earth tides can trigger shallow thrust fault earthquakes. *Science,* **306,** 1164–1166.
15. Khintchine A.Y. (1960) *Mathematical methods in the theory of queueing.* Griffin, London.
16. Clarke R.T. (1998) *Stochastic processes for water scientists.* John Wiley & Sons, Chichester.
17. Gabriel K.R., Neumann J. (1962) A Markov chain model for daily rainfall occurrence at Tel Aviv. *Quart. J. R. Met. Soc.,* **88,** 90–95.
18. Drton M., Marzban C., Guttorp P., Schaefer J. T. (2003) A Markov chain model of tornadic activity. *Mon. Wea. Rev.,* **131,** 2941–2953.
19. Aspinall W.P., Carniel R., Jaquet O., Woo G., Hincks T. (2006) Using hidden multi-state Markov models with multi-parameter volcanic data to provide empirical evidence for alert decision-support. *J. Volc. Geothermal Res.,* **153,** 112–124.

20. Bebbington M.S. (2007) Identifying volcanic regimes using Hidden Markov models. *Geophys. J. Int.*, **171**, 921–942.

21. Rabiner L.R. (1989) A tutorial on hidden Markov models and selected applications in speech recognition. *Proc. IEEE*, **2**, 257–286.

22. Falk R., Lipson A., Konold C. (1994) The ups and downs of the hope function in a fruitless search. In: *Subjective probability* (G. Wright, P. Ayton, Eds.). John Wiley & Sons, Chichester.

23. Sornette D., Knopoff L. (1997) The paradox of expected time until the next earthquake. *Bull. Seism. Soc. Amer.*, **87**, 789–798.

24. Matthews M.V., Ellsworth W.L., Reasenberg P.A. (2002) A Brownian model for recurrent earthquakes. *Bull. Seism. Soc. Amer.*, **92**, 2223–2250.

25. Embrechts P., Klüppelberg, Mikosch T. (1997) *Modelling extremal events*. Springer-Verlag, Berlin.

26. Woo G., Muir-Wood R. (1985) *North Sea seismicity*. Offshore technology report. Stationery Office Books, London.

27. Horner R.W. (1981) Flood prevention works with specific reference to the Thames Barrier. In: *Floods due to high winds and tides* (D.H. Peregrine, Ed.). Academic Press, San Diego.

28. Mandelbrot B.B., Wallis J.R. (1995) Some long-run properties of geophysical records. In: *Fractals in the Earth sciences* (C.C. Barton, P.R. LaPointe, Eds.). Plenum Press, New York.

29. Kondrashov D., Feliks Y., Ghil M. (2005) Oscillatory modes of extended Nile River records (AD 622–1922) *Geophys. Res. Lett.*, 32, L10702, doi:10.1029/2004GL022156.

30. Battjes J.A., Gerritsen H. (2002) Coastal modelling for flood defence. *Phil. Trans. R. Soc. Lond. A*, **360**, 1461–1475.

31. De Haan L. (1990) Fighting the arch-enemy with mathematics. *Statistica Neerlandica*, **44**, 45–68.

32. Gumbel E.J. (1958) *Statistics of extremes*. Columbia University Press, New York.

33. Tawn J.A. (1992) Estimating probabilities of extreme sea-levels. *Appl. Statist.*, **41**, 77–93.

34. Ashkar F. (1996) Extreme floods. In: *Hydrology of disasters* (V.P. Singh, Ed.). Kluwer Academic Publishers, Dordrecht.

35. Pickands J. (1975) Statistical inference using extreme order statistics. *Ann. Statist.*, **3**, 119–131.

36. Davison A.C., Smith R.L. (1990) Models for exceedances over high thresholds, *J.R. Statist. Soc. B*, **52**, 393–442.

37. Hosking J.R.M., Wallis J.R. (1987) Parameter and quantile estimation for the generalized Pareto distribution. *Technometrics*, **29**, 339–349.

38. Gilleland E., Katz R. (2011) New software to analyze how extremes change over time. *EOS*, **92**, 13–14.

39. Della-Marta P.M., Mathis H., Frei C., Liniger M.A., Kleinn J., Appenzeller C. (2009) The return period of wind storms over Europe. *Int. J. Climatology.*, **29**, 437–459.

40. Deligne N.I., Coles S.G., Sparks R.S.J. (2010) Recurrence rates of large explosive eruptions. *J. Geophys. Res.*, **115**, B06203, doi: 10.1029/ 2009 JB006554.

Chapter 6

1. Dirac P.A.M. (1929) Quantum mechanics of many-electron systems. *Proc. Roy. Soc. London*, **A123**, 714–733.
2. Nicolis G., Prigogine I. (1989) *Exploring complexity*. W.H. Freeman, New York.
3. Gawande A. (2010) *The Checklist manifesto: how to get things right*. Profile Books, London.
4. Kilcullen D. (2010) *Counterinsurgency*. C. Hurst & Co., London.
5. Coker C. (2009) *War in an age of risk*. Polity Press, Cambridge.
6. Woo G. (2009) Intelligence constraints on terrorist network plots. In: *Mathematical methods in counter-terrorism* (N. Memon, J.D. Farley, D.L. Hicks, T. Rosenorn, Eds.). Springer, New York.
7. Bennett R. (1997) *The catastrophist*. Headline Books, London.
8. Buldyrev S.V., Parshani R., Paul G., Stanley H.E., Havlin S. (2010) Catastrophic cascade of failures in interdependent networks. *Nature*, **464**, 1025–1028.
9. Vespignani A. (2010) The fragility of interdependency. *Nature*, **464**, 984–985.
10. Walras L. (1926) *Elements d'economie politique pure*. Pichon et Durand-Auzias, Paris.
11. Arrow K. (1972) General economic equilibrium: purpose, analytic techniques, collective choice. *Nobel Memorial Lecture*, Harvard University.
12. Caccioli F., Marsli M., Vivo P. (2008) Eroding market stability by proliferation of financial instruments. *Eur. Phys. J.* **B71**, 467–479.
13. Sorkin A.R. (2010) *Too big to fail*. Penguin, London.
14. Johnson N. (2007) *Simply complexity*. Oneworld Publications, Oxford.
15. Johnson N., Jefferies P., Hui P.M. (2003) *Financial market complexity*. Oxford University Press, Oxford.
16. Mantegna R.N., Stanley H.E. (2000) *An introduction to econophysics*. Cambridge University Press, Cambridge.
17. Soros G. (2009) *The crash of 2008 and what it means*. Public Affairs, New York.
18. Galbraith J.K. (1955) *The great crash*. Hamish Hamilton, London.
19. Lewis M. (1989) *Liar's poker*. Hodder, London.
20. Sornette D. (2003) *Why stock markets crash*. Princeton University Press, Princeton, N.J.
21. Buncefield Major Incident Investigation Board (2008) *The Buncefield incident 11 December 2005*. Health & Safety Commission, London.

22. Papan, P., Leblond, J., Meijer, P.H.E. (2002) *The physics of phase transitions.* Springer, Berlin.
23. Carver L. (2010) The physics of the flash crash. *Risk*, **23**, 91.
24. Bar-Yam Y. (1997) *Dynamics of complex systems.* Westview Press, Boulder, CO.
25. Klemm, K., Eguiluz, V.M., Toral, R., San Miguel, M. (2003) Global culture: a noise induced transition in finite systems. *Physical Review* E67, 045101 (R).
26. Woo G. (2006) Analysis of ancillary hazards associated with natural perils. *Proceedings of ESREL 2006: Safety and reliability for managing risk.* Estoril, Portugal.

Chapter 7

1. Kepel G. (2005) *The roots of radical Islam.* Saqi Books, London.
2. Tzu S., Liddell Hart B., Griffith S.B. (1971) *The art of war.* Oxford University Press, Oxford.
3. Gul I. (2009) *The most dangerous place.* Penguin, London.
4. O'Neill S. (2010) *The suicide factory.* Harper Perennial, London.
5. Haggstrom, G.W. (1967) Optimal sequential procedures when more than one stop is required. *Ann. Math. Statist.*, **38**, 1618–1626.
6. Ashby W.R. (1962) Principles of the self-organizing system. In: *Principles of self-organization* (H. Von Foerster, G.W. Zopf Jr., Eds.). Pergamon Press, London.
7. Gunaratna R. (2002) *Inside Al Qaeda.* Columbia University Press, New York.
8. Atwan A. B. (2006) *The secret history of al Qa'ida.* Saqi books, London.
9. Gul I. (2009) *The most dangerous place.* Penguin, London.
10. Storr J. (2010) Manoeuvre and weapons effect on the battlefield. *RUSI Defence Systems*, **13**, 61–63.
11. Dunne T. (2006) *Terrorism and the news media.* cpc@eastlink.ca.
12. Oliver A.M., Steinberg P. (2005) *The road to martyrs' square.* Oxford University Press, Oxford.
13. Lindley D.V. (1991) *Making decisions.* John Wiley & Sons, London.
14. Davis M. (2007) *Buda's wagon: a brief history of the car bomb.* Verso, London.
15. Cormie D., Mays G., Smith P. (Eds.) (2009) *Blast effects on buildings.* 2nd Edition. Thomas Telford, London.
16. Taylor P.J. (2004) *World city network.* Routledge, Abingdon.
17. Woo G. (2002) Quantitative terrorism risk assessment. *Journal of Risk Finance.* **4**, 7–14.
18. Tenet G. (2007) *At the center of the storm.* HarperCollins, London.
19. Kohlmann E.F. (2004) *Al-Qaida's jihad in Europe.* Berg, Oxford.
20. Wilkinson P. (1992) Interview. *The Daily Telegraph*, 1 September.
21. Brumfiel G. (2002) Homeland-security research: mission impossible? *Nature*, **419**, 10–11.

22. Watts D. (1999) *Small worlds*. Princeton University Press, Princeton, N.J.

23. Blass T. (2004) *The man who shocked the world*. Basic Books, New York.

24. Guare J. (1990) *Six degrees of separation*. Dramatists Play Service Inc., New York.

25. Woo G. (2010) The control of terrorism risk. *The Risk Report*. International Risk Management Institute, Texas.

26. Keeble H., Hollington K. (2010) *Terror cops*. Simon & Schuster, Sydney.

27. Bar S., Minzili Y. (2006) The Zawahiri letter and the strategy of Al Qaeda. *Current trends in Islamist ideology*, **3**. Hudson Institute, Washington D.C.

28. Shell G.R., Moussa M. (2007) *The art of Woo*. Penguin Group, New York.

29. Bonabeau E., Dorigo M., Theraulaz G. (1999) *Swarm intelligence*. Oxford University Press, Oxford.

30. Githens-Mazur J., Lambert R. (2010) Why conventional wisdom on radicalization fails. *International Affairs*, **86**, 889–901.

31. Christakis N.A., Fowler J.H. (2009) *Connected*. Little, Brown and Co., New York.

32. Granovetter M. (1978) Threshold models of collective behaviour. *Amer. Journ. of Sociology*, **83**, 1420–1443.

33. Kilcullen D. (2009) *The accidental guerilla*. C. Hurst & Co., London.

34. Baron-Cohen S. (1997) *Mindblindness*. MIT Press, Cambridge, MA.

Chapter 8

1. Diaconis P. (1978) Statistical problems in ESP research. *Science*, **201**, 131–136.

2. Moreno M., Rosenau M., Oncken O. (2010) 2010 Maule earthquake slip correlates with pre-seismic locking of Andean subduction zone. *Nature*, **467**, 198–202.

3. Ruegg J.C., Rudloff A., Vigny C. *et al.* (2009) Interseismic strain accumulation by GPS in the seismic gap between Constitución and Concepción in Chile. *Phys. Earth. Plan. Int.*, **175**, 78–85.

4. Liu D., Wang J., Wang Y. (1989) Application of catastrophe theory in earthquake hazard assessment and earthquake prediction research. *Tectonophysics*, **167**, 179–186.

5. Thom R. (1972) *Structural stability and morphogenesis*. W.A. Benjamin, New York.

6. Gilmore R. (1981) *Catastrophe theory for scientists and engineers*. John Wiley & Sons, New York.

7. Jordan T.H. (2006) Collaboratory for the study of earthquake predictability (CSEP). *5th Joint Meeting of the UJNR Panel on Earthquake Research*. Tokushima, Japan.

8. Zechar J.D., Jordan T.H. (2007) Testing alarm-based earthquake prediction. *Geophys. J. Int.*, **172**, 715–724.

9. Chen Q-F., Wang K. (2010) The 2008 Wenchuan earthquake and earthquake prediction in China. *Bull. Seism. Soc. Amer.*, **100**, 2840–2857.

10. Ma Z., Fu Z., Zhang Y., Wang C., Zhang G., Liu D. (1990) *Earthquake prediction: nine major earthquakes in China.* Springer-Verlag, Beijing.

11. Grant R.A., Halliday T. (2010) Predicting the unpredictable; evidence of pre-seismic anticipatory behaviour in the common toad. *Journal of Zoology.* 10.1111/j.1469–7998.2010.00700.x.

12. Diaconis P., Mosteller F. (1989) Methods for studying coincidences. *J. Amer. Stat. Assoc.,* **84**, 853–861.

13. Mohler G. (2010) The aftershocks of crime, *The Economist,* 21 October.

14. Zhuang J., Ogata Y., Vere-Jones D. (2002) Stochastic declustering of space–time earthquake occurrences, *J. Amer. Stat. Assoc.,* **97**, 369–380.

15. Console R., Murru M., Falcone G. (2010) Probability gains of an epidemic-type aftershock sequence model in retrospective forecasting of $M \geq 5$ earthquakes in Italy. *J. Seismol.,* **14**, 9–26.

16. Marzocchi W., Lombardi A.M. (2009) Real-time forecasting following a damaging earthquake. *Geophys. Res. Lett.,* **36**, L21302.

17. Sol A., Turan H. (2004) The ethics of earthquake prediction. *Science and Engineering Ethics,* **10**, 655–666.

18. Woo G. (2010) Operational earthquake forecasting and risk management. *Seism. Res. Lett.,* **81**, doi.1785/gssrl.81.5.778.

19. Tang L., Titov V.V., Chamberlin C.D. (2009) Development, testing, and applications of site-specific tsunami inundation models for real-time forecasting. *J. Geophys. Res.,* **114**, C12025, doi:1029JC005476.

20. Barnes L.R., Gruntfest E.C., Hayden M.H., Schultz D.M., Benight C., (2007) False alarms and close calls: a conceptual model of warning accuracy. *Weather and Forecasting,* **22**, 1140–1147.

21. Gilbert G.K. (1884) Finlay's tornado predictions. *Amer. Meteor. J.,* **1**, 166–172.

22. Murphy A.H. (1996) General decompositions of MSE-based skill scores – measures of some basic aspects of forecast quality. *Mon. Weather Rev.,* **124**, 2353–2369.

23. Smith D.M., Eade R., Dunstone N.J., Fereday D., Murphy J.M., Pohlmann H., Scaife A.A. (2010) Skilful multi-year predictions of Atlantic hurricane frequency. *Nature Geoscience,* **3**, 846–849.

24. Szöllösi-Nagy A. (1995) Forecasts applications for defences from floods. In: *Defence from floods and floodplain management* (J. Gardiner *et al.,* Eds.). Kluwer Academic Publishers, Dordrecht.

25. Calvo B., Savi F. (2009) Real-time forecasting of the Tiber River in Rome. *Natural Hazards,* **50**, 461–477.

26. Behrens A., Gunther H. (2009) Operational wave prediction of extreme storms in Northern Europe. *Natural Hazards,* **49**, 387–399.

27. Gain B. (2007) Predicting rogue waves. *MIT Technology Review,* 1 March.

28. Yeom D-I, Egerton B.J. (2007) Photonics: rogue waves surface in light. *Nature,* **450**, 953–954.

29. Zandi M. (2009) *Financial shock.* FT Press, N.J.
30. Voight B., Cornelius R.R. (1991) Prospects for eruption prediction in near real-time. *Nature*, **350**, 695–698.
31. Sigmundsson F., Hreinsdóttir S., Hooper A., Arnodóttir T., Pederson R., Roberts M.J., Oskarsson N., Auriac A., Decriem J., Einarsson P., Geirsson H., Hensch M., Ofeigsson B.G., Sturkell E., Sveinbjörnsson H., Feigl K.L. (2010) Intrusion triggering of the 2010 Eyjafjallajökull explosive eruption, *Nature*, **468**, 426–430.
32. Pralong A., Birrer C., Stahel W.A., Funk M. (2005) On the predictability of ice avalanches. *Nonlinear Processes in Geophysics*, **12**, 849–861.
33. Crosta G.B., Agliardi F. (2003) Failure forecast for large rock slides by surface displacement measurements. *Can. Geotech. J.*, **40**, 176–191.
34. Wegmann M., Funk M., Flotron A., Keusen H. (2003) Movement studies to forecast the time of breaking off of ice and rock masses. In: *Early warning systems for natural disaster reduction* (J. Zchau, A.N. Kuppers, Eds.). Springer, Berlin.
35. Kilburn C.R.J., Petley D.N. (2003) Forecasting giant, catastrophic slope collapse: lessons from Vajont, Northern Italy. *Geomorphology*, **54**, 21–32.
36. Hewitt K. (1999) Quaternary moraines vs catastrophic rock avalanches in the Karakorum Himalaya, Northern Pakistan. *Quaternary Research*, **51**, 220–237.
37. Tazieff H. (1983) Volcanological forecasting and medical diagnosis: similarities. In: *Forecasting volcanic events* (H. Tazieff, J.C. Sabroux, Eds.). Elsevier, Amsterdam.
38. Sackett D.L., Straus S.E., Richardson W.S., Rosenberg W., Haynes R.B. (2000) *Evidence-based medicine.* Churchill Livingstone, Edinburgh.
39. Williams S. (2001) *Surviving Galeras.* Little, Brown and Company, London.
40. Pearl J. (2000) *Causality.* Cambridge University Press, Cambridge.
41. Hincks T.K. (2007) *Probabilistic volcanic hazard and risk assessment.* University of Bristol, Ph.D. dissertation.
42. Bonita R., Beaglehole R., Kjellström (2006) *Basic epidemiology.* World Health Organization, Geneva.
43. Ginsberg J., Mohebbi M.H., Patel R.S., Brammer R., Smolinski M.S., Brilliant L. (2009) Detecting influenza epidemics using search engine query data. *Nature*, **457**, doi:10.1038/nature07634.
44. Jiang X., Neil D.B., Cooper G.F. (2010) A Bayesian network model for spatial event surveillance. *Int. J. Approximate Reasoning*, **51**, 224–239.

Chapter 9

1. Greene J.D., Sommerville R.B., Nystrom L.E., Darley J.M., Cohen J.D. (2001) An fMRI investigation of emotional engagement in moral judgment. *Science*, **293**, 2105–2108.
2. Sutherland S. (2009) *Irrationality.* Pinter & Martin, London.

3. Dijksterhuis Ap., van Olden Z., (2005) On the benefits of thinking unconsciously: unconscious thought can increase post-choice satisfaction. *J. Experimental Social Psychology*, **42**, 627–631.

4. Wiseman R. (2009) *59 seconds: think a little, change a lot.* Macmillan, London.

5. Klein G. (1998) *Sources of power. How people make decisions.* MIT Press, Cambridge, MA.

6. Gigerenzer G. (2007) *Gut feelings.* Penguin, London.

7. Franklin B. (1956) *The Benjamin Franklin sampler.* Fawcett, New York.

8. Miller T.P., Casadevall T.J. (2000) Volcanic ash hazards to aviation. In: *Encyclopaedia of Volcanoes (H. Sigurdsson, Ed.).* Academic Press, San Diego.

9. Comfort L. (1999) *Shared risk: complex systems in seismic response.* Elsevier, Oxford.

10. Thaler R.H., Sunstein C.R. (2008) *Nudge.* Yale University Press, New Haven.

11. Royal Commission (2010*) 2009 Victorian Bushfires.* Government Printer for the State of Victoria.

12. Wilcock P.R., Schmidt J.C., Wolman M.G., Dietrich W.E., Dominick D.W., Doyle M.W., Grant E.G., Iverson R.M., Montgomery D.R., Pierson T.C., Schilling S.P., Wilson R.C. (2003) When models meet managers: examples from geomorphology. In: *AGU Monograph Series*, **135**, 27–40.

13. Bush G.W. (2010*) Decision points.* Crown Publishers, New York.

14. Regnier E. (2008) Public evacuation decisions and hurricane track uncertainty. *Management Science*, **54**, 16–28.

15. Wilson R., Crouch E.A.C. (2001*) Risk-benefit analysis.* Harvard University Press, Cambridge, MA.

16. Marzocchi W., Woo G. (2009) Principles of volcanic risk metrics: theory and the case study of Mt. Vesuvius and Campi Flegrei (Italy), *J. Geophys. Res.,* **114**, B03213.

17. Opper S., Cinque P., Davies B. (2009) Timeline modelling of flood evacuation operations. (*First Int. Conf. Evacuation Modelling and Management, Hague, Netherlands), Procedia Engineering,* **3**, 175–187.

18. Parascandola M. (2010) Epistemic risk: empirical science and the fear of being wrong. *Law, Probability and Risk*, **9**, 201–214.

19. Aspinall W.P. (2010) A route to more tractable expert advice. *Nature*, **463**, 294–295.

20. Oreskes N., Conway E.M. (2010) *Merchants of doubt.* Bloomsbury, New York.

21. Surowiecki J. (2004) *The wisdom of crowds.* Little, Brown and Company, London.

22. Howe J. (2008) *Crowdsourcing.* Crown Publishing Group, New York.

23. Hicks T.E. (2009) *The gamble.* Penguin, London.

24. Myers D.G. (2005) *Social psychology.* McGraw Hill, New York.

25. Sunstein C. (2009) *Going to extremes.* Oxford University Press, Oxford.

26. Cooke R.M. (1991) *Experts in uncertainty.* Oxford University Press, Oxford.

27. Aspinall W.P., Woo G. (1994) An impartial decision-making procedure using

expert judgement to assess volcanic hazards. *International symposium on large explosive eruptions*, **112**, Accademia Nazionale dei Lincei, Rome.

28. Aspinall W.P., Cooke R.M. (1998) Expert judgement and the Montserrat volcano eruption. In: *PSAM4* (A. Mosleh, R.A. Bari, Eds.), **3**, 2113–2118.

29. Woo G. (1992) Calibrated expert judgement in seismic hazard analysis. *Proc. Xth World Conf. Earthq. Eng.*, **1**, 333–338. A.A. Balkema, Rotterdam.

30. Schulz K. (2010) *Being wrong*. HarperCollins, New York.

31. Daston L. (1988) *Classical probability in the enlightenment*. Princeton University Press, Princeton, N.J.

32. Tazieff H. (1989) *Earthquake prediction*. McGraw-Hill, New York.

33. Omand D. (2010) *Securing the state*. Hurst & Co., London.

34. Von Neumann J. (1961) Methods in the physical sciences. In: *Collected Works* (A.H. Taub, Ed.). Pergamon Press, Oxford.

Chapter 10

1. Shanklin E. (2007) Exploding lakes in myth and reality: an African case study. In: *Myth and geology* (L. Piccardi, W.B. Masse, Eds.), Geological Society of London, Special Publications, 165–176.

2. Doevenspeck M. (2007) Lake Kivu's methane gas: natural risk, or source of energy and political security? *Afrika Spectrum*, **42**, 91–106.

3. Lebow R.N. (2010*) Forbidden fruit*. Princeton University Press, Princeton, N.J.

4. Levy M., Salvadori M. (1992) *Why buildings fall down*. W.W. Norton, New York.

5. Woo G. (1995) Zonation based on kernel estimation of seismicity. *Proc. 5 Int. Conf. Seismic Zonation*, Nice, 526–532.

6. Bertero V.V. (2009) *Connections*. EERI Oral History Series, Oakland, California.

7. Stoyan D., Stoyan H. (1994) *Fractals, random shapes and point fields*. John Wiley & Sons, Chichester.

8. Perrow C. (1999) *Normal accidents*. Princeton University Press, Princeton, N.J.

9. Schultz C.H., Koenig, K.L., and Lewis R.J. (2007) Decision-making in hospital earthquake evacuation: does distance from the epicenter matter? *Annals of Emergency Medicine*, **50**, 320–326.

10. Jodidio P., Strong J.A. (2008) *I.M. Pei: complete works*. Rizzoli, New York.

11. Feld J., Carper K.L. (1997) *Construction failure*. John Wiley & Sons, New York.

12. Barton L. (2004) *Crisis management*. Harvard Business Press, Boston, MA.

13. Qa'idah Al-Jihad (2010*)* Operation hemorrhage. *Inspire*, Al-Malahem Media Production, November.

14. Krausmann E., Mushtaq F. (2008) A qualitative Natech damage scale for the impact of floods on selected industrial facilities. *Natural Hazards*, **46**, 179–197.

15. Box G.E.P., Draper N.R. (1987) *Empirical model-building and response surfaces*, Wiley, New York.

16.   Tukey J.W. (1962) The future of data analysis. *Ann. Math. Stat.*, **33**, 1–67.
17.   Fermi E. (1945) My observations during the explosion at Trinity on July 16, 1945. *Los Alamos National Laboratory memorandum.*
18.   Drake F. (1961) *Search for extraterrestrial intelligence* (SETI) lecture.
19.   Hawking S. (2010) *Into the universe with Stephen Hawking.* Discovery Channel, dsc.discovery.com.
20.   Lissauer J.J., Fabrycky D.C., Ford E.B. *et al.* (2011) A closely packed system of low mass low-density planets transiting Kepler-11. *Nature*, **470**, 53–58.
21.   Gleiser M. (2010) Drake equation for the multiverse: from the string landscape to complex life. *Int. J. Mod. Phys. D.*, **D19**, 1299–1308.
22.   Collins G.S., Melosh H.J., Marcus R.A. (2005) Earth impact effects program. *Meteoritics & Planetary Science*, **40**, 817–840.
23.   Odenwald S., Green J., Taylor W. (2006) Forecasting the impact of an 1859-calibre superstorm on satellite resources. *Adv. Space Res.*, **38**, 280–297.
24.   Irvine H.M. (1986) *Structural dynamics for the practicing engineer.* Allen & Unwin, Sydney.
25.   Pan T.-C., You X.T., Cheng K.W. (2004) Building response to long-distance major earthquakes. *13th World Conf. Earthq. Eng.*, Paper No.804, Vancouver.
26.   Wyss M. (2005) Earthquake loss estimates applied in real time and to megacity risk assessment. *Proc. 2 Int. ISCRAM Conf.* (B. Van de Walle, B. Carlé, Eds.), Brussels, Belgium.
27.   Earle P.S., Wald D.J., Jaiswal K.S., Allen T.I., Hearne M.G., Marano K.D., Hotovec A.J., Fee J.M. (2009) Prompt assessment of global earthquakes for responses (PAGER): a system for rapidly determining the impact of earthquakes worldwide. *USGS Open-File Report 2009–1131.*
28.   Inoue S., Wijeyewickrema A.C., Matsumota H., Miura H., Gunaratna P., Maduraperruma M., Sekiguchi T. (2007) Field survey of tsunami effects in Sri Lanka due to the Sumatra-Andaman earthquake of December 26, 2004. *Pure and Applied Geophysics*, **164**, 395–411.
29.   Peral-Gutierrez de Ceballos J., Turégano-Fuentes F., Pérez-Díaz D., Sanz-Sánchez M., Martín-Llorente C., Guerrero-Sanz J.E. (2005) 11 March 2004: The terrorist bomb explosions in Madrid, Spain – an analysis of the logistics, injuries sustained and clinical management of casualties treated at the closest hospital. *Critical Care*, **9**, 104–111.
30.   Ferguson, N. M., Fraser, C., Donnelly, C. A., Ghani, A. C., Anderson, R. M. (2004) Public health risk from the avian H5N1 influenza epidemic. *Science*, **304**, 968–969.
31.   Day T., André J-P, Park A. (2006) The evolutionary emergence of pandemic influenza. *Proc. R. Soc. B*, **273**, 2945–2953.
32.   Smith L.A. (2010) Extracting insight from predictions of the irrelevant: can the diversity in our models inform our uncertainty of the future? *28th IUGG Conf. Math. Geophysics,* June, Pisa.

Chapter 11

1. Dowding T. (2010) Learning to love Lloyds. *Reactions*, August, 23–25.
2. Samuelson P.A. (1963) Risk and uncertainty: a fallacy of large numbers. *Scientia*, 1–6.
3. Bennett, C. (1992) *Dictionary of insurance*. Pitman, London.
4. Chapman N.A., Tsuchi H., Kitayama K. (2009) Tectonic events and nuclear facilities. In: *Volcanic and tectonic hazard assessment for nuclear facilities (C.B. Connor, N.A. Chapman, L.J. Connor, Eds.)*. Cambridge University Press, Cambridge.
5. Meehan R. L. (1984) *The atom and the fault*. MIT Press, Cambridge, MA.
6. IAEA (2010) *Seismic hazards in site evaluation for nuclear installations*. Specific Safety Guide: No. SSG-9, IAEA, Vienna.
7. Cornell C.A. (1968) Engineering seismic risk analysis. *Bull. Seism. Soc. Amer.*, **58**, 1583–1606.
8. Mualchin L. (2005) Seismic hazard analysis for critical infrastructures in California. *Eng. Geol.*, **79**, 177–184.
9. International Conference of Building Officials (1994). *Uniform Building Code*. Whittier, CA.
10. Dowty S., Ghosh S.K. (2002) IBC structural provisions: a better alternative, *Building Standards*, May–June, 15–16.
11. California Department of Insurance (1995–1996) *California earthquake zoning and Probable Maximum Loss evaluation program*, Los Angeles.
12. Dominey-Howes D., Dunbar P., Varner J., Papathoma-Köhle M. (2010) Estimating probable maximum loss from a Cascadia tsunami. *Natural Hazards*, **53**, 43–61.
13. Grossi P., Kunreuther H. (2005) *Catastrophe modeling: a new approach to managing risk*. Springer, New York.
14. Woo G. (2002) Natural catastrophe probable maximum loss. *British Actuarial Journal*, **8**, 943–959.
15. Artzner P., Delbaen F., Eber J-M, Heath D. (1999) Coherent measures of risk. *Mathematical Finance*, **9**, 203–228.
16. Artzner P. (2000) Application of coherent risk measures to capital requirements in insurance. *North American Actuarial Journal*, **2**, 11–25.
17. Acerbi, C., Tasche, D. (2002) Expected shortfall: a natural coherent alternative to value at risk, *Economic Notes Banca Monte dei Paschi di Siena SpA*, **31**, 379–388.
18. Diers D. (2008) *Stochastic modeling of catastrophe risks in DFA models*. ASTIN Colloquia, Manchester, 13–16 July.
19. Buchanan, J.M. (1972) The Samaritan's Dilemma. In: Buchanan, J.M. (1977): *Freedom in constitutional contract*, Texas A&M University Press, Austin, 169–185.
20. Cummins J.D., Mahul O. (2009) *Catastrophe risk pricing in developing countries*. The World Bank, Washington D.C.

21. Ambraseys N.N., Melville C.P. (1982) *A history of Persian earthquakes.* Cambridge University Press, Cambridge.
22. Zolfaghari M.R. (2010) Application of catastrophe loss modelling to promote property insurance in developing countries. *Disasters,* **34**, 524–541.
23. Woo G. (2006) Diaspora disaster insurance. *Proc. International Disaster Reduction Conf.*, Davos, Switzerland, **3**, 646–648.
24. Churchill C. (2006) What is insurance for the poor? In: *A microinsurance compendium* (C. Churchill, Ed.). Munich Re Foundation, Munich.
25. Prahalad C.K. (2004) *The fortune at the bottom of the pyramid.* Wharton School Publishing, Philadephia.

Chapter 12

1. Bettencourt L., West G. (2010) A unified theory of urban living. *Nature*, **467**, 912–913.
2. Arrow K.J. (1971) *Essays in the theory of risk-bearing.* North-Holland, Amsterdam.
3. Trenerry C.F. (1926) *The origin and early history of insurance.* P.S. King & Son.
4. Cardenas V., Mechler R. (2005) The Mexico Cat Bond – a solution for countries at risk? *Munich Re Foundation Symposium: world disaster prevention – awareness is the key.* 16–17 November.
5. Andritzky J. (2006) *Sovereign default risk valuation.* Springer, Berlin.
6. Cox S., Pedersen H. (1997) Catastrophe risk bonds. *XXVIII ASTIN Colloquium,* 117–139.
7. Canter M.S., Cole J.B., Sandor R.L. (1997) Insurance derivatives: a new asset class for the capital markets and a new hedging tool for the insurance industry. *J. Appl. Finance*, **10**, 6–83.
8. Schmock U. (1997) Estimating the value of WinCAT coupons of the Winterthur Insurance convertible bonds. *XXVIII ASTIN Colloquium*, 231–259.
9. Froot K.A., Posner S.E. (2001) The pricing of event risks with parameter uncertainty. *Geneva papers on Risk and Insurance Theory*, 27, No.2.
10. Brookes B. (2009) Risk modelling and the role and benefits of Cat Indices. In: *The handbook of insurance-linked securities (P. Barrieu, L. Albertini, Eds.).* Wiley Finance, Chichester.
11. Kunreuther H. (2002) The role of insurance in managing extreme events: implications for terrorism coverage. *Risk Analysis*, **22**, 427–437.
12. Betlehem J. (2009) Emergency medical preparedness during the 2006 World Cup in Frankfurt, Germany. *Disasters*, **34**, 155–163.
13. Woo G. (2005) Current challenges in the securitization of terrorism risk. In: *Catastrophe risks and insurance.* OECD Publishing, Paris.
14. FIFA (2003) *Financial report.* Fédération Internationale de Football Association, Zürich, Switzerland.

15. Coriat S. (2009) Case study: a cat mortality bond by AXA (OSIRIS). In: *The handbook of insurance-linked securities* (P. Barrieu, L. Albertini, Eds.). Wiley Finance, Chichester.

16. Woo G., Martin C.J., Hornsby C., Coburn A.W. (2010) Prospective longevity risk analysis. *British Actuarial Journal*, **15**, 235–247.

Chapter 13

1. Rumsfeld D. (2002) Transforming the military. *Foreign Affairs*, **81**, 20–32.
2. Coker C. (2009) *War in an age of risk*. Polity Press, Cambridge.
3. Omand D. (2010) *Securing the state*. Hurst & Co., London.
4. Churchill W. (1895) *My early life*. Thornton Butterworth, London.
5. Beck U. (1997) *The reinvention of politics*. Polity Press, Cambridge.
6. Rittel H.W.J, Webber M.M. (1973) Dilemmas in a general theory of planning. *Policy Sciences*, **4**, 155–169.
7. Woo G. (1989) Is the risk of human intrusion exaggerated? *Proceedings of a Nuclear Energy Agency workshop on risks associated with human intrusion at radioactive waste disposal sites*. OECD, Paris.
8. Mumford D. (1999) The dawning of the age of stochasticity. In: *Mathematics towards the third millennium*. Accademia Nazionale dei Lincei, Rome.
9. Scheffer M., Carpenter S., Foley J.A., Folke C., Walker B. (2001) Catastrophic shifts in ecosystems. *Nature*, **413**, 591–596.
10. Scheffer M., Bascompte J., Brock W.A., Brovkin V., Carpenter S.R., Dakos V., Held H., van Nes E.H., Rietkerk M., Sugihara G. (2009) Early-warning signals for critical transitions. *Nature*, **461**, 53–59.
11. Drake J.M., Griffin B.D. (2010) Early warning signals of extinction in deteriorating environments. *Nature*, **467**, 456–459.
12. Schindler D.E., Hilborn R., Chasco B., Boatright C.P., Quinn T.P., Rogers L.A., Webster M.S. (2010) Population diversity and the portfolio effect in an exploited Species. *Nature*, **465**, 609–612.
13. Anderies J.M., Norberg J. (2008) Theoretical challenges: information processing and navigation in social-ecological systems. In: *Complexity theory for a sustainable future* (J. Norberg, G.S. Cumming, Eds.). Columbia University Press, New York.
14. Brock W.A., Carpenter S.R., Scheffer M. (2008) Regime shifts, environmental signals, and policy choice. In: *Complexity theory for a sustainable future* (J. Norberg, G.S. Cumming, Eds.). Columbia University Press, New York.
15. Waller I. (1954) *Nobel physics prize citation*. Nobel Committee, Stockholm.
16. Born M. (1949) *Natural philosophy of cause and chance*. Oxford University Press, Oxford.
17. Popper K. (1963) *Conjectures and refutations*. Routledge and Kegan Paul, London.

18. Edwards P.N. (2010) *A vast machine*. MIT Press, Cambridge, MA.
19. Houghton J. (2009) *Global warming: the complete briefing*. Cambridge University Press, Cambridge.
20. Oreskes N., Shrader-Frechette K., Belitz K. (1994) Verification, validation and confirmation of numerical models in the Earth Sciences. *Science*, **263**, 641–646.
21. Parker W. (2010) Confirmation and testing of scientific models, revisited. *28th IUGG Conf. Mathematical Geophysics*, Pisa, Italy.
22. Hennessy P. (2002) *The secret state*. Allen Lane, London.
23. Pielke R. (2010) *The climate fix: what scientists and politicians won't tell you about global warming*. Basic books, New York.
24. Leith N.A., Chandler R.E. (2010) A framework for interpreting climate model outputs. *Appl. Statist.*, **59**, 279–296.
25. Smith L. (2002) What might we learn from climate forecasts. *PNAS*, **99**, 2487–2492.
26. Pall P., Aina T., Stone D.A., Stott P.A., Nozawa T., Hilberts A.G.J., Lohmann D., Allen M.R. (2011) Anthropogenic greenhouse gas contribution to flood risk in England and Wales in autumn 2000. *Nature*, **470**, 382–385.
27. Stern N. (2010) *A blueprint for a safer planet*. Vintage Books, London.
28. De Mesquita B. (2009) *Predictioneer*. The Bodley Head, London.
29. Baker A., Woo G. (2004) Non-violence to the Palestinians' rescue. *Daily Star*, Beirut, 12 August.
30. Sharp G. (2002) *From dictatorship to democracy*. The Albert Einstein Institution, East Boston, MA.

Epilogue

1. Longfellow H.W. (1898) *The song of Hiawatha*. Hurst & Co., New York.
2. Carson B. (1990) *Mount St. Helens*. Sasquatch books, Seattle.
3. Perrow C. (1999) *Normal accidents*. Princeton University Press, Princeton, N.J.
4. Sherden W.A. (1998) *The fortune sellers*. John Wiley & Sons, New York.
5. Posner R. (2004) *Catastrophe, risk and response*. Oxford University Press, Oxford.
6. Nebeker F. (1995) *Calculating the weather*. Academic Press, San Diego.
7. Taleb N.N. (2010) *The bed of Procrustes*. Penguin, London.
8. Hennessy P. (2002) *The secret state*. Allen Lane, London.
9. Quéau P. (1986) *Éloge de la simulation*. Seyssel: Éditions du Champ Vallon.
10. Gell-Mann M. (1994) *The quark and the jaguar*. Little, Brown and Company, London.
11. Kent A. (2004) A critical look at risk assessments for global catastrophes. *Risk Analysis*, **24**, 157–168.

Index